# CONSERVATISM AND THE QUARTERLY REVIEW: A CRITICAL ANALYSIS

# The History of the Book

*Series Editor:     Ann R. Hawkins*

## Forthcoming Titles

*Contributors to the Quarterly Review: A History, 1809–1825*
Jonathan Cutmore

*Wilkie Collins's American Tour, 1873–1874*
Susan R Hanes

*William Blake and the Art of Engraving*
Mei-Ying Sung

# CONSERVATISM AND THE QUARTERLY REVIEW: A CRITICAL ANALYSIS

EDITED BY

Jonathan Cutmore

LONDON
PICKERING & CHATTO
2007

*Published by Pickering & Chatto (Publishers) Limited*
*21 Bloomsbury Way, London WC1A 2TH*

*2252 Ridge Road, Brookfield, Vermont 05036-9704, USA*

*www.pickeringchatto.com*

BRITISH LIBRARY CATALOGUING IN PUBLICATION DATA

Conservatism and The quarterly review: a critical analysis. – (The history of the book)
1. Quarterly review – History 2. Conservatism and literature – Great Britain
– History – 19th century 3. Politics and literature – Great Britain – History
– 19th century 4. Conservatism – Great Britain – History – 19th century
I. Cutmore, Jonathan
828.9'1209358

ISBN-13: 9781851969517

This publication is printed on acid-free paper that conforms to the American
National Standard for the Permanence of Paper for Printed Library Materials.

*Typeset by Pickering & Chatto (Publishers) Limited*
*Printed in the United Kingdom by Athenaeum Press Ltd, Gateshead*

# CONTENTS

For Sylvia

# CONTRIBUTORS

*J. M. R. Cameron*, formerly Dean of Education at the Northern Territory University, is Adjunct Professor in History at Murdoch University. He has published numerous articles on pedagogy and Australia's historical geography. His books include *Ambition's Fire: The Agricultural Colonization of Pre-Convict Western Australia* (Nedlands: University of Western Australia Press, 1981), *Letters from Port Essington, 1838–1845* (Darwin: Historical Society of the Northern Territory, 1999) and *The Millendon Memoirs: George Fletcher Moore's Western Australian Diaries and Letters* (Victoria Park: Hesperian Press, 2006).

*Jonathan Cutmore* is former Assistant Professor at the University of Toronto, Lecturer at Memorial University, St John's, Newfoundland, and a researcher on *John Stuart Mill Collected Works*. He has published several articles on the *Quarterly Review* and he is the editor of the *Quarterly Review Archive* on the University of Maryland's *Romantic Circles*.

*Boyd Hilton* is Professor of Modern History at the University of Cambridge and a Fellow of Trinity College. His books include *Corn, Cash and Commerce: The Economic Policies of the Tory Government 1815–30* (Oxford: Oxford University Press, 1977), *The Age of Atonement: The Influence of Evangelicalism on Social and Economic Thought, 1785–1865* (Oxford: Clarendon Press, 1988) and, most recently, *A Mad, Bad, and Dangerous People?: England 1783–1846* (Oxford: Clarendon Press, 2006).

*Lynda Pratt* is Reader in Romanticism at the University of Nottingham. The general editor of *Robert Southey: Poetical Works, 1793–1810* (London: Pickering & Chatto, 2004), she is also the editor of *Robert Southey and the Contexts of English Romanticism* (Aldershot: Ashgate, 2006).

*Sharon Ragaz* is a member of the English faculty, Oxford University. She is the author of articles on Scott and Maturin in the *Review of English Studies*, *Romantic Textualities* and *Cardiff Corvey: Reading the Romantic Text*, and co-author, with Peter Garside and Jacqueline Belanger, of *British Fiction 1800–1829: A Database of Production, Circulation, and Reception*, designer A. A. Mandal, <http://www.british-fiction.cf.ac.uk>.

*W. A. Speck* is Emeritus Professor of History at Leeds University and Special Professor at the University of Nottingham. His books include *Literature and Society in Eighteenth-Century England* (London: Longman, 1998) and *Robert Southey: Entire Man of Letters* (New Haven, CT: Yale University Press, 2006).

*Christopher Stray* is Honorary Research Fellow in the Department of Classics, Swansea University. He is the author of books, articles and introductions on nineteenth-century education and classics, including *Classics Transformed: Schools, Universities, and Society 1830–1960* (Oxford: Clarendon Press, 1998).

*Kim Wheatley* is Associate Professor of English at the College of William and Mary. She is the author of essays on early nineteenth-century periodicals and nineteenth-century literature in *Prose Studies, Nineteenth-Century Literature, Romanticism, Radicalism, and the Press* and *Studies in English Literature*. She is the author of *Shelley and His Readers: Beyond Paranoid Politics* (Columbia, MO: University of Missouri Press, 1999) and she is the editor of *Romantic Periodicals and Print Culture* (London: Frank Cass, 2003).

# ABBREVIATIONS

| | |
|---|---|
| article # | serial number derived from J. Cutmore (ed.), *The Quarterly Review Archive*, <www.rc.umd.edu> |
| Beinecke | James and Marie-Louise Osborn Collection, Beinecke Rare Book and Manuscript Library, Yale University Library, New Haven, CT |
| BL | British Library, London |
| BL Add. MSS | Additional Manuscripts, British Library, London |
| Clements | Croker Papers, William L. Clements Library, University of Michigan |
| Derbyshire | Wilmot Horton Collection, Derbyshire Public Record Office |
| Devon | Devon Public Record Office |
| *ER* | *Edinburgh Review* (Edinburgh) |
| *ER #* | *Edinburgh Review* article serial number, derived from *WI* (see below) |
| Houghton | Houghton Library, Harvard University, Cambridge, MA |
| Iowa | Leigh Hunt, Series 2, Murray-Croker, Special Collections, University of Iowa Libraries, Iowa City, IA |
| JM MS | John Murray Archive, formerly at 50 Albemarle Street, London, now at the National Library of Scotland, Edinburgh |
| Leeds | Earl and Lady Harewood deposit, West Yorkshire Archive Service, Leeds District Archives, Sheepscar |
| Liverpool | Autograph Letter Collection, Hornby Library, Liverpool City Libraries |
| Millgate | Millgate Union Catalogue of Walter Scott Correspondence, <www.nls.uk> |
| Morgan | Literary and Historical Manuscripts, The Morgan Library, New York |
| *NL* | *New Letters of Robert Southey*, ed. K. Curry, 2 vols (New York: Columbia University Press, 1965) |

| | |
|---|---|
| NLS | Sir Walter Scott Collection, National Library of Scotland |
| NLW | Llyfrgell Genedlaethol Cymru / The National Library of Wales |
| Northumberland | Society of Antiquaries of Newcastle upon Tyne deposit, Northumberland Public Record Office |
| *ODNB* | *Oxford Dictionary of National Biography*: <www.oxforddnb.com> |
| Perkins | Rare Book, Manuscript, and Special Collections Library, Perkins Library, Duke University, Durham, NC |
| PRO | Public Record Office, Kew, London (now the National Archives) |
| *QR* | *Quarterly Review* (London) |
| *QR* Letter | referring to the editor's unpublished edition of *Quarterly Review*-related correspondence. For a list of these letters and their sources, see Appendix A, pp. 179–88 |
| *SL* | *The Letters of Sir Walter Scott*, ed. H. Grierson, et al., 12 vols (London: Constable, 1932–7) |
| Smiles, *Memoir* | S. Smiles, *A Publisher and his Friends: Memoir and Correspondence of the Late John Murray*, 2nd edn, 2 vols (London: John Murray, 1891) |
| Trinity | Sanford-Monk Papers, Trinity College Library, Cambridge University, by permission of the Master and Fellows of Trinity College |
| Wellcome | Western Manuscripts, Wellcome Library, The Wellcome Trust, London |
| Westminster | Westminster School Library, Westminster School, London, by permission of the Governing Body of Westminster School |
| *WI* | *The Wellesley Index to Victorian Periodicals 1824–1900*, vol. 1, ed. W. E. Houghton (Toronto: University of Toronto Press, 1966) |

# INTRODUCTION

## Jonathan Cutmore

The essays in this collection contribute to a renewed scholarly commitment to explore the cultural impact of early nineteenth-century periodicals.[1] During the Regency, contemporaries credited the *Quarterly Review* with great power to influence literary opinion and the sale of books. Consequently, its many famous reviews – of Keats, the Shelleys, Byron, Wordsworth, Crabbe, Hemans, Hazlitt, Hunt, Austen and Scott – are quoted by reader-reception specialists, by literary historians, by biographers of Romantic-era figures and by students of book history. Also, because its political, foreign policy and economics reviews represented the cream of conservative writing in the period, and because some of its core contributors were connected with the highest levels of government, historians frequently cite the journal. It is perhaps surprising, then, that hitherto no critical study of the early *Quarterly Review* has appeared.

The preservation of thousands of relevant documents (in the John Murray Archive, the Sir Walter Scott Collection, and elsewhere) makes the *Quarterly* ideal for testing theories of the formation and conduct of early nineteenth-century periodicals. To facilitate such an experiment in the present instance, the editor supplied the contributing essayists with transcriptions of primary sources that relate to the journal during the editorships of William Gifford (1809–24) and John Taylor Coleridge (1825).[2] With each essayist addressing either a major topic (politics, classics, the business of reviewing) or a major contributor (Scott, Southey, Barrow), the collection strikes a balance between treating the journal as a monolithic cultural formation in which individual voices were editorially suppressed and as a collaborative enterprise that was shaped by the publisher's, editor's and contributors' sometimes competing motivations and interests. Whatever their positions on questions of theory, all of the essayists regard the *Quarterly* not as a cultural sampler, nor as historical background, but as a textual artefact worthy of detailed study.

This introduction begins with an overview of the nature and sources of archival *Quarterly Review* materials, it then reflects on the essayists' use of those and other materials, and it closes with a look at what the archives tell us about the publisher John Murray and his editor William Gifford, the two men primarily responsible for making the *Quarterly Review* a successful commercial venture and an effective instrument of conservative propaganda.

We can lament Gifford's stipulation in his will that upon his death his papers – he specified in particular his *Quarterly Review* papers – should be destroyed, for with them went an important part of the journal's history. There are, however, consolations. While Gifford dealt with many of the journal's minor writers and some lesser-known names, such as the Oriel College intellectual Edward Copleston, it was his publisher, John Murray, who was the constant correspondent of the *Quarterly*'s most prolific contributors, Sir John Barrow, John Wilson Croker and Robert Southey.[3] A number of their letters to Murray that are preserved in the John Murray Archive were made available to the essay writers in the form of the editor's transcription. The editor also supplied the contributors with annotated transcriptions of unpublished letters of Murray, Gifford and Ellis from the Sir Walter Scott Collection at the National Library of Scotland and from other major caches of Gifford correspondence, such as the twenty-seven letters to George Ellis at the British Library (BL Add. MSS 28099). The Gifford-Ellis letters cover almost the full period of Ellis's contribution to the *Quarterly Review* and are an invaluable source of knowledge about Gifford's editorial practice and of his handling of a senior, friendly contributor. Ellis was an intimate of three other co-founders of the *Quarterly* – Walter Scott, Richard Heber and George Canning – and he was well connected to the ruling class. As he was the reviewer of Scott and Byron, letters addressed to him by his editor are intrinsically interesting. We find in these letters information about Ellis's cooperation with Canning on a series of foreign policy articles and about his collaboration with Canning and Huskisson on essays on political economy. So these letters give us some insight into the *Quarterly*'s sources of authoritative information, the formulation and reception of its views on two of the great writers of the period, and how the journal served the interests of literary and political elites.

The mother lode of *Quarterly Review* materials is the John Murray Archive, formerly at 50 Albemarle Street, London, now permanently housed at the National Library of Scotland, Edinburgh. In the Archive we find caught as if in amber every letter related to the *Quarterly Review* that passed over the threshold of 32 Fleet Street and, from mid-1812, of 50 Albemarle Street, the offices of John Murray, Bookseller. John Murray II cast no letter aside and each of his successors, recognizing the value of what their forebear had preserved, kept the collection together. Most of the *Quarterly Review* letters at John Murray's, many hundreds of them, are naturally addressed to the publisher, including stacks of letters from Gifford, Barrow, Croker, Ellis and Southey, along with smaller collections of letters from a host of other contributors and supporters.

In addition to the boxes of Gifford letters to Murray and some Gifford odds and ends, the third John Murray pulled large groupings of Gifford's letters into the archive when he was contemplating a history of the journal (an effort that was absorbed into Samuel Smiles's project, his *Memoir of John Murray*). The Hay family gave John Murray III fifty-eight of Gifford's letters to Robert William Hay, an MP and civil servant who was well known to some of the journal's other principals, Canning, Croker and Barrow. The Gifford-Hay letters provide a view of the editor's handling of a prickly, talented civil servant and they supply further evidence of the extent of government cooperation in the production of political and diplomatic articles in the *Quarterly Review*. John Murray III also obtained Gifford's correspondence with John Taylor Coleridge, the *Quarterly*'s second editor. Coleridge, who was the poet's nephew and a close friend of John Keble and Robert Southey, was a Christian jurist – his letters to Gifford show that he was also a partisan moralist, the righteous scourge of the Cockney and Satanic Schools, of Hunt and Shelley.[4] Another valuable source in the Murray Archive is the firm's letterbooks. These preserve, some in Murray's own hand, copies of the publisher's correspondence. Because Murray was selective about what he copied in these books, their contents are of considerable interest. The editor made available to the essay writers his transcription of some of the letters in the letterbooks, of other letters in the Archive, of John Murray's register of books loaned to contributors, and of Murray's early *Quarterly Review* memoranda.

Also offered to the essayists were transcriptions of thirty-seven letters from William Gifford to Edward Copleston, the holographs of which are deposited at the Devon Public Record Office.[5] Through them we can trace Gifford's sometimes sycophantic, not always deft handling of an important contributor and collaborator. The other letters made available to the essayists by way of the editor's transcriptions are: Gifford to Murray and Murray to Croker from the Iowa collection;[6] Gifford to Canning from the Harewood deposit at the West Yorkshire Archive; Gifford to Horton from the Derbyshire Public Record Office; Gifford to Copleston from the Northumberland Public Record Office; Gifford to Copleston from the National Library of Wales; Gifford to George D'Oyly from the Wellcome Library, London; Peter Elmsley to Gifford from the Westminster School, London; Scott, Murray and Gifford letters from the Morgan Library in New York; Croker and Lockhart correspondence from the Clements Library, Ann Arbor, Michigan; Scott and Gifford letters from the Houghton Library, Harvard University; Canning to Gifford from the Beinecke Library, Yale University; and, from the Perkins Library, Duke University, Gifford to Canning letters and letters from Gifford to Canning's secretary, John Backhouse. Courtesy of Dr Henry Sanford and the Master and Fellows of Trinity

College, Cambridge, the editor and Christopher Stray learned much about Gifford's editorial practice from the fascinating collection of James Henry Monk letters that relate to the publication and reception of Monk's 1819 review of Brougham's education committee.[7] Naturally, the essayists supplemented the *Quarterly Review* documents with their already extensive knowledge of period-specific archival material and secondary sources.

In using these various materials, the essayists demonstrate the complexity of the early nineteenth-century conservative publishing milieu. They identify the range of conservatisms reflected in the *Quarterly*'s pages: the Canningite liberal conservatives, Oriel Noetics, Porsonian classicists, evangelical Saints and the Romantic Conservatives. We learn from the essayists that, while each of these groups attempted to use the *Quarterly* to market its version of conservatism, a degree of uniformity was imposed upon them, for although the journal's first editor accepted contributions from a broad spectrum of writers, he attempted to preserve in the *Quarterly*, as best he could, a distinctive liberal-conservative voice. The essayists debate just how successful Gifford was in his effort to produce a homogenized 'house voice' that represented the Canningite faction in Parliament.

Far from being discussed as a specifically liberal-conservative organ, the *Quarterly* is often mistakenly described as a reactionary agent of government control, the literary equivalent, as Hazlitt put it in his vitriolic *Letter to William Gifford* (1819), of the secret police. While the *Quarterly* partly fulfilled its promise that in its pages readers would have access to privileged and authoritative information, information from high government figures and from executive members of the civil service, the journal and the government were not hand in glove. As I state in my essay herein, while the *Quarterly*'s conductors supported 'principles English and Constitutional', they hesitated to promote specific government measures and, Canning excepted, most government men. Boyd Hilton shows that the *Quarterly Review* was top to bottom a political project, an ideological counterblast to the *Edinburgh Review*. But, as he points out, the journal's association with a political faction, the Canningites, and tensions between the publisher, the editor and one particular contributor caused the *Quarterly* to support the government's positions only inconsistently. Hilton demonstrates that for most of Gifford's tenure the *Quarterly* was out of step with the nation's evolving conservative constituencies. He shows that the editor was unsympathetic to the growing influence of evangelicalism and the High Church on British conservatism, while Croker, who greatly influenced the publisher's political sympathies, did not respond to the increasingly 'Burkean' tenor of conservatism in the 'Tory' party. Bill Speck reflects that with one of the *Quarterly*'s most prolific contributors, Robert Southey, adamantly opposed to the liberal economic policies favoured by Canning and his cronies, on some important issues the *Quarterly* did not consistently support the liberal conservatives' position.

A reason why during Gifford's reign the journal failed to achieve ideological coherence was that the aims and values of some of its core staff were in conflict. An aggressive editor, through his blue pencil interventions Gifford created the *Quarterly*'s imperious, self-assured style, but conditions on the ground ensured that he could not entirely suppress his better writers' individuality or completely resist Murray's efforts to dilute the journal's political character. Highlighting the negotiations that took place between the *Quarterly*'s co-founders during the lead-up to the publication of the first number and over the course of the journal's early years, Kim Wheatley and Sharon Ragaz explain that editorial power was distributed between Murray, Gifford and Scott. Wheatley points out that in debating the *Quarterly*'s tone and manner – specifically whether they should adopt the *Edinburgh*'s vituperative style – the *Quarterly*'s founders put political, literary, commercial and personal considerations into play. In her essay on Sir Walter Scott, Ragaz concentrates on the great man's sometimes difficult relationship with Gifford and Murray. She demonstrates that, regardless of the tentative nature of Scott's long-term association with the *Quarterly*, the journal found its footing in large part because Scott lent the conductors his 'experience, advice and prodigious efforts in the matter of contributions' and by that means 'helped to ensure good management, wise editorial policy and a high standard for the articles'.

In discussing Robert Southey's accomplishment as a *Quarterly* reviewer, in their complementary essays Lynda Pratt and Bill Speck highlight Southey's independence. They show that despite Gifford's effort to control him by excising from his articles whatever might give offence to liberal conservatives, Southey produced a distinctive and distinguished body of work. Pratt concentrates on Southey as a literary reviewer, in particular on the 'complex relationship between "Southey" the author and "Southey" the critic' that brought him into conflict with contemporaries such as Coleridge, Wordsworth, Byron and Shelley. Speck focuses on Southey's programme of social and political reform and on his relations with the journal's publisher. His essay examines how far Southey supported government policies while he defended his own views where they differed from government. Both writers qualify the impression Southey himself retailed, that his *Quarterly Review* articles were hopelessly distorted by Gifford's edits.

J. M. R. Cameron provides an example in his essay on the Admiralty's Second Secretary, Sir John Barrow, of how one powerful official cultivated his association with the *Quarterly* to further his and his department's interests and, in doing so, acted with a considerable degree of editorial independence. Cameron argues that, by virtue of the popularity of Barrow's articles, and their great number, far from being subsumed into the *Quarterly's* collective voice, the Second Secretary influenced the journal's character and reputation.

If individual personalities greatly shaped the journal's editorial complexion and its commercial fortunes, so did intellectual collectives in the Church and the universities. By examining the treatment of classics in the *Quarterly Review*, Christopher Stray demonstrates the impact of intellectual networks and *Sitz im Leben* on the periodical's content and manner. He argues that the history of the involvement of classicists in Gifford's *Quarterly Review* is in part that of the contrasting styles of the two universities: in Oxford, his own alma mater and the home of his advisor Edward Copleston, Gifford may have felt more comfortable; he was active, though, in recruiting like-minded reviewers from Cambridge. Stray also traces a complex history of interaction between the *Edinburgh Review* and *Quarterly Review*, one which involved both differences of belief and commercial rivalry.

As we have seen, then, collectively the essayists demonstrate that grounding discussion of theoretical questions in empirical evidence leads to a nuanced definition of the *Quarterly* as a conservative journal and to a recognition of the push and pull between individual and corporate voices.

The balance of this introduction epitomizes what we learn from the archives about the journal's day-to-day conduct and especially about the crucial relationship between John Murray and William Gifford. Because at the beginning of an enterprise and at points of transition men form alliances and lay bare their motives, the present volume's essayists tend to emphasize the *Quarterly's* formative years and the appointment of a new editor upon the first editor's retirement. Of particular note in the journal's early history is the often acrimonious relationship between Gifford and Murray. The tension between the two men stemmed from the competing sets of values that drove their participation in the journal. We find that, in setting up and conducting the *Quarterly*, Murray pursued commercial interests while Gifford represented his political patron, George Canning, in a defence of what he called 'the cause', the protection of the Constitution against the incipient threat of radical reform. Especially in the first few years, the *Quarterly* was consequently conducted under a divided command: the publisher was determined to safeguard his investment, while the editor, weakened by Canning's twelve-year exile from high office (1810–22), was unable entirely to resist Murray's editorial intrusions. Through the *Quarterly Review* materials we can trace how Murray and Gifford nevertheless achieved success and how they and their coadjutors benefited thereby.[8] We find that success rested on two pillars. It was the structure of the journal's relationship with government – and Gifford's handling of that relationship – along with its conductors' ability to attract talent that made the journal an asset to its political sponsors, and to its publisher, editor, writers and readers. The journal's prestige brought patronage benefits to some of Gifford's collaborators, while its conservative readership benefited by having their views defended and their prejudices confirmed in the periodical press.[9]

Strategically, the *Quarterly* was a project in Murray's long-term scheme to achieve commercial success by identifying his firm with the establishment. That he was 'anxiously and firmly attached to the government' (*QR* Letter 51)[10] and that he was conservative by temperament there can be no doubt; but it is not at all clear that he was a man of strong, perhaps any, core political convictions. We glean from the archival evidence that his alliance with government secured for him revenue, reputation and a stable lucrative market.

The other founders of the *Quarterly Review*, in contrast – Scott, Canning, Ellis and Gifford – were British nationalists whose primary motivation in establishing the journal was 'to further the cause' (*QR* Letter 3). Only in a narrow sense did they set up the journal to prop up a weak conservative Ministry; more broadly and generously they desired to advance a political and social vision. With a high degree of sincerity,[11] these men wished to promote a complex of conservative ideas, that Britain was a beacon of Christian civilization and that her glory was embodied in national 'establishments' – the universities, courts, Church, king and aristocracy, parliament, the unwritten Constitution, and, not least of all, the Anglo-Scottish literary tradition.[12] Historians of canon formation have noted that in the long eighteenth century British conservatives touted English and Scottish literature as an expression of *national* genius, as an 'establishment' on a par with the monarchy, parliament and the Church. In the wake of the Anglo-Scottish Union of 1701, the ideological tsunami of the French Revolution, and the 1800 Act of Union with Ireland, promoting the idea that there was a national literature was a component of the state-sponsored effort to articulate a distinctive British identity. The literary establishment, like other national establishments, was to be protected from erosion by foreign interlopers. As a manifestation of this effort to preserve and defend the nation, during the French Revolution and the Napoleonic era conservatives such as William Gifford partly defined British literature, character, manners and politics in contradistinction from French models. Christian British nationalism had a considerable impact on the *Quarterly* as it more or less directed Gifford's and his sympathetic contributors' choice and treatment of subjects for review.

As a principled conservative, the first editor of the *Quarterly Review* was not a partisan supporter of the conservative governments of the day; he thought that many of the 'Tory' ministers were weak and self-serving. Archival materials inform us, then, about the limits of government influence on the journal and about how much and in what ways the *Quarterly* served the establishment or was manipulated by it. We find that while Gifford, Murray and their gentlemen gave general support to Cabinet, their allegiance to 'the present men' was not slavish (*QR* Letters 4, 41, 75, 97, 140). From their earliest negotiations, the journal's principals – Murray, Scott, Canning, Heber, Ellis and Gifford – agreed that while the *Quarterly* would 'to a certain extent' serve the Crown (*QR* Letter 8) it was not measures and men but rational Christianity and the Constitution that the journal would actively support. Thus it was that in 1810 Prime Minister Perceval met with a surprise when he tried to have an article on the bullion question inserted in the *Quarterly Review*. Because the view he espoused conflicted with the position the journal had already taken on the matter, Gifford 'manfully vindicated [the *Quarterly*'s] independence' by turning away the first minister of the Crown (*QR* Letters 70, 71). In 1813 Prime Minister Liverpool experienced a similar rebuff when he tried to influence the *Quarterly*'s position on the renewal of the East India Company charter. As it is not in the nature of power to reward independence, Gifford's pluck, coupled with his association with Canning, in the long run probably damaged the *Quarterly*'s ability to attract contributions from high politicos and extract information from government (*QR* Letter 148). 'It is really astonishing that they [the Cabinet] will not take more advantage of us, and influence a great portion of the country which we have brought almost to their feet', Gifford wrote to Canning in 1817 (*QR* Letter 183). It was a complaint he uttered often (*QR* Letters 57, 111, 162, 180), but in doing so he forgot he had warned the ministers not to expect an automatic entrance into the *Quarterly Review*.

The *Quarterly Review* materials show, however, that Gifford and Murray were able to call upon government for practical help. Most importantly, high officials fed authoritative privileged information to the editor and his collaborators (*QR* Letter 187). While there is no evidence that the Treasury provided a subvention, the *Quarterly*'s connection with government brought indirect financial benefits, with ministries rewarding Murray and his writers with contracts, patronage and promotions (*QR* Letters 93, 229). Managing the journal also involved posting a massive amount of correspondence – 'I have 42 Letters before me to answer', Murray once complained (*QR* Letter 174). To ease this significant burden on themselves and the journal's contributors,[13] Gifford and Murray relied heavily on the franking privileges of men they knew in government and the civil service;[14] it seems that one of the journal's political sponsors, the chief administrator of the postal service, Sir Francis Freeling, also got involved, possibly to deflect Murray and Gifford's postage costs (*QR* Letter 160). For strategic reasons, though, no member of the *Quarterly*'s editorial group received direct financial support from government specifically for their work on the periodical – the *Quarterly* would have lost credibility with the public had it become known as a Treasury journal.[15]

Under Murray and Gifford's tutelage the *Quarterly* was not, then, in any facile way a government organ. It was, however, what the hyper-Protestant *Antijacobin Review* supposed it to be, a mouthpiece for the Canningites, which was another reason why governments under Perceval and Liverpool were somewhat wary of it.[16] Gifford initially agreed to serve as editor only as long as Canning remained in office. He accepted the position, he told Canning, 'because I know of no other whom you could securely trust – with me, you are perfectly safe' (*QR* Letter 3; cf. Letters 89, 257).[17] A definition of the *Quarterly Review* as a Canningite journal should, however, be qualified by Canning's formal disbanding of his party in 1813 and by the observation that the statesman's influence on the periodical was largely achieved through his surrogates, Gifford, Ellis and Heber. As an initiator of correspondence relating to the *Quarterly Review*, Canning is represented in few letters; and yet his silence, if properly understood, signifies not indifference or irrelevance but governing influence. Canning was involved in planning the *Quarterly* (*QR* Letters 10, 11) and, with Ellis, he wrote a number of articles; but for the most part he exercised control passively. He was the great man whose will Gifford and Ellis consulted before embarking on any article of political note (*QR* Letters 20, 114, 144, 148, 188). At a minimum, Canning's unwavering sponsorship of Gifford meant that Murray could not remove him, much as he wanted to upon occasion – at times of stress Murray tended to seek a scapegoat and, in the matter of the *Quarterly*, Gifford was always at hand to serve that purpose (*QR* Letters 59, 60).

Archival materials help us gain a nuanced view of government support for the *Quarterly Review*; they also help us measure the relative contribution of those who shaped its editorial character. The materials reveal that the production of any given article was a collaborative affair, as was the general conduct of the enterprise. Some contributors, such as Walter Scott and George Ellis, helped formulate editorial policy. Others helped sub-edit the *Quarterly*. To get through all the work that bringing out an issue involved, and to ensure that arcane topics were adequately treated, Gifford employed a legion of sub-editors. Many of his more reliable writers played this role: Barrow sub-edited Croker and Croker, Barrow; Gregory sub-edited Young and Young, Gregory; Copleston sub-edited Dudley; Heber, Scott; Scott, Erskine, and so on. Many of the same men who wrote for the journal or who undertook a sub-editorial role were also recruiters for it.

Collaboration did not mean that Gifford was editor in name only or that the *Quarterly Review* was merely the sum of its parts. After all, he directed this sub-editorial activity; he filtered the results; and, without exception, he vetted the journal's political content. The situation was complicated, however, for Gifford and Murray were engaged in a contest for executive control. Early on, Scott took sides with Murray, but as Sharon Ragaz points out in her contribution to the present volume, Scott was active in the journal for mere months. Despite his promises to Gifford that he would assist in the editorship and that he would be a steady supplier of articles and men (*QR* Letter 4), no sooner had the first issue appeared than Scott's interest trailed off. The archives also confirm, however, Scott's importance in carrying the project forward: he organized political and literary sponsorship; he articulated an editorial policy; he suggested a marketing strategy; and, perhaps most important of all, he inspired confidence in Murray, Canning, Gifford and the others that the project could succeed. But after the initial issue, published on 1 March 1809, he barely kept his hand in. Between the ninth number, published in April 1811, and the twenty-seventh number, published in March 1816, he contributed nothing. The reasons for Scott's withdrawal are complex: his energies were needed elsewhere – to manage his difficult business relationship with the Ballantyne brothers for instance – but a major consideration was that he found it an imposition constantly to be pressed for copy by Gifford, Murray and Heber. In any case he could persuade himself that the journal had achieved the goals he had set for it in October 1808 (*QR* Letter 4). By 1811 its success was assured, or at least the danger of its imminent collapse had passed; it had to some extent undermined Archibald Constable's power by diluting the novelty of the *Edinburgh Review*; and it certainly had successfully challenged the *Edinburgh*'s intellectual and ideological monopoly. The *Quarterly* was an important episode in Scott's life, but it was only an episode.[18]

Once Scott absented himself, Murray had one major competitor for top-to-bottom control of the journal, his editor. A contest of wills between Murray and Gifford was played out intensively in the period 1809 to 1811, with the selection of articles and the assignment and management of contributors as their chief battleground. The names Penrose, Kidd, Conybeare and Monk were flashpoints (*QR* Letters 27, 30, 45, 83, 195). These were men Gifford recruited or encouraged whose articles were either rejected by Murray or amended in circumstances that, in each instance, humiliated Gifford and caused him seriously to consider whether he should continue as editor. The answer always was, yes he would continue, but it was increasingly on Murray's terms. The best Gifford obtained from Murray was the delineation of separate spheres of influence. The older man, Gifford, would supervise the university crowd, the clerics and classicists, he would police articles for sloppy expression and lapses in 'taste' and, as Canning's agent, he would monitor the journal's political ethos. The younger man, Murray, would manage the prestige contributors – Southey, Barrow and Croker. It was an accommodation that Gifford was forced to accept because Canning's day-to-day influence was weak and because Murray's practical power over his editor was strong.

Delving into archival *Quarterly Review* materials, we discover that, during the journal's first years, John Murray transformed himself from a junior member of the British publishing fraternity and a peripheral member of the *Quarterly*'s editorial coterie into a man who, by 1815, was acknowledged as 'the Prince of Booksellers'[19] and who in 1817 claimed, without fear of contradiction, that he 'alone created' the *Quarterly Review*, 'the most formidable engine that ever was invented, in support of the laws and Religion of his Country' (*QR* Letter 216).

John Murray extended control over Gifford and his other gentlemen by using money strategically, to buy loyalty, to advertise success and to create dependencies. It was not market pressure or 'impulsive generosity'[20] alone that drove him to pay so well; his extravagance may have been risky, even foolish, but it was extensive and systematic. He used money not by threatening to withhold it, but by throwing it at his editor and contributors, by rewarding those of his gentlemen for whom, as Scott put it, receiving compensation of fifteen or twenty guineas was 'a matter of convenience to them' (*QR* Letter 4). He supplied gratis subscriptions to the men and women he wished to compliment, flatter or do business with. To the men upon whose loyalty he depended he sent gifts: to the inveterate bibliophile Richard Heber, fine first editions; to the voracious reader Southey, rafts of free books; in later years, to the ailing Gifford, permanent access to carriage, horse and driver; to Barrow and Croker, his most prolific contributors, Murray sent cheques so generous that both men felt obliged to return them. Money was an effective, if expensive, means of control.

Through his largesse Murray created, for those of his gentlemen who were susceptible, an 'income stream' and with it a 'lifestyle dependency'. Certainly Southey and Gifford were not immune. Judging by his complaint to Canning in 1824 that by his retirement from the editorship he would lose half his income (*QR* Letter 257), the payment Gifford received from Murray was more important to him than he otherwise let on. As for Southey, to secure the quality of research and writing that he brought to the journal, Murray paid his best writer the astonishing figure of £100 per article, regardless of length.[21] Southey resisted by asserting his dignity, but with his own and the poet Coleridge's children to feed, he could not practically refuse payment or, like Gifford, Croker and Barrow, insist upon being paid less:

> Your pay is very liberal, and the price which I receive for my writings is by no means a matter of indifference to me, but it can make no difference in the manner of my writing. The same diligence, the same desire, – and the same power (whatever that may be) were brought to the task when you paid me ten guineas per-sheet, as when you raised it to 100£ per-piece. This last is a great price, and it is very convenient to me to receive it. But I will tell you with that frankness which you have always found in my correspondence and conversation, that work at that price I say suspect my time might be more profitably employed (as I am sure it might be more worthily) than in writing for your journal at the even at that price. (*QR* Letter 196)

Despite his threats to stop contributing to the *Quarterly*, oft repeated, all he could do was bluster and enjoy the insults about Murray – an intolerable coxcomb, a secret drinker – that his friend Grosvenor Bedford retailed for his benefit: 'Murray's an ass as we well know and have agreed upon long ago – a liberal ass enough perhaps – but still an ass'.[22]

We see in the *Quarterly Review* materials that money was the most obvious, but not the only, form of currency Murray used to control his men. Foremost among his other means were the journal's fame and reputation, means that Gifford also used to achieve particular purposes. The *Quarterly* enjoyed a prestige that has few parallels in journalism, then or now. T. F. Dibdin, a noted contemporary bibliophile, described the fevered demand for the *Quarterly* in the 1820s:

> In the history of Literature, the subscription-book of Mr. Murray ... would cut a splendid figure: and the ease and dexterity with which each number is divided into allotments, and distributed according to the copies subscribed for (the payment being PROMPT) by the several great bookselling houses, would astonish a looker on ... At sun-rise, the QUARTERLY TREE reaches to the sky ... At sun-set, it is levelled to the earth ... and every man hugs his *log* (alias, number) with eager and undiminished delight. What a SUB-NOTE might be here appended, as to the *sensations* which certain numbers ... are known to have some times produced?[23]

Obtaining just such a degree of estimation with the public was a key strategic goal that Scott, Murray and Ellis agreed in their letters of October and November 1808 (*QR* Letters 4, 7, 8, 10, 11, 14). Archival materials give us an idea of how the *Quarterly* achieved success and how its principals used what they called the journal's 'credit' as a commodity of exchange. The journal held out the promise that in its pages readers would have access to privileged and authoritative information, information from high government figures, from executive members of the civil service, from the bishops and from the great minds of the nation's universities. Gifford also cultivated the *Quarterly* as a source of reliable historical information. To that end he incubated major well-documented treatises, such as the articles Robert Hay produced on Russia's entry into the war against Napoleon, the articles John Wilson Croker wrote that he based on the memoirs of French revolutionists, and the article the Duke of Wellington sub-edited on the battle of Waterloo. The Second Secretary of the Admiralty, Sir John Barrow, made use of official documents in his articles on voyages in search of a northwest passage and on history-making explorations of discovery in deepest Africa, the Himalayas and the South Pacific. It was just because his articles combined these two types of authoritative information – official and historical – that they were highly popular and brought great credit to the *Quarterly Review*.

Gifford stipulated that a primary reason he had joined the *Quarterly*'s van was to stand up for literature, the Constitution, the Church and Christianity. 'I had long seen', he wrote to Edward Copleston, 'with thousands besides, that the Government was calumniated, the great literary Establishment of the country depreciated, the Church insulted, and even Religion itself attacked [by the

*Edinburgh Review*] with the unfairest and most odious weapons: and I flattered myself that when a fair opportunity was afforded, the friends of Order, Morality and rational Piety, would muster in their defence' (*QR* Letter 30). Because he saw more clearly than most of the other members of the journal's editorial machine that the *Quarterly* was committed to defending these national 'establishments', Gifford perspicaciously insisted that classical and religious topics should form part of the journal's regular fare. Referring to reviews of Latin and Greek texts, Murray's verdict was that 'more than one ... *learned* Article clogs us sadly' (*QR* Letter 61). That was not Gifford's opinion. As an imitator of Horace and Persius and as a translator of Juvenal, Gifford was attracted to the classics, but the reason he went out of his way to admit Greek and Latin articles was to cater to an important recruiting pool, men at the English universities. As Christopher Stray points out in his essay herein, publishing esoteric reviews of Greek texts was also a coded language meant to reassure the journal's subscribers who read the ancients that the *Quarterly* supported the classical edifice of British culture.

Gifford also met forceful, even contemptuous resistance from Murray, Ellis and Erskine when he championed the insertion of religious articles in the journal (*QR* Letters 26, 29, 59, 61). The editor persevered because he alone among the journal's principals recalled that the *Quarterly* was in part set up to rally a defence of the established Church and rational Christianity. Encouraged by his hyper-orthodox best friend John Ireland, the Dean of Westminster, Gifford showed an awareness that many of the journal's patrons expected the *Quarterly* to be an engaging persuasive advocate for the Church, and to promote Christianity as one of the nation's core values (*QR* Letters 7, 89, 146).

Gifford believed that historical, religious and classical articles elevated the journal above ephemera and created a demand for second, third and fourth 'editions' (*QR* Letter 148). It was a demand that saw complete runs of the periodical sold in large numbers to the end of the century, runs that were then passed down from generation to generation.[24] While it is unknown how many subscribers who bought the *Quarterly* had no intention of reading it – such as the Earl of Buckinghamshire, the leaves of whose copies to this day remain uncut –[25] it is clear that he and others like him were purchasing prestige by association; they displayed the journal in their country homes or London flats to advertise their intellectual credentials, their allegiance to the conservative administration, and their loyalty to Church and king.

Because the *Quarterly*'s prestige also brought credit to its writers, between John Murray's gentlemen there was intense competition over the selection of books to review (*QR* Letter 58), over the matching up of books and contributors (*QR* Letters 47, 83), and over the ordering of articles in a given issue (*QR* Letter 194), including which articles would occupy the privileged positions of first and last (*QR* Letter 61). Successful contributors asserted or were granted possession of swaths of intellectual territory. In the case of George Ellis, this meant ownership of individual authors – Lord Byron and Sir Walter Scott; in the case of Sir John Barrow, mental dominion over real geography – China, the Arctic, Africa, the South Pacific. Only one man, Richard Heber, ever exercised complete independence from Gifford and Murray in the matter of commissioning contributors and assigning books for review (*QR* Letters 47, 48, 75, 91). That his exercise of this power was anomalous and deeply inappropriate is evidenced in its chaos-inducing results. Gifford was left in the embarrassing position of having to tell a key collaborator such as Ellis or Scott to stop progress on an article they had begun because Heber had assigned it to another writer. Heber got away with this behaviour because he was present at the creation, because he was an effective recruiter for Gifford, and because he was Canning and Scott's particular friend.[26]

Gifford himself had a practical use for the journal's credit – as a commodity to be traded for regular copy. Although the *Quarterly*'s success, he said, only served to alarm him – he feared it could not be sustained – it did offer to alleviate his 'perpetual dread lest any assistance should be withdrawn' (*QR* Letter 122). Gifford used the journal's prestige to attract and retain contributors, but in that regard he faced a challenge. The pride of association that he could hold out as incentive to potential contributors was a tricky asset. It was not easily convertible, for bragging rights accrued to contributors only if their authorship was known, and the *Quarterly*'s rule, at the time conventional among review periodicals, was that its authors remain anonymous. One of the purposes of secrecy was 'the production of a corporate voice and corporate responsibility';[27] anonymity also benefited the *Quarterly* by permitting the journal to imply a fine pedigree for its articles that they did not always deserve. Letting it get out that Canning, Scott and Southey were contributors created a significant advantage, for association with the good and the great helped cast a glow of privilege and quality over the whole journal (*QR* Letter 53). Anonymity could raise all boats; it could also – at least in the imaginations of readers – elevate the already good into the realm of the sublime. When Gifford was fortunate enough to find a writer whose contributions created a sensation – as Lord Dudley's articles did – the author's hidden face, Junius-like, became the object of fevered speculation. Readers constructed a charismatic personality for their author; the powers they attributed to him were beyond all reason: 'It is impossible that any *known* name could support the high character which our *anonymous* assistant sustains', Gifford gleefully informed Murray (*QR* Letter 63). Novelty and competence, nurtured by promotion and speculation, helped gain the *Quarterly* the inflated credit that is the natural concomitant of extraordinary fame.

While it was one thing to let it be known that great men wrote for the periodical or to encourage readers to get excited about its good writers, it was quite another to reveal that very ordinary men also wrote for the *Quarterly*. As Croker warned Murray in 1823, should that truth come out the benefits of anonymity to the individual writer and to the journal as a corporate enterprise would evaporate: 'If you were to publish', he said, 'such names as Cohen and Croker and Collinson and Coleridge, the magical WE would have little effect, and your Review would be absolutely despised – omne ignotum pro mirifico'.[28] The potential danger or disadvantage of revealing an author's name meant that Gifford only selectively permitted it. He shared his secret knowledge with a collaborator, or permitted an author to let his name be known, when he thought it would benefit the *Quarterly*.

The *Quarterly Review* materials present us with examples of the variety of ways Murray, Gifford and their correspondents maintained or manipulated the policy of anonymity. In some instances it was Murray and Gifford's writers who, often for political reasons, insisted that they vigorously *keep* their secret. In the most elaborate cases, such as those of Robert Grant and Lord Dudley, even the publisher and editor were not permitted to know their authors' identities. Grant's father, Charles Grant, a high official in the East India Company, was an associate of William Wilberforce, James Stephen and Lord Teignmouth – the so-called Saints. The Saints had interests – such as their parliamentary alliance with the radical 'Mountain' against slavery and the slave trade – that might have been compromised had it become known that Grant was writing for the *Quarterly*. After all, a slave owner, George Ellis, was one of its co-conductors; the journal might at any moment come out with an article that would contradict and embarrass the Saints. To hide his handwriting, Grant had his friend John Thornton transcribe his drafts. Reginald and Richard Heber, Lord Teignmouth and Zachary Macaulay conveyed drafts and proofs between Grant and Gifford. Even more than Grant, Lord Dudley was determined not to be discovered. We find in Gifford's letters that Copleston – who acted as mediator between Gifford and Dudley – directed the editor to go to extraordinary lengths to remain ignorant of the identity of his 'anonymous friend'. Dudley also used an amanuensis and Copleston compelled Gifford and Murray to employ servants as runners and a London bookseller, 'Mr Budd', to act as a blind post office (*QR* Letter 103).

Few authors were quite so particular about maintaining anonymity as these two men; indeed, many of the *Quarterly*'s writers itched to have their names known. Gifford did sometimes grant a writer permission to claim his article in public, but when he did so, he often had an ulterior motive. A good case in point is that of James Henry Monk, the primary author of an important article on education that appeared in 1819.[29] By permitting him to reveal his authorship, the editor used Monk as a screen. As was his wont, Gifford submitted Monk's article to Croker for sub-editing; Croker then showed the article to Lord Lonsdale, whose interests were alluded to in the article; Lonsdale insisted that the reference to him be deleted. Croker and others also supplied arguments and drew conclusions; Canning polished the article (*QR* Letter 204). Except for Canning's helpful additions, it had not been Gifford's idea to let these men manipulate Monk's article to such an extent. Indeed he fiercely resisted Lonsdale's interference and he tried to remove some of the added material, but Murray and his allies Croker and Barrow faced him down (*QR* Letters 201, 202, 203, 205). In so doing, they showed contempt for his authority and humiliated him into filling the ugly role that Hazlitt accused him of occupying, that of 'literary toad-eater to greatness, and taster to the court'.[30] Gifford now had to ensure that his masters' interventions would not become known: 'That a word proceeds from me' (by which he meant Monk's collaborators) 'must *never never* be hinted', Gifford gravely impressed upon his young contributor. Counselling discretion, he disingenuously permitted Monk to admit to relatives and close friends that he was the article's author (*QR* Letter 197). Gifford knew his man. Like a colt out of the gate, Monk giddily revealed his role to his girlfriend and to anyone else who cocked an ear in his direction; his letters make delightful reading (*QR* Letters 206, 209, 212, 214, 215).

Letting an individual contributor forgo anonymity was one thing. What Gifford seldom did was confide his personal knowledge of an author's identity. When he did so, it was usually to a member of the inner circle. The other founders of the *Quarterly Review* had access to this secret knowledge by right; Gifford did not and could not withhold it from them. It is telling, however, that he could and did make an exception with Murray. In part this was because he was in competition with his publisher, in part it was because, as publisher – Southey liked to point out that Murray was a mere 'tradesman' – Murray's status was different in kind from that of the other founders, but it was also because, as he warned Scott, he thought Murray could not be trusted: 'The vanity of being in a secret, is too great for him' (*QR* Letter 121).

Given the value Gifford placed on possession of even a *single* author's name, it is a wonder that he ever gave up the pearl of great price, the key to *all* contributors. The *Quarterly Review* letters reveal that by giving out this key Gifford brought only one newcomer into the journal's inner circle, the future provost of Oriel College, Edward Copleston, to whom he repeatedly insisted 'I have no secrets' (*QR* Letters 45, 92, 207). To understand why Copleston alone outside the co-founders was admitted to the elect, we need look no further than the great number of men he brought to the *Quarterly*: Blomfield, Elmsley, Mitchell, Monk, Penrose, Davison, Grey, Phillpotts, Whately, Senior, Berens, Mitford and Dudley. From the blunt flattery of Gifford's letters to Copleston (*QR* Letter 99), and from his giving up this precious possession, we can see that Gifford had found in this collaborator whom he called 'the man of men' an indispensable ally (*QR* Letter 34).

The power the *Quarterly*'s success gave Gifford was limited and he was not terribly adept at using it. Murray, though, employed the *Quarterly*'s assets aggressively: to negotiate favourable terms with other publishers who clamoured to be associated with his firm (*QR* Letter 51); to obtain commissions from government;[31] and to manipulate the men his success depended on, his authors and his editor. Murray, with Gifford's assistance, gained this power by increasing the *Quarterly*'s putative value. Following Scott's instructions (*QR* Letter 4), he boosted the *Quarterly* above Grub Street journalism by applying the lessons the *Edinburgh* taught him: he resisted the temptation to puff his publications by commissioning positive reviews of them in the *Quarterly*; he paid his writers handsomely and insisted that all contributors accept compensation regardless of their class or means; and, with Gifford, he published, among lighter fare, lengthy informative reviews which, contemporaries believed, qualified as permanent contributions to history, biography or literature. In each of these respects, the *Edinburgh* paved the way, but Murray and Gifford went where the *Edinburgh* could not go: they extended the reach of politically-focused journalism into respectable conservative households of the middle class and aristocracy, Hazlitt's 'mob of well-dressed readers',[32] and they made association with review journalism a desirable career move for aspiring conservative professionals in the Church, law, the civil service and government.[33]

Alone among the quality periodicals, the *Quarterly* benefited its writers to the extent of potentially qualifying them for major patronage.[34] During Gifford's tenure it was the conservatives who dispensed patronage, primarily of course to their confrères. So a man's association with the *Edinburgh* or another 'serious' journal that espoused questionable political opinions – the *Critical*, the *Monthly*, the *Westminster* – may have garnered him intellectual respect, but it is doubtful that it would have helped him gain a patronage appointment.[35] Writing for a conservative journal such as the *British Critic* or the *Antijacobin* might qualify one for patronage, but only of a minor sort, because even members of the same general political species held these journals in contempt.[36] To the extent that association with the *Quarterly* helped its men receive patronage – men such as Copleston, Ireland, Blomfield, Davison, Grant, Heber and Monk, to name a few – it did so because the journal's quality reflected well on their services to the Crown.

The success of those of John Murray's gentlemen who, as Gifford put it, 'wrote for promotion' (*QR* Letter 113), is good evidence of the journal's respectability and the marketable value of its fame. That association with the *Quarterly* commanded real benefits can be readily illustrated. To return to James Monk, it was generally acknowledged that his 1830 elevation to the bishopric of Gloucester was in part a reward for his 1819 article on Brougham's education committee. Monk's elevation was resented, however, because there was a suspicion – not unfounded, as we have seen – that he deserved diminished credit for the review. Monk, it was thought, had merely supplied the article's matter, its 'coarse cloth', whereas Canning had supplied its 'gold lace and spangles' (*QR* Letter 268). A less complicated, but also controversial, instance is that of the valuable *Quarterly*

*Review* writer the Reverend John Davison. In 1817, Lord Liverpool presented him to the vicarage of Sutterton, Lincolnshire, at £1,400 per year. So rich was this living that Davison thought there must have been a mistake and asked the Prime Minister for a clarification. The episode raised eyebrows at Oxford because Davison was appointed ahead of men thought by partisans to be more deserving.[37] As he was a man of relatively slight accomplishment, only his association with the *Quarterly* explains his receiving, repeatedly, the Prime Minister's patronage.

We see in the archival materials that in virtue of its success the *Quarterly Review* became a commodity of exchange to all who were associated with it, to its founders, conductors, writers and readers alike. For their part, John Murray's gentlemen clothed the regime in respectable dress and so qualified themselves for lucre and for fame. Its readers benefited by being informed and entertained, and by having their views justified and confirmed in a respectable periodical. In the end, by maintaining a degree of independence from government while at the same time obtaining the government's imprimatur, the publisher and his editor satisfied their sometimes competing aims: John Murray made money and became the 'Prince of Booksellers'; William Gifford paid fealty to his political master George Canning and, in doing so, promoted British nationalism and the liberal conservatives' political vision.

## Acknowledgements

I would like to express my appreciation to the essay contributors for, on short notice, generously responding to my request to contemplate the significance of the materials I had collected and for abiding with me when the project hit a rough patch in early 2007.

I give heartfelt thanks to my wife, Sylvia Jones Cutmore, who over the course of too many years has sacrificed time and treasure to the 'books'. I am grateful to my children, Benjamin, Laura and Philip, for struggling with me over many a hard-to-read word in the Gifford letters, and for being patient whenever I drew their attention to another and yet another *Quarterly Review* connection.

I also wish to thank Christopher Stray for his cheerful encouragement and ready assistance; Donald Reiman for initiating the publication of the *Quarterly Review Archive* on the University of Maryland's *Romantic Circles*; Iain Brown, Principal Manuscripts Curator at the National Library of Scotland, and his staff for guidance concerning the Sir Walter Scott materials; and Virginia Murray, John R. Murray and the late 'Jock' Murray for access to the John Murray Archive when it was at 50 Albemarle Street.

JC
April 2007

# 1 PLOTTING THE SUCCESS OF THE *QUARTERLY REVIEW*

## Kim Wheatley

A good plot good friends and full of expectation –
An excellent plot excellent friends

*QR* Letter 5

The exchanges of letters between John Murray and his gentlemen beginning in 1807 offer a revealing look behind the scenes of the *Quarterly Review*. Jonathan Cutmore's unpublished edition of these letters gives us a greatly enlarged impression of what Murray, Walter Scott (not yet Sir Walter Scott) and George Ellis thought they were doing as they worked in secrecy to found the *Quarterly* in opposition to the *Edinburgh Review* and enlist William Gifford as editor. I will be concentrating here on the letters written prior to the first issue of the *Quarterly* that discuss the founders' elaborate plans for the new periodical. Our new insight into the specificities of these plans deepens our understanding of the material conditions underlying Romantic-era print culture. Mixed in with references to other business matters, we can also find in the letters plenty of eye-opening general reflections about what these so-called 'Tory conspirators'[1] hoped to achieve. As Cutmore shows in his essay in the present volume, re-examining the formation of the *Quarterly* helps to challenge the myth of its ideological cohesiveness. In my essay, I will be looking both at freshly available and previously published letters to bring out the creative impulses behind this high-stakes enterprise. I have raised elsewhere the question of what it would mean for Romantic-era periodicals to be termed Romantic in the traditional aesthetic sense.[2] Many scholars have long considered the politically conservative *Quarterly* anti-Romantic because of its intemperate attacks on Percy Bysshe Shelley, John Keats, Leigh Hunt and William Hazlitt. However, certain articles in the *Quarterly* can be seen as contributing to even while they resist the emergence of canonical Romanticism – not so much in what they say as in how they say it. By contrast, the letters dealing with the founding of the *Quarterly* at first sight exemplify the nitty-gritty machinations behind the invention of a new product in the literary marketplace, appearing completely at odds with Romantic notions such as spontaneity, beauty and the 'deep self'. To the writers of these letters, 'transcendent' is merely a complimentary adjective to apply to a well-crafted article rather than a tribute to the sublimity of the imagination (*QR* Letter 137). Yet the 'success' pursued by these writers (*QR* Letter 1) – whether political, literary, financial or all three – verges on the mystical: success for the *Quarterly* in its early years constitutes, in William Wordsworth's phrase, 'something evermore about to be'.[3]

Recent criticism of early nineteenth-century periodicals has focused on the periodicals' shaping of their audiences and on the interplay between collective discourse and individual authorship. These same two issues intersect in this fascinating collection of letters. The chief preoccupation of the founders of the *Quarterly* is the influence that they hope the periodical will have on its readers. As William St Clair has recently emphasized, the Romantic era saw widespread debate over the effects of reading and, in particular, the power of the printed word. St Clair's book foregrounds sales and circulation figures to modify more text-based interpretations of Romantic-era print culture such as Jon Klancher's book on the carving out of distinct but overlapping readerships by different periodicals.[4] Not surprisingly since they are looking forwards rather than backwards, the founders of the *Quarterly*, by contrast, initially approach the creation of audiences from the point of view of production rather than reception: they imagine the responses of implied as opposed to actual readers. I am especially interested in the assumptions that they make about writing and reading as they plot to counter the (to them) lamentable brilliance of the *Edinburgh*. We will see that these writers slide back and forth between concerns with the propagation of political principles, literary merit, entertainment value and commercial viability. A central problem for them is whether the *Quarterly* should replicate the supposedly vitriolic prose of the *Edinburgh*. At times, the achievement of what the letter-writers euphemistically call a 'sprightly' style (*QR* Letter 8) comes to seem an end in itself.

Besides discussing how they hope to 'create' an 'ardent appetite in the public' (*QR* Letter 25), the letter-writers explicitly and implicitly address the relationship between establishing a corporate ethos and expressing the opinions of individual contributors. The complexities of this relationship have taxed recent commentators on Romantic-era periodical writing, many of whom use as their starting point Klancher's notion of a depersonalized 'transauthorial discourse'.[5] David Latané contends that 'any attempt to define unilateral corporate discourse' must be balanced against the effort to '[resurrect] the diffuse subjectivities of noncanonical writers'.[6] By contrast, St Clair warns against applying Romantic notions of solitary authorship, claiming that 'When reviewers employed the royal "we", they were implying that their views were those of the institution for which they were writing and of a constituency of the reading nation whom they claimed to represent, not just their own views'.[7] Other critics try to reconcile Romantic conceptions of authorship with a heightened awareness of the historical conditions of periodical production. Mark Parker and Nanora Sweet, for example, both stress the ability of individual editors to manipulate the overall effect created by their anonymous contributions.[8] As we will see, the *Quarterly* letter-writers are preoccupied by editorial power – both that of Francis Jeffrey, whom they regard as the almost preternaturally effective editor of the *Edinburgh*, and, in anticipation, that of the controversial figure of Gifford. Yet they remain aware that 'Jeffrey's best articles are ... the result of the studies and thoughts of several friends' (*QR* Letter 32). Meanwhile, we can interpret the letters themselves, though of course signed by individuals unlike the articles in the periodical, as an unfolding collaborative text, a shared work-in-progress. Weaving in and out of extensive spoken conversations, and in some cases intended for the eyes of more than one reader, these letters enact the subordination of individual to collective agency as their writers collaborate on something larger than the sum of its parts – literally, the establishment of the *Quarterly*, but more abstractly the quest for a sense of 'success' that remains always just around the corner. At the same time, attention to the language of the letters enables us to begin to recapture the human voices behind an ostensibly corporate product.

Aesthetic concerns and human idiosyncrasies admittedly at first glance seem nowhere in sight in the earliest letter proposing the creation of the yet-to-be-named new Review,[9] a plea for 'high patronage' from Murray to the Tory politician George Canning (25 September 1807; *QR* Letter 1). Yet much of the letter dwells on the near-magical success of the *Edinburgh*, a topic that recurs obsessively in the letters that follow. Tellingly, Murray does not begin his letter by mentioning his proposed new periodical, but by informing Canning of what he surely already knows – that 'a work entitled the Edinburgh Review' has 'obtained an extent of circulation not equaled by any similar publication' (*QR* Letter 1). Throughout their letters, Murray and the other founders of the *Quarterly* will wrestle with the question of how to define their publication against the *Edinburgh*, sometimes referred to simply as 'our rivals' (*QR* Letter 7) or 'the enemy' (*QR* Letter 4). The letter-writers will also anxiously aspire to match or surpass the *Edinburgh*'s circulation figures, for a mixture of ideological and economic reasons. For the moment, ideological concerns are in the forefront as Murray conjures up a spectre of almost demonic efficiency: 'The principles of this work are ... so radically bad, that I have been led to consider the effect which such sentiments so generally diffused, are likely to produce; and to think that some means equally popular ought to be adopted to counteract their dangerous tendency' (*QR* Letter 1). Couching political opposition in moral terms in his September 1807 letter to Canning, Murray does not pause to define the 'effect' or to identify the exact correlation between a large audience and the propagation of 'dangerous' ideas.

In that letter, Murray continues to elevate the 'publication in question' by describing it as 'written with ... unquestionable talent' and 'conducted with ... high and decisive authority'. These phrases leave no room for debate: the writers for the *Edinburgh* would seem too supremely powerful to challenge, except that this letter at the same time belittles the *Edinburgh* as a mere party 'organ'. Murray initially leaves vague the nature of his proposed counterattack: 'some means equally popular' may be easier imagined than accomplished. Yet in the course of the letter he shifts from the humble suggestion that his plan 'is not perhaps undeserving of one moment of [Canning's] attention' to an announcement of the extent of his ambition: 'my object is nothing short of producing a work of the greatest talent and importance'. The magisterial *Edinburgh* will it seems be surpassed. The same switch from humility to self-aggrandizement can be seen in Murray's comments on himself: his attitude to Canning is deferential throughout, but he closes the letter with a display of his credentials: 'the person who thus addresses you is no adventurer, but a man of some property inheriting a business that has been established for nearly a century'. The connection between the achievement of a 'work of the greatest talent and importance' and the long-standing nature of Murray's 'business' is left to be inferred, although the implication is that talent can be bought and respectability can be borrowed. The hint of a conflict between individual self-assertion and submission to a collective entity – the publisher defers not only to Canning but to his unnamed 'friends' – will be developed in later letters by writers other than Murray.

This conflict between corporate and individual enterprise is much more evident in a long letter of advice from Scott to Gifford written more than a year later (25 October 1808; *QR* Letter 4) once arrangements for the new Review were underway. As a defector from the *Edinburgh*, Scott was one of the *Quarterly*'s most enthusiastic proponents. According to his biographer John Sutherland, 'He wanted to control the operation, but he did not want to be seen to be in control'.[10] The topics covered in Scott's letter include financial matters, the political character of the new periodical and the duties of the editor, as well as the arguably more mundane matters of the publication's name ('any one which has little pretension might serve the turn') and how often it should appear (quarterly, like the *Edinburgh*, is the predictable suggestion). Claiming that he does not have 'the vanity to hope I can point out any thing of consequence', Scott purports to offer merely a 'few observations' in obedience to 'the commands of our distinguished friends'. On one side, the 'distinguished friends' are at the helm; on the other, Gifford's own 'literary experience and eminence' rule the day. Yet Scott's downplaying of his own agency is belied by the length of his letter (almost 2,500 words) and its apparently comprehensive scope. Similarly, his self-deprecating reference to his 'miscellaneous' thoughts is belied by the clear organization of the letter. Scott even wrote a full draft of the letter (*QR* Letter 4A), which he sent to Ellis, and the differences between the two versions reveal the intensity of his involvement with the new Review. Scott circulated his revised version of the letter to the Scottish Lord Advocate Archibald Campbell-Colquhoun and to the future *Quarterly* contributor William Erskine as well as to Canning. The letter thus appears less a one-on-one communication than a contribution to an ongoing group discussion. In line with the ostensible ceding of control, eventually Scott's letter drifts, like those of some other correspondents, into figurative language hinting at an aggression that may unsettle the group's shared agenda.

The achievement of 'success', according to Scott, will rely on emulation of the *Edinburgh*'s financial practices, which turn out to be fundamentally, though not unproblematically, bound up with deeper concerns. Scott begins his advice with an assertion that is questionable despite its parade of inside knowledge:

> The extensive reputation and circulation of the Edinburgh Review is chiefly owing to two circumstances. First that it is entirely uninfluenced by the Booksellers who have contrived to make most of the other reviews mere vehicles for advertising and puffing off their own publications or running down those of their rivals. Secondly the very handsome recompense which the Editor not only holds forth to his regular assistants but actually forces upon those whose rank and fortune make it a matter of indifference to them. (*QR* Letter 4)

Objectivity is of course part of the ethos of the *Edinburgh*, but the idea that the *Quarterly* could be considered as independent of 'bookselling-interference', as Murray later put it, may seem far-fetched given Murray's own admission that 'It were silly to suppress that I shall not be *sorry* to derive from it as much profit as I can satisfactorily enjoy' (*QR* Letter 8), though of course he was merely suggesting that he would not puff his own works in the new journal.[11] Two years afterwards, Murray downplayed his concern for profit, telling Gifford, 'I would rather it excelled all other Journals and I gained nothing by it than gain £300 a year by it without trouble if it were thought inferior to any other. – This Sir is true' (*QR* Letter 59). Profitable or not, the *Quarterly* would long be defined by its connection to Murray's publishing house. James Mill, in a searing attack on the *Quarterly*, would accuse it of having 'always displayed much more of the character of a bookseller's catch-penny, than the Edinburgh Review'.[12] Scott's other point, that the *Quarterly* contributors, like those of the *Edinburgh*, should be 'handsomely recompensed' rests on the premise that high pay guarantees a high quality of writing – or rather that the perception that this is so will appeal to the reading (and purchasing) public. The image of writers being 'force[d]' into accepting payment supposedly reinforces the ideal of objectivity, but the mention of 'rank' in connection with 'fortune' betrays the possibility of social bias, anticipating the *Quarterly*'s reputation for deference to the aristocracy (*QR* Letter 4).

Further on in his letter of advice, Scott offers another questionable reason for the *Edinburgh*'s wide circulation:

> From eight to nine thousand copies of that review are quarterly dispersed and with all deference to the information and high talents of the Editor (which nobody can think of more highly than I do) much of this popularity is owing to their <its> being the only respectable and independant publication of the kind. In Edinburgh or I may say in Scotland there is not one out of twenty who reads the work that agrees in political opinion with the Editor, but it is ably conducted and how long the generality of readers will continue to dislike the strain of politics so artfully mingled with topics of information and amusement is worthy of deep consideration. (*QR* Letter 4)

What exactly does it mean to be 'ably conducted'? Given his emphasis on the *Edinburgh*'s phenomenal popularity, Scott seems to be suggesting that its large number of readers actually like rather than 'dislike' the artful mingling of politics and other topics – unless he is referring back to his claim that 'the lucubrations of the Edinburgh Review' concerning 'Spanish affairs' (or more precisely the Peninsular War) 'have done the work great injury with the public'. The *Edinburgh* had lost some subscribers after its notorious 'Don Cevallos' article had appeared in October 1808, but 'great injury' sounds like wishful thinking. From the contemplation of reputation it is a quick step back to sales figures: Scott goes on to say, 'I think the sale of the publication might be reduced at least one half by the appearance of a rival review'. Perhaps mistakenly, Scott seems to measure the 'ascendance' of the *Quarterly* in terms of taking readers away from the *Edinburgh* rather than expanding the existing reading public. Historical evidence demonstrates that some individuals, at least, did not read one of the quarterlies to the exclusion of the other.[13] In a letter to Scott, Ellis later imagined the *Quarterly* attracting the *Edinburgh*'s readers rather than carving out a new audience of its own: 'indeed I consider the high fortune of our rivals as one principal ground of hope; because, as those who have perused the morning-post are anxious to read the morning-chronicle, so, when the Edinburgh Review shall have a professed rival, will all its readers be eager to compare the antidote with the poison' (*QR* Letter 7). Rather than hoping to surpass the *Edinburgh*, Ellis takes its 'high fortune' as a guarantee of the *Quarterly*'s success. The logic here is still somewhat shaky, because the writer fails to consider that readers might be content with the 'poison' that they are already enjoying.

Scott's remarks on the 'political character' of the new Review in his letter of advice to Gifford skirt around the question of the extent to which politics can be separated from other considerations. He says at one point that 'It would not certainly be advisable that the work should in its outset assume exclusively a political character'. The 'character' of its writing must come first. 'But', he adds in a heightened tone, 'as the real reason of instituting the publication is the disgusting and deleterious doctrine with which the most popular of these periodical works disgraces its pages it is essential to consider how opposite and sounder principles can be most advantageously brought forward'. How will this happen? 'Principles', it turns out, will be spread through 'accurate views of points of fact'. Scott emphasizes, 'This is the most delicate yet most essential part of our scheme'. According to him, 'On the one hand', a reputation for partisanship would damage the *Quarterly* while 'On the other hand', the key to success will be the new periodical's access to 'political information'.[14] Those 'who have the power of befriending us in this respect' will supply such information to reviewers via the editor. Scott leaves unexplained how the dissemination of facts would spread 'sounder principles'.[15] A telling assumption in his letter is the idea that the *Quarterly* will succeed because of its political affiliations while the *Edinburgh* succeeds in spite of its affiliations; evidently, Scott believed that there was a conservative audience nested in the *Edinburgh*'s subscription list that, craving a journal based on better principles, could be separated from it.

In a letter to Ellis written the following week, Scott implies that the *Edinburgh* is politically powerful because it is socially necessary:

> Of this work 9000 copies are printed quarterly and no genteel family *can* pretend to be without it because independent of its politics it is the only ~~independent~~ <valuable> literary criticism which can be met with. Consider of the numbers who read this work how many are there likely to separate the literature from the politics – how many youths are there upon whose minds the flashy and bold character of the work is likely to make an indelible impression and think what the consequence is likely to be. (*QR* Letter 5)

The term 'valuable' here carries an economic as well as a cultural resonance. Scott betrays a distrust of the periodical reader's perceptiveness in claiming that 'of the numbers who read this work' few are able or willing to disentangle political partisanship from 'literary criticism' (literary criticism in the sense of reviews of books on all subjects not excluding politics). Since the *Quarterly* is going to propagate 'principles English and Constitutional' (*QR* Letter 5) without betraying itself as a party tool or political organ, presumably it will rely on the same obliviousness among its readers. A letter from Murray to Scott takes such obliviousness for granted: if 'we can once fix ourselves upon public attention, honnied drops of party sentiment may be delicately insinuated into the unsuspecting ear' (*QR* Letter 8). Murray's image suggests a desire to outdo the *Edinburgh* at its own game. In a later letter to the American publisher John Bristed, Murray describes the ideal *Quarterly* article: it should make 'the reader ... if possible so insensibly to feel your opinions as to adopt them, believing them to be his own, arising from his own conviction' (8 June 1810; *QR* Letter 51). Who needs 'information' if one can rely on the insidious effect of 'party sentiment'? Murray does not pause to define how review articles can work 'delicately' and 'insensibly'. In his long letter of advice to Gifford, Scott recommends 'labouring the literary articles with as much pains as the political' so as to give the new periodical 'a decided character independant of [politics]' (*QR* Letter 4). But the distinction between literary and political remains hypothetical.

Scott's comments on the 'office of editor' in his letter of 25 October go back and forth on the question of the extent to which this 'character' should be the result of collective or individual (editorial) effort. Should the editor be omnipotent, or should he rely on his 'friends'? Scott offers Gifford somewhat conflicting advice in his discussions of what he sees as the dual aspects of the editor's role: selecting contributions and revising them. First, the editor, or rather Gifford himself since Scott implies that no one else would suffice for the post, 'must be invested with the unlimited power of controul for the purpose of selecting curtailing and correcting the contributions'. Scott predicts that finding contributors will be 'so difficult' that Gifford himself will 'be soon compelled' to write for the Review himself, presumably further putting it under his 'controul'. Yet Scott also offers to work 'as a sort of Jackal or Lions provider' in helping out with 'this troublesome department of Editorial duty'. Gifford's 'power' will it seems depend on Scott's aid.

Scott's advice concerning the revision of articles again seems to play up the influence of the editor only to dilute it. This section of his advice foregrounds its assumptions about marketing and prose style. In the same letter, Scott begins by recommending that Gifford imitate Jeffrey:

> One very successful expedient of the Edinr. Editor and on which his popularity has in some measure risen is the art of giving life and interest even to the duller articles of his Review. He receives for example a criticism upon a work of deep research from a person who has studied the book and understands the subject and if it happens to be written which may often be the case in a tone of stupefying mediocrity he renders it palatable by a few lively paragraphs or entertaining illustrations of his own or perhaps by generalising and systematising the knowledge which it contains. By this sort of *fineering* he converts without loss of time or hindrance of business an unmarketable commodity into one which from its general effect and spirit is not likely to disgrace those among which it is placed. (*QR* Letter 4)

The phrase 'stupefying mediocrity' does not exactly convey a high opinion of learned men of letters. The idea that such a 'tone' could be redeemed by 'a few lively paragraphs' perhaps assumes that readers skim rather than digest the *Edinburgh*.[16] The reference to Jeffrey's practice of *'fineering'* articles is defined in the draft as 'render[ing]' dull articles 'palatable by throwing in a handful of spice' (*QR* Letter 4A). This image seems to concede the desirability of the sporadic inclusion of malice or scandal. (I will return to the letter-writers' use of culinary imagery.) The draft also refers to unrevised articles as 'goods' which 'in their original state ... might hang in the market', an image that emphasizes Jeffrey's skills as a businessman (*QR* Letter 4A). Although Scott makes it sound as if the *Quarterly* could by analogy basically be a display of Gifford's 'talent', he adds, 'And I should hope many friends and well wishers to the undertaking would be disposed to assist in this part of the task and altho they might not have leisure to write themselves might yet revise and correct such articles' (*QR* Letter 4). At this point in the discussion, editorial control seems to fan out to encompass other collaborators. One begins to visualize an army of editorial assistants energetically rewriting other people's contributions, presumably each 'throwing in' their own brand of 'spice'.[17]

The implication that the *Quarterly* is more a collective than an individual project is at once reinforced and destabilized by the military and warfare imagery in Scott's letter. This imagery occludes the real conditions in which the founders of the *Quarterly* were working – penning copious letters and sometimes enjoying each other's hospitality during face-to-face meetings. The letter's first figurative expression stresses subordination to the common good: Scott asserts that Jeffrey 'acts on the principle that even Czar Peter working in the trenches must accept the pay of a common soldier'. It is not clear whether the 'Czar' therefore earns less or more than he deserves. Human agency momentarily disappears entirely when Scott claims that conservatives have made the mistake in the past of thinking 'their good cause should fight its own battle'. But, he notes, 'it is not too late to stand in the breach'. The first number of the *Quarterly* 'will burst among the Whigs (as they call themselves) like a bomb'. These images are relatively depersonalized. In contrast, Scott predicts that Gifford himself will have to appear 'in the field' instead of trusting the cause to 'auxiliaries', stressing that the *Quarterly* will have to rely on Gifford's personal forcefulness as a writer. A few pages later Scott returns to the idea of proliferating rather than concentrated energy: 'In the mean while I am for gliding into a state of hostility without a formal declaration of war and if our forces for one or two numbers be composed of volunteers and amateurs we will find it easy when our arms have acquired reputation to hire troops of condottieri and to raise and discipline regular forces of the line' (*QR* Letter 4). This passage implies that, given the secrecy in which the *Quarterly* was being hatched, the *Edinburgh* will soon be at war without even knowing it. Apparently 'volunteers and amateurs' may suffice for the moment, since the 'foe' will be taken by surprise when the 'first bomb bursts upon the public' (*QR* Letter 5). A makeshift army's acquisition of 'reputation' will enable the commanders to obtain 'troops of condottieri' *and* 'regular forces', suggesting that the *Quarterly* will be doubly strengthened by mercenaries and a standing army, neither of which are available at present.[18] Insisting on writing implements as weapons,

Scott later defiantly announced, 'I will fight upon my stumps, like Widdrington, and *to* the stumps both of my pen and my sword, if need be' (*QR* Letter 18).

But can a makeshift army prevail? Murray's 15 November 1808 letter to Scott insists that it cannot. Revealing anxiety about the need for efficient leadership, Murray modulates Scott's military imagery: 'Entering the field ... as we shall do against an army commanded by the most skilful generals, it will not do for us to leave any of our best officers behind as a reserve, for they would be of no use if we are defeated at first – ~~but~~ We must enter with our most able commanders at once' (*QR* Letter 8). At once modifying and reconfirming his optimism, in his long letter to Gifford, Scott had added, 'It is certain some push must be made at first for if we fail we shall disgrace ourselves and do great injury to our cause. I would not willingly be like my namesake, Walter the pennyless, at the head of a crusade consisting of a disorderly rabble and I judge of your feelings by my own. But "screw up your courage to the sticking place and we'll *not fail*"' (*QR* Letter 4). His image of himself at the 'head' of a 'disorderly rabble', invoking the ignominious end of the so-called Peasants' Crusade, confirms the sense of vulnerability behind the mixed messages about whether 'auxiliaries' are weak or will prove strong enough. Moving forward in the 'van of the battle' is glorious but of course dangerous (*QR* Letter 4). The (slightly misquoted) adjuration from Shakespeare could be a stirring call to victory but seems ominous given that these words are spoken by Lady Macbeth before the murder of King Duncan. (Scott's use in another letter of the doomed Hotspur's 'excellent plot' speech, quoted as my epigraph, sounds equally ominous.) The draft of the letter contains less colourful language – no 'condottieri', no 'Walter the pennyless', no quotation from *Macbeth*, suggesting that Scott chose to intensify his letter's note of urgency, perhaps through fear that Gifford might '*fail*'. For all his emphasis on the benefits of a group of people working together, one suspects that Scott would like to take the management of the enterprise entirely into his own hands.

Gifford's own reflections on the extent of his editorial power also offer mixed messages. On 12 October 1808, he had written a letter to George Canning ambivalently characterizing himself as at once eager to delegate and intent on taking control. Gifford begins the letter by stressing his unfitness for the role of editor: 'I am, like Othello, declined into the vale of years, and from nature and habit, very inert' (*QR* Letter 3). As an editor, he is prepared merely to 'arrange and overlook the various articles, and carry them through the press' – although of course these may be no small tasks. Yet as the *Othello* allusion hints, this impression of relative feebleness is misleading. Gifford, it transpires, is ready to 'rouse [him]self in [his] elbow chair'. This phrase nicely encapsulates the tension between Gifford's apparent desire to mastermind the *Quarterly* and his self-image as an uninvolved back-seat editor. The tone of slight reluctance is contradicted by Gifford's later avowal in the same letter that 'I must be endowed with a sort of

Dictatorial power over what comes before me'. This forthright assertion implies that Gifford will stamp the *Quarterly* with his personality. After promising to 'use' his 'power' with 'lenity, but with the strictest vigilance', however, Gifford backs down from the implication that he wishes to mastermind all aspects of the new periodical. He offers a tempered rather than an absolute commitment: 'The business of revising, altering, occasionally adding, and finally carrying a work of this kind through the press will occupy fully as much time as I can ever promise myself'. This claim raises the question of how Gifford's 'power' can be 'Dictatorial' if he is not always wielding the pen. In the event, despite his protestations to the contrary, Gifford wrote at least four *Quarterly* articles, including one or two for the first number, and collaborated on at least twenty more, in addition to his revisions of other writers' contributions. Gifford's hidden presence always loomed large in hostile readers' responses to the *Quarterly* – one thinks, for example, of Hazlitt's or Leigh Hunt's strictures, which treat the periodical and its editor as virtually interchangeable.

Gifford's reply, dated 9 November 1808, to Scott's long letter of advice, gives a much more elaborate impression of his lack of energy but, as in his letter to Canning, the 'picture of my mind', as he puts it, has blurred edges. Considering the recipient, this particular letter may stress Gifford's 'lethargy' over his demand for 'power' because of Scott's own aspirations to power. But Gifford may protest too much. He asserts,

> I have many and serious fears of myself. From habit, feebleness of constitution (for I never yet knew what health was) and, perhaps, from years, there is come upon me, in the language of Bottom such an *exposition* of dullness, that, if my friends did not sometimes stick pins in my cushion, and set me in motion, you would certainly read among the casualties of this or the following year, 'Died, of an elbow chair. Wm. Gifford'. (*QR* Letter 6)

This comical image of an invalid dependent for movement on rather sadistically pin-wielding 'friends' and so chair-bound as to be on the brink of death is not calculated to inspire confidence in Gifford's commitment to the role of editor. In marked contrast with his letter to Canning, he now hesitates openly over whether he is equal to the task he has undertaken: 'I, too adventurously, it is to be feared, engaged to occupy a station which would task to the uttermost infinitely more vigour and ability than I ever possessed'. Yet he counteracts this insistence on his weakness by his confidence in the contributors that Scott is supposedly assembling: 'I should utterly despair but for the powerful assistance of your Northern friends: They have activity, energy, habits of deep thinking and a shrewdness which peculiarly fit them for criticism'. That is, Scottish rather than English contributors to the *Quarterly* will challenge the supremacy of the *Edinburgh*. Gifford, one assumes, will merely watch from the sidelines. Reinforcing the impression that he is playing up his fragility, Gifford continues: 'On Scotland, therefore, rest all our hopes; and, for some time at least, we can only aspire to the name of weak auxiliaries. Thereafter, perhaps, we may come "to fill a pit as well as better men"'. Gifford's use of Falstaff's language from *1 Henry IV* adds to his humorous self-characterization; the idea that he is merely an example of what Shakespeare's character calls 'food for powder' could hardly be further from his demand for 'Dictatorial power'. The question of whether the *Quarterly* will use English talent to defeat the Scots or fight Scots with Scots recurs elsewhere in the letters.[19] Gifford goes on to express an exaggerated deference to Scott's judgement, offering a wholesale acceptance of the terms of his letter and assuring him that his 'regulations' will be 'made the Canon law of the Undertaking'. He wonders – understandably – why the 'better qualified' Scott does not want to be editor and begs him to be 'viceroy over me'. After re-emphasizing his weakness ('What can I do?'), however, he goes on to modify his tone of anxiety and wry self-deprecation by showing that he does have a few ideas of his own about the shape of the first number, including the suggestion that the *Quarterly* should have more articles than the *Edinburgh*, a suggestion that was followed, but only during the first year or two. As in Scott's letter to Gifford, the true impetus behind the *Quarterly* remains uncertain: is it Gifford himself with his overstated tone of feebleness, Scott with his professed willingness to rely on 'amateurs', or the perhaps equally vague energies of 'friends', whether Gifford's (English) or Scott's (Scottish)? The uncertainty is a symptom of the multi-causal origins of the *Quarterly*, but also of a mutual struggle to find a distinctive voice.

Given Gifford's account of himself as dependent on friends pricking his chair-cushion, one might expect those friends to help him assert or exert himself, but, during the build-up to the first number, Scott and his correspondents are afraid that he will do too much as well as too little. Writing to Scott, Murray and Ellis both express anxiety over Gifford's low level of 'activity' as editor (*QR* Letters 8 and 9), not surprisingly given Gifford's own emphasis on his lethargy. Yet their letters also reveal a dread of letting the *Quarterly* be led astray by Gifford's lack of judgement or more specifically dominated by Gifford's propensity for satire. In a letter dated 15 November 1808, Murray begs for Scott's 'arduous assistance', for Gifford, he fears, 'has lived too little in the world lately – to have obtained that delicacy of tact whereby he can feel at one instant, and habitually, what ever may gratify public desire or excite public attention and curiosity' – the key, according to Murray at this point, to the *Edinburgh*'s 'success'. Murray also pleads for Scott's 'assistance' in persuading Gifford that Robert Southey would not be the appropriate person to write 'a grand Article upon Spain' for the first number, and dissuading Gifford from including a review of a translation of Juvenal because that would necessitate a reference to Gifford's own translation, thus betraying 'an *individual* feeling – the least spark of which in our early numbers must both betray and ruin us' (*QR* Letter 8). These comments imply that Gifford is taking too much control and threatening to stamp the periodical with his '*individual*' reputation as a satirist. Here we see the extent of the concern to give the *Quarterly* an anonymous corporate voice – the confident tone of which, one assumes, will completely mask the 'fear' confessed in this letter.

Murray's next letter to Scott, dated 17 November 1808, takes a more optimistic stance in referring to Gifford as 'most obliging in his activity upon our hints'. (Gifford will receive plenty of 'hints'.) The same letter asks Scott to help 'fann Mr G into the activity which we require' (*QR* Letter 9). A letter from Scott to Ellis dated the next day asks, 'Now, *entre nous*, will not our editor be occasionally a little warm and pepperish?' Scott calls these 'essential qualities' but does not want them to 'constitute the leading character' of the 'publication'.[20] This danger, of being overwhelmed by Gifford's acerbic voice, conflicts yet coexists with the prospect of Gifford failing to lend a sense of direction. Scott himself says that Gifford 'will require ... both a spur and a bridle, – a spur on account of habits of literary indolence induced by weak health – and a bridle, because, having renounced in some degree general society, he cannot be supposed to have the habitual and instinctive feeling enabling him to judge at once and decidedly on the mode of letting his shafts fly down the breeze of popular opinion'.[21] The similarity of the latter thought to Murray's idea about Gifford's lack of 'delicacy of tact' is a good example of how these letters can congeal into the expression of a collective mentality. In his reply of 22 November 1808, Ellis agrees with Scott that Gifford will have to be helped, both to put himself forward and to restrain himself. Picking up on Scott's term 'pepperish', Ellis added that '[Gifford] is the readiest of mankind to sacrifice his pepper-box, even at the moment when his hand is raised to powder the dish with its contents, although his own fondness for the most poignant and even caustic spices is the distinguishing characteristic of his taste. The only difficulty will be to convey some such monitor to his elbow' (*QR* Letter 10). But can a man whose 'taste' is defined by a 'fondness' for 'caustic spices' really 'sacrifice his pepper-box'? One is left with an impression of Gifford's propensity for self-assertion rather than the reverse, even while Ellis's claim in his 22 November letter that 'Our supervisor will require the most attentive supervision' suggests that Gifford's individual power will be an illusion. The success of the *Quarterly* will depend not on the efforts of one man, but on what already appears to be an ever-widening circle of potential contributors, none of whom singly can carry the day, despite their 'personal activity' (*QR* Letter 12).

The fraught issue of whether spice (or pepper) is nice – or desirable – is bound up with the issue of how much Gifford's own character will be the character of the *Quarterly*, but it is also bound up with the degree to which the Review should resemble the *Edinburgh* and fight it on its own ground. At the heart of the latter issue is the question of how to attract an audience and whether it is the allegedly 'flashy and bold character' (*QR* Letter 5) of the *Edinburgh* that has created its popularity (as opposed to, say, its political doctrines). In suggesting that the *Quarterly* contain more articles than its rival, Gifford claimed that sometimes the *Edinburgh* 'has been tolerably dull' due to lack of 'variety' (*QR* Letter 6). For the most part, however, the founders of the *Quarterly* seem to agree that the liveliness of the *Edinburgh* is the greatest barrier to the success of the new Review. On 15 November 1808 Murray wrote to Scott, 'If our first numbers are not written with the greatest ability, upon the most interesting topics – it will not excite public attention – no man, even the friend of the principles we adopt, will leave the sprightly pages of the Edinburgh Review to read a dull detail of stail morality up or dissertations upon subjects whose interest has long fled'. This comment implies that sprightliness must be matched with sprightliness. Murray sees the task of achieving such readability and thus the task of attracting an audience in terms of recruiting 'talent'. In the same letter he worries over 'the immense difficulty of obtaining talent of sufficient magnitude to render success even *doubtful*'; he also frets that the *Quarterly* risks *increasing* rather than decreasing the success of the *Edinburgh* if the first number does not 'vibrate on the scale of excellence with the best of the Edinburgh Review': 'the increasing reputation of the Edinburgh Review will most certainly be inversely to our *unsuccessful* opposition'. As in Scott's long letter of advice to Gifford, the implication is that to fail would be far worse than doing nothing at all. Murray insists, 'Our first numbers must contain the most valuable and *striking* information in politics and the most interesting articles of general literature and science – written by our most able friends'. The proliferation of superlatives registers the mounting pressure to achieve 'excellence'. Despite his emphasis on attracting readers, Murray recommends that in chastising 'literary men ... let it be with the gentle hand of a parent rather than with the scourge of a slave master'. The same letter recommends that, once established, the *Quarterly* should give 'opinions opposite to those of the Edinburgh Review without appearing to notice them and when we are strong indeed we shall gradually advance to partial attacks upon their weakest points. The Sardonic Grin however will be our best weapon' (*QR* Letter 8). The *Quarterly* writers will wear a 'Grin' in that they will pretend that the *Edinburgh* does not exist, but they will also presumably resort to the 'quizzing' style of the *Edinburgh* (*QR* Letter 4A). Murray and his gentlemen will return to the question of at what point the *Quarterly* should actually *mention* the *Edinburgh*.

Ellis, in his letter to Scott dated 11 November 1808, also addresses the issue of an appropriate style as he contemplates whether the *Quarterly* should be like or unlike the enemy. He first addresses the *Edinburgh*'s selection of articles:

> My own idea is that the Edinburgh Reviewers have most shamefully departed from
> their original professions by passing over without notice some works of great value
> ... whilst they have frequently, in their eagerness to produce a premeditated essay of
> their own on some popular subject, selected, as an excuse for the introduction of
> that subject, any paltry pamphlet that without their notice might have been lost or
> mislaid in the printers' warehouse; – and yet that it may be perhaps quite necessary
> for us, in some cases, to follow their example. (*QR* Letter 7)

The *Edinburgh* reviewers are shamefully inconsistent in using 'paltry' publications as pegs on which to hang 'premeditated' articles – 'and yet' their practice should probably be imitated! Ellis goes on, however, in contrast with Murray, to argue that the *Edinburgh*'s style of writing should not be duplicated: 'it is still easier to obtain popularity for such a work by good-natured pleasantry and plain sense, than even by that ribaldry to which the Edinburgh Reviewers have so successfully employed against authors who, if they possessed equally extensive means of circulating their satire, would have often been an overmatch for their critics'. The 'ribaldry' of the *Edinburgh* is only successful because of the periodical's wide circulation. Yet what if the satire caused the wide circulation in the first place? Scott, replying to Ellis a week later, agreed that vitriol should be avoided: 'The truth is, there is policy, as well as morality, in keeping our swords clear as well as sharp, and not forgetting the gentlemen in the critics. The public appetite is soon gorged with any particular style.'[22] Scott's claim begs the question of whether a sword really can be 'clear as well as sharp'. And what if the *Edinburgh*'s 'style' is addictive rather than nauseating? In the same letter, Scott enlarges upon the choice of weapons and ingredients:

> The Edinburgh folks squeezed into their sauce plenty of acid, and were popular from
> novelty as well as from merit. The minor Reviews and other periodical publications,
> have *outred* the matter still farther, and given us all abuse, and no talent. But by the
> time the language of vituperative criticism becomes general – (which is now pretty
> nearly the case) – it affects the tympanum of the public ear no more than *rogue* or
> *rascal* from the cage of a parrot, or *blood-and-wounds* from a horse-barrack. This,
> therefore, we have to trust to, that decent, lively, and reflecting criticism, teaching
> men not to abuse books only, but to read and to judge them, will have the effect of
> novelty upon a public wearied with universal efforts at blackguard and indiscriminat-
> ing satire.[23]

Returning to images of ingestion, with 'acid' now replacing 'spice', Scott conjures up a scenario in which 'abuse' ceases to be effective because it is so widespread. But the notion may be another example of wishful thinking since perhaps 'acid' can be digested without satiety. The 'language of vituperative criticism' may never actually get stale: it may simply generate more of the same. A tamer sort of 'novelty' may not be so easy to swallow.

The gastronomical imagery of Scott's 18 November 1808 letter to Ellis carries over to an imaginary scene of writing that would, if realized, serve to anchor the collective voice of the *Quarterly*. Previous letters had already lamented the impossibility of George Canning finding time to contribute to the new Review because of his political duties. But Scott proposes to Ellis that Canning, 'though unquestionably our Atlas, might for a day find a Hercules on whom to devolve the burthen of the globe, while he writes us a review'. Scott continues, 'suppose he should, as great statesmen sometimes do, take a political fit of the gout, and absent himself from a large ministerial dinner, which might give it him in good earnest, – dine at three on a chicken and a pint of wine, – and lay the foundation at least of one good article?' As with the military metaphors, the actual work of reading, thinking and writing is occluded. A 'good article', it seems, will appear as if by magic from the self-sacrificing repudiation represented by the early dinner-hour, the scanty 'chicken' and mere 'pint of wine'.[24] In the event, Ellis responded to Scott that Canning 'is really so harassed by the number of his necessary occupations that [it] is impossible for me, who *see* him so worn down with fatigue, to put a pen into his hands and request him to use it in our service' (*QR* Letter 11). As with Gifford's frequent mentions of his poor health, the fantasy of what the *Quarterly* might be here collides with human limitations. This is not the only moment in the letters when the collaborative labour exacted by the *Quarterly* encroaches on the boundaries of domesticity and private life. At one point Ellis laments that household responsibilities prevent him from travelling to meet with Scott in person: 'If it were possible to *spay* one's female servants, and perform a similar operation on the males, it would be something' (*QR* Letter 31)! On another occasion, a letter from Gifford to Scott blurs the line between an apparently essential leisure activity and the task of enlisting new contributors: 'And you, my friend, when you have killed all the moor game, will, I hope, prowl about the city, with your gun in your hand if necessary, and compel some ingenious idler, to come in!' (*QR* Letter 27). One might think that Scott's time would be better spent penning an article of his own, but this humorous image of him coercing a random 'ingenious idler' at gunpoint to contribute material concedes a certain irrationality behind the drive to make the *Quarterly* advance from strength to strength when it is barely off the ground.

As they geared up for the publication of the first number, the founders' discussions of what constitutes an effective style continued to refer anxiously to the style of the *Edinburgh*, either as something to aspire to or as something to avoid. Murray's 1 December 1808 letter to Scott claims that the 'last Number of the Edinburgh Review' contains 'several very heavy abstract articles' that 'have put many of their readers to sleep' (*QR* Letter 12). As the 'machine' went into 'motion' (*QR* Letter 12), the letter-writers monitored each number of the *Edinburgh* in order to measure its probable level of effectiveness in comparison with the *Quarterly*'s. Murray's next letter asserts that even if the forthcoming *Edinburgh* is 'immaculate ... we have no reason at present to be very apprehensive of a comparison even then' (*QR* Letter 13) – a contrast with his previous doubts. After the publication of the first number Murray wrote to Stratford Canning, 'I find that, upon comparison with the *E.R.*, we are thought to want spirit, and we require a succession of novelty to attract public attention before we shall be sufficiently read to render our counteracting arguments and principles decidedly serviceable to our cause'. The word 'spirit' would seem to allude euphemistically to the notoriously author-mangling style of the *Edinburgh*, but the phrase 'a succession of novelty' suggests that an alternative mode is possible: the same letter goes on to explain that 'by giving an account of books and subjects which the *E.R.* cannot have access to we shall provoke public attention, and by this means be able to insinuate and to circulate our better doctrines in Church and State'.[25] Whether mere 'novelty' can 'attract' or 'provoke' the 'attention' of readers who have been stimulated for so long by the *Edinburgh*'s 'spirit' remains to be seen. Besides, the *Quarterly* has some 'spirit' of its own. Reflecting the vacillating priorities of these discussions, its reviews are sometimes humourless, sometimes sarcastic. Reporting on the reception of the first number, Gifford told Scott that his mocking review of Sir John Carr's *Caledonian Sketches*[26] 'has set half the town a grinning – Can not you find out some poor but presumptuous devil to laugh at again? Why will not blockheads be more alert, and do something to serve us?' By his own account, Scott had engaged in more than ridicule. He called the piece a 'whisky-frisky article' and 'flagellation' (*QR* Letter 20),[27] descriptions suggesting that '[h]umour and pleasantry' (*QR* Letter 26) can shade into 'vituperative criticism'. Perhaps, once flagellation has been employed, the very expectation of more serves to keep readers awake.

No sooner did the first number of the *Quarterly* appear than the pressure began to produce 'one or two powerfully commanding articles ... grappling with the Edinburgh in extent and depth of research ... in Number 2' (*QR* Letter 18). After the second number of the *Quarterly* was published, Murray continued to hope to ratchet up the level of 'talent', though claiming that only a 'very few degrees higher' would suffice to 'establish our reputation' (*QR* Letter 25). However, Ellis later agreed with Murray that the third number of the *Quarterly* 'was, perhaps, very *profound*, but most notoriously and unequivocally *dull*' (*QR* Letter 28). In the same letter, Ellis blames Gifford, yet also defends him in asking, 'can you or I assert that he rejected what was new and lively, and selected what was old and dull?' The problem, according to Ellis, is 'want of *variety*'; the third number needed 'two or three spirited and playful articles ... articles which might have been supplied in a few hours, but which, merely because it was so easy to do it, none of us thought of supplying' (*QR* Letter 28). Playful articles, in this account, are the work of the left hand, their writing so 'easy' and quick to accomplish that one forgets to produce them, even though they make all the difference between captivating an audience and putting them to sleep, like an earlier number of the *Edinburgh*. The implication is that the effect of the *Quarterly*'s lengthier and more '*profound*' articles can be improved merely by juxtaposing them with shorter, more frivolous reviews – a practice imitated from the *Edinburgh*. Apropos of an article he had co-authored with Canning, 'Short Remarks on the State of Parties',[28] Ellis later told Scott, 'I trust that a little piece of political *nonsense* ... will tend in some measure to enliven us'. Ellis urges Scott to find 'leisure to be nonsensical also' (*QR* Letter 31). The enlivening of the *Quarterly*, it would seem, will involve turning work into play or vice versa. Another correspondent of Murray's, John Thomson, pointed out that 'Success' will be difficult 'partly because it is much easier to write with spirit, and to please the reader by a universal and unmerciful system of attack, than by fair, candid, and enlightened criticism. Every one is delighted to see an author cut up.'[29] The founders of the *Quarterly* tend to accept the assumption that it is 'easier to write with spirit' and therefore beneath them even while they embrace the fantasy of replicating the *Edinburgh*'s 'spirit'.

The strategy for combating the *Edinburgh* includes a determination not to mention the rival in the pages of the *Quarterly*, to pretend, at least initially, that the *Edinburgh* does not exist. On 20 January 1809, discussing the contents of the first number, Gifford told Scott, 'S[outhey]. has rushed ense stricto on the Edinburgh Review. This shall be remedied' (*QR* Letter 15). Here we see the editor poised with his scalpel. A letter to Scott from John Bacon Sawrey Morritt, a would-be contributor to the *Quarterly*, takes issue with this unwritten policy. Morritt begins his letter by dismissing a book of 'French travels' on the grounds that 'I do not think that I c[an] make an article worth a farthing for the Quarterly Review out of the materials' – partly because 'they do not afford room for much fun'. The 'established canons of modern criticism' evidently necessitate 'fun'. According to this writer, pleasing the audience is vital because it is the means of ensuring the *Quarterly*'s ideological impact. In the second half of his letter, he relates that Gifford via Murray 'objected' to an article because 'it is *not* the Plan of the Review to introduce any *attack* upon the Edinburgh review, of which they wish to avoid the mention as much as possible'. Morritt comments, 'Whether this proceeds from cowardice or prudence I do not pretend to judge, but surely it is not a promising Augury for the future entertainment one should expect from the review, which I hoped was set on foot for the express purpose of unmasking the sophistry and counteracting the tendency of the Edinburgh wherever it appeared assailable'. This statement takes for granted that 'the wit and ridicule of the Host against which you are drawn up' can only be counteracted with more of the same. Morritt adds that 'besides this in the numbers hitherto published of the Quarterly this law of arms has been by no means adhered to, for the Edinburgh Review is named in several instances ... I should have tho[ugh]t that an avowed war with the Enemy as we have the choice of the ground of attack would have been more advantageous to the cause than a masked battery which after all may never reach the mark it is aimed at'. It is unclear in what sense the *Quarterly* has the 'choice of the ground of attack'. The *Quarterly* had in fact referred to the *Edinburgh* in its first number and again in its second.[30] Inconsistencies aside, the founders apparently preferred a 'masked battery'. Morritt advises Scott to 'put a little more of your own spirit into their sleepy hostility' (*QR* Letter 24). Scott did not follow this advice, but Gifford later reported to Ellis, 'Scott says that we have struck our fangs deep into the Edinburgh gentry – fox it! we will bite yet harder. I shall die unrevenged if they are not compelled to name us' (*QR* Letter 62). Here we see the corollary of the decision not to mention the *Edinburgh*: the desire to force the *Edinburgh* to mention the *Quarterly*. A month earlier, Gifford exulted to Scott, 'The Edin. Rev. begins to get terribly angry – this is excellent: we shall drive it to name us soon' (*QR* Letter 57). In the event the *Edinburgh* mentioned the *Quarterly* in its November 1811 number,[31] though only in passing, and not combatively.

In later letters the founders of the *Quarterly* continue to connect the 'progress' of the periodical (*QR* Letter 12) to the question of how far its style resembles the *Edinburgh*'s. They remain preoccupied with the importance of providing 'entertainment' even while they vacillate over its purpose: is 'fun' (*QR* Letter 173) a means of reaching a large audience or a means to a higher end? As before, the 'brilliancy and interest' of the *Quarterly* (*QR* Letter 179) is perceived to rely on the interweaving of serious with 'quizzing' articles. At the same time, the letter-writers express doubts over whether the 'sober and judicious' criticism of the *Quarterly* can compete with the *Edinburgh*'s 'brisk ribaldry' (*QR* Letter 57). Echoing Scott and Ellis's emphasis on pepper and spice, Gifford complained to George D'Oyly, 'the high seasoning of the Edinburgh Review has spoiled all taste for more solid and simple criticism' (*QR* Letter 67).[32] The *Quarterly*, like the *Edinburgh* itself, would of course offer both. Success, sometimes measured mundanely in circulation figures (*QR* Letter 173 reports that 7,500 copies of the *Quarterly* have been sold in four days), at other times is perceived by the founders more nebulously in terms of 'character', 'credit' (*QR* Letters 77, 88) or the smell of victory, remaining tantalizingly out of reach. Once a 'great circulation' (*QR* Letter 128) is attained, that fact is sometimes celebrated in the letters as if that alone constitutes success, regardless of the political impact of the *Quarterly*. Occasionally the letter-writers report other positive outcomes: they have forced the *Edinburgh* to deteriorate – 'The Edinburgh Review is indeed fallen off ... We have certainly humbled their tone' (*QR* Letter 97); more specifically, their 'laugh' at the *Edinburgh* reviewer Sydney Smith has driven him to leave town (*QR* Letter 42). Yet success, however defined, once apparently achieved, only generates more anxiety, as the writers become obsessed with the prospect of failure: 'We stand so high, that I feel uneasy lest we should not keep our elevation' (*QR* Letter 79); 'This success only terrifies me' (*QR* Letter 123); 'great exertions are necessary to maintain the proud eminence which we have reached' (*QR* Letter 171); 'The success of the last alarms me for what is to come. How shall we maintain our reputation?' (*QR* Letter 210). Such expressions of 'alarm' continue to be punctuated with Gifford's negative self-characterizations: he is a 'poor broken-winded hack' (*QR* Letter 32), a 'miserable invalid' (*QR* Letter 111) and a 'dead weight' (*QR* Letter 118). This behind-the-scenes state of nervousness and sense of insufficiency continued to accompany the *Quarterly*'s achievement of high sales figures and a reputation for political efficacy and its speedy rise to cultural prominence.

In discussing the problem of whether or not to imitate the *Edinburgh*'s alleged practice of savage reviewing, the founders of the *Quarterly* often give the impression that their choice is a matter of calculating the maximum political or financial effect. However, the choice is scarcely straightforward when it involves weighing 'solid criticism' against 'brisk ribaldry'. Both require skill, though of different kinds, but one is tempted to conclude, in contrast with the letter-writers themselves, that it may be even more difficult to write with briskness – 'life' and 'spirit' – than to produce 'fair, candid, and enlightened criticism'. Yet, in effect, the choice is not a real one, because as we have seen, the writers envisage pepper, spice, acid or other jolts of violence being interjected into their otherwise 'sober' prose. Imagining this heightening of aggression to be the task of the editor keeps their heads sober and their hands pleasantly clean. Meanwhile, their playing with the idea of 'fun' would seem to make these letters more than an exercise in the development of a commodity. In the letters, the prospect of amusing readers frequently eclipses any studied political payoff or even literary success. Nevertheless, producing entertainment often remains a matter of profit or political expediency even while it at once showcases and risks masking literary talent. Expressing the hope, after the publication of its third number, that the *Quarterly* will improve and thus become more politically effective, Isaac D'Israeli told Murray, 'Like our Constitution, it may contain in itself a renovating power'.[33] The *Quarterly*, once it has formed its sober *and* brisk style, may take on its own independent momentum. Murray's anxiety that attacking the *Edinburgh* in the *Quarterly* will serve merely to advertise the Whig journal hints at a larger possibility – that the burgeoning business of bookselling, rather than individual periodicals, may possess its own 'renovating power'. Marilyn Butler makes an analogy with present-day advertising: just as advertising promotes consumption in general as much as particular products, the reviewing periodicals created a taste not so much for particular books or opinions as for more 'literary intelligence'.[34] That possibility pulls writers who are ideologically at odds together in a common interest. Eventually, whether the success of the *Quarterly* is seen in materialist terms or as an elusive ideal, the ongoing shaping of taste transcends any collaborative effort by the writers of the *Quarterly*: in a sense, they collaborate with all their fellow-authors and reviewers, including the writers for the *Edinburgh*. Rival chefs and their assistants; commanders of the field, auxiliary troops and their opponents; miserable invalids and their enemies: they all get to share the fun.

# 2 'SARDONIC GRINS' AND 'PARANOID POLITICS': RELIGION, ECONOMICS, AND PUBLIC POLICY IN THE *QUARTERLY REVIEW*

## Boyd Hilton

When the four Pittite loyalists William Gifford, John Murray, Walter Scott and George Ellis combined to found the *Quarterly Review*, their purpose was entirely political. Although Scott thought it inadvisable 'that the work should in its outset assume exclusively a political character' (*QR* Letter 4), and Ellis was afraid that the insertion of articles on both Denmark *and* Spain in the first number would 'render our undertaking too obviously political' (*QR* Letter 11), privately Murray made it clear that the 'merely literary' articles would be so many spoonfuls of sugar to disguise the taste of the medicine. 'If we can once fix ourselves upon public attention, honnied drops of party sentiment may be delicately insinuated into the unsuspecting ear' (*QR* Letter 8). Their purpose was political because they were alarmed – at times almost hysterically so – by the success of the *Edinburgh Review*, which was founded in 1802 and had come to be recognized as the mouthpiece of the opposition Whigs in Parliament.[1] 'It is as a political engine that their work is seriously formidable', wrote Ellis of the *Edinburgh* reviewers (*QR* Letter 40). In going in to battle against such brilliant 'northern' wits, Gifford sometimes felt that his own 'troops' were mere 'amateurs' and 'volunteers' by comparison.

It might seem odd in retrospect that the Whig Party of Grey and Grenville should have been seen as such a serious threat, since (apart from thirteen months during 1806–7) it had been out of office since 1783 and would remain so until 1830. However, the situation looked rather different to Pittite loyalists in 1808. Pitt himself had died in 1806 and had begun to be invested with the mythical qualities of a national saviour, a type of conservative nostalgia that was actually rather frightening, since the more Pitt was lauded the more his loss seemed catastrophic. Fox had also died, in 1807, but since he was thought to have been a liability to the opposition Whigs, his departure brought no comfort to Pittite conservatives. Worryingly, the most recent general election had left the two sides of the House of Commons quite evenly balanced, Portland's conservative administration was becoming increasingly dysfunctional,[2] the war was going nowhere disastrously, and a commercial crisis was looming. Worse still, radicalism was rampant thanks to a scandal involving charges of corruption against the Commander-in-Chief, the royal Duke of York. In ordinary circumstances a resurgence of radicalism might have strengthened the hands of conservatives, by allowing them to argue that any concession to Whig reformers would put the country on a slippery slope, such as had happened in France during 1791–2. However, in 1808 the King's precarious health meant that his son might become Regent at any moment, in which case he might well use his prerogative powers to install Lord Grey in office, just as the King had sacked Fox and installed Pitt in 1783. 'If the new reign should commence, as it is supposed it will, with the elevation of Whitbread to a seat in the cabinet', Ellis wrote, 'I confess that I shall not feel very confident of a happy termination of the great struggle in which we are at present involved!' (*QR* Letter 98).[3] When these perspectives are taken into account, the *Quarterly*'s resort to 'paranoid politics' (to borrow Kim Wheatley's happy phrase) seems understandable.[4]

Even more worryingly, the *Edinburgh Review* had provided the opposition Whigs with an ideology, and the main point of the *Quarterly* was to counter it. 'As the real reason of instituting the publication is the disgusting and deleterious doctrine with which the most popular of these periodical works disgraces its pages it is essential to consider how opposite and sounder principles can be most advantageously brought forward' (*QR* Letter 4). The problem for the projectors of the *Quarterly* was to find some way of articulating those sounder principles. They wished to appeal to 'the friends of Church and State', or alternatively to 'the friends of Order, Morality and rational piety'. Unfortunately such people were inclined to consider their own principles as self-evident, and therefore thought it sufficient to leave the 'good cause' to 'fight its own battle' (*QR* Letter 4A). In other words, the reviewers were aiming at readers who knew what they felt in their bones, and their own task was to put literary flesh on those bones. 'There is a mass of good sense and right feeling in the country', Gifford assured Scott. 'It is dormant, but not dead. When roused, as in 1794, which I well remember, it can do wonders – and on this, I rely, if the worst should happen' (*QR* Letter 127).

What Gifford did not say was that the end of the first decade of the 1800s was very different from the late 1790s. At that earlier juncture the sense of ideological warfare between – to put it crudely – Paineites and Burkeites really had been palpable. It had therefore been easy to tar the Foxite Whigs as crypto-French revolutionaries and a very real danger to the Constitution, what with the prospect of a French invasion, the likelihood of mutiny in the navy and a militant radical menace that was all the more dangerous for having been driven underground by official repression. The danger was so obvious as to provoke waves of loyalism, patriotism, monarchism, Churchmanship and spiritual renewal, all of which had provided a backdrop to the brief but brilliant career of the *Anti-Jacobin; or, Weekly Examiner*, edited with government sponsorship by Gifford during its eight-month run in 1797–8. Then, thanks to contributions by the politicians George Canning, George Ellis and John Hookham Frere, wit and brilliance had for once been at the service of the government rather than the opposition. The success of this conservative trio in changing the intellectual climate was one reason why the Foxite opposition seceded from Parliament in despair during 1797–1801.

In seeking to replicate his success ten years later, Gifford could call on two of the same politicians (Frere, now an envoy in Spain, was unavailable). He could not call on government sponsorship, and often felt let down by lack of interest on the part of conservative politicians. ('It is really astonishing that they will not take more advantage of us, and influence a great portion of the country which we have brought almost to their feet'; *QR* Letter 183.[5]) More significantly he was not able to exploit a clear-cut ideological division as he had been in 1797–8. It is true that he and his contributors often *talked about* the 'fear of the growth of Jacobinism, and a strong feeling of the dreadful importance of all that is passing around us' (*QR* Letter 31). In speaking like this they contributed to those visceral fears of revolution that would continue to dominate the imagination of hidebound conservative reactionaries for another forty years. Such fears help to account for the success of the *The Antijacobin Review and Magazine, or, Monthly Political and Literary Censor* (1798–1821), a fairly crude rag run by another and unrelated Gifford, John. But the *Quarterly* was intended to be neither crude nor hidebound. It was meant to match the *Edinburgh*'s sophistication, a point signalled very early on by Murray when he promised that 'the Sardonic Grin ... will be our best weapon' (*QR* Letter 8), and the plain fact was that, with France an autocratic empire, support for or hostility to the war could no longer be presented in the starkly Manichaean terms of the 1790s.

In a sense Gifford and his collaborators were right in thinking that the *Edinburgh Review* was an ideological instrument that needed to be matched in like coin. Where they were mistaken was in supposing that its ideology had a capital 'I', or rather 'J'. In fact the *Edinburgh* was ideological in a more subtle way, meaning that almost every page expressed a particular way of looking at the world and a set of shared values. For Francis Jeffrey, its editor, everything was political and almost every one of its articles – whether about poetry, fiction, warfare, history, travel, science or religion – was doused in politics, even though there might be no explicit reference to parties or parliament. In other words, the *Edinburgh*'s ideological politics was rooted in culture – styles, values, loyalties, ultimately belief in progress – rather than in doctrine or policy. Gifford and his coadjutors by contrast distinguished between politics and everything else. Indeed, as stated above, the literary and learned articles were there as camouflage.

This helps to explain why the *Quarterly*'s approach to politics was top-down, a matter of parties, personalities and policies. A more immediate reason was the part played by John Wilson Croker who, although he mainly contributed literary and historical articles in Gifford's time, and only became the *Quarterly*'s leading political writer later under Lockhart, nevertheless exercised a profound influence on its political tenor from the first, albeit working in the background. Murray ran all the political articles past Croker, sometimes to Gifford's annoyance, and he often interfered by vetting what aristocrats and fellow MPs had written on public affairs.

According to the historian Keith Feiling, 'the booming gong in Croker's conventicle was the French Revolution'.[6] He abhorred and abominated it as a historical event, and he dreaded its re-enactment in Britain. Such paranoid anxiety might seem to make Croker an ideal candidate for *Quarterly* reviewer, and certainly he obliged Gifford in 1811 when he denounced the *philosophes'* 'literary machine' for having prepared the way for the storming of the Bastille in 1789.[7] Yet his take on the revolution was unusual and in some respects unhelpful. This was so partly because he was inclined to blame its descent into anarchy on an Orleanist conspiracy, which was a line mainly favoured by Whigs, including Jeffrey. But the main problem was that his interpretation of events was almost exclusively constitutional and high political. 'The first great error of the reformers was (as it must ever be of all who reform with the aid of an inflamed populace) their disregard of the ancient forms of their constitution'.[8]

That sentence encapsulates almost the entire contents of Croker's political philosophy, which Feiling not unfairly described as 'irascible stationariness'.[9] It amounted to saying that the Revolution was bad because it had destroyed the aristocracy. More specifically, in deciding at what precise point the Revolution had gone wrong, he made much of the fact that members of the National Assembly were excluded from sitting in its successor body, the Legislative, since it meant that established politicians like Robespierre, if they wished to remain in the public eye, had to seek more popular and therefore more dangerous stages on which to operate (in his case the Jacobin Club). It was a shrewd point, as was much of what he wrote about the operation of personal rivalry, envy and bribery among the Revolutionary politicians, but the cumulative effect was to diminish the horror of what had happened, and thereby to deny that the world had really changed between 1789 and 1793. The following critique of Croker's work by William Thomas, a historian far from unsympathetic to him, brings out just how bloodless was his assessment of the Revolution's central figure.

> He treats Robespierre as the leader of an extra-parliamentary opposition, stirring up popular opinion in the capital .... To the peculiarities of Robespierre's education and especially to the source of his political ideas, he is indifferent. He ... misses altogether

Robespierre's fatal debt to the theory of the general will. He has no psychological insight into Robespierre's motives .... Lacking an imaginative perception of the sort of man he was, he can convey none of the drama of the climax to the Terror. The struggle between the Gironde and the Jacobins becomes a mere fight between two sorts of ruffian, one cowardly and equivocating, the other single-minded and ruthless, but Croker does not consider the rival constitutional doctrines in the struggle, or the social backgrounds of the rival parties and their supporters. So for all his accuracy about dates and places, a reader gets almost no idea of the nature of the psychological or social forces which drove the Revolution into extremes of popular violence after 10 August 1792 nor why Robespierre became the person who articulated and guided the popular will.[10]

What seems to be missing from Croker's analysis is Burke. Croker admired that philosopher greatly, but he did not share Burke's deeper insights into the causes of the French Revolution, his horror of its 'incorporeal, pure, unmixed, dephlegmated, defecated evil', or his sense that it threatened the whole of humanity as well as just aristocrats.[11] His scepticism might have been justified, but it hardly fitted Gifford's vision for the *Quarterly*. When Ellis wrote in 1809 about the 'fear of the growth of Jacobinism' (*QR* Letter 31) he was almost certainly faking, but at least he was toeing the common line. Croker by contrast could not even see Jacobinism at work in France during the years of the Terror.

The *Quarterly* then, unlike the *Edinburgh*, was committed to a personal and structural approach to politics. It is also obvious from the private correspondence of Gifford's circle that it was intended to be a flagship for Canning. (There was a degree of symmetry here, since ten years earlier Canning had used the *Anti-Jacobin* to initiate a transformation in Pitt's reputation from its low point in 1797–8 to that of 'the pilot that weathered the storm'.) Among Gifford's friends the term used over and over again to describe Canning was 'genius'. 'You are, or at least, ought to be, *grande decus columenque rerum*' (the glory and keystone of the enterprise), cooed Gifford in March 1809 (*QR* Letter 19). Canning 'is not only the best speaker now in Parliament', he told Scott in November 1809, 'but the ablest and most spirited politician either in or out of it' (*QR* Letter 29). And certainly, at the point when the first number of the *Quarterly* was issued there was good reason to think that Canning's hour was about to come. In a splintered political system he commanded a party of about forty MPs, all blindly devoted to him, and since 1807 he had proved to be a vigorous, imaginative and efficient Foreign Secretary who, by urging the bombardment of Copenhagen and the invasion of Spain, had given a positive turn to the war at long last.

Unfortunately, by the time the fourth number of the *Quarterly* appeared in print, Canning had fought a duel with Castlereagh, both men had resigned, and the Portland government had collapsed. The *Quarterly* could hardly deny that the episode was reprehensible and a blow to national honour, but Ellis's article on the topic (largely written by Canning himself) tried to limit the damage by heaping blame on the challenger, Castlereagh, for having acted precipitately to perceived slights against him, when a pause for reflection on his part might have allowed matters to be smoothed over.

> The criminality which belongs to the choice of time, must fall exclusively upon the challenger ... His secret was in his own breast; he was at liberty to hasten or to delay the gratification of his intended revenge; the excuse of having acted under the sudden impulse of passion, cannot be pleaded in a case, in which, as it appears, an interval of twelve days elapsed between the provocation and the demand of satisfaction.[12]

For the next two years Gifford and his friends speculated despairingly about Canning's diminishing chances of reinstatement. Since he was so obviously 'the first person in the country' and 'above all rivalry as a politician' (*QR* Letters 135, 140), they fell back on that well-worn excuse of the disappointed, 'the prejudice against every *novus homo*'. 'If Pitt had only possessed talents, if he had not from birth and rank and experience acquired a sort of prescriptive right to govern, he might perhaps have died in opposition; so that some time of probation is perhaps necessary to any man who aspires to become his successor' (*QR* Letter 31). Whether, with Eton and Christ Church behind him, Canning was all that *novus* is open to dispute. At any rate he had the chance to play an important part in the administration Liverpool put together in 1812 but refused, ostensibly because he did not wish to serve in an inferior office to Castlereagh. He soon came to regret 'the station in Europe and in history, which I have thrown away ... having refused the management of the mightiest scheme of politics which this country ever engaged in, or the world ever witnessed, from a miserable point of etiquette'.[13] He referred of course to the Battle of Waterloo and the overthrow of Napoleon. That glory went instead to Castlereagh, a man whom the *Quarterly* had personally traduced and whose success it found it difficult to come to terms with.[14] Canning did re-enter Cabinet in 1816 (which at least meant that Gifford could have access to 'early and accurate information', something he had hoped to have from the outset; *QR* Letter 4), but it was in an inferior role, and in 1820 he was forced to quit again because of his one-time closeness to Princess Caroline. No wonder that when Croker reflected on the matter in 1821, the question of Canning's genius was looking somewhat problematic.

> His genius is a bright flame, but it is ... liable to every gust of wind and every change of weather; it flares, and it flickers, and it blazes, now climbing the heavens, now stifled in its own smoke, and of no use but to raise the wonder of distant spectators, and to warm the very narrow circle that immediately surrounds it. If he does not take care the Canning bonfire will soon burn itself out.

In the same letter Croker tacitly admitted that Castlereagh might after all be the more durable statesman. 'He is *better* than ever; that is, colder, steadier, more *pococurante*, and withal more amiable and respected.'[15] As things turned out, Castlereagh's suicide in 1822 allowed Canning to achieve high office once more, and by the time that Gifford relinquished the editorship he was on the point of establishing himself as the foremost statesman in Europe. Soon after his own death in 1827, friend and foe alike began to talk about 'Mr Canning's principles' and 'Mr Canning's system'. Indeed, the long-term nature of his ideological legacy can be gauged from the fact that as late as 1860 the four most eminent statesmen of the day (Gladstone, Disraeli, Palmerston and Derby) all acknowledged him as their earliest inspiration.[16] It was a clear case of promise fulfilled, but it all came too late for Gifford. Nor was it much help to later editors of the *Quarterly*, since the leading Canningites joined the Whigs in 1830, leaving Peel to hold the 'liberal Tory' candle.

Given Canning's prolonged state of suspended animation between 1809 and 1822, it was important for the *Quarterly* to develop a coherent and appealing message on what would today be called 'the issues'. Unfortunately it found it difficult to do this with respect to the three main areas of contemporary concern, namely: a spread of atheistic principles, which required Christians to reassert and redefine the ground of religious belief; a feared breakdown in social relations caused by the hectic pace of social and economic change; and the ambiguities of Britain's role in the world.

When the founders of the *Quarterly* appealed to 'the friends of rational piety', they were declaring themselves to be High Churchmen of the old 'high and dry' school. For them 'piety' meant that the lower orders should attend Church, where they could be instructed in the fear of God and the need to obey their betters. 'Rational piety' meant that the upper classes should reason with the plebeians in order to show them that it was in their own interests to behave themselves. An ulterior purpose of the *Quarterly* was to reassure conscience-stricken members of the elite that the existing social system really was for the common good, and that even the poor had reasons for contentment. In seeking to mount this propaganda drive, Gifford naturally looked for 'that assistance which can only be found in the Universities' (*QR* Letter 34). (He really meant Oxford, since whatever the context, Whiggish Cambridge – 'that hotbed of malignity ... from which spring your Critical Reviews, and other deleterious funguses' – was barely mentioned in the *Quarterly* but to be disparaged; *QR* Letter 6.) He did his best to win Oxford over by giving a regular platform to the clerical philosopher Edward Copleston, including an opportunity to defend that university against recent criticisms in the *Edinburgh Review*.[17] Despite this, in 1809 and again in 1819, Gifford was moved to lament that, Copleston and a few others apart, 'Oxford does nothing' (*QR* Letters 30, 210).

Gifford here revealed a blind spot since, at least in respect of religion, Oxford was actually doing more for the cause than the *Quarterly*. A striking effect of the

French Revolution in England had been to put conservative loyalists (including those at Oxford) in such a panic about religion as to provoke a genuine spiritual renewal among all sections of the established Church.[18] One manifestation was the evangelical movement, several of whose lay leaders, such as William Wilberforce and Henry Thornton, sat in Parliament, where they were ironically known as 'the Saints'. Having been brought to public prominence by the so-called Clapham Sect, evangelicalism was now proliferating cell-like from parish to parish and family to family. Its mouthpiece was the *Christian Observer*, founded in the same year as the *Edinburgh Review*; it had an outstanding popularizer and publicist in Hannah More; and it was rapidly establishing footholds in elite areas of national life such as the City, the navy, the universities, and the civil service. Slightly in evangelicalism's wake was the High Church revival, often associated with Hackney, and as far removed in its spiritual intensity as it was possible to be from Gifford's 'high and dry' High Churchmanship.[19] Evangelicals and new High Churchmen quarrelled fiercely over the former's willingness to associate with Nonconformists in their missionary endeavours, and they differed over the priority which the latter gave to the Church as an institution and to matters of liturgy and ritual, but they were at one in despising highness and dryness, and also in rejecting what they saw as the tolerance amounting to indifference of the old Latitudinarian tradition. However, by 1800 this third species of Churchmanship, while retaining an undogmatic and relativist approach to scriptural truth, was also becoming more fervent in its approach to worship, the outcome being referred to sometimes as liberal Anglicanism, and in an Oxford context known then as Noeticism. With varying degrees of intensity evangelicals, new High Churchmen and liberal Anglicans all practised 'vital religion'. That is to say, they believed in a superintending (but for the most part law-bound) providence, original sin, judgement and the promise of salvation by faith. They did not always wear their religiosity on their sleeves (though evangelicals did so to a greater extent than the others), but for the first time in a century it became commonplace to regard Christian belief as central not only to the battle for personal redemption but to the conduct of public affairs as well.

If this claim seems far-fetched, consider the ludicrous way in which the Bishop of Lincoln (Pretyman-Tomline), George Rose, the *Morning Chronicle* and later *Blackwood's Edinburgh Magazine* all attempted to convince Parliament and the public that Pitt had been fuelled by 'a religious principle' throughout his life, and that on his deathbed he had 'taken the Sacrament with the most fervent and edifying piety'.[20] None of it was true. Pitt was and remained to his last breath a sceptic, but it was necessary to pretend that he had been devout in an evangelical sort of way if his memory was to function as a rallying-point for nineteenth-century conservatives. More specifically in 1809, when the *Quarterly* was launched, Britain was experiencing a 'revival within a revival' in religious terms, in part because the Duke of York scandal seemed to confirm a widespread feeling that successive military failures might really be providential chastisements inflicted on a nation that was immoral from the top down. One outcome was the founding in the same year of the Alfred Club, which provided a venue for young conservative politicians such as Peel, Goulburn, Robinson and Croker to meet each Wednesday. Described by one historian as 'a haven of liberal Toryism in economic matters',[21] it was also a haven of evangelical religion and earnest discussion.

In view of these developments it might be thought that anyone who wanted to create an intellectual organ for conservatism would have to pay at least lip service to natural theology, the operations of Providence, the importance of Christian apologetic, the requirements of personal faith and the relevance of all these subjects to public policy. This was especially necessary in Gifford's case, given the support he had received from several of the 'Saints' in getting the *Quarterly* off the ground, and especially from his evangelical friend Lord Teignmouth, who was President of the British and Foreign Bible Society (1798–1834) and one of the journal's 'patrons' (*QR* Letter 146). However, the evangelicals' moralistic agenda was out of step with the editor's pre-eminent desire to emulate the *Edinburgh*'s wit and verve. Besides which Murray and Ellis, and to a lesser extent Gifford, had an antipathy to public displays of religious conviction. Murray was wont to complain about 'the tediousness of metaphysical and polemical divinity, and of religious subjects generally' (*QR* Letter 128); while all four of the founding fathers particularly disliked self-righteous evangelicals. 'Mr Gifford is equally sensible as you', wrote Murray to Scott, 'of the danger of allowing any preponderance to the Saints, and will carefully guard against them' (*QR* Letter 12). This was unwise since evangelically-inclined Anglicans would make up a large part of the journal's readership. When Number 7 was found to contain a disparaging article about Teignmouth and the Bible Society by a high and pretty dry Anglican dean, Gifford was 'deluged by letters complaining that this was an attack on the Saints'.[22] Having been bitten on this occasion, he was inclined to fight shy of religion altogether – hence numerous letters to Copleston apologizing for the *Quarterly*'s relative neglect (for example, *QR* Letter 89). He gave the game away, however, when he wrote privately that he hated William Roscoe and longed to 'have him mauled. He is a devil of a Saint, and never cuts a throat without a prayer ...' That he could have mistaken such a well-known Unitarian for someone of the very opposite religious persuasion reveals how unsure Gifford's touch was in matters of theology (*QR* Letter 54).

Even the despised *Antijacobin Review*, edited by the other Gifford, was more adept in exploiting the conservative religious revival, albeit in a negative way, since one of its main *raisons d'être* was to denounce Unitarian, socinian and suchlike literature.[23] However, a more interesting point of comparison is with the

*British Review and London Critical Journal*, edited by an evangelical lawyer and passionate Pittite, William Roberts. Launched in 1811 as a protest against the secular flippancy of the *Edinburgh* and the desultory coverage of religion in the *Quarterly*, it looked almost identical to them and discussed some of the same publications, but it was essentially a one-man-band, with Roberts writing most of the articles. It lacked financial backing and a wide readership and it folded in 1825, an event that drew from the *Christian Observer* the lament that the religious world was insufficiently literary and the literary world insufficiently religious to sustain it.[24] A good deal of it, certainly, was taken up with the latest theological writings, including works on prophecy and eschatology, and to that extent it failed to match the *Quarterly*'s worldly appeal. Intellectually, however, it caught the new conservative mood much earlier. A volume by Copleston on 'the divine economy and government of the world' was said to be the best work on natural theology since Bishop Butler,[25] while Hannah More's *Practical Piety* was praised for showing that Christianity was 'an internal religion, and not merely a religion of forms and decencies'.[26] In return More approved of the fact that Roberts not only noticed religious publications but also reviewed secular works 'in a Christian spirit'.[27] One such was the House of Commons Poor Law Report of 1817, mainly written by William Sturges Bourne and representative of Canningite social policy at that time. Its theme was that the existing poor laws (known by the name of Speenhamland) were over-generous. In Roberts's words, they interfered with the dispensations of providence, gave 'additional force to all the depraved corruptions of our nature' and offered 'an incentive to vice, an encouragement to improvidence, and a bounty to pauperism'.[28] The relevance of this is that Sturges Bourne was a friend of Canning and Huskisson, and his severely moralistic 'stand-on-your-own-feet' approach to the poor was representative of Canningite policy at that time.

This 'liberal Tory' call for a reduction in the amount of legislative provision for the poor would soon be taken up by the famous Scottish evangelical preacher Thomas Chalmers, for whose writings Roberts reserved his most lavish and extravagant praise. The *Astronomical Sermons*, for example, were described as one of the 'finest productions of modern genius'. 'Dr Chalmers is no meteor, but a fixed star in that firmament of science, which he has taught to shine with the radiance of the gospel.'[29] The praise was timely, for it was about now that the Scottish luminary entered on his career of quite extraordinary celebrity, especially in evangelical and 'liberal Tory' circles. 'All the world wild about Dr Chalmers', noted William Wilberforce, and his opinion was very widely corroborated.[30] Moreover, no one was in wilder raptures than Canning, who attended several of the great man's sermons.[31] The *Quarterly*, however, was unimpressed. Chalmers's earlier volume on *The Evidence and Authority of the Christian Revelation* (1814) had been dismissed in a patronizing way by the antiquarian Thomas

Dunham Whitaker, one of Gifford's hack writers. As for the *Astronomical Sermons*, which allegedly sold 20,000 copies in a few months, when Bishop George Gleig submitted an appreciative review Gifford rejected it as 'rambling and imperfect' (*QR* Letter 182).

The significance of all this must not be over-stated. Enthusiasm for Thomas Chalmers was a straw in the wind, not yet a defining issue of 'liberal Toryism'. Nevertheless, it is important for editors to sniff the wind, and this was a scent that Gifford was slow to pick up. That he did pick it up eventually is clear from changes in the way that the *Quarterly* treated the fashionable not to say portentous subject of geology. In 1818 the reverend and gentlemanly geologist Thomas Gisborne published a mainstream work of evangelical natural theology in which he argued that 'the earth, as to its exterior strata, is not at present in the same condition in which it was when it came forth from the hand of its Creator; but has manifestly undergone universal and violent and overwhelming convulsions of such a nature as to spread general destruction among the animated inhabitants of its surface'.[32] This version of theodicy was the standard evangelical strategy – to defend God against the charge that he had created a poverty-stricken and otherwise miserable world by attributing all injustice and unhappiness to the Fall. Gifford sent the work to Whitaker, whose hostile review was written in tones of affronted incredulity: 'According to [Gisborne] the whole landscape of human life is overspread with gloom and sorrow and suffering – and almost all the appearances of nature bear testimony to the wrath of God against the sin of man'.[33] Though Whitaker failed (or pretended to fail) to see it, Gisborne's real message was meant to be reassuring, being based on the premise that geological evidences (including floods, earthquakes and volcanoes) were theoretically compatible both with the goodness of God and with scriptural revelation. Two years later William Buckland, an Oxford evangelical, went further by arguing in *Vindiciae Geologicae* that recent scientific findings had empirically corroborated the biblical story of Noah's flood. Gifford sent that volume to John Barrow. Then in 1823 Buckland produced a more emphatic version of the same theme, *Reliquiae Diluvianae*, which Gifford sent to Copleston for review. Possibly Murray queried the choice of reviewer. At any rate, Gifford felt called upon to explain. 'Mr Buckland, I know complains that he has been treated solely as a geological writer – but he aspires to something higher, and it was this which made me wish for a more philosophical view of the subject.' 'This is just what is wanted, as our friend Barrow has already given us the technical part of it; which is but a narrow contemplation of a great question sufficiently important in many respects'.[34] Copleston duly obliged by affirming that Buckland had 'introduced new and convincing proofs of providential design – of that system of final causes, which is deeply impressed on the whole mechanism of nature'.[35] His review probably contributed to a groundswell of acclamation for Buckland, especially in 'liberal

Tory' circles, for in elevating him professionally, first Lord Liverpool and then Sir Robert Peel praised him for having held the line against those who would argue that recent scientific findings disproved the Bible narrative.

Provost of Oriel College, Oxford, subsequently Bishop of Llandaff, and a serious theologian of the Noetic party, Copleston was as near as anyone to being a Canningite or 'liberal Tory' intellectual. He also advised Peel and Huskisson on economic and social policy and yet, despite his being available to Gifford from the beginning, the *Quarterly* was slow to get the message on economics just as it was on religion. The problem was compounded by the fact that economics was one of the *Edinburgh*'s strong points, thanks to their Scottish contributors Francis Horner and Henry Brougham. The first big issue facing Gifford was the 1810 Bullion Report, co-authored by Horner, the evangelical Henry Thornton and William Huskisson, a Canningite MP and financial expert. If 'liberal Tory-ism' had its ethical roots in the evangelical natural theology of More, Chalmers and Gisborne, its origin in secular terms might well be traced to this report. An obvious way for the *Quarterly* to deal with the issue was by 'reviewing' an important pamphlet that Huskisson had written on the subject, and since he, Ellis, Canning and Copleston were all in the editor's pocket, there was no short-age of expertise. (Indeed, with Murray's and Gifford's connivance, Huskisson's pamphlet and the *Quarterly*'s critique were concurrently planned and executed. See *QR* Letters 66, 68–71.) The problem was rather a political one – that, while the *Quarterly* would cleave to the line taken by Huskisson in the Bullion Report and call for the gold standard to be restored at the earliest possible moment, Prime Minister Spencer Perceval and his key economic ministers (Castlereagh and Vansittart) were committed to the opposite line, both as a matter of eco-nomic theory and as a matter of practical policy. Now Gifford and his friends were used to lamenting the 'reign of mediocrity' under Perceval (*QR* Letter 31), but nevertheless they were anxious to support the King's government against the Whigs, so this divergence of view was an embarrassment.[36] Meanwhile, to make matters worse, the *Edinburgh* had not surprisingly come out in favour of the bul-lionist position. Gifford was therefore in a bind.

> I am truly grieved to find that ministers have on this question embraced what seems palpably the wrong side, and have started away from truth and reason ... in order to ally themselves with bigotry, wrong headedness, Sir John Sinclair, and the Bank Directors. Under these circumstances, the ground is delicate for the Quarterly ... [F]rom the Edinburgh ... I have no doubt that we may look for a strong decisive, and coarse assertion of what I conceive to be the right doctrines on money, mixed with some of their accustomed bearish reflections on ministers. The difficulty for the Quarterly will be to support substantially the same doctrines in quite another spirit. (*QR* Letter 68)

The lesson Gifford ought (but seems not) to have drawn was that the stark dichotomy he believed existed, and wished to further cement, between the government party and the opposition Whig party, simply did not correspond to the way in which opinion divided on several important issues. As will be seen, both parties were polarized on most areas of policy, and especially on economic policies including the currency.

From the very beginning much of the *Quarterly*'s comment on social and economic matters was provided by Robert Southey, and this posed another difficulty. As a youthful republican and proponent of Pantisocracy in the 1790s, Southey had been a leading butt of the *Anti-Jacobin*. That he had since 'turned his coat, and would have turned his skin' (as Byron cruelly put it in *The Vision of Judgment*), and was now a fierce loyalist, made him quite a catch for the journal. Gifford embraced him because he supported war in the Peninsula, because he saw social and moral value in the union of Church and state, and because as a prolific writer of more than decent prose he would bring literary prestige to the project. In many ways Southey enjoyed a special position as the *Quarterly*'s 'sheet anchor', and certainly Gifford allowed him more leeway than he did other contributors. (This was partly because Gifford was a self-confessed ignoramus on economic issues. On the bullion question, for example, he admitted, 'I confess that this is a subject which I have tried to understand well and failed in: either because I am stupid or because the subject demands an habitual acquaintance with money transactions'; *QR* Letter 75.) Even so, Gifford was often moved to wonder about the quality of Southey's conservatism, and he was right to worry, not because of any bad faith on the latter's part, but because his views were idiosyncratic and in some respects far removed from those of political conservatives like Gifford, Scott and Canning. For example, Southey believed that 'at this moment nothing but the army preserves us from the most dreadful of all imaginable calamities, – an insurrection of the poor against the rich' (*QR* Letter 125). Now all conservatives feared revolution, but they preferred to blame the danger on the poison spewed by radical journalists and conspirators, and not like Southey on discrepancies of wealth and (by implication) the justified grievances of the poor.

The tone was set in Southey's *Letters from England* (1807), in which he castigated commercial society and the manufacturing system, not out of any agrarian nostalgia but because the poor were little better off than they had been in the middle ages, which was alarming for someone with his continuing belief in progress and improvement. The problem with manufacturing was that it exacerbated inequalities of wealth, depressed the rewards of labour, impaired health and morals, and left too little leisure time for the moral and religious education of the people. Now there was certainly a need for a periodical that peddled a conservative type of anti-political economy based on paternalism, protectionism and public philanthropy, and from 1817 onwards it was supplied by *Blackwood's*, whose main economic spokesmen were David Robinson and Edward Edwards. Unfortunately, it was not a line the *Quarterly* could take, given its deference on such matters to Canning and Huskisson, successive MPs for the port of Liverpool and instinctive supporters of commercial progress and freer trade. But, apart from that, Southey's paternalism was different from that of *Blackwood's*-type conservatives. As already noted he was not an agrarian, he believed in economic progress, and he actually hoped that the spread of machinery would be beneficial. He also wanted to redistribute wealth by means of a general rise in wages (though he was not clear on how this would be achieved); and, most significantly of all, he advocated an increased role for the central state, including a hefty dose of public works and other schemes for creating employment.[37] Yet almost all genuine conservatives, whatever their views about free markets, wanted a central state that was limited in its functions.

The central question facing any journal purporting to deal with social and economic problems was Malthus's principle of population, which more than any other theory seemed to imply that God had created a world of misery and suffering. Now as it happens Murray's original intention had been 'to count upon Malthus for the department of political œconomy' (*QR* Letter 4), despite the latter's Whig sympathies and the fact that he occasionally contributed to the *Edinburgh Review*. Ellis too had commented beforehand on the need to publicize 'certain works of great value (for example Malthus's book)' (*QR* Letter 7). It is therefore both significant and surprising that Southey should have taken up the role instead, given that Southey reviled Malthus. By pouring cold water on hopes for moral and material progress, the latter's *Essay on the Principle of Population* had impugned the character of God, destroyed Southey's own utopian idealism, and indicated a brutal indifference towards the poor.

> Respecting Malthus I can speak without the slightest doubt or hesitation. The book is as worthless as it is mischievous, as much to be despised as it is to be detested ... [S]hould there be a new edition published ... I will take the opportunity, and give a death blow to this philosophist, or philosophicide, – the most mischievous of all the breed: – not for his abilities, – but because his system accords so well with the feelings of a selfish and sensual generation. (*QR* Letter 46)

Against Malthus's notorious contention that God had invited too many mortals to nature's feast, Southey claimed that thousands of years must elapse before the earth ran out of food.

> Till that time the first commandment which man received from his Creator stands unrepealed, – and if ever that time should come the Creator may then be trusted: meantime it is the truest policy and the highest duty to improve the condition of the poor. The better the people are instructed, the happier and the better they will

become; the happier they are, the more they will multiply; the more they multiply, the greater will be the wealth, and strength, and security of the state; and these maxims are as certain as the laws of nature and of God.[38]

The above quotation comes from a *Quarterly* article of 1816, one which according to Murray 'absolutely electrified every one who has read it', including apparently the Chancellor of the Exchequer Vansittart, who shared Southey's interventionist instincts (*QR* Letter 173). It might well have encouraged the latter to introduce the Poor Employment Act of 1817 and also the Church Building Act of the following year.

However, it was not sustainable for the *Quarterly* to go on taking a line on the most important social issue of the day that was antipathetic to that of the Canningites (not to mention Copleston, Chalmers and other conservative intellectuals). An opportunity to tack tacitly came with the publication of the evangelical John Bird Sumner's *Treatise on the Records of the Creation, and on the Consistency of the Principle of Population with the Wisdom and Goodness of the Deity*, also in 1816. As the title implies, this work consummated the reconciliation between natural theology and Malthusian theory, and paved the way for Chalmers and a hundred others to do likewise. The historian Patricia James has suggested that Sumner made Malthusianism 'theologically respectable' and 'certainly changed the attitude of the *Quarterly Review* towards him'.[39] Precisely how deliberate this change of attitude was is not clear, but it is significant that when the next (1817) edition of Malthus's *Essay* appeared it was reviewed, not by Southey who so much wanted to do it,[40] but by Sumner. Indeed the ensuing review must have been anathema to Southey, for Sumner endorsed and praised population theory, regretting only that Malthus had not gone on to point out that the miseries people faced in life were kindly designed for their own good.

> We cannot help regretting that the same masterly hand, which first pointed out why equality, and plenty, and community of goods were unattainable to beings constituted like mankind,[41] had not also proceeded to show that they were no less undesirable; that the same powerful guide, who first checked, in her untried course, the frail bark of universal happiness, sailing as she was 'with youth at the prow and pleasure at the helm', and pointed out the unforeseen bank on which she could not fail to split, had not also taken the pains to prove that the course human nature was forced to pursue is also the best it could pursue, when the object and end of the voyage are added to consideration.[42]

From an eschatological point of view there was something a bit lily-livered – that is to say, a bit lacking in Hell-fire – about the last comment, but Sumner was having to feel his way with a possibly sceptical readership, which may be why his article was full of tactful 'ifs' ('if Malthus is right', 'if this be true'). Still, it was an important article, signifying not only the *Quarterly*'s new attitude to Malthusianism[43] but also a new attitude to evangelicalism, at least in terms of its stance on public policy.[44] Of course, this could hardly be acknowledged in so many words, but before very much longer Malthusian attitudes would become deeply ingrained in conservative circles. For example, no one in 1817 would have anticipated just how evangelical-*sounding* Croker would gradually become, as when talking like this about the poor laws.

> It is the first Law of nature, the primal curse of an angry, but all-wise Creator, that we should earn our bread in toil and pain, and by the sweat of our brow ... It is meet and right, and our bounden duty, to help the weak, and to alleviate distress, as far as our means allow; but to tell the working classes that any power can relieve them from their state of want and dependence is to impugn, as it seems to me, the dispensations of Providence.[45]

On the face of it, foreign policy offered the *Quarterly* a more straightforward opportunity to rally conservative forces. After all, the most obvious difference between Pittites and Foxites was their attitude to the war against France, the former almost entirely enthusiastic for the fray, the latter equivocal when not thoroughly hostile. The struggle against and then victory over Napoleon, the growing sense of British identity, and the awareness of belonging to a burgeoning maritime empire would surely work in favour of those sounder political principles that Gifford and his colleagues wished to encourage. And up to a point this was true. On the other hand, matters were not quite so clear cut as in the 1790s, when the war had threatened imminent invasion and conquest. In such a context, irrespective of what one might think about the rights and wrongs of Jacobinism, sympathy for the enemy could reasonably be interpreted as treason. By 1809 the situation had become much more fuzzy. For a start the battle of Trafalgar, though it did not completely remove the fear of invasion, undoubtedly lessened the likelihood. Honour demanded that Britons fight to the death, and there was little doubt that continued French domination of the Continent would be very bad for this country in the long run. On the other hand, the war could also be said to be crippling the economy in the immediate term, in which case the question of what was in the 'national interest' became more ambiguous than in the 1790s. Recent scandals over the Convention of Cintra, the disastrous Walcheren expedition, and the Duke of York imbroglio had at the very least led to a degree of cynicism about the commitment of the political establishment to the war effort. Then again, whereas the navy had been able to touch the nation's heart strings, the Army – whose turn in the limelight it now was – never enjoyed the same degree of affection, which is why Wellington never received anything like the adoration Nelson had enjoyed (even while he was alive). In 1816, following the great victory at Waterloo, Liverpool's ministers expected to be able to bask in political esteem for a year or two at least; in the event their period of grace lasted no longer than the debate on the King's speech.

Nor was it altogether helpful that when the *Quarterly* was founded the big issue was the war in Spain. In October 1808 Scott had predicted that 'a distinct and enlightened view of Spanish affairs' would 'establish the character' of the new journal (*QR* Letter 4). This was because the *Edinburgh Review* had been giving vent to the belief of Brougham and other prominent Whigs that the Peninsula campaign was 'madness'. Against them Gifford intended to give support to Canning's conviction that the best way to defeat Napoleon was in the Peninsula. The stakes were drawn rather as they would be for Churchill and his Dardanelles strategy a century or so later. Unfortunately, before the first issue of the *Quarterly* could appear the retreat and death of Sir John Moore had caused widespread despondency, and was a major factor in the Portland government's unpopularity. Even after Wellington began to win victories in Spain and Portugal, the issue never proved to be the touchstone between the parties that Gifford still predicted,[46] if only because the waters were muddied in a number of ways. First, a voluble section of Whigs, including Horner and Holland, were also enthusiastic about the Peninsula adventure. Then again, for many conservative loyalists enthusiasm for the war of liberation was tempered by the thought that the French enemies were in many ways more civilized than the Spanish guerrillas, whose reported atrocities turned stomachs even though they were fighting on the same side as the British. Then again, success came at a price, namely the success of the *Liberales* party in the Spanish constitution of 1812. As Holland observed, 'even Mr Windham, with all his ardour for war and hatred of the French, was at moments startled by the apparition of liberty which the [Spanish] patriots occasionally summoned to their aid, and ... was scared at the notion of resisting Napoleon himself by anything approaching to democratic principles'.[47] One can imagine that Gifford and his friends felt just as queasy.

But here was a startling thing – Canning seemed keen to proclaim Britain's mission in the world as one of national liberation.

> Wherever this country has exerted herself, it has been to raise the fallen, and to support the falling; to raise, not to degrade, the national character; to rouse the sentiments of patriotism which tyranny had silenced; to enlighten, to re-animate, to liberate. Great Britain has resuscitated Spain, and re-created Portugal: Germany is now a nation as well as a name; and all these glorious effects have been produced by the efforts and by the example of our country.[48]

When Canning made that statement, and for many years afterwards, he played only a peripheral role in policy-making. This meant that the *Quarterly* could enjoy the years of victory and peace-making without taking too much notice of its hero's rhetoric. But by the time Gifford retired as editor, Canning was once more at the forefront, and was engaged in a series of struggles against Wellington, having emerged as a champion of South American independence and an irritant of Europe's more reactionary regimes. The historian Halévy described him as 'successfully dividing, teasing, and flouting Governments so reactionary, so mean, and so mischievous that they were objects of scorn and hatred to every generous heart'.[49] Even at the time the presiding genius of European reaction, Prince Metternich, described Canning as 'a malevolent meteor' and 'a whole revolution in himself alone'. It is impossible to tell from the pages of the *Quarterly* exactly what its first editor thought about this. No doubt Gifford was delighted that Canning had become such a powerful force at last. Moreover, he was willing to follow Canning in defending Spain from renewed military aggression by France, and in supporting liberal nationalist independence movements in the Tyrol, Greece and South America. Whether he also approved of his hero's frequent appeals at the bar of public opinion, and occasional public speeches in Liverpool and other large towns, seems more doubtful.

Nevertheless, with Copleston's review of Buckland and Malthus's first article coming just one year after Canning's assumption of power in 1822, Gifford could claim that he had at last managed to shunt his magazine on to the right 'liberal Tory' lines. And if he had been slower to sense which way the wind was blowing than his *Edinburgh* counterparts, that was probably because he turned fifty-two in 1808 whereas Horner, Brougham and Jeffrey had an average age of only thirty-two. The author of *The Baviad*, *The Maeviad* and other rollicking satires could be forgiven for failing at first to notice that the eighteenth century had given way to the era of sermons and soda water.

Finally, what about the *Quarterly*'s impact on the political world more generally? In a scabrous assessment one historian has described Croker as a 'death-watch beetle' inhabiting a political and social fabric in decay, presiding over and assisting in its 'hidden decomposition', and prolonging its agonies.[50] Hyperbole aside, it could no doubt be argued that the journal for which he wrote also sought 'to stabilize, to cabin and confine' the country.[51] In fact a more complex assessment is called for, a clue to which is provided by another and only slightly less hostile historian, Hedva Ben-Israel.

> [Croker] believed that men were born Whig or Tory, that political principles were inherent and not a matter of theory, that there are two antagonistic principles, stability and change, at the root of all government. 'The former is Tory and the latter Whig; and the human mind divides into these classes as naturally ... as it does into indolence and activity' ... Since political principles were inherent, Croker neither questioned nor expounded them. He fought his political battles to conquer and not to convert, and he fought them on practical issues.[52]

To a lesser extent this comment could also be applied to Gifford and his friends, and also indeed his enemies. By their mutual and at times almost juvenile antagonism and rivalry, the *Quarterly* and the *Edinburgh* together helped to keep the political world polarized between Pittites and Foxites, conservatives and Whigs. This meant that the party system remained locked in a pattern that corresponded to the important policy divisions of the 1790s and (to a lesser extent) the 1800s. As a consequence it failed to correspond to many of the policy divisions that emerged in the following decades, including the most pressing questions of economic and social policy. As a result it was obvious by 1826 that both sides of the House of Commons were hopelessly divided on those sorts of issues. In the words of Lord Holland,

> Political parties are no more. Whig and Tory, Foxite and Pittite, Minister and Opposition have ceased to be distinctions, but the divisions of classes and great interests are arrayed against each other, – grower and consumer, lands and funds, Irish and English, Catholick and Protestant.[53]

An attempt to realign the parties along the economic lines referred to by Holland occurred in 1827 when Canning, having been deserted by several members of the former Liverpool administration, formed a coalition government with sympathetic (i.e. economically liberal) members of the opposition. There was a more significant realignment in 1830 when a number of Canning's main surviving followers joined Grey's nominally Whig ministry. And there was a more or less complete realignment in the decade following the conservative split of 1846, when a majority of the Peelites gravitated over to the Liberals. Yet this development might have taken place thirty years earlier, had the traditional Pittite-Foxite struggle not been kept alive by personal and tribal loyalties. Given his intense and fully reciprocated dislike of Perceval, Castlereagh, Vansittart, Eldon and Sidmouth, for example, Canning might well have joined with Grey and other Whigs to form a government in 1812. In an interesting analysis of the current scene offered at a late point in Perceval's ministry, even Gifford recognized the possibility of such a realignment:

> I have not much comfort for you on the side of politicks ... Perceval has lost strength on the side of government, and constitutes in himself almost all the weight and talent of [the] ministry. Fortunately for him and for the country, the baseness, idiotism, and madness of Whitbread and other violent men of the opposition party keep Lord Grenville and his immediate friends out of power; and this is something. – An opposition of firm and moderate men, who would uphold the spirit of the nation, and recommend directing all its energies against Buonaparte (for that is the popular feeling) would be formidable indeed – nor do I think that it would be long resisted. But I am talking above the clouds. There is no chance of any such thing. Opposition is split into two and threes – into weak, suspicious, and gaming squads, and appear to have no common point of sentiment or union. Canning, evidently the first man in

the country, might do much for us: *but it could only be by the opposition going over to him, and not by his going to them* – which, I do not think, and I am sure that I hope – he never will do. (*QR* Letter 124; italics added)

Of course he never did, and they never did. The existing two-party system, largely based on attitudes to France and to Pitt's repressive policies, not only survived but grew ever more intense, stoked by the paranoid politics of the journalists. As a result neither party was remotely united on many important issues arising out of social and economic change, which meant that divisions between different sectors of the community could not be directed into safe parliamentary chan-nels. The political instability that resulted from this simple fact was one reason for the 'crisis of reform' that unfolded seven years after Gifford's resignation, a crisis in which – so it seemed to Croker – the monarchy, the Church and the aristocracy were all but overthrown.[54]

# 3 A PLURALITY OF VOICES IN THE *QUARTERLY REVIEW*

## Jonathan Cutmore

In the waning hours of his short-lived editorship of the *Quarterly Review*, John Taylor Coleridge wrote to John Murray, the journal's publisher: 'I have now put the finishing hand to my last number, and return you with this the little key of your paper box for Mr Lockhart's use' (*QR* Letter 264). The *Quarterly Review* letterbox, preserved in the John Murray Archive, is a portal to the past. Open it and we find wonderful things. In addition to a lock of William Gifford's hair,[1] the box now holds a remarkable document, an ancient memorandum book, torn in half, at some point slated for destruction. Murray began to use the notebook only a few weeks after his early October 1808 visit to Walter Scott at Ashiestiel, the famous meeting during which the two men discussed setting up a journal to rival the *Edinburgh Review*. Murray's memoranda include subjects and books for review and, most interesting of all, lists of prospective reviewers.[2] These lists help demonstrate that for moderate conservatives the commencement of the *Quarterly* was the opening of a hope chest, a chest they had begun to fill in 1802 with the publication of the first number of the *Edinburgh*. By meditating on the lists, we can consider how well Murray and his gentlemen managed the textual wedding of a number of conservative constituencies, and, by surveying the early history of the journal, how well that marriage turned out.

The lists represent various conservative networks: academic, philosophical, political, legal, ecclesiastical, scientific and military. Among the 123 names listed, we find some familiar ones: the Lake Poets, William Wordsworth, Samuel Taylor Coleridge and Robert Southey; clergymen-academics such as Thomas Robert Malthus, Edward Copleston and Peter Elmsley; scientists and mathematicians, including Thomas Young, Sir Humphry Davy and James Ivory; the evangelical philanthropists William Wilberforce, James Stephen and Henry Thornton; and famous statesmen, George Canning, Lord Aberdeen and Lord Hawkesbury (later Lord Liverpool).

The names in the memorandum book are grouped under those of the journal's editorial coterie – Walter Scott, William Gifford and John Murray himself.[3] Scott would recruit contributors from north of the Tweed; Gifford would contact literary and political cronies he had accumulated over his lifetime as a conservative periodical contributor and editor; and Murray assumed responsibility for authors he knew as a London bookseller and publisher. Other documents in the John Murray Archive provide an interpretive context for the lists. We commence with a 5 October 1808 letter John Murray wrote to his wife, Annie, in which he records details of the Ashiestiel meeting (*QR* Letter 2).[4] From it, we find that two other men were in attendance: the Edinburgh printer James Ballantyne, Murray's new business partner, who had arranged the meeting; and Richard Heber, a noted bibliophile and intimate of George Canning. In the men who were present at this foundational meeting, several Regency economies of power were represented – commercial, literary and political – that can also be detected in Murray's lists. Murray and Ballantyne were members of the conservative publishing fraternity that, while it supported the establishment, catered to middle-class aspirations for self-improvement, for moderate social, political and moral reform, and for economic and political stability. Scott was prominent among the Romantic conservative literary circle whose poetry and prose self-consciously served social, political and economic ends. Heber represented the Canningite liberal conservatives,[5] whose political complexion and social philosophy were remarkably close to that of the older Romantics.

Murray's planning notes, then, confirm the long-held impression that nineteenth-century periodicals, the *Quarterly Review* included, issued from interest groups, social or political networks, or existing cultural formations. With the *Quarterly's* starting point being identifiable party interests – the Canningites and, in Scott, the Scottish unionists – and with a largely sympathetic readership,[6] we might expect that the *Quarterly's* discourse was monologic, that the journal resisted dialogue, that in the culture wars initiated by the French Revolution it was an instrument of conservative nationalist propaganda.[7] And yet a reading of the journal's context challenges the idea that the *Quarterly's* editorial coterie was of one mind and that its writers spoke with a single voice to a homogenous audience. By studying Murray's lists and the principals' conduct of the journal, we discover in the *Quarterly* the truth of Laurel Brake's observation that it was *apparent* homogeneity and a unified sectarian readership that early nineteenth-century journals depended on to attract contributors and assure sales.[8] Rummaging about in the day-to-day operations of the periodical – the editor and publisher's negotiations with each other and with the journal's contributors – we find that, within the limits imposed by Gifford's editorial interventions, the *Quarterly's* discourse was dialogic.

In this essay, I will examine four factors that frustrated Gifford in his desire to make the *Quarterly Review* the wooden end of a Canningite ventriloquist act: namely, the paucity of liberal conservative writers that forced Gifford to look far afield for contributors; John Murray's character and his business ambitions that caused him to attempt to mute the journal's political voice; the evolving state of conservatism during the Regency that made the *Quarterly* a lyceum for a plurality of voices; and the complex intermixing of conservative and liberal social networks that saw a relatively large number of Whigs, liberals and even some radicals become writers for the *Quarterly Review*.

The editorial character of the *Quarterly Review* was distorted when the projectors' early expectation that Gifford would be *'encumbered* with help' (*QR* Letter 12) was not borne out. Gifford had trouble finding suitable Canningite contributors, so when writers of other conservative stripes sought admission to the *Quarterly*, the editor by necessity had to let at least some of them in. Also, driven by business imperatives and by his need to control his gentlemen, Murray habitually interfered 'with the œconomy of the work' (*QR* Letter 48),[9] which made it difficult for Gifford to develop and execute an editorial plan. He pressed Gifford to attract as broad an audience as possible by drawing into the journal contributors from across the political spectrum. As there were multiple conservatisms in the Regency period, it was impractical to think that the *Quarterly* could ever speak with a single voice. In our period of coverage what we now call conservatism consisted of an amalgam of groups from various sectors of British society – religious, political and cultural – groups that disagreed on some fundamental political and religious questions. It was inevitable that the *Quarterly* would reflect these groups' various views. Consequently, at the end of Gifford's tenure when the balance of power in conservatism shifted from liberal conservatism towards High Toryism, the *Quarterly*'s editorial slant began to change as well.

## John Murray's Advertisement

The advertisement John Murray placed in newspapers in January 1809 announcing his new venture attempts to give the impression of a 'mandarin'[10] periodical pretending to broad political, social and cultural agreement between its editorial coterie and its contributors. What follows is the advertisement's second version:

Speedily will be published, the First Number of
THE QUARTERLY REVIEW.
By John Murray, 32, Fleet-street, London.
In announcing this New Literary Journal, the Publisher requests that the First Number may be considered as the Prospectus; while, however, he holds out no prom-

ise, he can confidently assert, that the Gentlemen[a] who have engaged in this Review have long enjoyed the esteem of the Public, and, could their names be given without injury to the freedom, and the truth of Criticism, they would[b] be an honorable pledge of the[c] zeal, the[d] liberality, and the[e] attachment to the interests of Literature, with which this British Journal will be conducted.[f11]

Instead of receiving an impression of homogeneity, however, readers might have sensed tentativeness, anxiety, even embarrassment, especially if they noticed the advertisement's multiple interpretations of the journal's raison d'être as centred in novelty, literature or patriotism. A key variation between the advertisement's two versions – the transformation of 'Authors' into 'Gentlemen' – suggests that originally Murray had been reticent to place the *Quarterly's* political dimension at the forefront of his marketing strategy. Someone, probably Gifford acting as Canning's substitutionary presence, pointed out that 'Authors' implied that an exclusively literary coterie lay behind the *Quarterly*. For most readers of a 'New Literary Journal' this was perhaps not a bad recommendation. But for those in the know, excluding the journal's non-literary supporters (George Canning foremost among them) was an oversight Murray paid money to correct.

There are additional indications in the advertisement's rhetoric that Murray's purposes and those of the *Quarterly's* political backers were in some way in conflict. The text seeks to assure readers of the respectability of the journal's parentage, yet the publisher strangely states that he 'holds out no promise' – does this mean that he cannot trust the staying power of those 'Gentlemen who have engaged in this Review', or is he reserving the right to replace them? (In either case, this is a bizarre qualification for an advertisement.) If anything, Murray appears to mean the latter, for it must be his gentlemen that he is addressing: nineteenth-century convention dictated that articles be published unsigned. As periodical reviewing was an anonymous affair, readers would never know when or if Murray fulfilled his promise to publish articles from men high in public esteem. When we read between the lines, then, we see that the publisher was conscious of a gap between the journal's other projectors and himself.

In the advertisement, we especially locate tension between the publisher and the *Quarterly's* political sponsors where Murray plays a shell game with the prospectus, the sine qua non of early nineteenth-century periodical publishing. Journals such as the *Quarterly Review* established legitimacy and authority by pretending to discursive unity, a pretence achieved in the first place by the issuing of a ringing manifesto, a prospectus. Through such an instrument, the conductors spoke as if with a single voice to an audience clearly defined. The prospectus, an invitation to readers to survey the journal's point of view, is in Murray's advertisement self-consciously deferred. The circumstance begs the question, why was no prospectus issued?

Murray was the originator of the unlikely notion that the journal should be introduced in '*secrecy*', without 'any other annunciation than the dispersing [of] a certain number of gratis copies' (*QR* Letter 5). The publisher suggested this novel plan to Scott at the October 1808 Ashiestiel meeting.[12] Surprisingly, Scott accepted and even embraced the idea, though in his imagination he degraded Murray's marketing strategy into a street kids' prank. He told Gifford that the first number would be 'compiled without ~~any~~ the plan taking wind … [so as to] burst among the Whigs (as they call themselves) like a bomb' (*QR* Letter 4). The designated editor raised no objection; after all, Scott presented Murray's strategy as a fait accompli. It is remarkable, though, that the projectors stuck with the strategy even after it lost whatever utility it may have had – by mid-December, the *Edinburgh Review*'s editor Francis Jeffrey and other men knew that Scott was preparing a journal to oppose the *Edinburgh*. We are left to question why the *Quarterly*'s projectors persisted in the plan.[13]

The probable answer leads us back to the summer of 1807, to the Foreign Office in Downing Street when George Canning, the Foreign Secretary, read and approved a prospectus for a London-based journal to be called the *Quarterly Review*. A few days or weeks later, a copy of the prospectus arrived at 6 James Street, Buckingham Gate, the residence of Canning's literary protégé William Gifford; he too thought well of it. It was the Foreign Secretary's younger cousin Stratford Canning who, with some friends, a year and a half before the Ashiestiel meeting had come up with the idea of a journal to combat the *Edinburgh Review*. It was he who presented the prospectus to Canning and Gifford.[14] Later that year, Stratford Canning met with John Murray; then, in early 1808, he put Murray in contact with Gifford and with other members of the old *Anti-Jacobin* group.[15] Given this history, it is obvious that when Murray met with Scott he was aware of Stratford Canning's prospectus and he knew that William Gifford and George Canning had given it their imprimatur. We can reasonably conclude that Murray, in effect, *suppressed* a prospectus that already existed.[16] To what purpose? Setting aside Stratford Canning's prospectus gave Murray an opportunity to claim to be the journal's instigator; he may also thereby have subverted a document that committed the journal to a political programme or party.

That Murray would think to do such a thing matches his passive-aggressive personality and his pattern of behaviour:[17] to secure his investment, he sought to make the *Quarterly* as much a literary as a political journal and he strived to gain moral as well as legal proprietorship over it. By his own determined efforts, Murray's status grew between November 1808 when George Ellis spoke of Walter Scott, not Murray, as the 'first instigator of our enterprize' (*QR* Letter 28), and May 1819, when the publisher claimed to be the 'man who has *alone* created and succeeded by perseverance in finally establishing the most formidable engine that ever was invented, in support of the laws and Religion of his Country' (*QR*

Letter 216; emphasis added). It is no surprise, then, that a dominant theme in the correspondence is Murray's evolving status in the group that founded the *Quarterly* – 'our little band' (*QR* Letter 258)[18] William Gifford called it – as he moved from the periphery to the centre. That movement is subtly but convincingly evidenced in his and his gentlemen's use of the possessive pronouns 'my' and 'our' to reflect their sense of individual or corporate ownership. In letters of late 1808 that record the founders' negotiations, Scott, Gifford, Ellis and Murray generally use the language of 'our scheme', 'our plan' and 'our Review'. Soon, though, we begin to see Murray speak of 'my plan' and 'my Review'. His use of such language is neither casual nor incidental: he wanted the other projectors to see him as the journal's primary founder. In subsequent years the idea that the *Quarterly* was 'Mr Murray's Review' was implicitly accepted by men who were not present at the creation – Sir John Barrow, John Wilson Croker and Robert Southey. The journal's founders, however, Gifford in particular, generally resisted or ignored Murray's claim to primacy; they only ever saw Murray as 'our publisher'.[19]

Murray's shifting language, and some of his gentlemen's resistance to it, is a sign that the publisher stood in a fundamentally different relationship to the journal from that of his co-founders. At the core of his motivation, Murray was a businessman risking capital in the expectation of gaining profits and commercial prestige. While the others had complex reasons for their involvement – including political and career considerations, and in Gifford's case pecuniary ones – the correspondence confirms that the men with whom Murray worked to bring the *Quarterly Review* into existence were British nationalists motivated by a desire to defend Church, king and nation. True, there was an accommodation between Murray and his gentlemen on the journal's liberal conservative political ideology and the group for the most part worked harmoniously and productively to achieve one of the major publishing successes of the nineteenth century. But the meaning of much of what appears in the correspondence remains opaque until we recognize that there was a fundamental conflict of values between Murray and the journal's other projectors.

The commercial motivation that drove Murray's involvement is evident in his letter to George Canning of 7 September 1807, the famous letter that marks the documentary commencement of the journal (*QR* Letter 1).[20] In this letter we see the young publisher awkwardly navigating between two worlds as he attempts to implement his strategy of marketing to rich and powerful patrons. His starting point is the entrepreneurial world of contract, capital, risk and profit; his desired destination is the establishment world of hierarchy, deference, patronage and obligation. Murray lays out his strategy, if unconsciously, in the letter's coda: 'Permit me sir to add that the person who thus addresses you is no adventurer, but a man of some property inheriting a business that has been established for nearly a century. I therefore trust that my application will be attributed to its proper motives, and that your goodness will at least pardon its intrusion.' It is startling to see Murray in these sentences deny that his 'proper' motive ('proper' in the sense of 'true') is the pursuit of profit; by definition, the motivation of a merchant 'adventurer' is one who risks money in the expectation of personal reward, which exactly describes Murray's interests and his actions. That the publisher saw a strategic advantage in denying his 'proper' motive is clear; by distancing himself from the world of money and speculation he sought acceptance by those who valued inheritance and property, who disdained capital and labour, to whom profit was not a 'proper' motive ('proper' in the sense of 'socially appropriate'). Murray thereby elevated his motive from the self-interest of the capitalist to the noblesse oblige of the aristocrat.[21] Some years later, in 1812, the publisher moved his headquarters from the grubby environs of Fleet Street to elegant West End apartments on Albemarle that he purchased from William Miller, another publisher who marketed to well-heeled customers. Southey then captured Murray's strategy sardonically and precisely: 'I wish you all the success from your prospective removal which you can anticipate. Miller has made his fortune by publishing for the rich. It is a sure method, – and if Government will act with sufficient vigour to protect the rich, I trust you will soon find it so' (*QR* Letter 125).

In future years, Murray used his September 1807 letter to Canning to buttress his claim to be the primary founder of the *Quarterly Review*. In the publisher's telling, which he oft repeated and which made its way into Smiles's biography, his letter was one of two pillars upon which rested the legitimacy of his claim to be the journal's instigator. The other was his meeting with Scott at Ashiestiel in early October 1808, an event that is documented in Murray's 5 October letter to Anne Murray (*QR* Letter 2). Whereas in his 1807 letter to Canning the young publisher adopts the sycophantic tones of the suppliant, in his letter to his wife, 'Annie', he speaks in his native voice as husband and businessman. He excitedly reports that the first reward of his deftly managed alliance with James Ballantyne, an audience with Walter Scott, has ended wonderfully. 'I am truly happy', he triumphantly announces, 'in being able to assure you of the most complete satisfaction which I derive from my visit to Mr Scott and it has now realized or [is] likely to do so, all that had been agitating in my mind for this last Twelve months'. The chain of activity that followed Scott's agreeing to participate in a plan for a conservative journal to rival the *Edinburgh Review* led straight to the publication in March 1809 of the first issue of the *Quarterly Review*.[22] So by any assessment the Ashiestiel meeting effectively marked the journal's commencement. Yet it is worth asking if that meeting was the direct outcome of Murray's twelve months of plotting and planning and that he was therefore, as he later claimed to be, the journal's moral owner.

As we have seen, the *Quarterly Review* had a significant history prior to the Ashiestiel meeting, a history in which Murray played a subordinate if important role. The journal was formed in the convergence of a set of men and events, each necessary but none sufficient to create this cultural artefact at just this time. When Murray met Scott at Ashiestiel, the idea of establishing a periodical to combat the 'eternal Jacobinism' of the *Edinburgh Review* was a general one among British conservatives (*QR* Letter 7).[23] Walter Scott and James Ballantyne were already deeply involved in planning the *Edinburgh Annual Register* to prevent Archibald Constable issuing a similar, Whig-oriented periodical. Richard Cumberland would bring out his *London Review* a month before the first appearance of the *Quarterly*. The Saints too, Lord Teignmouth, Zachary Macaulay, Henry Thornton and James Stephen, had formulated a plan for a rival to the *Edinburgh*, a plan they shelved only when Gifford brought them in as sponsors and potential contributors to the *Quarterly*.[24] So it is clear that the plan agitated by Murray was by no means original; Stratford Canning had the idea first and other men as well intended to act on their discontent.

Among the founders, Murray alone believed that the original plan was his. At the time of their October 1808 meeting, Scott saw Murray, at best, as a messenger, the bearer of news that an English political consortium wished to find literary sponsorship for a new conservative journal. To Scott, Murray was a recruiting agent for men who wanted to canvass him (Scott) as someone who by his reputation and connections could attract a body of regular contributors. To get the journal started, Scott and Canning were essential to the enterprise. Murray, on the other hand, was a functionary, 'our publisher' (*QR* Letters 6, 10), in status and dignity on a level with that of the editor, replaceable if need be.

That the *Quarterly* was a vessel that Scott, not Murray, had launched,[25] was an idea Scott himself encouraged in a 2 November letter to Ellis:

> During Heber's stay John Murray the Bookseller in Fleetstreet who has more real knowledge of what concerns his business than any of his brethren at least than any of them that I know came to canvass a most important plan of which I am now in 'dern privacie' to give you the outline. I had most strongly recommended to our Lord Advocate to think of some counter-measures against the Edinburgh Review which politically speaking is doing incalculable damage. (*QR* Letter 5)[26]

In this letter Scott broke the cause and effect relationship between his and Murray's actions; he took credit for the project and he now took the initiative. It was Scott, not Murray, who after the Ashiestiel meeting maintained the project's momentum. Though he was not the journal's 'master strategist'[27] – that was a role he shared with Gifford, Ellis and Canning[28] – in the immediate aftermath of the meeting he inspired confidence among the journal's projectors that the game was worth the risk. By the time Scott and Murray next communicated with each other,[29] Scott had confirmed Canning's participation and he had decided not to be editor. Encouraged by Scott, Archibald Campbell-Colquhoun, the Scottish Lord Advocate, had written to Canning with a request that he back Scott's venture.[30] Canning had replied in the affirmative and then, without informing anyone, let alone Murray, he approached Gifford, who agreed to be editor. Gifford, acting on Canning's instructions, immediately contacted high political men, Hawkesbury, Long and Huskisson, and he corresponded with Scott (*QR* Letter 6). Shortly thereafter, Scott enlisted Ellis, who had already heard about the project from Canning (*QR* Letter 5).[31]

In contrast to Scott and the participants whose actions he inspired, in the crucial weeks after the Ashiestiel meeting Murray contributed nothing; he was in transit between Edinburgh and London 6–16 October, and for the balance of the month his activities were at best ineffective.[32] It is no wonder, then, that in the following few months the others largely ignored Murray. For weeks he was kept in the dark about Gifford's appointment (*QR* Letter 8). In late November when Canning, Ellis and Gifford met to plot strategy, Murray was not invited (*QR* Letters 10, 11). And it was not until early December 1808 that Gifford saw fit to introduce Murray to Canning in a pro forma meeting.

Murray's response to thus being sidelined reveals that his occasional sycophancy with Canning and Scott was a pose, that he thought well of himself, his talents and his contribution, and that he was determined to assert himself and protect his investment. In early November 1808, he began a campaign to move himself to the centre of the enterprise. After he found out that Canning had some weeks before appointed Gifford to the editorship, on 15 November he wrote to Scott forthrightly claiming credit for the idea of the new review. In the letter he refers to the *Quarterly Review* project as 'my plan' (*QR* Letter 8).[33] As there is no direct record of the conversation at Ashiestiel, we cannot know if Murray's statement sounded presumptuous to Scott or repeated a claim he had made earlier. In any case, at the beginning of the letter Murray humbly admits that his idea was by no means original: 'The propriety, if not the necessity of establishing a journal upon principles opposite to those of the Edinburgh Review has occurred to many men more enlightened than myself' (here he perhaps expresses consciousness of Stratford Canning's role). Yet later in the letter he claims to have had the 'the idea of a new Review' for 'nearly *two* years'[34] (thus predating Stratford Canning's efforts), and states that he 'addressed Mr Canning upon the subject' (though he fails to mention that George Canning did not answer his letter).

Undoubtedly Murray was sincere in regarding himself as an indispensable participant. After all, most of Stratford Canning's activities had centred on him and, moreover, it was Murray alone who kept the plan alive after the younger Canning left for the Continent on a diplomatic mission in the late spring of

1808; Ballantyne enacted Murray's strategy when he set up the meeting with Scott; and – Murray in later years did not let his gentlemen forget this – he willingly put his reputation and money and 'in hazard' (*QR* Letters 58, 60, 66).

Murray asserted himself with increasing shrillness when he saw that the other projectors were continuing to act beyond his control. Whatever high status these men enjoyed by merit or appointment, he was not about to be cowed by them; their independence increased the risk to his capital and so, starting with Gifford, he meant to rein them in. In February 1809, Murray told James Ballantyne that he believed it was 'indispensable that the management must rest with one individual'. A divided command would lead to 'the conductor' having to deal with 'a thousand distracting desires' (*QR* Letter 17). The situation Murray faced was, indeed, far from ideal, for in its first years the *Quarterly* was conducted by a triumvirate: Murray himself, who acted in the interests of his firm; Scott, who functioned more or less on his own; and Gifford, whose power of independence rested mainly on his association with the journal's chief political sponsor, George Canning.

Murray had to deal with Scott for only a brief period. Gifford, though, intended to stay. As witnessed by his arbitrariness and, paradoxically, by his early exit, Scott was a force unto himself, unmoved by Murray's attempts to influence him (*QR* Letters 8, 9, 12, 13, 53). Yet, despite his promise that he would assist Gifford in the editorship and that he would be a steady supplier of articles and men (*QR* Letter 4), from April 1811 Scott ceased to take much interest in the journal. As for Gifford, he promised Canning that he would remain in the editorship and defend his master's interests for as long as Canning was in office (*QR* Letter 3). After the planning stage had passed, Canning was not involved in the conduct of the periodical, but because he continued to sponsor Gifford he nevertheless drew power away from Murray, a circumstance the publisher could not abide. So, by putting his solicitor Sharon Turner forward as a writer on politics and foreign policy, like a moth to the flame Murray tested Gifford's determination to make the journal 'safe' for Canning (*QR* Letters 3, 257).[35] Gifford passed the test. Backed by Ellis, he would not permit Murray, through his solicitor, to speak for the *Quarterly* on government topics. After complaining to his wife that Ellis and Gifford were driven by 'a determined jealousy of Turner',[36] Murray backed off, but in the end he was undaunted: he formed an alliance with John Wilson Croker that eventually saw Croker become the journal's main political writer.

In the meantime, besides politics and foreign policy, Murray permitted Gifford exclusive control over only two departments: religion and the classics. Initially when Gifford insisted upon including these topics, Murray, who thought that both types of articles were detrimental to the journal, enlisted Scott, Ellis and Erskine to persuade the editor to publish fewer of them (*QR* Letter 61). To

Ellis, Murray complained, '*one* Religious Article in each Number ... would be serviceable – but more of this – and more than one (and that a *very* able) *learned* Article [on classics] clogs us sadly' (*QR* Letters 25, 61). He confessed to Ellis, 'my Ledger ... advises me a little upon these points'. Indeed, it was only after about 1812 when the *Quarterly's* subscription list increased and he began to turn a large profit that he finally let Gifford have his way.

Otherwise, Murray involved himself in every aspect of the periodical's conduct,[37] because he was a busybody, but also, as he saw it, to compensate for Gifford's disorganization, pedantry and indolence.[38] Especially in the early years, he officiously bypassed Gifford: he hired contributors, assigned books for review and cancelled commissions, all without consulting his editor. Of course the situation was untenable, but it was not until Gifford threatened to resign that Murray finally became, in the editor's words, 'more modest and tractable' (*QR* Letter 30).[39] Gifford would be permitted to handle his three departments – religion, classics and politics – to add spice to dull submissions, to finesse the articles' language and to see them through the press. For his part, Murray continued to monitor his editor's activities and he actively managed the journal's most prolific writers, Barrow, Croker and Southey. No wonder that Gifford disparagingly referred to his publisher as 'lord paramount' (*QR* Letter 41).

If Gifford's sloppy business practices gave Murray an excuse to interfere in the editorial conduct of the journal, his fear that Gifford would push an intemperate and divisive party line caused him to try to draw power away from his editor. Murray therefore attempted to mute the *Quarterly's* polemics and its political signature – which partly explains the presence of radicals in his lists of prospective contributors, men such as James Mill and Leigh Hunt, and by the fairly large number of liberals who in the end contributed to the journal. In 1810, Murray even second-guessed one of Canning's surrogates, Ellis, by ordering him to remove from one of his articles an allusion to the *Edinburgh Review*.[40] Murray's approach was paradoxical: he wished the journal to advocate a political point of view but not be overtly political. He told an American correspondent: 'I do not profess to be, nor am I willing to become a *political* Publisher – but I am so anxiously and firmly attached to the government that I am always disposed to publish any thing decidedly able and respectable that may be written in their favor' (*QR* Letter 51). As a loyal subject and as a businessman, his interest lay in supporting the forces of stability, so while he by no means forced his editor to avoid politics entirely, he mitigated his investment risk and managed Gifford by emphasizing the *Quarterly's* literary character: the alternative, a stridently political journal, he assumed would mean narrow audiences and low sales. After he discovered that Gifford was to be editor, to Scott he advanced the idea that the conductors 'fix [themselves] upon public attention' through the publication of high quality literary articles. Only then, he thought, should 'honnied drops of party sentiment ... be delicately insinuated into the unsuspecting ear' (*QR* Letter 8). By recommending the 'Sardonic Grin', Murray was pulling his coadjutors back from a strident declaration of political principles and positions. He wanted Gifford and his contributors to use guile because, for business reasons, he wanted to place a governor on the *Quarterly* as a political journal.

A shift in emphasis from politics to literature is detectable in Murray's correspondence of 1807 and 1808. In his invitation to George Canning he obviously had in mind a periodical in which politics and the Constitution would be discussed. During the planning stage, in late 1808, he often wrote about the need to have the journal's political sponsors support the *Quarterly* with authoritative information. Looking ahead, we find that the shift was temporary; in the right circumstances he was not averse to expressing strong political views at all. When Lockhart took over the editorship, at the beginning of 1826, Murray was perfectly happy to see his ally Croker steer the journal towards High Toryism and to represent the government's position uncompromisingly. While we should not, then, overemphasize Murray's aversion to politics – as Kim Wheatley points out in her essay in the present volume, like the other projectors Murray slid 'back and forth between concerns with the propagation of political principles, literary merit, entertainment value and commercial viability' – it is clear that during Gifford's years Murray wished to de-emphasize the political dimension of the *Quarterly Review*.

The reason he did so is that his plan did not unfold quite as he had intended. When he left Scott at Ashiestiel he expected the project would take time to gestate and apparently he supposed Scott might yet accept the editorship.[41] At the meeting, the two men agreed that Scott would come to London, meet with high politicos, and at that time 'urge some very formidable plan into activity'.[42] Scott's energy and decisiveness took the publisher by surprise and Murray did not expect or welcome Gifford's appointment. In his conversations with Gifford in early 1808, Murray had taken the measure of the man and had found him wanting. The publisher wrote to Scott on 15 November worried that Gifford had 'lived too little in the world lately – to have obtained that delicacy of tact whereby he can feel at one instant, and habitually, what ever may gratify public desire or excite public attention and curiosity' (*QR* Letter 8).

Up to November 1808, Murray accepted that the purpose of the journal was primarily political. But when he found out that Gifford was to be at the helm, he instinctively began to emphasize literature, where Gifford because of his withdrawal from the world was weak, over politics, where Gifford because of Canning's sponsorship was strong. Murray then told Scott that 'the department which will be our ultimate and only solid resort – is Literature' (*QR* Letter 8). In private memoranda recorded in late 1808, he mused that in the journal politics should be only one topic among many. Murray categorized the journal's audience:

> The Parson – Soldier – Lawyer – Statesman – Farmer – Merchant – General Reader
> – Artist – Man of Letters – Scholar – Scientist

His conclusion was that 'there should be one article in every number appropriate to each of these classes – the rest to be filled up with subjects of general interest and importance'.[43] By the time he announced in his January advertisement a 'New *Literary* Journal', he seems to have committed himself to producing something more along the lines of a literary magazine than a political-literary periodical similar to the *Edinburgh Review*. The model he may have had in mind was a magazine he and the poet Thomas Campbell tried to set up in 1806 with Scott's help.[44] Consciously or not, by placing politics on a level with literature and everything else Murray led away from Gifford's high card, his political connections.

## The Saints, Sydney Smith and the Formation of the *Quarterly Review*

If the ideological coherence of the *Quarterly Review* was distorted by business imperatives and its publisher's personality, it was even more so by the agendas of the groups that came together to form the periodical's body of contributors. To characterize the *Quarterly*, then, is to understand each group's history with the journal. As an apt demonstration of Gifford's difficulties in moulding into a homogeneous Canningite text the disparate voices of often competing conservative interests, we can look at the participation in the *Quarterly Review* of one group, the 'Saints'.[45] Identifying how the Saints came to be associated with the *Quarterly* will help us locate their motives in wishing to join John Murray's gentlemen. Uncovering their agenda will help us analyse the problems they faced in getting Gifford to accommodate their aims. And describing their participation will deepen our understanding of the events and personalities that converged in late 1808 to produce a new 'British Journal'.

The Saints' role in the history of the *Quarterly Review* was an important one. In his 1808 planning notes, Murray listed four first-generation Saints: Lord Teignmouth, William Wilberforce, Henry Thornton and James Stephen. Three second-generation Saints also appear in his lists: James Stephen's nephew, Henry John Stephen, and two brothers, the younger Charles Grant and Robert Grant, sons of a powerful East India Company chairman, the elder Charles Grant. Another first generation Saint, Zachary Macaulay, met with Gifford in early January 1808 to discuss the role he could play in the new journal. He briefly became involved as a subeditor.

In the *Quarterly's* first years, the Saints participated most effectively through the contribution of Robert Grant, a barrister and soon-to-be parliamentarian who ended up as the Governor of Bombay. At his father's instigation, Grant had contributed to the *Edinburgh Review* a series of brilliant articles on India. But as the quintessential liberal conservative, he was more at home in the pages of the *Quarterly Review*. For Gifford he wrote articles on economics, politics and literature that garnered praise and attracted subscribers. One of his submissions, his 1810 review of John Gifford's *Life of William Pitt*, was by unanimous agreement the early *Quarterly's* central document. Gifford, who called it 'a masterly article', regarded it as 'a sort of Manifesto of the Pitt-principles' (*QR* Letter 32).[46]

Except for Grant's articles, however, the Saints played their most important role during the prehistory of the *Quarterly Review*.[47] The immediate cause of the Saints' participation in the *Quarterly* was the Reverend Sydney Smith, who in the January and April 1808 numbers of the *Edinburgh Review* published a concerted attack on evangelicalism and Christian foreign missions.[48] Smith's bravura performance roused the Saints' ire and it also incensed Robert Southey. Understanding the origins of the Saints' participation in the *Quarterly* therefore takes us some way towards understanding why Southey was determined to 'hoist the bloody flag, down alongside that Scotch ship'.[49] Like Southey, the Saints had been considering for some time before the formation of the *Quarterly* how best to answer the *Edinburgh Review*.

A letter from John Murray to Walter Scott dated 19 November 1808 reveals that at about the time the two men met at Ashiestiel, the Saints themselves were contemplating a journal to counter the *Edinburgh*. Murray received this news from Gifford, who had been speaking with a leading Saint, his friend Lord Teignmouth. Upon hearing of Murray's project, Teignmouth unhesitatingly pledged the Saints' support. The evangelicals' plans were well enough advanced that Teignmouth could offer Gifford a list of Saints who could be relied on to contribute articles – the names Murray dutifully recorded in his 1808 memorandum book: Thornton, Macaulay, the Stephens, Wilberforce and the Grants. Murray characterized Gifford's news as 'important',[50] no doubt because he recognized the moral and political weight the Saints carried with significant political and religious constituencies. It was fortunate, Murray told Scott, 'that we intend opening with an article on missionaries, which, as it will be written in opposition to the sentiments in the Edinburgh Review, is very likely to gain that large body of which Wilberforce is the head'.[51] The article in question, 'Account of the Baptist Missionary Society', Robert Southey's first contribution to the *Quarterly Review*, directly rebutted the Sydney Smith articles offensive to both him and the Saints.

When Murray told Scott that the evangelicals were on board, however, he reassured him that 'Mr Gifford is equally sensible as you of the danger of allowing any preponderance to the Saints, and will carefully guard against them' (*QR* Letter 12). Murray's caution, and the fact that in his answer to the publisher's letter Scott responded negatively to Gifford's news, are early indications of the indifference, and in some cases hostility, the evangelicals eventually met from the *Quarterly Review*'s editorial coterie. There was thus a potential problem in Gifford's strategy of enlisting a group mainly because it was the enemy of his enemy: when the opinions of his primary sponsors conflicted with those of one of his other constituencies, the junior partner in the alliance lost out. The predictable result was that eventually the Saints were alienated from the *Quarterly Review*.

By the time Gifford retired, at the end of 1824, the Saints had been repeatedly buffeted in the *Quarterly*, just as they had been in the *Edinburgh*. Besides numerous sniping remarks about evangelical practice,[52] the *Quarterly*'s offences towards evangelicalism took three forms: negative portrayals of evangelical leaders, both Nonconformist and Church of England; criticism of evangelical organizations, in particular the British and Foreign Bible Society and, though it was not named, the Church Missionary Society; and challenges to public policies that the Saints advocated or supported, such as the evangelization of India and the rapid abolition of slavery. Gifford even permitted Sir John Barrow to express exactly the same objections to Christian evangelization that Sydney Smith had raised in his *Edinburgh Review* anti-missions articles.[53] The last few years of Gifford's tenure also saw the emergence in the journal of overtly anti-evangelical articles, most damagingly William Gilly's 'Martyn's Memoirs' in Number 50 and John Philips Potter's 'Newton and Scott' in Number 61.[54] The Saints even more greatly lamented, though, the *Quarterly*'s failure to support the abolition campaign. The few articles that touched upon the question expressed qualified sympathy for the West Indian planters, demonstrably because some of Canning's close associates, including George Ellis, were plantation owners whom Gifford did not wish to offend.

A major reason why the evangelicals were roughly treated in the *Quarterly* was because Gifford, Murray and Scott were more comfortable with the other major branches of the established Church than they were with the evangelicals – the Erastian Orthodox ('high and dry'), the pre-Tractarian High Church and the Broad Church parties.[55] Given the principals' wariness of the Saints' enthusiasms, then, we might well ask if there was anything besides having a common enemy that would explain the joint participation of moderate evangelicals[56] and liberal conservatives in the *Quarterly Review*. We discover that in some respects the two groups were ideologically compatible and, as might be expected when comparing socially contiguous groups that crossed categories (religious and political), their personnel overlapped.

To begin with, the Saints and the Canningites shared political convictions and were strong and affectionate allies in and out of parliament. Many, indeed a majority of the *Quarterly*'s contributors were pious Christians. At a minimum, Canning was an orthodox Christian – his orthodoxy is asserted by both his biographer and his eldest son and is amply demonstrated in the manuscript record. He was also close to a number of evangelicals. He enjoyed a friendship with the Saints' leader, William Wilberforce, which was predicated on their mutual admiration of William Pitt. (Canning was Pitt's protégé; Wilberforce had been one of Pitt's closest friends.) Canning numbered among his associates other evangelicals as well, including Lord William Bentinck, Viscount Granville and Henry Thornton; he was even known to rub shoulders with extreme evangelicals such as Lewis Way and Edward Irving. Also, other *Quarterly Review* co-founders and sponsors had connections to the evangelicals: John Hookham Frere's brother James was a prominent evangelical premillenialist; Richard Heber and his half-brother Reginald were intimate with the Thorntons and the Grants; and, as we have seen, Gifford was a friend of Lord Teignmouth. It was through Reginald Heber that Robert Grant secretly conveyed his *Quarterly Review* contributions to Gifford. So we can see that, although Gifford was doubtful about the evangelicals' fraternization with Nonconformists and although he sometimes mocked their piety, at a personal level the Canningites and the Saints were surprisingly acceptable to one another.

Despite the appeal of working with men with whom they shared bonds of sympathy and affection, the Saints only took the decision to abandon the *Edinburgh* after they had suffered a long series of provocations from that journal. By locating the Saints' reasons for deserting the 'Northern Blast',[57] we can identify some of the grievances conservatives expected the *Quarterly* to redress. The Saints had enjoyed a long-standing relationship with the *Edinburgh* primarily through Henry Brougham, the dynamic parliamentarian who was a member of the *Edinburgh*'s editorial coterie. As early as June 1803, immediately upon his relocation to London from Edinburgh, Brougham sought an introduction to the leading Saints as he wished to participate with them in the slave-trade abolition campaign.[58] By October 1808, partly as a reflection of this relationship, but also as a tribute to the Saints' prominence, some thirty-four articles of immediate interest to the Saints had been published in the *Edinburgh*, including articles on slavery and critiques of evangelicalism. Saints had supplied information for seven articles the Edinburgh 'Northern light'[59] had published in support of abolition. The *Edinburgh* reviewed the publications of several Saints, including Wilberforce, Teignmouth, Thornton and Stephen.

While none of those articles caused offence, a few other reviews were the source of considerable friction between the *Edinburgh* and the Saints. Brougham led parliamentary opposition to the Orders in Council and James Stephen (the Orders' primary author) allowed two articles that Brougham published on the matter to sour their friendship; those bad feelings did not, however, prevent the two men from continuing to work together on abolition. Before the publication of Smith's articles, the most serious rift to open between the Saints and the *Edinburgh* was the result of an 1804 article by a friend of Brougham's, James Loch.[60] His criticism of East India Company management angered the elder Charles Grant, at the time the Company's Deputy Chairman. Brougham could hardly contain his annoyance. The outcome of his strenuous efforts to smooth Grant's ruffled feathers was Robert Grant's series of *Edinburgh Review* articles on India, mentioned above. A mutual determination to patch up differences for the sake of abolition had led to a good result. But this and similar episodes sowed seeds of discord and contributed to the Saints' eventual dissociation from the northern journal.

From the *Edinburgh Review*'s inception, in 1802, to the appearance of the *Quarterly*, in early 1809, conservatives such as Walter Scott, Bartholomew Frere and Robert Grant contributed to the journal. As long as its liberalism remained muted, they were willing to put up with the odd anti-establishment indiscretion. By 1808, largely under Brougham's influence, though, the journal became increasingly sympathetic to democratic and even republican ideas, a development that culminated in the 1808 article 'Don Cevallos',[61] the *Edinburgh*'s anti-aristocratic manifesto that has often been credited with launching the *Quarterly*. And yet long before then leaders of conservative networks, including the Saints, the Canningites and the Scott-Southey literary circle, had found reason to be discontented with the *Edinburgh*, so much so that they warned Jeffrey that he was straining their patience.

The Saints and other conservatives' complaints centred on three main issues: what Robert Southey called the *Edinburgh*'s 'peacemongering' policy on the war with France; the journal's acerbic and uncharitable literary reviews, especially Jeffrey's reviews of the Romantic poets; and its anti-religious tone. At the time of the first appearance of the *Quarterly Review* there was agreement among conservatives about which of the *Edinburgh*'s articles had been the most troubling: in literary circles, Jeffrey's reviews of prominent poets, particularly of Wordsworth, Scott and Southey caused offence;[62] in religious circles, reviews of the evangelical poets Cowper and Montgomery produced howls of anger and contempt;[63] in political circles, a review of Cobbett's *Political Register*, one on Whitbread's anti-war pamphlet *Letter on Spain* and the 'Don Cevallos' article deeply disturbed the journal's conservative subscribers.[64] Of all the articles against which conservatives set a black mark, Jeffrey's review of Montgomery was the most lamented. Among the tamer things the editor said about this good man's bad verse was that he had initially ignored the philanthropist-poet because he mistook him for 'some slender youth intoxicated with weak tea, and the praises of sentimental Ensigns and other provincial literati, and tempted, in that situation to commit a feeble outrage on the public'. Obviously, Jeffrey was not above employing homophobic innuendo and rape metaphors, but Southey summed up his crimes as emotive and material: 'He wounds a man in his feelings and injures him in his pocketbook'.[65]

When the time came for conservatives to gain their revenge on the *Edinburgh*, Southey led the vanguard; besides Jeffrey's attacks on the Romantic poets, the articles that disturbed him most were the same articles that bothered the Saints. To judge by his correspondence and his early *Quarterly Review* submissions, the Montgomery review was first in the list of articles that motivated his vendetta.[66] Almost as high were Smith's attacks on evangelicalism in the January and April 1808 numbers, 'Ingram on Methodism' and 'Indian Missions'.[67] In Smith's anti-evangelical articles, the nagging combination of obvious genius with a 'petty censorious spirit'[68] disgusted Southey who found unpalatable the fact that Smith treated religion in a flippant, paltry and satirical manner. The Reverend Sydney Smith raised Southey's ire because a clergyman satirizing a religious group represented an offensive combination of the sacred and the profane.[69]

Until Smith's articles appeared, the Saints had only suffered pot shots from the materialist, anti-dogmatic *Edinburgh* reviewers. These had stung, however, because, with Brougham at their side, the Saints expected that when it came to evangelical interests the *Edinburgh* would at least be neutral. While the Saints were certainly uneasy in their relationship with the *Edinburgh*, they were unwilling to give up such a valuable ally in the abolition campaign. Smith's articles, though, represented an open challenge that even for the sake of abolition they could not ignore. His articles were to the Saints what 'Don Cevallos' was to the Canningites, the occasion for a concerted response.

Brougham, who believed that Smith was never more offensive than in his attack on the evangelicals,[70] pointed out in his remembrance of the episode that the evangelicals faulted Smith for not distinguishing between Nonconformists and Church of England evangelicals.[71] Smith had indeed used 'evangelical' indiscriminately as a synonym for the eighteenth-century term 'enthusiasm' to describe religious irrationality of whatever stripe; his use of 'evangelical' in this way was both his method and his message. Measuring his opponents by the Enlightenment virtues of decorum and propriety, in his articles he satirically portrayed Methodists and Church evangelicals as stepping, respectively, above and below their proper social stations. 'Consecrated cobblers' (Marshman and his fellow Baptist missionaries to India) or men of wealth and influence acting like Nonconformist ranters (Wilberforce and his fellow Saints) represented a mixing of social genres offensive to Smith's Augustan mind. In this respect, 'Ingram', 'Indian Missions', and his 1809 article 'Styles on Methodists and Missions' can be read as a set. The first two articles satirize the Saints for stepping below their proper station; the third satirizes the Methodists for stepping above theirs.

Besides strategically confusing persons and terms, Smith dissected and dev-astatingly criticized evangelical belief and practice. He warned that evangelical 'gloom', stemming from an unorthodox theology of retribution, soured the life of the individual and made him unfit for society; that the evangelicals' emphasis on the doctrine of Special Providence led to a too familiar use of sacred words and forms; that the evangelicals' belief in Perfectionism – the idea that sin is rooted out at conversion – often led to antinomianism, self-righteousness and hypocrisy; and that evangelical leaders, driven by megalomania, inevitably sought power and were ultimately a danger to the State.

Finally, and at great length, Smith brought the implications of his general criticisms home by showing his readers that evangelical doctrine and practice could have serious negative consequences for the nation. He did so by high-lighting the July 1806 Vellore mutiny in India that had proved embarrassing to the Saints and had undermined a policy they were pursuing, the Christian evangelization of the Indian subcontinent. By mentioning, in the peroration to his January 1808 article 'Ingram on Methodism', the Saints' domination of the East India House under Charles Grant and their call to evangelize India, Smith alluded to the public debate just then raging over Indian missions. The particu-lar focus of the debate was the role of missionaries in exacerbating conditions prior to the mutiny at Vellore and the subsequent massacre of British soldiers and expatriates.

In his second article, the April 1808 'Indian Missions', Smith made even more direct use of this debate to support his contention that evangelicalism could endanger national interests. Smith wrote that on the subject of evangelism Grant and his friends were 'quite insane, ungovernable; they would deliberately, piously, and conscientiously expose our whole Eastern empire to destruction'. The Saints were therefore 'not to be trusted for a single moment'. The power of the Saints at home as an articulate, moneyed, parliamentary interest, and their alliance with Nonconformist missionaries abroad, had already resulted, Smith argued, in damage to British interests in India and might lead to even worse con-sequences in the future, to the destruction, perhaps, of the empire itself.

Smith spoke powerfully and persuasively to an audience already well aware of what was at stake; for some time evangelical propaganda had saturated public discourse with calls for the conversion of India. A national debate on Indian mis-sions had commenced in 1803 when Claudius Buchanan, one of the so-called 'pious chaplains' in India, pushed the question of Indian evangelization onto the national agenda.[72] In an 1805 *Memoir* published in Calcutta, Buchanan chal-lenged the East India Company's long-standing policy of non-interference in native religious practice by demanding the establishment of an Indian episco-pacy. Two years earlier, he had instituted £100 and £500 prizes at several British universities for the best poem or essay on the topic of Indian evangelization.

As Buchanan hoped, his *Memoir*, and what one periodical reviewer called his 'truly oriental munificence', attracted public attention at home.[73] These events embarrassed Charles Grant at the India House by associating him through his reputation as a Saint with a position he did not necessarily hold, and with a strategy for advancing policy, an appeal to public opinion, that he did not at the time condone.[74]

Buchanan caused real damage to the Saints' interests when news of the Vellore mutiny arrived in England in early January 1807.[75] Grant's opponents saw in the mutiny an opportunity to diminish his power and undermine the Saints' ability to influence the terms of the East India Company Charter, up for parliamentary renewal in 1813. The anti-evangelical forces seemed to gain the upper hand when news reached England in March 1807 that investigating authorities claimed that missionaries had unintentionally instigated the mutiny. The authorities alleged, falsely as it turned out, that evangelical missionary zeal had led the sepoys to believe that a policy of forced conversion to Christianity would soon be adopted.[76] In October 1807, in the chambers of the India House men such as John Scott-Waring and Thomas Twining raised the cry against missions. Some of the journals – the *Critical*, the *Antijacobin* and the like – then proceeded to throw fuel on the fire and prominent evangelicals responded to their goad, Lord Teignmouth among them.

In Parliament, meanwhile, as well as in the East India Company, a determined opposition had been growing against the extraordinary influence of Charles Grant and his lieutenant and fellow Saint, Edward Parry. Between them, Grant and Parry had been Chairman or Deputy Chairman of the Company five times in the period 1804 and 1808; together they controlled the votes of as many as two-thirds of the Company proprietors; and they could depend upon the support of most of the Company Directors. In the Company, the Saints represented one faction, the 'Company interest', while Warren Hastings and his henchman John Scott-Waring led the opposition, the 'Indian interest'.[77] For the Indian interest, the idea of converting the Indians was 'downright madness', as one of their number, David Anderson, expressed it to Hastings.[78] In the midst of the anti-missions uproar Buchanan awarded yet another of his exorbitant prizes.

Despite the handicap the intemperate Buchanan represented, by the end of December 1807 Grant and Parry again demonstrated their grip on the Company by beating back the opposition. The pamphlet war that had raged for three months fell into a lull; then Smith's 'Ingram on Methodism' appeared. Immediately, public opinion turned against the evangelicals, giving Grant's opponents a renewed mandate.[79] Between the publication in the *Edinburgh Review* of Smith's 'Ingram' in January 1808 and his 'Indian Missions' in April, another inflammatory anti-missions pamphlet appeared and the bitter pamphlet combat resumed.

Wilberforce and Grant concluded that the year-long assault on their India policy had perceptibly undermined their broader influence.[80] The immediate harm to the Saints' interests was the defeat of the Curates Salaries Bill that was before Parliament at the time of the appearance of Smith's 'Indian Missions' article. (Bishop Porteus had devised the bill as part of a campaign the Saints supported against ecclesiastical pluralities.) During debate on the bill in the House, the opposition attacked with vigour, with a prominent Whig leader, Creevey, echoing the tone of Smith's articles. He claimed that a sinister puritanical conspiracy lay behind the bill, led by 'members [of] the Foreign Bible Society, the Society for the Suppression of Vice' (societies founded and conducted by Saints), 'and those dealers in missionaries who had nearly overturned the power of Britain in the late conduct in India'.[81] The Saint-Whig parliamentary alliance that had proved so fruitful in the passage of the slave-trade abolition bill only the year before was evidently at risk. It was in this context, then, that the Wilberforce circle found especially galling the publication in the October 1808 number of the *Edinburgh Review* an article in which Smith flippantly criticized the Curates Salaries Bill. Smith began his diatribe in that article with a memorable if infamous line, 'The poverty of curates has long been a favorite theme with novelists, sentimental tourists, and elegiac poets'. This and most of the other equally facile points in the article gratuitously echoed, though admittedly with greater wit, the recent parliamentary debates that, as we have seen, had themselves been inspired by Smith's anti-evangelical articles.[82]

Such were the circumstances that led the evangelicals to desert the *Edinburgh* when in late 1808 Gifford informed Lord Teignmouth that Scott and Canning were projecting a new journal. The Saints and other moderate conservatives welcomed the *Quarterly* because they saw it as an opportunity to sublimate hurt personal feelings, to counter the political and religious heterodoxy of the *Edinburgh Review*, to model a 'moral' alternative in reviewing, and to present to the public a moderate conservative voice. Although Brougham, and through Brougham, Jeffrey, had promised to suppress those aspects of the *Edinburgh* that the Saints and others had found most offensive,[83] by late 1808 the *Edinburgh*'s conductors had not only failed to inject what Southey called 'morality' into the journal's essays, but the Saints had been openly and repeatedly insulted in Smith's articles. His unguarded sarcastic references to evangelical interests – India, foreign missions and abolition – the Saints considered the final blow to their relationship with the *Edinburgh Review*.

The Saints found it possible to consider cooperating with the projected *Quarterly Review* because it represented to them an alternative forum that would be, again in Southey's words, 'orthodox and loyal'.[84] At the time they had reason to hope that they could also make it an abolitionist journal. When they first heard of the project, in October 1808, no articles had been written, and the periodical's policies on specific issues were yet to be established. A promise was held out that Sydney Smith's articles would be rebutted. They could not have anticipated how considerably the *Quarterly Review* would disappoint them by its treatment of evangelicalism, by its adopting the carping, uncharitable tone of the *Edinburgh* in its literary reviews, and by its failure to support abolition.

## A Plurality of Voices in the *Quarterly Review*

Gifford's treatment of the evangelicals points to a fundamental problem in his conduct of the journal: partly for the practical reason that he needed a steady stream of contributions, it was impossible for him to draw exclusively from Canning's circle. Therefore, with conservatives of various temperatures wishing to be represented in the *Quarterly*'s influential pages, Gifford found it necessary to admit at least some writers he had doubts about. That is why four sets of contributors made their way into the *Quarterly* during Gifford's tenure that were to some extent incompatible with the aims and purposes of the journal's Canningite projectors: the Saints, anti-Erastian High Churchmen,[85] High Tories and liberals (Whigs and radicals both). As we have seen, Gifford admitted the Saints, but he placed shackles on their contribution by restricting them to topics of a non-religious nature; in addition, he counterbalanced their voice by publishing anti-evangelical articles. Given conditions on the ground, it was perhaps inevitable that High Churchmen and High Tories would eventually find a place in the *Quarterly*; it should be noted, however, that very few High Tories contributed to the journal in its early years.

The presence of Whig and radical contributors in the *Quarterly Review* is entirely anomalous and requires an explanation. (It is startling to see Gifford admit a Whig such as Francis Hare-Naylor, for with the Whigs setting themselves apart not only by their politics but also by their social behaviour, circles of acquaintance, and even their speech, what he was doing must have been obvious to himself and to everyone else involved.)[86] For the most part it was for personal reasons, or to satisfy Murray, or because the contributor in question wrote on an ideologically neutral topic that he permitted liberals or radicals such as Hare-Naylor, James Pillans, Henry Matthews, John Herman Merivale, Henry Hallam, Thomas Arnold, William John Bankes, Charles James Blomfield, Octavius Gilchrist, John Hoppner, Peter Elmsley, Macvey Napier, Richard Chenevix, John Symmons and Robert Bland to become writers for the *Quarterly Review*. It would be wrong, however, to exaggerate the impact of these men's presence in the journal; after all Gifford rejected any of their submissions that 'would have given displeasure to all [his] friends'[87] and made certain that in what he did publish their liberal propensities did not show.

Liberals aside, under Gifford the *Quarterly*'s supporters and contributors consisted of men from six groups, each an amalgam of conservative religious, ecclesiastical, philosophical, economic, political and constitutional positions. Making allowances for some overlap in personnel, the groups were: the Canningites, conservative Romantic writers, Orthodox Churchmen,[88] moderate evangelicals, anti-Erastian High Churchmen and Broad Churchmen (the Oriel Noetics).[89] That we can use a Church party label to identify all but two of these groups is a measure of the importance Gifford and Ireland placed on the *Quarterly*'s defence of the Christian dimension of the unwritten British Constitution. Indeed, it was chiefly that aspect of the *Quarterly*'s editorial ethos that attracted the attention of men from across the conservative spectrum and caused them to want to have a presence in the journal.[90]

The one major group that Gifford virtually excluded from the *Quarterly Review*, the High Tories, triumphed in the end. In addition to Robert Southey, who after 1810 deserved the label, Gifford admitted only one bona fide High Tory, George Gleig, into the roster of contributors. (John Wilson Croker is a special case. His High Toryism must be qualified, and in any case during Gifford's tenure he bided his time by steering clear of politics in the *Quarterly*; under Gifford he largely confined his reviews to literature, memoirs and histories.) As each of the groups that dominated the *Quarterly* to some extent defended the political and social status quo, they had that much in common with the High Tories. But, again demonstrating the importance to Gifford of constitutional religious questions, it was the High Tories' Protestant constitutionalism, their disdain for Catholic Emancipation, which caused the editor generally to exclude them. The High Tories remained in the wings for most of Gifford's tenure because the editor stood his ground against their admittance, but also because there was little incentive for them to press for representation: they had a number of alternatives open to them, the *Antijacobin*, *Blackwood's* and *John Bull*. (*Blackwood's* in particular provided an outlet for the High Tories' best writing talent.)

The transition to High Churchmanship and High Toryism in the *Quarterly* that was (with some qualifications) achieved under Lockhart was partly the result of happenstance.[91] It was almost by default that editorial control over the *Quarterly* was temporarily gained by, of all people, Robert Southey when for a season his nominee, the lay High Churchman John Taylor Coleridge, succeeded Gifford. Murray had wanted William Haygarth, a man who had no significant connection with the *Quarterly*'s major constituencies, either in the Church or in Parliament, whose politics were more liberal than conservative, and who appealed to Murray for just those reasons: he would probably muddle the journal's conservative character without overthrowing it and be dependent upon Murray alone for his position. It was also just for those reasons that Gifford spurned Haygarth. The men Gifford preferred were liberal conservatives, but he was too ill in 1824 to push hard for them. Though Gifford distrusted Robert Grant's Saintliness, he was at the top of the retiring editor's list to replace him in the editorship. Grant was offered the post, but, as Gifford expected, he 'proved timid'.[92] Gifford's next choice was the Erastian High Churchman Reginald Heber; he too declined – 'wisely, perhaps' was Gifford's weary verdict (*QR* Letter 234). Finally, starting with Nassau Senior, Gifford mulled over the whole set of liberal churchmen, the Noetics, but he could not settle on anyone. In the matter of a successor, Gifford was certain of one thing, he did not want Murray's candidate, whoever that might be. The publisher finally hired the only person with a serious claim on the editorship who was neither Gifford's nor his own candidate, John Taylor Coleridge.

After a single year in the position, during which time he fought with Croker and left Murray unimpressed, Coleridge moved aside in favour of Sir Walter Scott's son-in-law John Gibson Lockhart, whose reign lasted to 1853.[93] Now Murray had what he had wanted, a cooperative malleable editor and the journal's political department in the hands of a man with whom he had had a close personal and working relationship. Murray depended upon Croker to guide the journal's political direction; Lockhart deferred to Murray.[94] The young editor's one important sponsor, Scott, was far distant and he was otherwise preoccupied with his own considerable financial troubles. Lockhart was therefore stranded in London, his career and his pocketbook at the mercy of a publisher who knew how to manipulate a man while he made it look as if he was doing him a favour.

The *Quarterly* fell into the hands of anti-Erastian High Churchmen and, to some extent, High Tories, then, because moderate conservatives gave up the game. While Gifford and Canning stood by and watched, Murray exercised his own preference, which happened to fall at just that moment on Lockhart. What was an entirely personal choice largely devoid of ideological content nevertheless reflected the spirit of the times, for Lockhart's ascendance mirrored a shift in the balance of power in English conservatism that took place during the 1820s, from Liverpool's liberal conservatism to Eldonite High Toryism.[95] Key *Quarterly* reviewers, Scott, Gifford, Copleston, Heber, Barrow, Sumner and Grant, represented an urbane and generally mild form of conservatism. These were men who advocated the tenets of political economy and were willing (albeit grudgingly) to accept some reform measures, including, in order to buttress the union with Ireland, Roman Catholic Emancipation. In a November 1817 article in the *Quarterly*, William Gifford permitted Richard Wellesley to qualify liberal conservatives' commitment to the status quo: 'We are no more the panegyrists of legitimate authority in all times, circumstances, and situations, than we are the advocates of revolution in the abstract'.[96] Other early contributors, Southey and Croker in particular, were harbingers of the paternalism and resistance to political reform that became the preferred view of many young Tories from the late

1820s. Their extreme conservatism was destined under Lockhart and Croker so to mark the *Quarterly* that many scholars, sometimes unthinkingly, refer to the journal as 'reactionary'.

The *Quarterly* might have avoided that fate had Robert Grant accepted the editorship when it was offered to him in 1822, for he would have seen virtue in the *Quarterly*'s plurality of voices. He may have declined the editorship because, to make the journal 'popular', Gifford had followed Jeffrey by injecting 'spice' into some of the journal's reviews in the form of vitriol and sarcasm. He thereby offended the important constituency to which Grant belonged – the Saints – along with Southey and the better angels of the High Church party. In attempting to accommodate Canning's immediate political needs, too, he had excluded support for abolition and, to satisfy his Orthodox constituents, Gifford had allowed the evangelicals to be openly criticized. Similarly, to keep a valued contributor such as Southey, he permitted the journal to deviate from liberal conservative tenets in its treatment of political and social issues and policy, such as in its coverage of political economy, in particular of Malthus's prescriptions on the Poor Law. By forming an alliance with John Wilson Croker, and by pushing aside a man he could not well control, John Coleridge, Murray, too, played a part in shifting the tenor of the *Quarterly* to a less temperate and accommodating breed of conservatism. Some voices in the chorus, liberals, Saints and Noetics, that – though muted and distorted by editorial control – had found a place in the *Quarterly Review* under Gifford, were seldom if ever heard in the *Quarterly Review* under Lockhart.[97]

# 4 POLITICS, CULTURE AND SCHOLARSHIP: CLASSICS IN THE *QUARTERLY REVIEW*

## Christopher Stray

On 15 November 1810, William Gifford wrote to George Ellis: '– redit labor actus in orbem. The wheel is come round, and we are again in the press. In what state is your first article?' (*QR* Letter 68). On 29 December, sending back a review to Walter Scott, he warned him, '... you must not keep it beyond a fortnight – our labour, you know, like the husbandman's redit actus in orbem, and I wish to put your review as forward as possible' (*QR* Letter 75). On both occasions, Gifford was quoting from Virgil's account in the *Georgics* of the farmer's year: *Redit agricolis labor actus in orbem*, 'The work of farmers, once performed, comes round again'.[1] It was to a classical quotation that Gifford went to encapsulate the recurrent demands of a periodical publication. In so doing, he will have reached not for a dictionary of quotations, but simply into his memory, which like that of many other educated men of the times was well stocked with Latin and (to a lesser extent) Greek phrases which summed up situations, feelings and rules of conduct.[2] Such phrases were convenient resources with which to introduce or drive home a point. Boswell, discussing Johnson's use of quotations, commented that 'a highly classical phrase [may be used] to produce an instantaneous strong expression'.[3] Editing a quarterly journal involved a seasonal cycle of work which might aptly be compared to that of the husbandman; but even within a season, the editor's dealings with several contributors necessitated the repetition of letters of request, encouragement, reminder or rebuke. It is appropriate, then, that the invocation of Virgil's classical reference to the farmer's round should itself 'come round again', made first to Ellis and then to Scott.

The *Quarterly Review* during Gifford's editorship was published at a time when classical scholarship was still deeply embedded in English high culture, though its authority had declined in the previous two centuries.[4] The use of Latin as an international language of scholarly communication had withered, surviving only in the ritual and ceremony of Church and university. In the 1690s, Newton had written his *Principia* in Latin, but in the same decade, Locke had complained of the difficulty of finding tutors who had a good command of the language. Challenges to the authority of classics as the exemplar of polite learning had not been wanting in the following century, and from the 1750s demands for the teaching of more 'useful' subjects, including English, had mounted. The new bourgeois groups who rose on the back of the industrial revolution, however, looked for badges of respectability at a time when classical knowledge, or the appearance of it, still constituted the prime source of such things. In the reformed public schools such as Rugby under Thomas James (1778–94) and Shrewsbury under Samuel Butler (1798–1836), the sons of these families were stripped of their provincial accents and armed with useful social connections and with classical learning. In many cases, this would not have enabled them to do more than read a few easy sentences of Latin, and to spout a small number of classical tags learned by heart. But such activities carried with them the assumption that Latin and Greek belonged to gentlemen, marking them off from their inferiors, who communicated only via the ambiguously named 'common language', English. Until well after the period with which we are concerned, English, modern languages, mathematics and natural science hardly appeared in the curricula of public schools. When science teaching began there, it was through public lectures by visiting teachers. French was taught by laughable 'Monsewers' as a social grace, rather like fencing. As for English, it was not taken seriously until late in the nineteenth century.[5]

The mounting waves of protest against classics in the 1750s coincided with the visit to Athens of James Stuart and Nicholas Revett, whose accounts of Greek architecture were to spark off a neo-Hellenic revival.[6] As romantic Hellenism gathered force in the 1780s and 1790s, ancient Greece took over from Augustan Rome as a dominant cultural exemplar in Britain. In the early nineteenth century, the writing of Keats, Byron and Shelley drew on this inspiration to create powerful English poetry based on Greek models. The world of Pope and Latinate satire was left behind in favour of the new paradigm, though the three poets I have named of course covered a wide range of styles and genres. The climactic event of the worship of Greece, in one way, was the arrival of what are now commonly called the Elgin Marbles at the British Museum in 1816. They are controversial today, as the battle goes on between those who would return them to Greece and those who either believe their return would set a dangerous precedent, or that they might suffer from conditions in Athens. But they were controversial in a different way in 1816, when some critics did not believe they were worth buying or displaying.[7] Stuart and Revett had been funded by the Society of Dilettanti, a club of gentlemen founded in 1734 whose activities combined travel with antiquarian collecting. The activities of Lord Elgin in Greece were characteristic of dilettante practice, as was the collecting of Edward Clarke of Cambridge, who brought back to England what he claimed was a statue of

Ceres; his accounts of his travels were reviewed in the *Quarterly*.[8] This was in effect the tradition of the virtuoso continued; what we might now recognize as 'scientific' archaeology, with systematic excavation, record-keeping and dating, came only with the work of Charles Newton in the 1850s.

## Schools and Universities

As in the life of the educated gentleman, so in the endowed and public schools which usually provided his schooling, classical learning was a fossilized relic of the Latinate literary republic of Europe. Typically it involved the memorizing of passages of Horace and Virgil and of Latin grammars written in dog-Latin, and the constant practice of composition in Latin. Greek was begun later on in a boy's school career but learned in the same way, the Greek grammar also being written in Latin. Boys who went on to Oxford or Cambridge from the public schools often had behind them ten or more years of exposure to classical literature. But it should be emphasized that almost all of this was an exposure to texts taught not as literature to be explored, discussed and appreciated, but as linguistic corpora to be learned by heart and to be analysed ('parsed') according to mechanical rules of grammar and syntax which were themselves learned by rote. The Eton Latin grammar (*Introduction to the Latin Tongue*, 1758) and its Greek counterpart (1768) lay at the heart of this process; the prestige of Eton ensuring that they were used by most English schools. The widespread use of the Latin grammar had led to its being pirated in the 1790s, but from the 1820s it was subjected to an increasing barrage of criticism. Not only were it and its Greek sibling written in Latin, they were confused and internally contradictory; reform was however blocked by institutional pride, and they were not abandoned until the 1860s. During the period we are concerned with, translations of the Eton Latin grammar into English began to appear, in part reflecting the growth of a wider reading public, and of aspirant social groups eager to acquire gentlemanly knowledge. The changes in the quarter-century after 1820 were nicely captured by De Quincey in 1846:

> Everything in our days is new ... *readers* ... being once an obedient race of men, most humble and deferential in the presence of a Greek scholar, are now becoming intractably mutinous, keep their hats on whilst he is addressing them, and listen to him or not, as he seem to talk sense or nonsense! ... [the] vast multiplication of readers within the last twenty-five years has changed the prevailing character of readers. The minority has become the overwhelming majority; the quantity has disturbed the quality. Formerly, out of every five readers, at least four were, in some degree, classical scholars; or if *that* would be saying too much, – if two of the four had 'small Latin and less Greek' –, they were generally connected with those who had more or, at the worst, who had much reverence for Latin, and more reverence for Greek ... But now-a-days the readers come chiefly from a class of busy people who care very little for ancestral crazes.[9]

From this schooling, boys in their late teens could go on to Oxford and Cambridge, which in 1824 were still the only universities in England. As the educational wings of the Anglican Church, the ancient universities imposed religious tests on students, though with varying strictness. At Oxford one could not matriculate (register on entry) without subscribing to the Thirty-Nine Articles; in Cambridge this was required only at the point of graduation. This technical difference reflected a more general contrast in religious and political opinion, Oxford being a more conservative and more High Church institution than Cambridge. In curricular terms, the two universities were mirror images of one another. At Oxford, classics was dominant, the mathematicians being in a minority; in Cambridge, the reverse was the case. The university examinations set up in Oxford in 1800 included both classical and mathematical subjects (the latter were hived off in 1807). College teaching centred on classics, and in the 1800 statute this was extended to university level. Underlying this move was a concern to secure a firm system of moral as well as intellectual discipline, to act as a bulwark against Jacobinism.[10] At Cambridge the situation was very different. Fuelled by Newton's reputation, mathematical physics had since the early eighteenth century come to overshadow its competitors and it was comfortably allied to natural theology. By 1809, when the *Quarterly Review* was founded, the university's only honours examination, the Senate House Examination, was dominated by mathematics, though it also included papers on logic and on moral philosophy.[11] Classical learning was, as at Oxford, encouraged in the colleges, and tested in their undergraduate examinations.[12] At university level, however, the only rewards for classical proficiency were a handful of endowed prizes and scholarships which were irregularly available and hedged with restrictions. After his appointment as Regius professor of Greek in 1808, James Henry Monk campaigned for a classical examination to be set up, but without success. This came only after Christopher Wordsworth's appointment as Master of Trinity (the college of both Monk and C. J. Blomfield) in 1820; the Classical Tripos was founded in 1822 and first examined in 1824, the final year of Gifford's editorship. Trinity was not only the largest college in the university, but also its leading centre of classical scholarship. During Monk's tenure of the Greek chair (1808–23 – almost identical to Gifford's reign at the *Quarterly*), it was in addition the home of a group of scholars known as the 'Porsonian school'. Pupils and disciples of the great Greek scholar Richard Porson (d. 1808), Monk's predecessor in the Greek chair and Gifford's friend, they followed his style of work, focusing on the minutiae of language and metre, especially in the editing of Greek tragic drama.

In 1812, Monk, Blomfield and some Cambridge friends founded a journal to promulgate the Porsonian style of scholarship: *Museum Criticum, or Cambridge Classical Researches*.[13] John Murray offered to publish the journal 'on the same terms as the Quarterly Review: i.e. to defray the whole expence of publication,

& then to divide the profits with the editors'.[14] The first issue of the *Museum* appeared in May 1813. It sold reasonably well, but the intervals between issues soon increased from six months to a year. The editors' main problem was that they could not retain their fellowships if they married; and if they were given livings they were unlikely to have time for scholarship. Blomfield's first substantial living came in 1817; Monk was appointed Dean of Peterborough in 1822. Both ended up with sees, Monk as Bishop of Gloucester and Bristol, Blomfield as a celebrated Bishop of London.[15] The *Museum* did not long survive their preferments: Number 7 did not come out until 1821, five years after the previous issue, and the eighth and final number was published only in 1826.

The Porsonians formed a recognizable school, one which was identified as such soon after Porson's death by Samuel Butler.[16] Butler was a fellow of St John's College, and the rivalry between St John's and Trinity underlay the tensions between Butler and the Porsonians. But it was reinforced by political and religious differences, Monk and Blomfield being more conservative and High Church than Butler and his friends. Another basis for disagreement was the rivalry between the *Museum* and its major competitor the *Classical Journal*, published by Abraham Valpy since 1810. This has some claim to be the first journal in England devoted to the subject. It contained a variety of matter: erudite articles on textual scholarship, inscriptions, book reviews, prize poems from Oxford and Cambridge and lists of forthcoming books. Valpy saw himself as the new Aldus Manutius, and gathered round him a group of classicists, most of whom were not university-based. The most prolific contributors included Edmund Henry Barker and George Burges, who were similar in their combination of considerable learning and lack of judgement. Barker had been an undergraduate at Trinity, but had left without taking a degree, probably because of religious scruples. He waged a long campaign against Monk and Blomfield, even going to the length, apparently, of publishing complimentary reviews of his own work over Monk's initials ( J. H. M.).[17]

Gifford's early university connections were with Oxford, notably with Edward Copleston, but through Copleston he made contact with like-minded men in Cambridge. Monk and Blomfield were both High Churchmen, and in this and in their commitment to classical scholarship were apt candidates for recruitment to the *Quarterly*. If we include the probable as well as definite identifications, Monk contributed two reviews, Blomfield ten; among other things, they reviewed each other's editions of Greek plays.[18] It seems likely that Monk was contacted first and then brought in Blomfield. Their correspondence in this period shows that Monk often urged Blomfield, whom he regarded as a more accomplished and effective writer, to provide articles and reviews Monk thought should be published; and this helps to explain the disparity in the numbers of their reviews. In 1813, Monk wrote to Blomfield, 'We will make out an article between us; tho' to say the truth, I shall principally rely upon you. Nature has given me the dangerous powers of satire with a very sparing hand – you can wield the weapons effectually.'[19]

'We will make out an article between us': this was clearly a common procedure with *Quarterly* reviews, and it bedevils attempts at attribution. But Monk's estimate of his and his friend's powers was a just one, and this helps in the task of identification. Consider an 1820 article which reviewed E. H. Barker's incoherent diatribe against Blomfield after the latter's crushing review of Valpy's edition of Estienne's Greek Thesaurus.[20] Cutmore comments that this is either Blomfield assisted by Monk or vice versa. We can assume that the eulogies of Blomfield are by Monk; but our knowledge of their respective talents adds to this by allowing us to ascribe the finer passages of sarcasm to Blomfield: for example, 'In the same spirit of knight-errantry in behalf of dunces in distress ...'[21] The best guess that can be made, then, is that rather like the attack on Brougham in 1819,[22] this review was drafted by Monk and then embellished and spiced up by a more entertaining writer – in this case Blomfield.

## Oxford and Cambridge, London and Edinburgh

The role of classics in Oxford and Cambridge, and the differences between the two universities, formed part of the background to the development of the *Quarterly Review*. Not only were they important sources of both contributors and readers, they played an important part in the *Quarterly*'s battle with the *Edinburgh Review*. Just after the *Quarterly* was founded, its great rival in Edinburgh launched an onslaught on Oxford, criticizing its curriculum, its teaching and its religious restrictions.[23] Payne Knight's scathing review of Thomas Falconer's edition of the Greek geographer Strabo and Sydney Smith's broader attack on Oxford, including a criticism of its failure to teach political economy, brought a powerful response from Edward Copleston in the following year. In a series of three pamphlets, he seized on flaws in his opponents' case and was regarded in Oxford as having crushed its opponents.[24] In fact the *Edinburgh* reviewers had a strong case, but they did not make the most of it. Among the points at issue was the use of Latin in scholarly editions, a remnant of the once widespread use of the language for communication between European scholars. Latin continued to be used for editorial introductions and for textual notes until the middle of the nineteenth century, and mistakes in its use in such contexts were often seized upon by critics. The *Edinburgh Review*'s onslaught on Oxford in 1809 was typical of this tendency, as were Copleston's replies. The *Quarterly* reviewer of the *Edinburgh* response to Copleston made great play with the defective command of Latin shown by the *Edinburgh* writers.[25]

Copleston's role as the champion of the more conservative and higher Anglican of the ancient universities against the Scottish onslaught made him the ideal advisor for Gifford in the university world. It is not surprising, then, that Gifford used him as a source of counsel and as a conduit to other contributors, and that, as Cutmore has noted in his Introduction, he was willing to share his deepest secrets, the identities of other contributors. The recruits brought in via Copleston included Monk and Blomfield. Blomfield had been a regular classical reviewer for the *Edinburgh Review* since 1809, but broke off relations in 1813. On 31 August 1813, he complained to a fellow-classicist, Peter Elmsley, that he had asked Jeffrey to return an article Blomfield had sent him: 'I told him candidly that I could not lend my feeble aid to a Journal, the tone of which was so offensive to men of religious feeling'. Despite this, Blomfield went on, Jeffrey had printed his article 'in the 42nd number'.[26]

In other fields, too, the picture of classics one gains from the *Quarterly Review* in this period suggests the continuation of an eighteenth-century tradition on the eve of new developments. There is almost no sign of the crucial contemporary movement, the emergence of Altertumswissenschaft (the systematic study of the ancient world) in Germany, sparked off at the end of the previous century by Friedrich August Wolf.[27] His study of the Homeric epics employed techniques originally developed for biblical criticism; and the philological seminar which became a characteristic feature of classical training in German universities was modelled on the seminars founded for the training of ministers. The appearance of the 'higher criticism' of ancient literature was viewed with alarm in conservative quarters in Britain, since it was clear that techniques formulated to assess the literature of the Greeks and Romans could also be applied to sacred literature. These alarms, however, belonged largely to the later 1820s onwards. During the early years of Gifford's editorship, the continental blockade severely hindered scholarly contact with the Continent, and this in turn was reinforced by isolationist feelings in England after the Revolution, the Terror and Napoleon's conquests.

The history of *Museum Criticum* and of the *Classical Journal* (which ran until 1829) shows that there were relatively specialized outlets for classical publishing available during Gifford's reign at the *Quarterly*. This raises the question of the relationship between this more specialized publishing and the *Quarterly* and other general reviews. The question is not an easy one to answer, except by saying that the reviews confined themselves to reviewing. The more specialized journals included original articles, translations, prize poems, notes on texts, inscriptions, lists of recent books and a whole host of other features whose nature placed them beyond the remit of the *Quarterly* and the *Edinburgh*. A comparison of the reviews published in the two groups of journals reveals very little difference. Reviews of classical editions typically consisted of opening remarks, sometimes including a survey of previous editions; a statement of the leading features of the book under review, and the reviewer's opinion of these; and finally a long (sometimes very long) list of comments on individual textual details.[28] A modern reader may wonder how many contemporaries stayed the course to the end of such reviews; and it is clear that Gifford and Murray were also concerned. It was important to include articles on classical topics, if only because the *Edinburgh* did so; and this in turn reflected the continuing centrality of classical learning in gentlemanly culture. Literary articles were also needed for a fundamental reason that Elmsley's and Southey's friend Grosvenor Bedford made very clear: 'To avoid even the appearance & to repel any charge that may be made against the work on the score of ministerial influence all pains will be taken to make it [the *Quarterly*] complete as to scholarship, literature & science'.[29] Anything more than a sprinkling, however, was too much, and this applied especially to reviews of editions of classical texts. It was surely the realization of this limiting factor, inter alia, which prompted Monk and Blomfield to set up their own journal.

On 25 September 1810, Murray wrote to Gifford:

> Greek Articles are not read generally even by those who are capable of understanding them – I don't think you or Mr E[llis] or Mr C[anning] would read them in any other Journal – they should therefore be refused. I can concede to very important Works … by the very first classical scholars. – A Greek article should be very able indeed so as to excite attention at the Universities where almost alone it is read … If provided too – *one* good religious article in each number would render us more service than two or three – but we should always have one. (*QR* Letter 60)

Murray reiterated the point to George Ellis on 2 October 1810, in relation to articles on religious subjects: 'If we could compound for *one* Religious Article in each Number it would be serviceable … and more than one (and that a *very* able) *learned* Article clogs us sadly' (*QR* Letter 61).[30] Murray's remarks make it clear that the problem was not confined to classical topics: he saw his market as lying partly within, partly without the universities, and was concerned not to include more academic articles than a wider readership would tolerate. This resonates with the tensions between the Porsonians and their rivals: for this was partly founded on the distinction between the Cambridge academic base of the *Museum Criticum* and the metropolitan location of the *Classical Journal*, run by a printer (albeit one with high cultural pretensions) and supported by scholars from outside the universities, such as Edmund Barker and George Burges.

Especially in the case of Greek topics, the use of Greek type (in printers' terminology, an 'exotic' type) constituted a clear visual signal that some readers would be unable to appreciate large parts of a review. The second half of Blomfield's review of Monk's edition of Euripides's *Alcestis* in April 1816 was devoted to comment on textual detail. At the end of his article Blomfield declared, 'We make no apology to our readers for the length and minuteness of these criticisms. Those who take no interest in such matters have only to transfer their paper-knife to the next article.'[31] Blomfield was well aware that he was catering for a small minority. Four years earlier he had written to Elmsley, 'I believe that Jeffrey's notions with regard to classical criticism are nearly such as you describe them; for having observed that my article would occupy 30 pages, he adds, "while on a liberal computation, there are about as many persons who will understand it". In the same letter, he confirmed that he had published the fragments of the minor Greek writer Sophron in Valpy's *Classical Journal*, and added, 'I wish to continue the Fragments of Sophron, but I have no leisure to transcribe them for the press; nor do I think that when they are printed more than ten people will understand them'.[32] Here Blomfield was in fact echoing the language of an earlier letter from Elmsley: '... there are about ten men in England who really study the *minutiae* of Greek, and of these few, four or five do not write'.[33] The theme had been adumbrated, in fact, by Gifford himself, in the first classical review to be published in *Quarterly Review*, in February 1809. He opened by confronting the problem head on: 'Though the reading population of this country has been long on the advance, the number of classical scholars by no means increases in the same proportion. An indifference to classical learning seems to be gaining ground in society ....' His response is to link classical learning as a traditional cultural formation with the *Quarterly*'s task of defending tradition: '... we feel, in common with every Englishman, a partiality approaching to veneration for that discipline which is consecrated by long usage, and guarded by bulwarks coeval almost with the constitution of the country ....'[34]

## Classics, *Quarterly Review* Style

It is time to consider what kind of classical work was represented in Gifford's *Quarterly Review*, and what relation it bore to the classical teaching and research of the period. What Gifford included is of course far from being a simple reflection of classical work. Nor could a reflection in any case be a simple one, given the variety of the strands of classics – antiquarianism, Porsonian text criticism, archaeology, the study of myth, travel, composition and translation – practised between 1809 and 1824. We can assume, though it does not get us very far, that 'Quarterly Review classics' was influenced, though not created, by the books which came to the attention of Gifford, John Murray and his (other) 'gentlemen'. Here already some kinds of classical practice were filtered out: those which tended not to result in publication. An obvious example is the great mass of verse compositions in Latin and Greek which were produced at Oxford, Cambridge and elsewhere. Some of these were written for prize competitions, of which there were several at Cambridge; the relative paucity at Oxford reflected the embedded strength of the subject and hence the lesser need of encouragement.[35] During Gifford's editorship only two volumes of such work were reviewed, the first being *Musae Cantabrigienses* of 1810.[36] This collected successful entries for the Browne Medal, founded by Sir William Browne in 1774 and restricted to Greek and Latin odes and epigrams. The title of the book does not mention Browne's name, nor does its title page identify the editors; they were in fact C. J. Blomfield, soon to become a regular reviewer, and his friend and co-founder of the *Museum Criticum*, Thomas Rennell. The publication of the book in 1810 might be seen as part of the self-conscious assertion of the Cambridge tradition of scholarship in the wake of Porson's death in 1808.[37] If so, it is ironic that Porson himself despised most modern attempts at Latin and Greek composition, or at least their publication; he praised an earlier Greek scholar, Richard Dawes, for choosing 'rather to read good Greek than to write bad'.[38]

The second collection to be reviewed was of a very different kind: a volume of compositions by pupils of the Royal High School, Edinburgh, edited by their headmaster James Pillans (who afterwards confessed that the publication was premature). The book was sympathetically reviewed in the *Edinburgh Review* in November 1812 by Francis Jeffrey,[39] and this may have prompted Gifford to commission an article in response. The review in the *Quarterly* listed the Edinburgh schoolboys' errors at length: 'We had at first determined to collect all the errors against syntax and prosody contained in this little volume; but we found the task Herculean'.[40]

One of the most obvious filters through which books were selected for review was Gifford's own tastes. Like Porson he came from humble origins and owed his education to a series of rich patrons. The two men also shared a taste for satire and polemical writing. Their politics, however, were very different. Porson was a supporter of the French Revolution and a member of the London Corresponding Society, whereas Gifford made a reputation as a vitriolic Tory satirist with the *Baviad* (1791) and the *Maeviad* (1795),[41] culminating in his editorship of the *Anti-Jacobin* in 1797–8. His scholarly work centred on his editing of English authors (Ford, Massinger, Jonson and Shirley); his translations were made from Roman satirists (Juvenal in 1802, Persius in 1817 – the latter author he had taken as his model in the *Baviad*). The picture of Gifford we gain from this is very much that of a late eighteenth-century figure, his tastes formed by the Augustan period with its liking for Latin authors and satire, before the surge in Romantic interest in Hellenism from the 1780s. One might, with caution, link the contrasting literary tastes of Gifford and Porson to their university allegiances: an American visitor who studied classics at Cambridge in the 1840s suggested that 'The Cantabs are stronger in Greek, the Oxonians in Latin'.[42] Gifford's predilections are seen most clearly in the reviews he wrote himself: three articles concerned with Roman satirists are all probably by him.[43] It was in precisely in this area that Gifford himself had published. His own hopes of bringing out a translation of Juvenal by subscription in 1781 had been dashed. He eventually published it in 1802, with some success, though it was unfavourably noticed in the *Critical Review*, prompting his *An Examination of the Strictures of the Critical Reviewers on the Translation of Juvenal* (1803). Gifford may therefore have felt some fellow-feeling towards the anonymous author of *Specimens of a New Translation of Juvenal*, which appeared in 1812. If so, it did not stand in the way of his denouncing it as a 'petty publication' whose author was not up to the task. Nor was he very complimentary to the unfortunate author when, two years later, he published his complete translation.[44] From Gifford's review, it is clear that the anonymous *Specimens* were the work of Charles Badham: a fact of which we should otherwise be ignorant.[45]

The *Quarterly*'s treatment of classics of course depended in large part on its choice of reviewers. Both Murray and Gifford, with the help of Walter Scott, began with lists of possible contributors, and, as we might expect, these included friends and acquaintances. A good example is John Ireland, later to be Dean of Westminster 1815–42; a schoolboy friend of Gifford's and the executor of his will. Ireland was not productive as a classicist, and the *Quarterly* articles attributed to him deal exclusively with religious issues; but he founded prizes at Oxford (the Ireland Prize, 1825) and at Westminster School to promote the practice of classical composition. Ireland's conservatism will have endeared him to Murray, and the same is true of the antiquarian Samuel Seyer of Bristol, a minor figure. A cleric and son of a cleric, Seyer ran a school in Bristol, was an accomplished local historian, and wrote a number of Latin textbooks. He was an Oxonian, but graduated three years before Gifford matriculated; he may however have come to Gifford's attention through his *Latium Redivivum*, published (by Murray) in 1808, the year in which the lists of potential *Quarterly Review* contributors were drawn up. In his book, Seyer proposed the restoration of Latin as the language of international diplomacy, in part as a way of rolling back the advance of French, the language of the Revolution and of Napoleon's empire.[46] Seyer is not known to have contributed to the *Quarterly*, and the same is true of the Norfolk antiquarian William Stevenson, also on Gifford's list: he was probably included as a frequent contributor to the *Gentleman's Magazine*. Murray's own list includes 'Pillans', and this is presumably James Pillans of Edinburgh, later to contribute three articles.[47] Pillans is an interesting figure in this context, since he was an Edinburgh Whig. He had recently worked at Eton College as an usher, and this may have brought him into contact with Murray; but his review of a translation of Juvenal for *Edinburgh Review* in April 1808[48] will also have attracted Gifford's attention. Two Oxford scholars figure in the lists: Thomas Gaisford and Peter Elmsley. The latter was a prolific contributor of reviews, though as we shall see his liberal views and his connections with the *Edinburgh* were a potential problem for Gifford and Murray. Gaisford was quite different, a hard-working scholar who devoted his career to bringing out editions of difficult authors, but he had no wider ambition than this, and actively avoided ecclesiastical preferment as a distraction from scholarship. In his dogged persistence he can best be compared with another Christ Church man of the period, Henry Fynes Clinton, author of enormous and detailed accounts of ancient chronology.[49] Clinton's autobiography reveals him as a man of precision who loved to count: even the amount of Greek and Latin he read each day was noted to the page and line, and annual totals drawn up in pride or mortification.[50]

Among those listed by Walter Scott was a man on whose judgement Gifford came to rely: Edward Copleston of Oriel College, Oxford, a classical scholar and, as we have seen, the great champion of his university (and Gifford's) against 'the calumnies of the *Edinburgh Review*'. It is likely that other Oxonian reviewers were recommended by Copleston. Similarly, at Cambridge Gifford was as we have seen in touch with Monk and Blomfield, both of Trinity. The impression one gains from Gifford's letters, however, is that his links with his own alma mater were always stronger.

## The Classical Articles in the *Quarterly Review*, 1809–24

Fifty or so articles published during Gifford's tenure can be described as 'classical'; about 7 per cent of the total. There are several cases which are more or less marginal: for example, an article on Jerningham's *The Alexandrian School; or a Narrative of the First Church Professors in Alexandria* deals with ancient history, but its concerns are essentially with Church history, as the book's subtitle makes clear: '*with Observations on the Influence they still Maintain over the Established Church*'. A review of Woodhouselee's anonymous *Historical and Critical Essay on the Life and Character of Petrarch* is concerned with the Renaissance, and not directly with the classical world. In another article, C. J. Blomfield reviews W. M. Leake's *Researches in Greece*; almost the whole review is devoted to the status and nature of modern Greek, with only an initial paragraph or two discussing the wider aspects of Leake's book.[51] This review reflected Blomfield's current interest in contemporary Greek, which unusually he saw as a resource for understanding the classical language; his interest however appears to have waned later in 1814.[52] This may explain Gifford's assignment of a later review in this area (of Coray's Ἑλληνικη Βιβλιοθήκη *With Observations relating to the Modern Greek Language*) to Robert Walpole.[53] 'Coray' is in fact Adamantios Koraës,[54] a crucial figure in the development of modern Greek language and literature, then living in Paris.

The articles which can be called 'mainstream classics' fall into distinct clusters. First, there are reviews of editions and translations of Greek or Latin authors. (The distinction is not always easy to maintain, as some translations included critical notes.) There are about two dozen of these, that is about half the total number of classical articles. Some patterns are very clear. Greek authors preponderate – eleven authors and eighteen articles, compared to five Latin authors and as many articles. This is not surprising in a period when Romantic Hellenism was in full swing; but another factor may be the strength of the Cambridge contingent in the *Quarterly* reviewing team. The most reviewed author is Euripides, with three reviews of editions of single plays and one of a collection of three. This was an Oxford edition of 1811 of the kind known as 'variorum': that is, it includes selections of notes and other material by several scholars who had previously published on the plays. In this case one of them is highlighted: a leading English classical scholar of the eighteenth century, Jeremiah Markland (1696–1776). The variorum style was, by 1811, rather old-fashioned and it may be significant that this edition was produced on large paper. It was intended, that is, as much for country gentlemen who liked to have visually and socially impressive large-format volumes as for classical scholars in the universities. As a whole, this volume sits slightly oddly among the other editions reviewed in the *Quarterly*, which are fairly recent. In its backward-looking quality and in its use of a variorum format it belongs to a period when the presses of both ancient universities were out of touch with the leading contemporary scholarly views. The best-known example is the edition of Aeschylus which Porson refused to undertake in 1782 because the University Press would not fund a visit to Italy to collate manuscripts – the Vice Chancellor commented, 'Let Mr Porson collect his manuscripts at home'. (Porson later referred scornfully in print to scholars who did not understand the difference between collating and collecting.)[55] Samuel Butler, headmaster of Shrewsbury, agreed to undertake the task on the Press's terms; the result was a massive four-volume variorum edition, based on Thomas Stanley's text of 1663, which began to appear in 1809, when it was severely criticized by Blomfield in the *Edinburgh Review*.[56]

After his death in 1808, as has been mentioned, a cult of Porson had developed. His pupils and followers tended the fire at his shrine in several ways. First, they produced editions of his unpublished notes. On 6 April 1810 the Master and Seniors of Trinity College agreed 'that the Porsonian Collection of Mss, lately purchased, be published, for the Benefit of the College ...'.[57] The first result was the publication of Porson's adversaria by Monk and Blomfield in 1812.[58] Monk's successor as professor of Greek, Dobree, published Porson's notes on Aristophanes in 1820 and his Photius in 1822. Another Trinity admirer, Thomas Kidd, in 1815 published Porson's *Tracts and Miscellaneous Criticisms*. Second, they published editions of their own in the Porsonian style. Third, they made clear their reverence for the great man in reviews and other publications. Some of these books, and these reviews, appeared in the *Quarterly*.[59] The attitude taken to Porson is indeed of use in determining authorship in some cases: adulation is to be expected from Monk or Blomfield, but not from Elmsley.

The wider ripples of Porson's fame can be detected later on. In her correspondence with Hugh Boyd, the blind Greek scholar who coached her, Elizabeth Barrett at times becomes 'Porsonia'.[60] The virtuous English governess in Catherine Sinclair's moral tale *Female Accomplishments* (1836) is called 'Miss Porson'. As late as the 1930s, a shy young man in McDonell's *England Their England* is, to his embarrassment, named Porson Wilamowitz Jebb – three eminent Greek scholars in one. Even in 1961 the poet and librarian Philip Larkin, reviewing an annotated record of Louis Armstrong tracks, could refer to the annotator as 'the Porson of early jazz'.[61] The use of 'Porsonian' and the identification of a Porsonian school of scholarship began quite soon after Porson's death; the earliest appearances of 'Porsonians' and 'Porsonian school' are in Samuel Butler's *Letter to C. J. Blomfield* of April 1810. Butler was a fellow of St John's, the neighbour and great rival of Trinity, and the references can be compared with the more fantastical alternatives he also coined: Porsonianians, Porsonaccians, Porsonulettes. Some of these appear in letters to another scholar with mixed relations to Porson's followers, Peter Elmsley, who himself coined 'Porsoniasm' to refer to the cult of the master's style.[62] The Porsonian types were cut by Richard Austin in 1807–8 and first used (a few words only) in E. D. Clarke's *Greek Marbles brought from the Shores of the Euxine* (1809); the first substantial use was in Blomfield's edition of Aeschylus's *Prometheus Vinctus* (1810), reviewed in the *Quarterly* by Elmsley in February 1811.[63] In his review of Monk's *Hippolytus* in September 1812, Blomfield provided a summary of the school's characteristics: a conservative attitude to emendation, the use of analogical reasoning and a condensed and cogent style of annotation. He concluded that 'the Porsonian school' is 'but another term for the *best* school of Greek criticism'.[64]

## Classics, the *Quarterly Review* and the *Edinburgh Review*

The *Quarterly Review* was of course founded as a counter to the *Edinburgh Review*, and it is easy to find evidence for a rough division of the literary world between the reformist supporters of the *Edinburgh* and the conservative contributors to and readers of the *Quarterly*. For example, James Monk wrote to John Murray in 1817 that the Dissenter Sir James Smith, against whom he had published a pamphlet, '... has links with some Edinburgh Reviewers'.[65] It would be a mistake, however, to see them as simply two separate and polarized entities. For one thing, there were authors who contributed to both. Elmsley contributed six articles to the *Edinburgh* between April 1803 and February; he then published one review in the *Quarterly*, in July 1812.[66] An article of September

1812,[67] previously regarded as being probably by Elmsley, was in fact by Blomfield; who wrote to Elmsley on 1 December 1812:

> My dear Sir
> The facts relative to my review of Monk's Hippolytus are these. I drew it up in considerable haste early in the Summer, & wrote twice to Jeffrey, requesting him to insert it in the last No. of the Edinburgh. Not receiving any answer to my application, and having understood from you, that you had relinquished the intention, which you once entertained, of reviewing it, I sent it to Gifford through the medium of a friend of mine at Cambridge who is a regular contributor to the Quarterly.
> My only motive for concealment is, that, as I am known to be a personal friend of the author, I might be suspected of partiality in the laudatory parts of my review.[68]

As we have seen, Blomfield abandoned the *Edinburgh Review* in 1813, having had one article published which he wished to withdraw, and another ignored which he wished to publish.[69] The cooling-off may have been mutual: the letter from Blomfield quoted earlier shows that Elmsley did not see Jeffrey as an enthusiastic publisher of classical reviews, at least of the kind he had received from Blomfield and Elmsley: detailed evaluations of editions, including lengthy discussion of textual minutiae. Elmsley may have abandoned the *Edinburgh Review* because he realized Jeffrey was not keen to continue publishing reviews which attracted only a small minority of the review's readership, and which would entail an uphill struggle against the *Quarterly*. His motivation, however, probably had more to do with his political and religious beliefs than with his scholarship. By the time the *Edinburgh Review* launched its onslaught on Oxford in 1809, Elmsley had already published in it, though not recently (his three articles had all appeared in 1803), and he went on, as the review continued to criticize his old university, to publish in it again in November 1810 and November 1811.[70] His articles were all reviews of classical editions – no mention in them of wider issues of education or religion – and this might be thought to lessen his offence. In fact, he was probably felt to be allying his Oxford-based scholarship with precisely those who had criticized it. No wonder Copleston, busily engaged in defending Oxford against the Scottish onslaught, described his fellow-Oxonian's link with the *Edinburgh Review* as 'an unnatural confederacy' (*QR* Letter 87). Elmsley's situation was difficult in any case, since he was known to be a Whig and to have Grenville as a patron. This may be why he turned in 1811 to the writing of articles on ecclesiastical policy; but his offering to Gifford, on the burial of Dissenters, was rejected as being sluggish and boring (*QR* Letter 113); it would also have offended the more evangelical readers of the *Quarterly Review*. Elmsley then offered an article to Jeffrey, on Clarendon's view of Catholics, which was published in February 1812.[71] This was a sensitive issue, as the liberal minority in Oxford, to which Elmsley belonged, was pressing for the admission of Catholics, a policy which became the touchstone of liberalism in the university.[72] His views contributed to his failure to gain two posts in 1812: first, the Regius chair of Greek at Oxford, which went to a safe man, Thomas Gaisford, younger and less distinguished;[73] second, the preachership of Gray's Inn, which despite the conservative vote being split was won by William Van Mildert, later Bishop of Durham.[74] In October 1813, Elmsley wrote to Samuel Butler that he had not sent articles to the *Edinburgh* for two years: 'The irreligious tone and the Jacobinism of some of its articles have compelled me to withdraw from it'.[75] In the same letter he told Butler that, having contributed an article to the *Quarterly Review*, 'I have private and personal reasons for not contributing to it again, at least for the present'. He had asked Murray for permission to turn one of his articles into a pamphlet but was refused; Murray had a rule against allowing reprinting and was unwilling to break it. Elmsley thereupon declared that he would not write for the *Quarterly Review* again.[76] To Monk and Blomfield's dismay, he at first extended this prohibition to the *Museum Criticum*, since it was published by Murray. They were, however, able to persuade him that Murray had no say in the journal's content, and by November 1813, Monk was able to report to Murray that 'Elmsley promises material for no. 3'.[77]

Peter Elmsley, the most distinguished Oxonian classicist of his generation, received no further preferment (he had been given a small rural living in 1797). Not until 1823, two years before his death, was he appointed Camden professor of ancient history and principal of St Alban's Hall. In the previous year, his appointment as Regius professor of divinity at Oxford had been blocked by Prime Minister Lord Liverpool, an opponent of Catholic Emancipation and a close friend of Canning, and he himself refused the see of Calcutta, thus becoming 'probably the only recusant Greek play bishop'.[78] Elmsley's career and writing provides an interesting case study of the relations between scholarship, politics and religion in the early nineteenth century, and the two reviews clearly formed part of that complicated nexus.

## Telescopes across the Tweed: The *Quarterly Review* and the *Edinburgh Review*

On 31 August 1813, Blomfield complained to Elmsley about Jeffrey's refusal to return a review and his subsequent publication of it in the *Edinburgh*:

> I consider this conduct of Jeffrey as extremely indelicate, to use no harsher term – but I have now no redress ... Immediately upon my discovering the circumstance, I wrote to Gifford, begging him not to scruple withholding my remarks on your Heraclidae to a future No. of the Quarterly, in case he should feel any difficulty from the appearance of my contribution in the TransTweedian journal ...

Gifford clearly had no such qualms (or no substitute article to hand), since Blomfield's review of Elmsley's *Heracleidae* duly appeared in the July number of the *Quarterly*.[79] He may indeed have been keen to match the *Edinburgh Review*'s performance, as his letters suggest this was a constant concern. In *QR* Letter 83, Gifford reported that 'I have for the next a Review of Blomfield's Aesch[ylus] somewhat elaborate; but the article in the last Edinburgh has forced us to exert ourselves a little'. This is a case of special interest, since the two reviews[80] were of the same book: Blomfield's edition of Aeschylus's *Prometheus Vinctus*. Competition could hardly be harder-pressed than this. Blomfield and Copleston, as we have seen, were corresponding with one another (they were first in touch in January 1812), and to a degree were able to coordinate their reviewing, the former being in touch with policy in Edinburgh and the latter with *Quarterly Review* plans. Contrast the low-profile and chalcenteric Gaisford, who worked away in Oxford with very little knowledge of the politics of the reviews; as he himself acknowledged in February 1811, when he told Elmsley, 'I have no knowledge of the editor or contributors to the Edinburgh Review'. A letter of January 1815 confirms this impression of isolation: Gaisford wrote that 'I respect the Museum Criticum but have neither time nor inclination to contribute to it nor to any other work of that kind, except to point out some rare tract &c'. He added that Valpy had spoiled an article Gaisford sent him for the *Classical Journal* by printing it wrongly; as a result Gaisford had ceased corresponding with him.[81]

One way to assess the interaction of the two journals in the classical field is to look at the rate and nature of their production. Of the 452 articles published in the *Edinburgh* before the *Quarterly* first appeared, 16 were on classical subjects – about 3.5 per cent. During the period of Gifford's editorship of *Quarterly Review*, a further 613 articles appeared in the *Edinburgh Review*, of which 20 were classical; again, about 3.5 per cent. Compare this with the *Quarterly Review* figures: about 50 classical articles out of a total of 733 (14.5 per cent). As so often, however, overall figures offer only crude pictures of policy and preferences. A closer look at the *Edinburgh*'s record reveals that no classical reviews appeared between July 1813 and January 1820. It seems clear that, with the departure of Blomfield and Elmsley, Jeffrey abandoned the classical field altogether for more than 6 years. When he returned to it, he published on classics at a rate of about 5.5 per cent – hardly more than a third of the *Quarterly Review*'s percentage, but still a significant amount. Of *Edinburgh Review*'s first 16 classical articles, 6 were on Latin topics; of the 20 which Jeffrey brought out during Gifford's reign at the *Quarterly*, none. In the *Quarterly*, by contrast, of the two dozen or so reviews of editions and translations, 6 were on Latin topics. It could be argued that Jeffrey trimmed to sail parallel to Gifford's course: in other words, that he veered towards a preponderance of Greek topics to match the *Quarterly*'s tendency. But any such argument has to allow for the vagaries of the availability of books and of reviewers; the varying ability of the latter to submit reviews on time; and the kind of internal conflict, as between Murray and Gifford, which is evident in Gifford's letters. We can be more confident about the large-scale patterns, such as the disappearance of classical reviews from the *Edinburgh* between July 1813 and January 1820.

Most of the discussion so far has been concerned with the reviews of editions, especially those of Greek tragedians. The other classical reviews covered a wide range, but one area which deserves separate mention is the activity of British gentleman abroad, going on the Grand Tour, writing accounts of their travels and bringing back antiquities. Among those with connections to the *Quarterly* were the Cambridge-educated philhellenes William Haygarth, Thomas Smart Hughes and Robert Walpole. Haygarth[82] was a friend of Byron whose first visit to Athens led to his publishing a long poem on Greece.[83] His interest in the historiography of Greece and Rome was evidenced not only in a history of the Roman Empire (left unpublished at his death), but also in reviews of Mitford on Greece and Bankes on Rome.[84] Mitford's conservatism and distrust of democracy made him congenial to the *Quarterly* reviewers, but this did not stop Haygarth protesting at the unattractiveness of his prose style.[85] Thomas Hughes, similarly, went to Greece and published an account of his travels. Robert Walpole followed the same pattern, but also investigated the Herculaneum papyri, on which he published with Sir William Drummond.[86]

The best-known example of this kind of travel was the extensive tour carried out by the antiquary and mineralogist Edward Daniel Clarke of Jesus College, Cambridge (1769–1822), mentioned above. Much of continental Europe being inaccessible in wartime, he and his companions travelled north in 1799, via Sweden and Russia, to Constantinople, the Troad, and finally to mainland Greece, returning to England in 1802. Between them Clarke and his pupil John Cripps brought back more than 150 cases of antiquities. Clarke collected a thousand ancient coins, which were eventually sold to Richard Payne Knight; some valuable Greek manuscripts, which were bought by the Bodleian Library; and a vast statue weighing nearly two tons from Eleusis, which he (mistakenly) believed was of the goddess Ceres. The statue was badly eroded, and dismissed by some critics as being hardly worth preserving. Clarke's account of his travels was published in six large-format volumes between 1810 and 1823, and was very successful. The interest shown in his account is reflected in the *Quarterly Review* record: Volume 1 was reviewed in 1810, Volume 2 in 1813 and Volumes 3–4 in 1817.[87] The first two of these reviews followed hard on the heels of reviews in the *Edinburgh* of August 1810 and February 1813, and the first one was clearly designed to match the *Edinburgh* offering.[88]

If Clarke's 'Ceres' attracted derision in some quarters, the statuary brought back by Lord Elgin from the Parthenon (the 'Elgin marbles') provoked a controversy at the highest levels, as I mentioned earlier. A Select Committee of the House of Commons was appointed in 1816, recommended purchase, and the marbles were bought for the nation in the same year for the enormous sum of £35,000. Elgin's removal of them from Athens was itself controversial, but some claimed in addition that they were not distinguished works of art and so not worth acquiring.[89] Croker's review of the Select Committee report and other documents, published in May 1816, followed an *Edinburgh* review of the previous October by Jeffrey.[90] That, however, had as its subject the *Remains of John Tweddell*. The Elgin and Tweddell stories had by then become deeply entangled. Tweddell, a young, talented and politically radical fellow of Trinity College, Cambridge, had set out for Athens in 1796, made hundreds of drawings of antiquities, and died of a fever in 1799. Some of his drawings were destroyed in a fire, but others were entrusted to the care of Elgin, who appears not to have brought them back to Britain. Tweddell's brother and memorialist accused Elgin of shabby conduct, and the object of the two *Quarterly Review* articles on the topic[91] seems to have been to publicize Elgin's side of the case. The first article was largely by Blomfield, the second by Croker, but it is clear that Elgin was also invited to contribute, and that Blomfield and Croker were shown each other's texts at some point; a procedure at which the latter protested (*QR* Letter 170). One might think that Blomfield would take the side of the dead Tweddell, a fine classical scholar and fellow of his own college; but Tweddell's political radicalism would not have appealed to him. Yet Blomfield's hero Richard Porson had also been politically radical in the 1790s – and a drunk in the 1800s. In fact Tweddell had recanted his Jacobinism after the Terror, and Blomfield's discussion proceeds comfortably, his major criticism being directed at the over-enthusiastic annotation provided by Tweddell's brother.[92]

## Conclusion

In 1903, A. E. Housman declared that the great age of English scholarship which had been initiated by Bentley towards the end of the seventeenth century 'was ended by the successive strokes of doom which consigned Dobree and Elmsley to the grave and Blomfield to the bishopric of Chester'.[93] What Housman called 'scholarship' was the kind of scholarship that mattered to him: the study of the linguistic aspects of classical texts. As we have seen, this kind of scholarship was cultivated by the Porsonians, led by Monk and Blomfield, and it figures prominently in the classical articles in the *Quarterly*. The narrowing of interest promoted by Porson led to a split between this 'critical' or 'pure' scholarship and the study of ancient history and archaeology. These were cultivated by travellers like Clarke and Tweddell; they were also practised at Oxford, whose classical curriculum took on a broader form than that at Cambridge.[94] Peter Elmsley, fine textual scholar though he was, also had interests in these wider topics (and in a sense can be counted as a traveller, given his journeys to France, the Netherlands and Italy to inspect manuscripts). The history of the involvement of classicists in Gifford's *Quarterly Review* is in part that of the contrasting styles of the two universities: in Oxford, his own alma mater and the home of his advisor Edward Copleston, Gifford may have felt more comfortable; though as we have seen he was active in recruiting like-minded reviewers from Cambridge.

Another and sharper contrast of styles obtained between the two English universities and their five Scottish counterparts. North of the border, philosophy and political economy loomed large, while Greek was taught to mixed classes, some of whose members were complete beginners. This contrast needs to be remembered when evaluating the political and religious contrasts between the two reviews. In this essay I have hardly scratched the surface of what was clearly a complex history of interaction between the *Edinburgh Review* and *Quarterly Review*, one which involved both differences of belief and commercial rivalry. As far as classical reviewing was concerned, however, the overall pattern is clear. Gifford was concerned from the beginning to match and surpass the *Edinburgh* in his classical contributions, and this doubtless had something to do with the close links between the scholarship of Oxford and Cambridge and the conservative political-religious establishment. The attacks on Oxonian scholarship in 1809, just as he entered on his reign at *Quarterly Review*, will have spurred him on in this quest. He appears to have been successful for a considerable period, since as we have seen his rivals abandoned any attempt to compete in this sphere between 1813 and 1820.[95]

# 5 WALTER SCOTT AND THE *QUARTERLY REVIEW*

Sharon Ragaz

Walter Scott had a remarkable talent for immersing himself in any project that engaged his imagination and sense of purpose, even – or, perhaps, especially – when he was also heavily committed to a great many other tasks and projects. The period from 1808–10 was a busy and fertile one for Scott. He had behind him the phenomenally successful publication of *The Minstrelsy of the Scottish Border* (1802–3) and *The Lay of the Last Minstrel* (1805) but the rate of his output was only increasing. In addition to his usual legal employment, the works for which he was partly or solely responsible during these years included major editions (with biographies) of Jonathan Swift, John Dryden and Anna Seward, the *Edinburgh Annual Register* (first published in 1810 but underway from 1808), several miscellaneous verse collections, poetry (*Marmion* in 1808 and *The Lady of the Lake* in 1810) and fiction (the first attempt at *Waverley* and the completion of Joseph Strutt's *Queenhoo Hall*).[1] That these activities coincided with intensive and wide-ranging work on behalf of the fledgling *Quarterly Review* points to a very great degree of interest in and commitment to the new periodical and, although later Scott was to distance himself somewhat from the venture, his early involvement was crucial for its planning and success. It may be too much to claim that without Scott there would have been no *Quarterly*. It is certainly the case that his enthusiastic participation in the initial stages was highly significant for the management and content of the review, and may well have prevented the venture from stumbling at the outset. The story of his involvement is important in terms of Scott's own evolving career, literary and social connections, and interests during this period. But it is in respect of the history of the *Quarterly* that it is particularly telling, illuminating not only the initial planning but also the sensitivities, beliefs and fine distinctions of opinion amongst those who united for a shared cause and enterprise.

## Initial Stages and Planning

From the first it was John Murray who was intent on securing Scott's assistance for his project of establishing a periodical to rival the influential and very successful *Edinburgh Review*. Murray's determination to inaugurate a new periodical emerged from a complex of political and business motives and was shaped throughout by his aspirations as a young publisher, eager to make his name and establish profitable alliances. His initial courting of Scott was occasioned by an awareness of his Tory political affiliations and the recognition that Scott was well placed in the Edinburgh (and Scottish) literati to wield considerable influence among those whose support would be advantageous. Having Scott on board would strike a direct blow at the *Edinburgh* where he was known to be an occasional contributor and an acquaintance of the editor, Francis Jeffrey. Such involvement in the rival establishment and Scott's own predilections for keen observation and business management meant that he was thoroughly knowledgeable about the *Edinburgh*'s inner workings. According to John Gibson Lockhart, Scott's son-in-law and editor of the *Quarterly* from early 1826, by 1808 Murray had been watching Scott's affairs with interest for some time and was eager to further the relationship and the two men's common interests. He saw in the new venture an opportunity to enlist Scott not only for the periodical but also as an author for his publishing firm.[2] Murray had a quarter share in *Marmion* and had published *Queenhoo Hall*, and as a shrewd businessman was certainly aware of Scott's future earning potential and the financial and social benefits accruing from a close association with him.[3]

The relationship did not develop entirely as Murray envisaged – largely due to factors not under his control. Although Scott flirted with the idea of an alliance with Murray to publish his works, his enduring commitment was to the Edinburgh house of Archibald Constable, and to maintaining ties between that company and the printing firm of James Ballantyne where Scott was a secret partner. There were other factors too. Despite the *Quarterly*'s origin as an opponent to the *Edinburgh Review*, it eventually developed into an essentially London-based publication and Scott's allegiances remained securely in Scotland. And, although Scott was initially enthusiastic about the periodical and remained committed to its success, in the long term he never meant it to predominate over his many other interests. He also quickly became aware of some jostling for influence by other players in the *Quarterly* venture – most notably the editor, William Gifford – which occasionally expressed itself in attempts by Gifford to minimize control by Murray and Scott while still capitalizing on their expertise.

When Murray first broached the subject of a new periodical in autumn 1808, Scott was certainly ripe for considering the idea. This was so because a fortunate confluence of events predisposed him to join the venture.[4] It is impossible now to estimate the relative importance of any one of these. Taken together, though, they clearly influenced and nourished Scott's imaginative engagement with the new periodical, causing him to seize on it with his customary enthusiasm for any project that would expand the publishing, literary and reading cultures of the day. In no particular order, the following circumstances played a role in furthering Scott's interest.

Despite the success of *Marmion* when it was published early in the year, 1808 marked a low point in Scott's relationship with his Edinburgh publisher, Constable.[5] Although Scott blamed the temporary rupture on the uncivil behaviour of Constable's partner, Alexander Hunter, rather than on the publisher himself, the net effect was a prolonged cooling of their relations and a rivalry with several important consequences. In the first place, Scott endeavoured to set up John Ballantyne – James's younger brother – as a publisher who would issue his works and generally act for him in Constable's place. He knew that such a venture required a London associate and his preference was for one more prepared to take risks than Longman and Company – Constable's co-publishers – had shown themselves to be. Second, at about this time Scott and James Ballantyne were developing plans for an Edinburgh equivalent to the *Annual Register* – a scheme which, under the circumstances of Scott's break with Constable, gave additional satisfaction by successfully pre-empting the publisher's scheme for a similar venture. Third, Murray's plan for a new *Quarterly* periodical doubtless acquired piquancy from the fact of Constable being the publisher of the *Edinburgh Review*. That the *Edinburgh* had recently printed Francis Jeffrey's hostile review of *Marmion* does not seem to have contributed to Scott's dissatisfaction with Constable – who, in any event, would himself scarcely welcome the contraction in sales that might result from a negative review.[6]

In Scott's estimation of the *Edinburgh*, any minor private grievance that he felt about the periodical's response to his poem was overshadowed by a much more serious problem: its strongly expressed political stance on the war in Spain. Like many other readers, Scott found the *Edinburgh*'s October 1808 article on Don Pedro Cevallos particularly offensive, and as a direct consequence he withdrew as a subscriber and – a still more serious loss for the periodical – as a contributor.[7] At such a time of extreme anxiety over Napoleon and the condition of Spain, the radical views articulated in the Cevallos article were a red flag for Scott: they demonstrated that the Whig political bias of the *Edinburgh* had become intolerable and intensified his existing sense of the need for a corrective expressing a more patriotic view of events.[8] The desire to give voice to another perspective on Spain was certainly rooted in Scott's Tory politics, but these should not be narrowly understood. Although Scott firmly adhered to one viewpoint on the matter of Spain and Napoleon's aggression, he recognized that there would be other ways – however misguided – of seeing the matter. It was simply that he wanted the various positions to find expression in published form and thus be set side by side to lobby on equal terms for the hearts and minds of the reading public. Scott understood the expansion of this reading public to be limitless and he also believed in persuading by example and by moderate, reasonably expressed opinions that would persuade without being shrill or overstated.

Although the breaking point with the *Edinburgh* came over the Cevallos article, for Scott politics suffused daily life and, importantly, coloured his responses to literature. His interest in the new periodical was, therefore, also an interest in forging an alternative to the *Edinburgh*'s hitherto dominant voice of literary criticism, since that too reflected its political ideology. Scott dismissed as beneath notice the kind of reviews that regularly featured in other contemporary periodicals because they tended to be either 'puffery' – pieces placed by publishers to increase sales – or abusive; and, as he wrote to his friend George Ellis, the public was 'wearied with universal efforts at blackguard and indiscriminating satire'.[9] While he knew that the *Edinburgh* reviews were clearly of a consistently much higher calibre than others available at the time, he saw them as reprehensibly tinctured by Jeffrey's Whig politics. In contrast, he seems to have believed that reviews in the new periodical would counter those in the *Edinburgh* by appearing politically neutral: they would teach individuals 'to read and to judge' books by modelling a 'decent, lively, and reflecting criticism' – thinking that any criticism from the Tory side, when mildly and reasonably expressed, would seem both correct and non-partisan. Another important aspect of Scott's interest in the literature side of the new periodical was his conviction that developing critical modes of appreciation in readers would strongly stimulate the growth of an informed and discriminating national readership.

The final but not insignificant factor in Scott's enthusiasm for the new review was his ongoing concern to find publishing outlets for his friends and family. With regard to the *Quarterly*, this was certainly allied to his goal of attracting contributors whose Tory political affiliation could be counted on.[10] Beyond this was his habitual concern for those like his hapless brother Thomas, for whom Scott repeatedly attempted to find work to ease his penury, or the antiquary Charles Kirkpatrick Sharpe, who would benefit from regular employment and literary contacts. In this sense, the new review looked to Scott like a capacious vessel in which many could securely float.

Whatever role the various circumstances obtaining in autumn 1808 had in shaping Scott's mindset, they meant that he was receptive to the idea of a periodical, as Murray was gratified to find. For the initial approach, Murray astutely recognized that the most promising avenue was through James Ballantyne. Although the details of Scott's partnership with Ballantyne in his printing company were not publicly known, it was clear to observers that the two had close business ties and mutual interests. Murray was also anxious to propose a reprint series of novels to be edited by Scott, and so the three men – or four with the addition of John Ballantyne – had several excellent reasons for communicating with each other.[11] Believing that a personal discussion was preferable to negotiations by letter, Murray travelled to Scotland. In Edinburgh he met with Constable and James Ballantyne over dinner on 20 September. Murray walked back to his lodgings with Ballantyne and it was during the private interview afforded by this walk that Murray broached the idea of the review and met with a thoroughly responsive audience. Reporting on the meeting in a letter to his wife of 27 September, Murray described his immense satisfaction on finding that he and Ballantyne shared 'the same views respecting the connexion which we might form with each other' (*QR* Letter 2). During the encounter with Ballantyne, he also confirmed his suspicions of the breakdown in relations between Scott and Constable, which cleared the way for consideration of Murray's proposals and a potential new publishing alliance.

Murray had good reason to congratulate himself on his meeting with Ballantyne, through whom he had secured favourable and influential access to Scott. For his part, Ballantyne, with his privileged knowledge of the various circumstances shaping Scott's mindset, knew that the time was right for a proposal of just the kind Murray had in mind. With Ballantyne's urging, Scott invited Murray to his residence at Ashiestiel where Murray was able personally to advance his cause in exploratory discussions and planning sessions with the famous author.[12] This three-day meeting with Scott, Murray, Ballantyne and Richard Heber – Scott's and Canning's friend who happened then to be on a 'flying visit' – must be regarded as foundational for the *Quarterly* project. It represents the moment when hitherto inchoate ideas for the periodical coalesced to a point where they could be put into practice. It is highly significant that the initial discussions and planning meetings were held in Scotland and that Murray early on identified Scott as key to the success of the proposed venture. The sustained importance of Edinburgh as a centre not only for publishing but also for informed debate on literary, political and social issues – the *Edinburgh* had marked out the territory geographically as well as culturally – meant that strong Scottish support was a prerequisite at least in the short term if the new review were to succeed in challenging the dominance of its rival. Securing Scott meant advice and practical assistance from one of Britain's pre-eminent literary figures, who also happened to possess considerable business and legal acumen. A bonus was the prestige of having on-side a notable defector from the contributors' list to the *Edinburgh* – one bringing all the advantages of his insider knowledge of the workings and management of that periodical.

## Scott's Letter to William Gifford and his Visit to London

That Scott facilitated and presided over the inaugural meeting at Ashiestiel demonstrates the high level of his initial enthusiasm for the project, and his support remained unstinting in the early stages after the meeting of 2–5 October 1808.[13] Nevertheless, with an eye to his multiple other commitments, Scott was from the first clearly determined to set limits. Notably, he declined the post of editor that Murray appears to have asked him to take up and thereby paved the way for the appointment of William Gifford to the editorship. After the early October meeting, Scott confined his participation to four key areas: identifying the principal elements of the review's mission and its modus operandi; communicating these to the editor, William Gifford, and offering to serve in an ongoing capacity as his advisor; suggesting items for review and writing contributions; and attempting to secure other contributors in order to build up a stable from which Gifford could reliably draw.

The central statement of Scott's conception of the review is found in his letter of 25 October 1808 to Gifford (*QR* Letters 4, 4A).[14] Here, Scott laid out plans, including editorial guidance and business arrangements and established principles that were to define the review in its early stages and contribute to its enduring success and stability. Before discussing the contents of this pivotal letter it is worth briefly rehearsing the circumstances under which Gifford became editor, since these were to have a later impact on the relationship between him and Scott. Sensitivities emerged at this time that later may have been contributing factors in Scott's apparent decision further to limit his participation.

George Canning offered Gifford the position of editor in early October. He accepted on 12 October on the condition that he would not be required 'to take a leading part in the composition' because, as he stated, '[t]he business of revising, altering, occasionally adding, and finally carrying a work of this kind thro' the press will occupy fully as much time as I can ever promise myself' (*QR* Letter 3). However, the offer to Gifford was conditional on Scott's decision; it appears that when Murray left him at Ashiestiel Scott was still considering the option. It seems possible that there was some disagreement – stated or unstated – between the various interested parties about the merit of Scott becoming the editor. It must have been obvious to all concerned that the political interests of the new periodical required a London-based editor, and Scott's other avocations made it impossible that he would even consider relocating. Murray possibly introduced the suggestion that Scott become the editor in the belief that he would refuse, so as to clear the way for his extensive involvement and advice – as, in the event, proved the case. By 23 October Scott had declined to take up the position; a letter from William Erskine to the Lord Advocate, Archibald Campbell-Colquhoun, notes that the refusal was made 'very properly' as Scott was already so busy with other projects and because, for the review to be strongly countenanced and supported by the appropriate political forces, the editor must be resident in London.[15] Moreover, Erskine's letter registers his belief that Gifford 'is the person Canning has in his eye'. Canning chose Gifford, but both Murray and Scott were wary, anticipating future problems with this undeniably gifted but also habitually unreliable valetudinarian.

Read against this background, Scott's long letter to Gifford of 25 October must be regarded as a calculated intervention intended to establish terms for the new review before Gifford had any opportunity or time to act or, indeed, to think much about the requirements of his new position. Although it begins modestly by disclaiming any right to instruct Gifford in his new office and ends by describing the contents as miscellaneous observations, Scott's letter to Gifford is both prescriptive and programmatic. A determined attempt to set the rules of engagement, the letter is notable not least for its attempted soothing of Gifford. The apparently haphazard ordering of its various topics makes the letter resemble a collegial conversation rather than – as in reality it is – a blueprint for the review and a minutely detailed job description for the editor. In the opening, Scott justified his letter by calling on the joint authority of the Lord Advocate and Canning: the letter is written by order of 'our distinguished friends'. He also deployed flattery clearly intended to disarm Gifford and ensure compliance. That Gifford agreed to be editor 'goes no small way to insure success to the undertaking' and there is nothing that would 'not have readily occurred to a person of Mr. Gifford's literary experience and eminence'. Only after establishing the terms by which it is to be understood does the letter move on to substantive issues.

The fine detail in which a programme for the periodical is described shows Scott to have been an astute observer of the strengths and weaknesses of the *Edinburgh Review* and of contemporary periodical culture, which was dominated by self-interested booksellers. The letter attributes the 'extensive reputation and circulation' of the *Edinburgh* to two features unusual for the period that must be adopted wholesale by the new enterprise. First, it had remained independent at a time when review periodicals were notorious for being run by booksellers or publishers as vehicles for puffing their own publications and damning those of rivals.[16] Second, it treated all contributors equally with regard to remuneration and thus ensured timely receipt of well-considered articles from authors who were treated as professionals. By recommending adoption of this practice, Scott was insisting upon the primary importance of having a body of dedicated reviewers who received payment for their labours. The principle of fair payment for literary work was always an important one for Scott who, with regard to his own writing, never sought to represent himself other than as a man who worked for a living and certainly never shied with gentlemanly disdain from negotiating the highest possible price. His insistence that the new periodical adopt a policy on remuneration was part and parcel of a deeply held belief that a flourishing literary marketplace is dependent on adequate financial benefit to authors. In the specific context of the letter to Gifford, however, this arrangement is examined not from the authors' viewpoint, but from the editor's: the letter argues for the merits of a business-like arrangement endowing the editor with discretionary powers to accept, reject or revise contributions. Final responsibility for articles must belong to an editor who is not constrained to court gentlemen contributors whose willingness to offer services gratis would never compensate for their casual disregard of deadlines or for inferior submissions.

Turning to the all-important matter of the editor's duties, the letter spells these out in uncompromisingly legalistic terms. The editor must have 'unlimited power of controul for the purpose of selecting curtailing and correcting the contributions; and as the person immediately responsible to the Public and to the Bookseller that each Number shall be published in its due time it will be the Editors duty to consider and settle the articles of which ... it shall consist and to take early measures for procuring them from the persons best qualified to write upon the several subjects of criticism'. Given the subsequent history of repeated publishing delays under Gifford's management, it is entirely possible that Scott hoped to forestall any problems that might stem from Gifford's dilatory nature. His letter also argues for following Jeffrey's rule of reserving the right to rework and edit submissions so as to render 'palatable' those of 'stupefying mediocrity'. This practice is averred to have several benefits. It ensures not only that articles are pleasant to read but also that they conform to a consistent and identifiable style. And it facilitates publication by allowing articles to proceed into print without the loss of time entailed by returning them for emendation to the contributor – perhaps another guard against Gifford's anticipated unreliability.

Having established these general rules for managing the review, the letter addresses more fraught or potentially divisive issues of content and tone. Given that the as-yet unnamed review was proposed as a political counterweight to the Whiggish *Edinburgh*, it may seem surprising that Scott counselled against assuming too zealous a character at the outset. Probably, however, he was striking preventatively against Gifford starting off with so belligerent and uncompromising a tone that readers were alienated before the review had established both its credibility and its willingness to judge issues on merit rather than on a partisan basis. Scott insisted that the quality of the articles themselves must be the paramount consideration, although he agreed that, given the motives behind the enterprise and the doctrines it was formed to counter, 'it is essential to consider how opposite and sounder principles can be most advantageously brought forward'. Also, the review's political allies must promptly furnish information 'upon topics of national interest'. Being first to publish such items would confirm the review's legitimacy and close connection to the centres of power, and establish it as the primary organ for rapid and accurate dissemination of 'correct' political views. Nevertheless, it is also and unequivocally decreed that the review must maintain an independent identity and resist becoming a mere political tool:

> This is the most delicate and yet most essential part of our scheme. On the one hand it is certainly not to be understood that we are to be tied down to advocate upon all occasions and as a matter of course the cause of administration. Such indiscriminate support and dereliction of independence would prejudice both ourselves and our cause in the eye of the public. On the other hand the work will obtain a decided ascendance over all competition so soon as the public shall learn (not from any vaunt of the conductors but from their own observation) that upon political subjects the new critics are possessed of early and of accurate information.

The sensitive issue of political affiliation – or, rather, the subtlety with which that affiliation should be made known to the public – is at the heart of Scott's letter to Gifford. He returned to the topic towards the letter's close, after discussing practical matters such as the review's name, the frequency of publication and the date of first issue. In advocating stealth, Scott used a martial metaphor to underline his point: 'I am for gliding into a state of hostility without a formal declaration of war'. That the largest part of the letter is concerned with promoting moderation in managing the review's political character strongly indicates that Scott – and possibly also the men who had urged him to write to the new editor – saw in this the key to success and the issue for which guidelines and a consensus were essential.

The final words of the letter touch on another issue close to Scott's own heart and identify the territory in which he was to excel as a contributor over the coming years: the literary articles. In Scott's view, this area deserved to receive equal attention with other matter in the review's pages, and the letter states this to be an issue of good policy. Care taken in the literary aspect will accrue benefit by establishing and consolidating readers' conviction of the worth and good sense of the periodical generally. An appearance of being motivated exclusively by partisan politics would be obviated 'by labouring the literary articles with as much pains as the political and so giving to the review a decided character independant of the latter department'. More simply, it will also ensure that enjoyment and pleasure are to be derived from reading it.

Scott's 25 October letter to Gifford is evidence for the kind of behind-the-scenes negotiation between sets of individuals characterizing the review's early days. It also suggests reasons why difficulties could and did arise. Scott was in contact with the Lord Advocate, William Erskine, and George Ellis; Murray with Gifford and also with Scott and Ballantyne; Gifford with Canning and Ellis. The sets overlapped: Scott was of course also in touch with Gifford. But there were primary alliances and, even when adroitly handled, the circuitous manner in which communication occurred tended to exacerbate existing sensitivities. Gifford's temperament was not particularly amenable to intervention or advice and there is some evidence that the letter from Scott was interpreted as unnecessary meddling despite its attempts at soothing flattery. Just a week after writing the letter, Scott wrote to Murray to describe the contents – although he assumed, incorrectly, that Gifford would already have communicated them – and to reiterate his certainty of the periodical's success and his willingness to assist in any way deemed useful.[17] That on 2 November he wrote again and more urgently on the same subject indicates some anxiety on Scott's part over Gifford's continued delay in answering his letter. The second letter to Murray pointedly affirms that the Lord Advocate approved Scott's programme for the periodical, but also more doubtfully states, 'I suppose you will very soon hear from Mr. Gifford specifically on the subject' and stresses that something must be done to implement plans without further loss of time.[18] Gifford eventually wrote, but only on 9 November, by which time he may have been responding to requests from Murray himself (*QR* Letter 6). The delay in Gifford's replying might, of course, be of no significance and after all is not so very great – a matter of several weeks only. However, given Scott's two intervening letters to Murray, there is likely more to the matter. Certainly, with the personalities involved, it is far from improbable that Gifford was irked by the opening reference in the letter to others having urged Scott on his task of instruction and advice, or thought the letter belittled his considerable experience. Gifford was a proud man who, unlike Scott, did have expertise as editor of a periodical and would understandably bridle at any suggestion that he was ill-equipped for the position or – worse yet – a mere puppet-editor with Scott the invisible hand behind the enterprise.

The matter requires more disentangling. The letter of 12 October to Canning from Gifford indicates that by that date he had already been approached about the editorship. That is, he had been asked prior to Scott's declining the post, although he was made aware that Scott had first refusal. To Canning, Gifford wrote: 'when you hear more you will let me know', probably referring to Scott's pending decision. Soon after, so it appears, Scott refused the post but he nevertheless then wrote the letter to Gifford outlining plans and prescriptions for the project. When Gifford replied on 9 November, he acknowledged a delay in his response but claimed that it was occasioned by his discussing Scott's remarks with Canning (*QR* Letter 6). Now, since Gifford had already been in communication with Canning, and because Scott's letter states that he wrote at the behest of Canning who therefore could be expected to know something of the contents, the explanation seems at least somewhat tenuous. Moreover, although Gifford's reply begins by acknowledging Scott's 'most friendly letter', it does not directly address the letter until halfway through where the suggestions about content but, notably, not the advice about editorial tone are discussed. Gifford's letter certainly takes care to express modesty; does it also reflect apprehension about interference in a job that he, after all, had accepted where Scott had declined?

As events developed, reservations on this score were actually directed less at Scott himself than, through him, at Murray, whose own relationship with Gifford was far from straightforward. Murray was concerned about Gifford's ability to meet the practical requirements of his position and on several occasions – perhaps unwisely – he wrote to Scott on the matter, asking his advice and support.[19] For his part, Gifford regarded Murray as a mere publisher and tradesman, whose control over the editorial aspects of the venture should extend no further than warranted by his status. Although Scott was a primary force behind the initial organization of the review, his role during the early months was often that of middleman who had to absorb, deflect or soften many of the worries, irritations and vexations that inevitably developed between the other parties.

The complexities of the matter may perhaps be overstated – it is hard now to read between the lines of what are ostensibly perfectly proper and polite letters. But it is clear that the relationship between the various players in the new enterprise was not entirely what it seemed on the surface. There are evident fault lines that would deepen into cracks when worst fears proved accurate and difficulties emerged with Gifford's management, notably the recurrent delays in publication. What we see at the early stage is a mixed group of strongly egotistical individuals who, although sharing a sense of the high worth of their common project, were diverse in their motivations, backgrounds and personal goals. What is remarkable is that Scott, having declined the editorship and doubtless registering ongoing signs of Gifford's touchiness, remained fully committed and determined, in the short term, to throw his energies and resources behind the periodical.

Whatever tensions did exist at this stage, they found only oblique expression. Gifford's letter is far from hostile; indeed, it is at pains to praise Scott and expresses a strong wish that he, having declined the editorship, should adopt a 'viceregal' role over Gifford. By far the most salient fact is that, with this exchange of letters and confirmation of the roles to be taken by the various individuals, the great project was finally and unmistakably underway. The exchange marks the pivotal moment when debating the project gave way to planning the inaugural issue, eventually published in March 1809. Soon after its publication, Scott travelled to London and stayed there from April to June, during which time he met with a number of the principal players in the *Quarterly* – Murray, Gifford, Canning and John Wilson Croker.[20] The significance of the London visit for Scott's connection to the *Quarterly* is incalculable. Beforehand, he assured an anxious Murray who was worried about sales of the first number that he would hold a personal discussion with Gifford while in London.[21] But while Scott certainly did meet with Gifford, it is harder to say what discussions took place and what effect any intervention may have had. In the main, it seems that the importance of the visit was in Scott meeting the other players in the enterprise, and reaffirming his support and role as the Scottish connection. The meetings seem to have been affable and mutually congratulatory. The review had been launched and was well on its way. And, having pronounced in the letter to Gifford on the duties of the editor and the tone the periodical should take on political matters, and met his London-based collaborators, Scott subsequently confined himself to securing contributors, identifying items for review and writing articles himself.

## Subsequent Involvement: Recruitment and Contributions

As far as the question of recruiting contributors was concerned, Scott had in mind not only those whose allegiance would harmonize with the intended political slant of the periodical but also friends and relations he wanted to assist. Thus, for example, he solicited contributions from his friend the antiquary and artist Charles Kirkpatrick Sharpe, writing to him on 30 December 1808 and again on 13 January 1809 to urge the matter.[22] He pointed out that benefits would be both financial and personal: Sharpe would be well paid and made 'more intimately acquainted with a very pleasant literary coterie'. He argued for Sharpe's involvement in particular because the *Quarterly* was likely to be 'a very well managed business'. Sharpe was reluctant but did eventually contribute an article on Hector MacNeill's *Pastoral or Lyric Muse of Scotland*. However, his apprehension was borne out when the piece was rejected by Gifford – who first insisted it had been received too late for the inaugural number and subsequently laid it aside despite Scott's strong endorsement.[23] Gifford's behaviour in this instance may have been a warning sign of his touchiness and insistence on editorial prerogative with regard to Scott in particular. Gifford similarly rejected an article written by John Bacon Sawrey Morritt after Scott approached him as a contributor in mid-January 1809.[24] Ever alert for remunerative tasks to be taken up by his hapless brother, Thomas, Scott also recommended that he make a submission and offered to vet and revise any article he wrote; in this case the suggestion seems never to have been taken up. Recruitment of Robert Southey and William Erskine for the first number was more successful, with the former being responsible for 'Periodical Accounts Relative to the Baptist Missionary Society' and 'Vindication of the Hindoos', and the latter writing 'Speeches of the Right Honourable John Philpot Curran' with Scott's assistance.[25] Both men subsequently became major contributors to the periodical. In 1809 Scott put Murray in contact with the Reverend William Greenfield, whose conduct while he was professor of rhetoric at Edinburgh University had led to disgrace and exile from Scotland. In the event, Greenfield contributed just one article.[26] Aside from those reviewers directly recruited by Scott, throughout the inaugural period his name undoubtedly served as a drawing card for others and helped in this crucial time to establish the credibility of the enterprise as a joint Scottish-English venture.

Through his various activities directed at establishing the new periodical, Scott was certainly a significant factor in its success. But once the initial planning stage had passed, his most important role was in writing articles himself. While later he allowed himself to contribute to other periodicals from time to time, in the early years of the *Quarterly* he kept exclusively loyal to the institution he had helped to found. The scope of Scott's other commitments and activities during the infancy of the *Quarterly* make the degree of his involvement as reviewer impressive. The achievement is the more remarkable given the quality and range of the articles themselves. In all Scott contributed at least twenty-four articles to the *Quarterly* in the period of Gifford's tenure as editor, with the majority of these appearing during the early years. Although numerically he contributed fewer articles under John Gibson Lockhart's management, the density of his output for that time is greater, with at least eleven reviews appearing in the years from 1826 to Scott's death in 1832. However, the single year when Scott's presence is most notable is 1809, when he was responsible for nine articles. The only number of the first volume in which he does not feature is that for August. His articles especially sustain the first number, for which he wrote three of the total eighteen reviews in addition to helping William Erskine with a contribution and being principal author of one article, which was amended by Gifford. No other individual – including Gifford – contributed so extensively to the inaugural issue and this, in combination with the major role he had in the planning, established Scott as one of the most significant voices behind the periodical at this stage.

Scott's contributions under both Gifford and Lockhart fall under three broad headings. The majority are either items of Scottish interest – appropriately since Scott's involvement was sought in part as a Scottish ally – or belles-lettres, although the two categories naturally overlap. Scott's own interests and expertise are in clear evidence: the Scottish articles focus on law and history, while the belles-lettres address fiction and poetry. A third and much smaller group of articles is miscellaneous but also shows the author's interests, including as it does reviews of books on fly fishing, estates' management and military bridges. This last in particular is unexpectedly knowledgeable and minutely detailed.[27]

Read in the light of Scott's prescriptions for the new periodical, his contributions show how these might be put into practice. Throughout his life, Scott firmly adhered to a belief in the power of example and never confined himself merely to theorizing. In the present instance, he recognized that the most valuable means for him to ensure not only the present success of the review but also its power to endure in a highly competitive market was by writing articles that set a standard and showed the way. Doubtless he wanted his early contributions to pad out the first volumes while giving time to secure ongoing contributors to carry the project forward: there is no indication that Scott expected to continue as a major contributor. But he was also determined to leave his stamp on the new periodical with regard to the quality of the articles, and wanted to show what could be achieved through deployment of a rhetorically deft but almost conversational tone.

Implicit in Scott's early attempts to model an acceptable voice for the *Quarterly* is an awareness of the potential peril of adopting the more divisive or even vituperative tone for which Gifford was justly famous. In his letter of 18 November 1808 to George Ellis, Scott commented that Gifford required both a 'spur and a bridle', referring both to the new editor's habitual lethargy and satiric bent.[28] Many years later, on the occasion of Gifford's funeral in 1827, Scott was to note in his journal that, although Gifford was 'a man of rare attainments', he alienated readers by his critical severity: 'he flagellated with so little pity that people lost their sense for the criminal's guilt in dislike of the savage pleasure which the executioner seemed to take'.[29] The remark indicates that Scott did not object to justified criticism: it was a question of the degree of severity with which an author was treated, and of avoiding invective. Certainly he was conscious that in adopting a tone of high seriousness and sobriety, the *Quarterly* risked seeming sententious or, worse, merely dull. Scott's own articles often do take a strong line that reflects the reviewer's thorough engagement with his topic, especially with regard to literary matters and to a controversial author like Lord Byron who, despite his great popularity, divided the reading public on moral grounds. But while the reviews can be razor-sharp and lively, they avoid descending into rancour. In a letter of 21 January 1810 to Lady Abercorn, who had queried his authorship of a particularly trenchant review of Sydney Owenson's *Ida of Athens*, Scott admitted to having twice deviated from his policy of reviewing only where he had something positive or serious to convey:

> The few essays I have made in the craft of reviewing are either of a grave cast or refer to books which I could conscientiously praise. There are I think in the *Quarterly Review* only two exceptions. In the one case I was provoked by the insufferable petulance of the author and in the other by the extreme want of candour of a certain author who, having loaded me in private with undesired and undesirable flattery chose to abuse me without temptation or provocation in his next book ...[30]

The petulant author is Richard Cumberland whose *John de Lancaster* Scott reviewed in the second number, singling out for criticism the author's 'assumed contempt of public applause'.[31] In fact the review is fairly mild given the harsh criticism Scott meted out to Cumberland in private correspondence.[32] The author wanting candour is probably Robert Hartley Cromek; Scott's review of his Burns edition is described in more detail below.[33] Despite his assurance to Lady Abercorn, for the first numbers Scott was willing to write whatever was required 'to stop up gaps' because of the dearth of other contributors. As a result, the proportion of his negative reviews is higher in the first numbers; nevertheless, even where they are most critical, Scott's articles resist the kind of remorseless satire or pillorying that occasionally characterizes those by Gifford or John Wilson Croker, among others.

That said, Scott's first published article in the *Quarterly*, the review of Cromek's *Reliques of Robert Burns*, certainly makes known his distaste for what Scott viewed as an editor's parasitism in relation both to the author he edited and to previous scholarship.[34] It is strongly informed throughout by scepticism about Cromek's motives and editorial principles.[35] Scott's reviews typically survey both the work at hand and the wider issues at stake. In the case of the Cromek article the larger issue is the merit of publishing an author's trivia; the review debates whether the volume enhances existing knowledge of Burns and if the new poems included deserve separate issue in this form. Scott's own view is unequivocal: the contents are merely 'gleanings ... the refuse and sweepings of the shop' and so properly not 'reliques' at all. He also points out that of the very few original poems included, one had already been published in James Currie's edition (a work to which Scott implied that Cromek had a largely unacknowledged debt) but was then found not to be by Burns at all. The review simply states these facts and lets the reader draw the necessary inference about Cromek's qualification for the task he has undertaken. That is, although the review is pointed, it exemplifies Scott's preferred method of letting the facts – as he drew them out – be eloquent for his opinion. However, one is aware throughout that it is only by considerable effort that Scott resisted bluntly expressing his opprobrium. The article's tonal register of restrained distaste combines with the evidence of close familiarity with the state of Burns scholarship to make it all the more damning. The conclusion declares the only possible justification for Cromek's publication to be the enrichment of Burns's impoverished family.[36] The final, well-chosen quotation from Chaucer's 'Pardoner's Tale' leaves no doubt as to Scott's conviction that charity was not one of the editor's motives.

If Scott's contributions for the first numbers were shaped by an urgent need to fill space, later ones, written when he could be discerning in the topics he took up, tend to be more reflective. Of these several are especially notable both in their content and for shaping contemporary and later opinion about the works under review. The strongly appreciative and sharply perceptive review of Jane Austen's *Emma* in 1815 is a much-quoted early assessment of Austen's powers and the particular virtues of her fiction.[37] It surveys not only the work at hand but also Austen's earlier works (with the exception of *Mansfield Park*) and it therefore alerts readers to other books by an author whom Scott is clearly eager

to promote. Its interest lies both in what it says about Austen and in being written by Scott at a time when he was in the beginning stages of his own long career
as a novelist. The reviews of Lord Byron's *Childe Harold's Pilgrimage* Cantos
III and IV have importance for their commentary on the genius of the poem
and its author, and – as Byron gratefully acknowledged – for publicly expressing
sympathy at a time when the campaign of rumour and moral indignation against
Lord Byron was at its height.[38] The review of Canto IV in particular shows Scott
the critic at his best. It uses the publication of *Childe Harold's* conclusion as
an opportunity to range widely over the entire poem, and to issue a farewell
to the serially-issued poem that is prophetic of its future critical status: it will
'claim its proper place amid the poetical galaxy'. That Scott intended his reviews
to have practical consequences not only in shaping public opinion but also in
helping out an author's career is shown by the 1810 review of Charles Robert
Maturin's *Fatal Revenge*.[39] His article begins humorously by announcing itself to
be an attempt at introducing the kind of 'light and airy articles which a young
lady might read while her hair was papering'. But there is a serious motive at
work: Scott surveys the contemporary fiction scene, lights on Maturin's novel
and, after dispensing some strongly-worded advice to the author, urges him to
seek a mentor. On learning that Scott had written the review, Maturin followed
up on the suggestion by contacting Scott – a fact that materially benefited his
subsequent literary career.

No assessment of Scott's role as contributor to the *Quarterly* could be complete without mention of his January 1817 self-review of the anonymous *Tales
of My Landlord*.[40] Although Scott had originally intended *Tales of My Landlord*
to seem as if it was by a different author from the one who had penned *Waverley*,
*Guy Mannering* and *The Antiquary*, speculation on the question of the author's
identity had been widespread, with many reviews and readers inferring that the
same man had written the novels. Directly responding to such rumours, the
review begins by unequivocally pronouncing the works to be all by the same
author. In fact Scott's review itself was yet another ploy in the ongoing game of
maintaining his anonymity as 'the Author of Waverley': rumours of his authorship of the review would, it was hoped, trump rumours of Scott's authorship
of the novels themselves. The review also pre-empts criticism by immediately
registering flaws such as the novels' slovenly approach to structure and plotting
and the insipidity of the heroes: '[i]n addition to the loose and incoherent style
of the narration, another leading fault in these novels is the total want of interest
which the reader attaches to the character of the hero'. The review also distrib-
utes praise, however, and singles out 'Old Mortality' for special attention. In so
doing, it takes up an issue close to Scott's heart by attempting to address the concerns of those Scottish readers who had been offended by the novel's portrayal of
the Covenanters. Scott's motives for writing the review were therefore twofold:

he hoped to scotch rumours of his authorship of the novels, and the article was a platform for responding to published criticisms of the book on grounds of historical inaccuracy.

## Later Stages and Conclusion

Scott was proud of his connection with the *Quarterly* and retained respect for it as an institution throughout his life. However, during the early period of his association, his concerns about Gifford's editorship did not abate and he continued to find himself in an intermediary position between editor and publisher. If worries about the frequent delays in publishing the review under Gifford's management were paramount, Scott had also undoubtedly been irked by the slight regard accorded some of those he had sought as contributors. Another problem directly affecting Scott's own early articles was the rush with which articles were often pushed through the press.[41] Looking over proofs for the first number, he described them as 'horribly incorrect'. He asked Murray in a letter of 28 January 1809 to ensure that Gifford 'look over the sheet very carefully as it will require accurate revising the corrections being so numerous' – a further instance of circuitous communications that doubtless did nothing to soothe Gifford.[42] In another letter to Murray, of 25 February, Scott says, 'I hope our hurry will not be such another time as to deprive me of the chance of doing the best I can which depends greatly on my seeing the proofs. Pray have the goodness to attend to this.'[43] Scott's anxiety about such matters was understandable and stemmed in part from a feeling of being at a distance from the centre of operations and unable to maintain a close watch over the progress of his writing into print – something that he was always able to do in Edinburgh because of his connection to James Ballantyne. But his manner of urging Murray to the position of intermediary seems unlikely to have helped matters particularly since Gifford already felt that both Scott and Murray had an unacceptable propensity to interfere with his authority. After the first number appeared in March 1809, Murray wrote to complain about Gifford's management and asked Scott for help in dealing with the problem. In his reply, dated 19 March, Scott states, 'I have written a long & most pressing letter to Mr Gifford which I hope may have some effect'.[44] It was as a consequence of perceived problems with Gifford's management that Murray was eager to have Scott visit London in the spring of 1809; once again, though, it is not difficult to imagine Gifford's resentment at being taken to task by Scott – particularly if he knew that it was at Murray's request.

Throughout the early years of the *Quarterly*, Scott evidently did feel able to maintain a more open relationship with Murray than he enjoyed with Gifford, and it is true that his character likely had more in common with the publisher than with the editor. But, although there was never an explicit rupture, even this relationship cooled rather markedly after the mixed experience of Murray publishing *Tales of My Landlord* in 1816. Scott felt that the publication had not been well handled, and problems arose with later editions of what proved to be a phenomenally popular work. These problems led to a vituperative correspondence between Murray and William Blackwood on one side and Constable and James Ballantyne on the other. Although Scott remained in the background and Murray and Blackwood were never conclusively let in on the secret of his authorship of *Tales*, he was not well-pleased with what he saw as Murray's and Blackwood's attempt to wrest publishing control from him. After concerns on this score came to a head in 1819, the frequency of Scott's correspondence with Murray decreased, although the number of his contributions to the *Quarterly* had declined earlier, with the publication of Number 9, in April 1811, and picked up again only for a brief period in 1816 to 1818 and when Lockhart became editor.[45] Scott also began contributing to other periodicals (including the *Edinburgh Review*) and on at least one occasion – with Mary Shelley's *Frankenstein*, which was harshly reviewed in the *Quarterly* by John Wilson Croker – used the opportunity to write critical responses where he put forward a strongly opposing view.[46]

Dwelling on the negative side of Scott's relationship with William Gifford, on the rupture with Murray or on Scott's evident decision to spread his favours among other periodicals after the years of loyalty to the *Quarterly* may give the impression that in the end his connection with the periodical turned sour. This would be a mistake: there is no evidence that Scott felt unkindly towards the periodical he had helped to found, and a strong sign of his positive view is his recommendation of Lockhart to the post of editor. Indeed, it must have been an object of considerable pride to Scott that the institution he was instrumental in founding had not only survived but prospered and certainly had well succeeded in its aim of establishing a credible voice to oppose the *Edinburgh*. And there is no doubt that Scott's experience, advice and prodigious efforts in the matter of contributions had been crucial: they had helped to ensure good management, wise editorial policy and a high standard for the articles. Scott seems never to have intended a prolonged intensive commitment to the *Quarterly*, and he did not retreat until he was certain that the periodical was securely afloat. The story of his involvement brings one particular aspect into telling focus: the periodical founded to oppose the *Edinburgh* and therefore conscious of its need to establish a secure Scottish base eventually outgrew its origins and succeeded as a London-based publication. If Scott moved away from the *Quarterly* and on to other projects, it is also true that the *Quarterly* gradually came to have need of him only as an occasional contributor. And that events transpired in this way was in fact a tribute to the periodical's great success – one in which Scott played no small role.

# Notes on Scott's Contribution to the *Quarterly Review* under Gifford

## *'Reliques of Robert Burns', 1:1 (1 March 1809)*[47]

The review is a fine example of Scott's ability to be critically scathing while retaining a measured tone, and his distrust of Cromek's motives and scholarship is clearly evident. Although some items of interest are found in the volume under review, in general the contents are properly to be regarded as mere 'gleanings ... the refuse and sweepings of the shop'. The volume includes letters, memoranda, and a very few original poems – one of which the review notes as previously published in Dr Currie's edition of Burns and long discounted as a Burns original. The review ends acidly by stating that the only possible justification for publication would be the enrichment of the poet's family and quoting from Chaucer's 'Pardoner's Tale' to indicate the unlikelihood of this being the present case.

## *'Chronicles of the Cid', 1:1 (1 March 1809)*[48]

Scott elegantly summarizes the narrative in some detail, assuming that his readers will be unfamiliar with it. He notes in conclusion that, while the contents are surely partly fictitious, the chronicles remain 'exceedingly valuable as a singular picture of manners of which we know little or nothing'. Style and the length of the work are occasionally criticized on the basis that although Southey was not engaged in a task of translation he did not take advantage of his license to amend or compress passages. With that minor caveat, Southey is thanked for 'a most entertaining volume, edited with a degree of taste and learning, which few men in England could have displayed'.

## *'Barrett's Swift', 1:1 (1 March 1809)*[49]

At the time of writing the article, Scott was at work on his own edition and biography of Swift. Accordingly, the review reflects a close familiarity with the subject, and begins by taking issue with Barrett's title since the book is almost exclusively concerned only with a single episode of Swift's early life: his expulsion from Trinity College, Dublin, for misconduct. The *Essay* is an investigation into the truth of various allegations about the episode and the confusing circumstances surrounding it. Scott's legal mind is at play here in weighing the evidence. The review also comments on poetical pieces, taken from a manuscript in the Trinity library, which are first printed in the book; Scott judiciously considers the likelihood of Swift being their author. He praises the inclusion of two new Swift letters, which he finds to be 'highly valuable and characteristic'. The article concludes on a sarcastic note by suggesting that Barrett's leisure in his academic position has granted him time to fashion too ingenious an argument.

*'Caledonian Sketches', 1:1 (1 March 1809)*[50]

This is Scott's 'whisky-frisky article on Sir John', as described to John Murray in a letter of 28 January 1809.[51] The entire article is written with the tongue firmly in cheek – including in the mention of the *Edinburgh*'s response: 'we, novices in criticism, are taught compassion by our elder brethren of Edinburgh'. Scott does find occasion to praise the work for its sketches of the Highlands and discussion of the problems of emigration, but he is strongly critical of much imprecision in the style. The review, although good-natured, is in the 'whipping' mode (hence the ironic reference to the *Edinburgh* brethren). Scott's mention of it as a 'flagellation' in a 30 January letter to Murray[52] is echoed in the article itself which ends by advising Sir John to take his travels more distantly in the future and making comparison with a top that becomes stationary when it narrows its gyrations: 'the remedy to restore its activity, and enlarge its circuit, is a tight flagellation'.

*'Gertrude of Wyoming', 1:2 (30 May 1809)*[53]

This is Scott's first contribution on a work that is wholly literary – and one that shows him commenting on a publication by a poet, Thomas Campbell, whose popularity rivalled his own. In this context, there are two particularly interesting features: the opening, which discusses the critical standards necessarily employed in assessing a new work by an already established and highly-regarded writer, and the opinion expressed about the danger that an author's too extensive rewriting of his poem will deaden rather than improve the work. Mention of the popular poet who throws his effusions before the public with the attitude of an ostrich is surely self-referential. Scott is critical of advance publicity for *Gertrude*, which not only announced the subject but also proclaimed the work Campbell's masterpiece. While the interest of the Wyoming massacre as a theme is acknowledged, Scott's patriotism shows in the expression of hope that in the future Campbell will choose an episode 'more honourable to our national character'. The organization of the narrative is faulted for paying too little attention to readerly expectations. The shorter pieces included in the volume are received more favourably than the title poem.

*'John de Lancaster', 1:2 (30 May 1809)*[54]

The review is valuable for showing Scott's reflections on novels and novel-writing at just the time when (as is now conjectured) he was making a first attempt at *Waverley*. It begins by discussing Cumberland's literary career, finding his main claims to fame in his periodical writing and his translations from ancient Greek. His novels, however, are described as being merely above the usual stock of a circulating library. The criticisms in the review's conclusion are justified by reference to Cumberland's own bitter reflections on the contrast between the excessive financial rewards earned by adherents of the Gothic fashion in novels and the more paltry sums offered to writers who adhere to nature. Scott finds characterization in Cumberland's novel to be just as incredible as anything in Gothic writing, and states that his 'assumed contempt of public applause we cannot but consider as an unworthy affectation' since 'few men have shewn more eagerness to engross the public favour'. However, Cumberland is also saluted for continuing to amuse readers at his advanced age.

### 'The Battles of Talavera', 2:4 (23 December 1809)[55]

The review begins by lamenting the indifference of contemporary poets to current events. The work under review is an exception, and the poet is praised for his choice and in particular for making occasion to praise and celebrate Lord Wellington. The execution is also praised and, although it is pointed out that his use of irregular Pindaric measure derives from Scott's *Marmion*, its use in this case is entirely appropriate and just. The review summarizes the contents of the poem but declines to point out all the flat rhymes because of the poet's admirable choice of topic.

### 'Wallace', 3:5 (31 March 1810)[56]

The case for considering the work an imitation is debated at the outset, with these observations deriving from the poem's notable similarity to *Marmion*. However, the work is far inferior, showing no signs of the 'romantic lore' or 'strong powers of conception and description' animating Scott's poem. Although Scott was hostile to attempts to capitalize on his fame, the high praise accorded to him here may indicate that this review is not in fact by him (or, not solely at any rate). There is a summary of the poem's contents with criticisms especially of its diction and the probability of some of the incidents. The poet (male authorship is assumed) is not without ability but has not taken the care and labour to acquire the appropriate skills.

### 'Fatal Revenge, 3:6 (21 July 1810)[57]

The article is significant for having prompted Charles Robert Maturin to write to Scott soliciting his advice (the review suggests that he seek a mentor); Scott's subsequent intercessions on Maturin's behalf were crucial in furthering his literary career. If *Fatal Revenge* seems an unlikely subject for the *Quarterly* to review, it is chosen because of criticisms of dullness which led to a resolution to review 'not only the grave and weighty, but the flitting and evanescent productions of the times'. A history of the novel as a genre is given, where it is claimed that the reviewer accidentally came across Maturin's book in the course of his researches into the novel. A summary of the narrative is followed by criticism of the use of the supernatural in winding up the story. Overall, the abilities of the author are found to be impressive although his taste is 'inferior to his powers of imagination and expression'.

### 'Pursuits of Agriculture', 3:621 (July 1810)[58]

The review begins by humorously commenting on the spirit of improvement common to the age. The poem under review is a satire on 'improvers', although the poet is also eager not to be seen as unfriendly to rational attempts to improve husbandry. The author is pronounced 'no unsuccessful pupil of the Hudibrastic school'.

### 'Old Ballads', 3:6 (21 July 1810)[59]

The review groups several similar works together and compares them; it also gives a history of minstrel verse in Scotland and of contemporary imitations. It is noted that R. H. Evans, in revising his father's original publication, judiciously omitted some and so opened room for the inclusion of some genuine ancient ballads – which, however, are not very worthy specimens. Dr Aiken's work is also a republication, and Scott owns the originals of the works under review and the new editions so he has a basis for comparison. In particular he compares Aiken's earlier reflections on song-writing with his later ones. Scott comments in passing on degeneracy in most modern songs and finds Aiken's collection a refreshing escape from this.

### 'The Curse of Kehama', 5:9 (10 April 1811)[60]

A summary of the debate between critics and poets through the ages concludes by suggesting that critics have often mistaken merely accidental matters such as subject, incident or the conduct of the story for those aspects essential to poetry. Southey's poem is described as interesting in its nature and subject but also 'wild and uncommon' as a story, the telling of which requires a measure new to narrative verse. The narrative based on Hindu mythology is summarized and found powerfully interesting, but 'it is difficult to adopt any certain rule of criticism with respect to a production so anomalous'. The review is at once a meditation on what it means to criticize poetry and a review of Southey's poem. Scott can make no guess as to the likely popularity of a work so unusual whose faults are evident but whose 'beauties are infinite'. He ends with a note of approval about the method of printing whereby each line is set on the page so that the margins remain equal; this is found to be pleasing to the eye and should establish a precedent for future publications.

### 'Latin Verse', 8:16 (5 March 1813)[61]

The subject is a collection by James Pillans of the Edinburgh High School of schoolboy Latin verse. Allegedly, the boys' tutors corrected the verses, but the reviewer finds this implausible given the abundance of errors. The review in general is heavily critical of the entire enterprise. That the reviewer himself shows an extensive and intensive knowledge of the language and prosody might cast doubt on Scott's authorship of this review: his knowledge of Latin was serviceable at best.

### 'Letters of Mrs Elizabeth Montagu', 10:19 (18 December 1813)[62]

Scott's support of women writers and his talent for friendship with them shine through in this review, which is the occasion for praising the advance of female literacy and the resultant high achievements of women authors. The betterment of women's situation is found to be a social good, and in particular it is noted that women's general improvement in education means that the stereotype of the woman pedant has lost currency. The review argues too that better education for women must stimulate improvements in learning for men who formerly, no matter how ignorant, could always claim superiority in knowledge over women.

### 'Emma', 14:27 (12 March 1816)[63]

Likely the most often reprinted of Scott's articles, this highly favourable and sensitive review was influential in establishing Austen's reputation. The opening history of novel-writing and reading has special interest since by 1815 Scott had written two novels of his own. The history concludes by welcoming recent development in naturalistic fiction that focuses on real, daily life. The result of these developments, however, is that every reader feels free to be a critic. Moreover, if the morals, events and scenes are ordinary, what must be remarkable is the telling of the story, and in this Austen excels. The review accounts for *Sense and Sensibility* and *Pride and Prejudice* in addition to *Emma*, but does not mention *Mansfield Park*. Although the novels are highly praised, a plea is entered at the end for the role of romance in the moral and emotional development of youth.

### 'The Culloden Papers', 14:28 (18 May 1816)[64]

The book under review is the occasion for an excursive but concise history of the Jacobite rebellion and the system of clanship in the highlands, which demonstrates the level of knowledge informing Scott's own Scottish novels. The review ends by arguing against the highland clearances, pointing out that while some highland proprietors have attempted to introduce new modes of cultivation and provide employment for families, in other cases 'the glens of the highlands have been drained ... of the whole mass of the inhabitants, dispossessed by an unrelenting avarice'. The review thus effectively refutes claims that Scott supported the clearances.

### 'Fair Isabel', 14:28 (18 May 1816)[65]

Polwhele was a tiresomely frequent correspondent of Scott's, and sought his intercession with the publication of several of his works. The manuscript of *Fair Isabel* was first sent to Scott and was for a time accidentally locked up in his bureau, and Polwhele records this event at the poem's outset. Scott, as reviewer, attributes to this accident the similarities with *The Lady of the Lake* in such matters as stanzaic introductions; he also comments on Polwhele's 'wonderful improvement' in having his characters frequently sing to each other. He wonders if the poem was for a time closeted with some work by Byron since there are similarities there too – but again Polwhele is said to have improved on the original since he cannot be accused of hurrying his readers on with the interest of the narrative. The review ends with the recommendation that the author stick to antiquarian research and leave off writing verse.

### 'Childe Harold', 16:31 (11 February 1817)[66]

Scott's favourable review at a time when Byron was being depicted as a monster of depravity was a remarkable intervention and justly earned Byron's lifelong gratitude. It begins with an eloquent description of Byron's character, terming him 'afflicted' with sufferings that must be linked to his possession of the poetic temperament – a 'dangerous gift'. A history of Byron as poet and *Childe Harold* and its reception follows. As in Scott's earlier review of Campbell's *Gertrude of Wyoming*, not revising so extensively as to efface powerful originality is recommended. The review includes an important discussion of similarities among all Byron's heroes, and the tendency of the public to read them as figures for the poet. Scott notes his strong disagreement with Byron on the subject of Waterloo, but does not dwell on the subject. He also praises the shorter pieces – notably 'The Prisoner of Chillon' and 'The Dream' – that are included in the volume, although the subject of the first is found too despairing for poetry and the latter is seen to invite too ready application to the poet himself. The review ends with some advice to Byron, urging him to look on the world not as an enemy but as 'a doubtful and capricious friend' and to remember that his well-wishers are legion.

### 'Tales of my Landlord', 16:32 (17 May 1817)[67]

Scott is anonymously reviewing himself as the author of the anonymous *Tales* – and being in no small measure critical. William Blackwood, who co-published the novel with Murray, had sought a review from Henry Mackenzie that was laid aside in favour of this by Scott and Erskine (the extent of Erskine's involvement is not known but seems to have been minimal). The problem of the insipidity of the Scott heroes is first identified here. The review is fleshed out with reference to various historical authorities. After a summary of the novels, their popularity as historical fiction is discussed. There is an attempt to defuse the strong contemporary criticism of Scott's portrayals of the Cameronians in *Old Mortality* by pointing out that this ultra-radical sect had long since ceased to exist in a tolerant age, and no criticisms of moderate Presbyterianism are to be understood by the portrayal of historical events in the novel. Authorship of the review was much-debated along with the authorship of the *Tales*, as Scott intended.

### 'Essay on Military Bridges', 18:36 (9 June 1818)[68]

The article begins by urging the patriotic duty of all those who have knowledge of such matters as the book under review to place their expertise at the service of the country to further national security. The expert discussion of hydraulics indicates that Scott did not write this unaided, although his presence is evident in the more narrative portions. The six sections of the book describe various types of military bridges, and a conclusion identifies the implements that may be used to construct these under circumstances of battle. The writing style of the book is described as 'plain and manly, as it should be'.

### 'Secret and True History of the Church of Scotland', 18:36 (9 June 1818)[69]

Scott was a good friend of the editor, Charles Kirkpatrick Sharpe. The review acquits Sharpe of having any motives other than those suggested by an inquiring mind into his task of editing a work previously available only in manuscript but nevertheless mined extensively for quotation by partisan historians. Apparently the notes in Sharpe's edition are most diverting where the material itself is most dull. Included in the volume are biographical details about Kirkton himself and an account of the murder of Archbishop Sharpe, which do not appear in the original manuscript. The history informs both Scott's *Old Mortality* and his *Heart of Midlothian* which he was writing concurrently with the review. His comment on men who still 'cannot divide their just attachment to the Kirk of Scotland from a doting and depraved admiration of men who, far from having put on religion, seem, from their own narrative, to have stripped themselves of every ordinary feeling of humanity' may reflect his view of the vitriolic reaction in some quarters to his depiction of the Covenanters in *Old Mortality*.

### 'Letters from the Hon. Horace Walpole', 19:37 (26 September 1818)[70]

The review begins with a commentary on Walpole's 'extraordinary and strangely blended character' which mixes affectation, inconsistency and theatricality. However, he is acknowledged to be unrivalled in his memoirs and correspondence, especially for his descriptions of passing scenes. A letter describing the funeral of George II is quoted in illustration of Walpole's talent for creating a sense of immediacy and particularity. It is noted in particular how the characters from high society become lastingly memorable through his accounts of them.

### 'Childe Harold IV', 19:37 (26 September 1818)[71]

Scott uses the publication of the final canto of *Childe Harold* as an occasion for expressing melancholy regret that such an impressive literary event, which had enraptured the nation, was now concluded. He looks back over the poem in its entirety and considers the circumstances that made it so popular. Byron is the first poet since Cowper who appeared directly before the public in his works and, although Byron himself always insisted on a distinction between poet and protagonist, his power over his audience partly derived from an identification of the two. Public feeling is aroused by a sense of 'familiarity with a mind so powerful'. The power and genius of the poet are commented on, and *Childe Harold* is described as hovering between a philosophical and a descriptive poem. Quotations are chosen to illustrate how the fourth part sustains the reputation of the whole, but a difference is detected in that the conclusion reflects less passion and more deep thought, and a greater sublimity. The review concludes with strongly-voiced criticism of the republican political slant of John Cam Hobhouse's notes, which Scott chooses to consider as independent from the poem and not, therefore, as specifically approved by Byron.

*'Letters to and from Henrietta, Countess of Suffolk',* 30:60 (28 August 1824)[72]

The review is strongly appreciative of the editor's judicious handling of the material, and is as much a commentary on that as on the contents of the letters themselves. It begins with an interesting reflection on public interest in collections of letters through which the writers seem again to live and breathe; it is also noted that the publication of actual documents from the time serves in this case effectively to refute scandal or establish a more accurate portrayal of the facts. The correspondents of the Countess included a number of literary men (Gay, Pope, Swift and Arbuthnot) who sought access to royal patronage through her; the edition does great service in publishing their letters. A number of letters are quoted here in part or in their entirety to show the range included in the edition. The review concludes with thanks to the editor for what is described as an exemplary work.

# JOHN BARROW, THE *QUARTERLY'S* IMPERIAL REVIEWER

## J. M. R. Cameron

John Barrow (1764–1848), traveller, author, colonial administrator, influential member of the Royal Society, co-founder of the Royal Geographical Society and Second Secretary to the Admiralty for forty years, was a major contributor to the *Quarterly Review*, writing more than two hundred articles between 1809 and 1841, three quarters of them while Gifford and Coleridge were editors. In a widely repeated anecdote written one year before his death, Barrow attributed his involvement to an invitation from George Canning, then Foreign Secretary, and his subsequent discussion with Gifford. When Barrow offered to review Louis-Chrétien de Guignes's recently published account of his experiences in east Asia while he was the French representative in Canton (1784–1800),[1] Gifford agreed readily as 'it is one at your fingers ends, and one that few know anything about ... and I am gasping for something new'.[2]

Barrow's remembrance is undoubtedly correct as far as it goes, but, like so many of his reminiscences, it holds back more than it reveals. As Canning knew but Gifford probably did not, Barrow and his protégé George Thomas Staunton, then on leave from his post with the British East India Company at Macao and Canton (Guangzhou), were actively negotiating a second British embassy to the Chinese imperial court.[3] Canning may have suggested that the *Quarterly* provided an excellent forum for generating popular support. In any event, Barrow focused his review[4] on de Guignes's report of the Dutch embassy to Peking (Beijing) in 1794–5, for which he had been interpreter – and which followed the first British embassy (1792–4) led by Lord Macartney – to highlight his conviction that the British, unlike the Dutch, had not failed in their objectives. In his view, the favourable treatment of Macartney's entourage, in such contrast to the denigration and humiliation heaped upon the Dutch, was clear evidence of the high regard and respect the Chinese held for the British. More importantly, the embassy had contributed significantly to increased knowledge of China. It was, therefore, most unfortunate that this had not been built upon by the East

India Company, whose exclusive preserve China was, but that could be expected because of the Company's narrow interest in commercial and personal advantage for a select few. Of all of its servants, only Staunton had acquired knowledge of Chinese manners, customs and language, despite ample opportunity for other Company employees to do so.

Barrow made no reference to the desirability of a second British embassy but had no need to do so. Six weeks before the publication of his review on 23 December 1809, and after a meeting with Robert Dundas, then President of the Board of Control, a jubilant Barrow had written to Staunton: 'We have done the deed; and I most heartily congratulate you on the almost certain prospect of your going to Pekin as the King's ambassador'. Staunton then discussed the nature of the embassy with Charles Grant, the powerful chairman of the East India Company, and plans were set in train for a modest ambassadorial retinue, perhaps twenty in number, to sail with the next China fleet.[5]

The embassy did not happen, but the idea was not forgotten. Following his appraisal of French exploration in the Indian and Pacific oceans and a review of Malté-Brun's French translation of his *Cochinchina*,[6] both of which he considered to be convincing proof of French designs in eastern Asia, Barrow used his review of Staunton's translation of the *Ta Tsing Leu Lee* or 'The Laws of China' to mount a strenuous attack on East India Company mismanagement and the adverse effect of its patronage system. The ignorance of China by Company employees, with the sole exception of Staunton, was fraught with great danger as it denied the possibility of ever establishing effective trading relationships with the Chinese and necessitated immediately 'a conciliatory mission to the court of Pekin, to endeavour to place our connections with the Chinese at Canton on a more respectable footing'. Staunton had the necessary experience for this task.[7] Once more, Barrow's and Staunton's hopes were dashed by political manoeuvring beyond their control, and Barrow waited until early in 1815 before making his next attempt.[8] This time he succeeded, if only in part, because this embassy was to be led by Lord Amherst. In the unlikely event that he died, Staunton would succeed him. Barrow celebrated his small victory by reviewing de Guignes's recently-published Chinese dictionary.[9]

This skilful use of the *Quarterly* to promote the careers of servants of empire such as Staunton, or Thomas Stamford Raffles at a later date, to generate public support for maritime or polar or African exploration, or the destruction of the slave trade, to explain or justify government policy, particularly in relation to naval affairs, or to encourage emigration or imperial expansion more generally, is a central characteristic of Barrow's relationship with the journal, its editors and its owner. His surviving correspondence concerning the *Quarterly*, which was mainly with Murray rather than the editors, reveals little interest in influencing editorial directions, but the volume of his contributions, shaped as they were by his experiences, orientations and intentions, gave to the *Quarterly* a distinctive quality that distinguished it from its rivals. Many of the topics Barrow selected, such as his attack on London's shipping interest or Britain's armed conflict with the United States,[10] his treatment of them and his obvious access to confidential government information helped to convince the *Quarterly's* readers that it reflected government policy accurately. This was certainly true of the first arrivals in the Swan River Colony (1829–30),[11] who were confident that the British government would alleviate their woes because it was Barrow who had encouraged them to emigrate through his rapturous account of the site selected for settlement in the April 1829 issue of the *Quarterly*.[12] Equally unsuccessful settlers on South Africa's frontier held similar views a decade before because of Barrow's promotion of the Albany settlement.[13] Yet, six years after submitting his last contribution, Barrow claimed that he avoided all political commentary.[14] He may have believed this to be the case, certainly when compared to his close friend and colleague John Wilson Croker, but his writings were marked by a pronounced xenophobia and by the liberal conservative perspective espoused by George Canning and his supporters. These had been shaped by his experiences on the outer edge of the British Empire and progressively refined and sharpened through his long service as a senior imperial servant.

Barrow had an established reputation as an author and commentator on public events long before he became a contributor to the *Quarterly*. He was born on 19 June 1764 in the hamlet of Dragley Beck on the edge of Ulverston, Lancashire, the son of a journeyman tanner who had acquired a small property through marriage. Recent critics such as Cranmer-Byng, Peyrefitte and Fleming point to this humble background as the source for Barrow's overwhelming ambition,[15] forgetting that this was a period when bright young men with energy and enterprise could make their own way in the world, providing of course that they had a powerful protector. Barrow did not forget, and in his *Auto-Biographical Memoir*, written when he was eighty-three years old, he laid out the clues to what he believed explained his progress to high office.

A precocious scholar, Barrow emerged from the local grammar school at the age of thirteen proficient in Greek and Latin. He was later to add proficiency in French, Dutch, Chinese, Portuguese and Spanish, although his strong Lancastrian accent ensured that he never acquired (or sought) native fluency. He enhanced his proficiency in mathematics with additional tuition from a local farmer and traded this proficiency with a young midshipman who taught him the fundamentals of navigation. He applied both sets of skills to a survey of the nearby Conished Priory estate. Intended for the Church by his father but lacking the means for acquiring the necessary formal education, Barrow opted to work as a book-keeper in an iron foundry in Liverpool. His employer's failing health led to Barrow taking increased responsibility for its management, but the promised partnership vanished with his employer's death. Seeking further adventure, aged eighteen, he served on a Greenland whaler for a year, in the process developing a lifelong interest in the discovery of a passage through the north polar ice linking the Atlantic and Pacific oceans. On his return, life at Dragley Beck could no longer sustain him and he shifted to London where, through the intercession of his mathematical farmer friend Mr Gibson, he gained a teaching post at the Reverend Mr James's Academy at Greenwich, attended by the sons of such notables as Lord Anson and others preparing for a naval career.[16]

Barrow is circumspect about this period but it is clear that he entered the fringe of London's intellectual society and came under the influence of the Scottish historian and classicist John Gillies, a member of the Macartney-Staunton circle. He may also have become a Freemason at this time. Barrow had already produced a small treatise on the use of surveying instruments which incorporated exercises used in his own teaching[17] when he was approached by Sir George Leonard Staunton to tutor his son George Thomas, equally precocious and thirteen years younger than Barrow. Staunton's influence with his friend and colleague Lord George Macartney led to Barrow's appointment as comptroller of household to Macartney's embassy to China (1792–4).

Barrow's role in this embassy, although hinted at in both Staunton's official account (1797) and in Macartney's journal,[18] has never been fully documented. As comptroller, or civilian quarter-master, his major task was to take care of and demonstrate the celestial globe, planetarium and other scientific instruments intended as gifts for the Chinese emperor. However, Macartney drew increasingly upon Barrow's wide interests and talents in the gathering of the commercial and strategic information which formed the second set of objectives for the embassy – the first being the establishment of a permanent British presence at the imperial court in Beijing. Barrow's assessments of the fortifications at Rio de Janiero, the commercial and strategic significance of Cochin China (Vietnam) and the desirability of establishing a trading centre at Chusan (Zhoushan), among others, although unacknowledged publicly, formed the basis of several confidential reports Macartney forwarded to Henry Dundas, the future Lord Melville, then president of the Board of Control. Staunton was more gracious in his acknowledgement[19] and his account of the embassy draws heavily on Barrow's activities and observations. Barrow's greatest tangible contribution, however, was through ten of the eleven maps and three of the forty-four illustrations he prepared for Staunton's 1797 publication. Elegantly designed and carefully annotated, these demonstrate his considerable cartographic, artistic and observational skills.

On the return of the embassy in September 1794, Barrow became Staunton's librarian and amanuensis, serving as the link between Staunton, who suffered a severe stroke shortly after his return, the President of the Royal Society Sir Joseph Banks, officials within the East India Company, which had financed the embassy, and Staunton's publishers. His experiences in China had pointed to severe deficiencies in his scientific training and he set out on another round of self improvement, particularly in biology and geology. As a member of Staunton's household, he became part of Macartney's larger intellectual and social circle. He was planning to accompany Staunton junior on a tour of Europe when a grateful Dundas offered Macartney the governorship of the recently annexed Dutch colony at the Cape of Good Hope which they both saw as the key to control of the Indian and Southern Atlantic oceans and thus of major commercial and strategic significance. An equally grateful Macartney offered Barrow one of his two personal secretaryships.

Macartney's entourage reached Cape Town on 4 May 1797. In less than two months, Barrow was on his way to Graaff-Reinet in the eastern Cape. His immediate objectives were to settle the disturbances among the frontier Boers and install the *landdrost* Frans Bressler, ejected from Graaff-Reinet by the Boers some months before. He was also to make contact with the Xhosa peoples along the edge of European settlement to attempt to delineate a clear boundary between the two groups in an effort to reduce if not remove the inter-racial conflict which had underpinned the Boer unrest. His more important task, however, was strategic reconnaissance. He was requested by Macartney, at Dundas's behest, to make an inventory of available timber and other naval stores, assess the fitness of the land for producing hemp and flax, determine the suitability of Algoa Bay as a British naval base, estimate the fishing potential along the coast, and identify any actual or potential mining developments. He was also to gauge the nature and extent of commerce among the native peoples he encountered and determine whether a 'commerce or intercourse might be carried on' with them 'with safety, propriety and advantage'. While Macartney indicated that these were his major concerns, he gave Barrow an open brief to examine any other things 'which will naturally suggest themselves, and which your turn of mind and desire for knowledge, will not be neglected by you'.[20]

With the exception of a brief respite at Cape Town during the height of summer, Barrow spent the next twelve months on this task, criss-crossing the colony, delineating its boundaries, checking the accuracy of earlier accounts, and everywhere observing, recording and mapping. At the end of the period, he produced two major reports for Macartney – 'A General Description of the Colony of the Cape of Good Hope' and 'Of the Revenues of the Cape of Good Hope'[21] – as well as a map which one analyst has described as the first modern map of southern Africa.[22] He made only one further expedition, again to the eastern Cape, in March 1799 in an unsuccessful attempt to unravel the increasingly tangled and violent confrontations between the frontier Boers, the Xhosa and the Khoi.[23] His competent handling of the troops under his command, however, earned him the approbation of Major General Francis Dundas who was then acting governor in the interregnum between Macartney's departure and the arrival of Sir George Yonge.

Promoted to the post of Auditor General by Macartney in September 1798, Barrow set out, under Macartney's direction, to overhaul the finances of the colony through a Board of Revenue to which the Receiver of Revenue, the Receiver of Land Revenue, and the Receiver of Customs and Tithes made monthly reports which were then evaluated by Barrow and reported upon to the governor. Barrow settled down to life as a colonial official, became a landed proprietor, took control of the botanic garden, completed the manuscript of his travels and forwarded it to Staunton to arrange publication,[24] and, after a cautious courtship lasting two years, married Anna Maria Trüter, the daughter of a member of the Council of Justice and part of a well-established and influential Cape Dutch family. Significantly, and unlike many of his British colleagues, he employed no slaves, despite ample opportunity to do so. His career suffered a setback during Yonge's governorship but, following Yonge's departure in disgrace, blossomed under Francis Dundas, again acting governor, who relied heavily on Barrow's advice and appointed him to two major commissions of inquiry as well as to the editorship of the *Cape Town Gazette and Commercial Advertiser*, the Cape's only newspaper.

It was therefore with a sense of betrayal and personal loss that Barrow received news in August 1802 of the return of the Cape to the Dutch as a result of the Treaty of Amiens. To add insult, it was Barrow and Acheson Maxwell, his friend from the embassy to China, who arranged the handover of government to the incoming Batavian administration. It would have been some consolation, had he known it, that Commissioner de Mist singled out Barrow and his management of the office of Auditor General as worthy of emulation by the new Dutch government.[25]

Barrow arrived back in Britain in mid 1803 with solid achievements in colonial administration, an already established reputation as a cartographer, geographer and author, experience in journalism, and sufficient wealth through marriage and judicious property dealings to sustain a writing career. He had begun work on his *Travels in China*[26] while still at sea, but further employment prospects were bleak. He had been strongly recommended to Melville by both Macartney and Francis Dundas but Pitt, and thus Melville, were out of office. Nevertheless, Macartney arranged a dinner with Melville and Pitt so that Barrow could outline his views on the strategic significance of the Cape.[27] Melville encouraged him to put his thoughts into print. His second volume on South Africa followed, appearing before the end of 1804.[28] On Pitt's return to office, Melville offered Barrow the second secretaryship at the Admiralty on 15 May 1804, a position he was to hold, except for a brief period between 10 February 1806 and 7 April 1807, until 28 January 1846 when he retired at the age of eighty-one. During his temporary unemployment, Barrow completed his *Voyage to Cochin China* (1806), revised his *Travels into the Interior of Southern Africa* (1806), and produced a *Life of Earl Macartney* (1807).

All of these publications were well received. Writing in the *Edinburgh Review*, Francis Jeffrey observed that Barrow's *Travels in China* was the 'most sound, judicious and candid' account that had yet appeared on that country and 'set the example of sobriety and moderation'. He had been less impressed with *Travels in Southern Africa* because of the argument that was put forward for its retention, and said of *Cochin China*: 'We have come to the dregs of Mr. Barrow now. He must travel again before we allow him to publish any more travels', but, despite this, Jeffrey concluded: 'In point of sound sense and sagacity, we are disposed to rank him at least as high as any modern traveller'.[29] This was a widespread assessment. Among most reviewers, including those in the *British Critic* and *Antijacobin*, there was general agreement that Barrow had established a standard for travel writing against which other future travellers would be judged.[30]

Although largely forgotten now (except among book collectors, by whom they are highly valued), his publications were also influential. For example, and reflecting the view of many modern South African commentators, Michael Streak singled Barrow out as the person most responsible for the negative attitudes held by the British towards, first, the Boers and then, subsequently, towards Afrikaners. Michael Adas has argued that Barrow's opinions, along with those of his contemporaries de Guignes and John Davis, 'formed the nucleus of a cluster of ideas about China that informed virtually all nineteenth-century accounts of the Qing empire'.[31] Zhang Shunhong came to a similar conclusion in his analysis of British views on China between 1790 and 1820, and observed that Barrow's account of the Macartney embassy marked a watershed between the generally positive and increasingly critical British assessments of Chinese culture, governance and achievements in the sciences and arts.[32]

Once established in London, Barrow began to extend his influence, the foundations for which rested on three pillars held firmly in place by a series of interlocking professional and personal networks. Undoubtedly, the most important of these was his official position within the Admiralty and thus within government circles, but this was reinforced by his involvement in the major scientific associations of his day, particularly the Royal Society and the Linnaean Society, and extended by his continuing literary activities, including active membership of the Literary Club. Bonding them together was the force of his dynamic personality and the breadth of his interests. He became very much a man of business in a wider imperial sphere.

When Barrow arrived at the Admiralty, Britain was well on its way to establishing naval supremacy, although eleven years of conflict remained, including an economic war of attrition and the troubling War of 1812. His wartime experiences convinced him that Britain would never be a major land-based power in Europe. Supremacy depended on sea power which, in turn, depended upon possession of a numerically and qualitatively superior fleet and control of the world's sea lanes upon which international trade, the key to security and dominance, revolved. He thus became heavily involved in a wide range of activities for which the *Quarterly* became an important forum. These included the development of naval infrastructure, encompassing ship design, the development of dockyards and their associated support facilities, and the treatment of dry rot in ship timbers,[33] all of which required him to work closely with the prominent scientists and engineers of the period, notably the ships architect Robert Seppings, the Brunels, John Rennie and his sons, and James Watt.[34] He also advocated aggressive, pre-emptive annexation of strategic locations such as Mauritius or retention of possessions seized during the recent wars.[35] His successful advocacy through the *Quarterly*[36] and elsewhere of the annexation of Fernando Po so that it became the base in West Africa from which to attack the slave trade led the Colonial Secretary Lord Bathurst to complain to his colleague Wilmot Horton: 'if coveting islands is a breach of the ten Commandments, then he is the greatest violator of the Decalogue in the Kingdom'.[37] This was a characteristic that Jeffrey had drawn attention to at least two decades before when reviewing his *Cochin China*. Fernando Po was only one of the many sites Barrow targeted. Malta, the Ionian Islands, Zanzibar, Western Port, Melville Island, New Zealand, Ceylon, Hawaii, the Ryukyu Islands and Port Essington all had a place in his vision of a greater empire.[38]

Barrow's appointment to the Admiralty broadened his circle of professional and personal colleagues. The Admiralty's First Secretary, the noted orientalist William Marsden, introduced him to other former East India Company notables – men such as James Rennell,[39] the former surveyor general of India and a recognized geographer, former author-governors like Stamford Raffles and Mountstuart Elphinstone,[40] soldier-diplomat-explorers like Malcolm, Pottinger, and Kinneir and Morier,[41] and the incomparable East India Company hydrographer James Horsburgh. Through Charles Yorke, when First Lord, Barrow came to know and work closely with Henry Salt,[42] the British consul at Cairo, with whom he actively promoted the sustained looting of Egyptian antiquities, as well as the irascible Henry Warrington[43] at Tripoli who became an essential link in his promotion of the search for the Niger.

Routine work brought him into regular contact with senior officials in the Foreign Office, the Colonial Office, the Board of Control, the Board of Trade, the Navy Board and the Treasury, with many of whom, such as Benjamin Hobhouse, William Hamilton, Joseph Planta, Henry Goulburn, Wilmot Horton and Robert Hay, he formed lasting friendships of considerable significance for his imperial activities. Without doubt, however, his closest working relationship was with John Wilson Croker, the Admiralty's First Secretary from 1810 to 1830, with whom he enjoyed a lasting friendship, cemented through marriage between Croker's adopted daughter and Barrow's eldest son George. Their friendship survived considerable differences in their views on the role of the post-war navy and imperial expansion. Through Croker, Barrow became a confidant of Robert Peel, but he had already established a web of influence among rising politicians among whom could be counted Canning, Castlereagh, Aberdeen, Huskisson, Robert Dundas (the second Lord Melville), Charles Grant (Lord Glenelg) and Frederick Robinson (Lord Goderich-Earl of Ripon). In time, he was to include Palmerston among those who regularly sought his advice. As he survived eleven First Lords, part of Barrow's influence can be attributed to his longevity, but he had an incomparable knowledge of naval traditions and organization, which was put to effective use in the overhaul of naval administration during Sir James Graham's term as First Lord (1831–5). More significant, however, was his knowledge of remote corners of the world. He became the government authority on Britain's imperial geography and was regularly consulted by colleagues in both the Colonial Office and Foreign Office. It was to Barrow that Napoleon owed his incarceration on St Helena.[44]

Barrow's role in the formation and early development of the Royal Geographical Society is well known, if understated.[45] Less well known is his involvement in the Royal Society, which had been an important scientific adjunct to the Admiralty since the establishment of the Royal Observatory, over which, with the Board of Ordnance, they had joint responsibility. The three bodies also had responsibility for the Board of Longitude, established in 1818 under an act introduced by Croker to promote polar exploration and associated scientific discovery, particularly in the field of magnetism.

The relationship between the Admiralty and the Royal Society was mutually beneficial for both exploration and science, particularly from the time of planning Cook's voyages onward and more particularly during the period of Sir Joseph Banks's presidency (1778–1820).[46] It was especially fruitful for Banks and Barrow. While few details of joint ventures are recorded in the minutes of the Royal Society, strong evidence from other sources shows that Barrow enlisted Royal Society support to initiate Tuckey's Niger expedition in 1815, the first of his planned forays into Africa,[47] as well as the series of polar voyages begun in 1818.[48] In turn, Banks used Barrow to obtain employment for promising young men such as Phillip Parker King, the son of an old friend and a former governor of New South Wales. King's survey of the Australian coastline (1818–22) surpassed that undertaken by Flinders – another Banks–Admiralty initiative of two decades before.

Although George Leonard Staunton had proposed nominating him in 1801, Barrow did not join the Royal Society until early 1805. Three years later, he was welcomed into the Royal Society Club, the inner sanctum of the Society which never contained more than forty of the most prominent and 'clubbable' of its members and which met for dinner prior to all normal meetings. The Club was an important forum for the determination of Society policy and served as an information gathering and disseminating node, and a locus of influence. As Admiral W. H. Smyth, a Barrow protégé prominent in geographical circles, observed in 1860, it was 'a true *hospitum publicum* for labourers in the scientific vineyard, and an elegant resort for the more general admirers and patrons of human knowledge'.[49] Barrow became a member of the council for the first time in 1815 and, for the next fifteen years, alternated his membership with Croker to ensure an Admiralty presence. He was appointed a vice president several times thereafter.

Barrow's original nominators – ambassador and colonial governor Lord Macartney, orientalist William Marsden, naval hydrographer Alexander Dalrymple, geographer and marine engineer James Rennell, the chemist and fellow Literary Club member Charles Hatchett, naval physician Gilbert Blane and historian John Gillies, among others – indicate the position he had already created for himself in literary, geographical and East India Company circles. His subsequent involvement in the nomination of fellows – more than 170 over the next 42 years – demonstrates the consolidation of his status and the extension of his interests and influence: he was at the forefront in the election of young explorers and promising colonial and imperial officials and used his influence to ensure the presence of a strong naval lobby. He must have been sufficiently confident in the strength of his power base when he and Croker, with the acting president Davies Gilbert, the foreign secretary Thomas Young and Barrow's close friend Thomas Amyot, schemed to have Peel appointed as president in 1826 after Humphry Davy announced his intention to retire. His involvement in the election of the Duke of Sussex as president in 1830 is more covert. The rift this created between the amateur and professional scientists may have been a factor in his agreeing to assist Francis Beaufort and William Henry Smyth in the formation of the Royal Geographical Society.

As a *Quarterly* reviewer, Barrow's interests ranged widely. In addition to topics emerging out of his work at the Admiralty, such as naval construction and scientific and technological advances, he commented on the insurance industry, the standardization of weights and measures, begging, Egyptian antiquities, and foreign investment. The slave trade, which he abhorred, was a particular focus.[50] All of his articles were imbued with the notion of progress and the superiority of British civilization. Nearly seven-eighths of his articles had a geographical focus, usually with an underlying imperial theme. His early interest in Asia (61 articles) dominated, with 17 articles being devoted to China alone, but he wrote extensively on North and Central America (32 articles), Australia and the

Pacific (17 articles), and the eastern Mediterranean (7 articles). His interest in the promotion of exploration of Africa led to 38 articles, while polar exploration contributed a further 17. Of the far flung parts of the globe, only South America escaped his close attention, Robert Southey claiming that as his particular interest. No significant explorer in Africa, Asia, Australia or the Americas escaped his scrutiny.

His output was prodigious. In a 32-year span from 1809, he contributed more than 200 articles and in excess of 2.5 million words to the *Quarterly*. From 1812 until early 1830, Barrow's output averaged 10 articles a year. Thereafter, following a major rift with the then editor John Gibson Lockhart, his contributions declined sharply and he wrote, commonly at John Murray's specific request, only when a subject sufficiently seized his attention, usually to do with polar exploration, the colonies, China, emigration, slavery or the Russian threat in central Asia. Never completely happy with Lockhart as an editor, the break came through Lockhart's perceived failure to support him over his disparagement of his friend Sir Rufane Donkin's theorizing about the geography of north Africa,[51] and his rejection of Sir Howard Douglas's claim that it was his father who was responsible for Admiral Rodney's decision to 'break the enemy's line' in the Battle of 12 April.[52] Murray encouraged Barrow to write books instead. The first of these, for which Barrow received a fee of £300, was *Mutiny of the Bounty*, written in less than four months in the summer of 1831. This was followed by biographies of Barrow's personal heroes Peter the Great (1832), Admiral Earl Howe (1838) and Admiral Lord Anson (1839). A summary of polar exploration undertaken through his initiatives was published in 1846, too early to document the fate of the Franklin expedition he had set in train with Royal Society support three years earlier. Barrow completed the final pages of his *Sketches of the Royal Society* on 29 October 1848, less than a month before he died, at the age of eighty-four.

Barrow also contributed seventeen lengthy articles to Macvey Napier's *Supplement* to *The Encyclopaedia Britannica*, between 1814 and 1824, including major descriptions of Africa, Australasia, China and the Pacific, all of which were revised and expanded later for inclusion in the seventh edition of the encyclopaedia, published in 1842. Napier had approached him specifically to write on fisheries following Barrow's analysis of the British fishing industry in the eighteenth number of the *Quarterly*.[53] Using Captain Basil Hall as an intermediary,[54] Napier also recruited Barrow as an *Edinburgh* reviewer after Barrow's final break with Lockhart over the latter's refusal to publish an unsolicited review by George Barrow of his younger brother's book of travels.[55] Barrow wrote five articles for Napier between 1841 and 1844, the first being a review of Hall's *Patchwork*, which was followed by reviews of Beechey's and Belcher's travels, and biographies of Admiral Keppel and Admiral Lord St Vincent.[56]

As could be expected from this output, the quality of his observations varied enormously. He typically wrote in the evening in a small office in his official residence in Spring Street, New Gardens, or less commonly and more leisurely over the summer during his break from official duties, often at Leigh Park, George Thomas Staunton's exotically-landscaped estate near Portsmouth. He wrote quickly, submitting first drafts for typesetting, usually making corrections and, sometimes, quite substantial changes at the first or second proof stage. At times, his writing appeared unnecessarily prolix but that was a reflection of the speed at which he wrote rather than his writing style. He once told Napier that the article he was forwarding was so long only because he did not have time to make it shorter.[57] At its best, his writing exhibits the excitement of discovery, and a mastery of the available information, combined with acute insights into its strategic significance. As an example, his account of the Australian colonies, written in 1841 and his last contribution to the *Quarterly*, is a masterly summary of what was then known, including information drawn from official documents unavailable to other writers, interwoven with a deep appreciation of the nature and effects of (British) government policy and a call for further expansion and development.[58] His explanations of the Chinese language have no contemporary parallel. But it was his description of the geographies of previously unknown areas of the globe that made their greatest impact. Only Hugh Murray, a compiler of accounts of discovery and a contributor to the *Edinburgh Review*, came close to rivalling his geographical output, and he lagged far behind. In his obituary address, George Thomas Staunton summarized his contribution in these terms:

> During a long series of years, whenever an article illustrative of science or enterprise appeared in the *Quarterly*, the public at once recognised the hand from which it proceeded, and valued it accordingly. He had, indeed, not only a remarkable facility in composition, but, what was of still more importance, that of detecting, sifting, arranging, and applying all those dispersed and often obscure materials which were essential to the elucidation of his subject, but, which, however important in themselves, had been in their crude state, almost worthless and valueless.[59]

Like Barrow, Staunton held back more than he revealed. Barrow certainly had an urge to expand bodies of knowledge and to share this knowledge with a wide reading public, but, as Staunton knew to his advantage, this was often done with an underlying, frequently unstated, purpose. Barrow was as concerned to influence as he was to inform. Significantly, his 1841 account of Australia was a veiled attempt to generate support for the small and isolated settlement at Port Essington on Australia's northern coast, recently devastated by a severe tropical cyclone. This public utterance was matched by intense lobbying within both the Admiralty and the Colonial Office. The occupation of Port Essington in 1838 had been his initiative, and followed his earlier efforts to safeguard nearby military outposts on Melville Island (1824) and Raffles Bay (1826), both abandoned in 1829. For Barrow, all three settlements were key stakes in a notional 'ring fence' he and his Colonial Office colleague Robert William Hay had helped to erect in the 1820s and 1830s to keep out foreign invaders, by which they meant the French and Americans, and so secure the Australian continent solely for the British.[60] It may be mere coincidence that orders to abandon Port Essington were issued a month after Barrow's death in November 1848.

An examination of how Barrow translated his interest in exploration into action after the defeat of Napoleon provides an even more compelling illustration. The *Quarterly* was the vehicle Barrow used to arouse public interest in the renewal of African exploration. Mungo Park's journals from his second, fatal attempt to trace the course of the Niger having been recovered, they were edited by Bryan Edwards, the African Association's secretary, and published early in 1815. The planning by Banks, representing the African Association and the Royal Society, Marsden, Rennell, Goulburn of the Colonial Office and Barrow of a new expedition along the Niger, to be undertaken by Major Peddie and fully supported by Lord Bathurst, was well advanced when Barrow's review hit the streets of London on 20 June 1815. Holding out the prospect of the glory to be won by British courage and initiative and the advantages to be gained for British science, Barrow stoutly defended Park's reputation from accusations by the African Institution, published in the rival *Edinburgh Review*,[61] that he was opposed to the abolition of slavery and asserted that successful suppression was dependent upon the knowledge of the slave trade that Park's account and that of future explorers revealed. A third of the review was devoted to expounding his own theory that the Niger, from the last point seen by Park, turned south to flow into the Zaire, also known as the Congo.[62]

The groundwork having been laid, and as preparations for the Peddie expedition were being finalized, Barrow gained Bathurst's and Goulburn's support for a complementary expedition to determine the source of the Zaire[63] and enlisted Banks's support to convince the Admiralty Lords that this should be a naval venture and that steam power should be used. Captain James Hingston Tuckey, well known to Banks and Barrow for his surveys in southern Australia and for his recently-published *Maritime Geography* (1815), was selected for this task.[64] Banks's and Barrow's friend, the engineer John Rennie, supervised the experiments with the *Congo*, the steam vessel designed specifically for the shallow waters expected on the Zaire, but concluded by late January 1816 that the engine was under-powered and consumed too much fuel.[65] The *Congo* was then converted to sail and Tuckey finally departed in February 1816.

While neither expedition succeeded, they reveal the essential attributes of post-war exploratory activity that Barrow set in train, typically with Banks's support. The expeditions had been planned cooperatively, the Colonial Office taking primary responsibility for, and meeting the expenses of, land-based exploration, while the Admiralty took responsibility for maritime activities. The wider scientific community, primarily but not exclusively the geographically-oriented members of the Royal Society, served as a reference group by providing support for the initiative, assisting in the selection of key personnel and helping to shape the explorers' instructions. Barrow linked these elements and, as he prepared the instructions for both expeditions, put his particular stamp on the form they were to take. The key element, upon which all the others depended, was the use of the *Quarterly* to generate and maintain public support.

Renewed interest in the search for the North-West Passage followed a similar path to the renewed search for the Niger. When reports arrived in London from returning whalers that the waters surrounding the Greenland fishing grounds were more free of ice in 1817 than any could remember, and particularly the reports Banks received from the whaler-scientist William Scoresby, Barrow wrote a lengthy article in the October 1817 issue of the *Quarterly* which reviewed Britain's past contribution to the search, outlined his views on the likely location of the passage, and urged the nation to take up the challenge.[66] The effect on the public was electric. At Murray's request, Barrow followed up with a book-length version which appeared early in 1818.[67] Banks's support and the weight of the Royal Society were enlisted once more, and the moribund parliamentary act 16 Geo. III, c. 6 was revamped to provide a princely reward of £20,000 for the discoverer. At the same time, the Board of Longitude, the joint responsibility of the Admiralty, the Board of Ordnance and the Royal Society, was reconstituted to more adequately supervise the experiments with magnetism that were to be a central feature of the renewed search.[68] By the spring of 1818, two expeditions, one under the command of Captain John Ross, the other under the command of Captain David Buchan, were sent forth. They failed to penetrate the ice and were back in Deptford in November, but Barrow, keeping interest alive through the pages of the *Quarterly*,[69] ensured that Parry, Ross's second in command, was sent out again in the next season, and that this was followed by a succession of voyages, despite lack of success and increasing cost, until John Franklin's final and fatal expedition. Edward Parry, introduced to Barrow by Acheson Maxwell, his friend from their time together in China and southern Africa, returned from his third voyage to become acting hydrographer to the Royal Navy and went on to an illustrious naval career, finishing his days as captain-superintendent of Haslar Hospital. John Ross had a major disagreement with Barrow and the group of young officers he had recruited for his Arctic adventures. Ross received no further sponsorship by the Admiralty. Scoresby, among the most experienced and competent of the Greenland whalers, was not a naval officer and could not expect to command a naval vessel. When he declined a subordinate position, his involvement ceased.

Although it failed to achieve its objectives, the Tuckey expedition left an important legacy. With the successful publication of Tuckey's manuscript, which he edited, followed very closely by publication of the several accounts of the Amherst embassy, in which he also had a major role, Barrow encouraged John Murray to produce a remarkable sequence of explorers' accounts which in time developed into the equally successful series of travel guides produced by Murray's son. Barrow played a central role in this development, not infrequently recruiting authors, advising them on how to write, introducing them to Murray, and assisting them to negotiate a publication fee, acting as a referee for their manuscripts before editing them, and then publicizing the finished work through the pages of the *Quarterly*.[70] In this way, and in his reviews in the *Quarterly*, Barrow was able to put his stamp on what may be called the 'explorer genre' that emerged in this period. What Barrow supplied in his own travel books he also looked for in the books he reviewed and in those of authors he helped through the press. Two criteria, narrative and novelty, were central. The story of the journey had to be presented in a simple, unaffected style in a way that unfolded new knowledge about the natural and human world. Comment on the manners and morals of the people encountered, the resources they had access to and the potential of those resources for Britain were also essential. The explorer was there to observe accurately and comprehensively and report skilfully, for which he needed sound training in cartography and the natural sciences, particularly geology and biology, as well as an ability to convey through his writing a sense of the drama and excitement that accompany all discovery. Thus, Barrow's *Travels in South Africa* (1801) and the strategic reconnaissance upon which it was based remained his ideal model, totally appropriate for an expanding British role in a post-Napoleonic world. The *Quarterly* became an important vehicle for ensuring a wide readership for books that met his criteria. Barrow made it abundantly clear that it was not the explorer's role to theorize. That was for others, presumably armchair geographers like himself, to do. Even though he otherwise admired Alexander von Humboldt for the scope of his discoveries and his modesty in presenting them, Barrow made him a particular target for criticism for his propensity to theorize and because 'he spreads too much canvass, and stows too little ballast', that is he generalizes too readily from a limited factual base. This was a weakness in continental exploration more generally.[71] Barrow never felt similarly constrained and ended his celebration of the Royal Geographical Society's first anniversary by reaffirming the value of 'hypothetical or speculative geography' which kept curiosity alive and justified Britain's continuing exploration of unknown lands.[72]

Murray agreed to publish three accounts of the Amherst embassy to China in 1815–17, by John McLeod, surgeon on the *Alceste*, Henry Ellis, one of the three commissioners, and Captain Basil Hall of the Royal Navy, an accomplished author. He may well have commissioned the works before the embassy left Britain. In early September 1817, Barrow wrote to Murray:

> I sat up last night over Mr. McLeod's narrative til I nearly got through it, which proves at least that it interested *me*; and I am much deceived if it will not interest others. There is no pretension of science or fine writing; but the story of the voyage and the description of the *Leou-Keou* [Ryukyu] islands in particular are told in a plain intelligible and unaffected manner. It will certainly make a very interesting and most readable *Octavo* volume; and will afford a very pretty little article for the Review; so that you have it in two ways; and as it will not in the least interfere with the Ellis *Quarto*, I should suppose you might have it out in 6 weeks or a couple of months – neither will it much interfere with Hall's, tho it will take off the edge of curiosity with regard to the friendly reception and kind manners of the Oriental Islanders.[73]

Highly favourable notices in the *Quarterly* accompanied their publication.[74]

Despite his voluminous public writing, Barrow remains somewhat of an enigma, in part because he destroyed his private correspondence as he dealt with it. His *Auto-Biographical Memoir* is stripped of his personality and, although he observes with obvious pride the prominent positions achieved by his three surviving sons, no reference is made to his wife, who continues to be highly regarded in South Africa for her landscape painting,[75] or his daughters. Yet, he was a devoted family man. He regularly dined at the Athenaeum, the Literary, the Royal Society and Raleigh clubs and at several of the more prominent houses around London, yet appears to have entertained rarely at home. That he was a kind, trusted and an entertaining companion is attested to by his many enduring friendships. Yet, he was a vengeful and unrelenting opponent, as the polar explorer Captain James Ross and others who disagreed with him discovered to their cost. He had an active and enquiring mind, but was opinionated, dogmatic and aggressive when challenged. He was both deferential to and assertive with his superiors and attracted the loyalty and affection of his subordinates, many of whom contributed to the remarkable monument erected in his memory on Hoad Hill at the head of Morecambe Bay, overlooking his birthplace. The three surviving portraits reveal a man of middle height, sturdy build, straight backed and stiff necked, and with a striking face, complete with forward thrusting chin and penetrating gaze, surely a preferred self-image.

Two verbal portraits which survive are more revealing. The first comes from an entry in the diary of Lord Glenbervie, who had been considered at one time as Macartney's replacement as governor at the Cape:

April 2 [1818], Thursday, 6.30 am, in bed, Argyll Street. – We dined yesterday at Sir J. Stanley's and met there Doctor Holland and Mr. Barrow. This was the first time of my being in company with him. He is very cock-a-hoop with the success of his paper in the last Quarterly Review on the North Pole business. He is a goodish talker, and well acquainted with his own subjects, with rather good manners for an author-secretary in office. But he has a strong north country accent and voice; and besides I have a grudge to him for his review of the first Report of the Commissioners of Woods and Land Revenue which he thought fit to damn with faint praise.[76]

The second comes from Lady Anne Barnard, wife of Macartney's colonial secretary at the Cape, written to her former suitor Henry Dundas, and describing her encounter on top of the Cape's Table Mountain:

'And now,' says I, 'Mr. Barrow, thou man of infinite charts and maps, explain to me all that I see before me, and what I do not see – what is this – what is that – where are the different bays I hear you all wrangling about – where can we effect junctions – why cannot we sail around this continent with as much ease as we sail around other coasts? – shew me the roads by which grain and cattle, and wine come from the interior of the country, and do not suppose that I am to clamber to the top of Table Mountain for nothing.'

What he told me Mr. Dundas – all is now forgotten. I only remembered that he explained everything so intelligibly as to prevent me from appearing very ignorant afterwards, when the subject was discussed.[77]

# 7 HUNG, DRAWN AND QUARTERLYED: ROBERT SOUTHEY, POETRY, POETS AND THE *QUARTERLY REVIEW*

Lynda Pratt

In 1809 Robert Southey outlined the economic realities facing any would-be 'man of letters', that only 'two branches' of literature provided 'adequate remuneration ... writing for reviews, or for the stage'.[1] Whilst he did not dismiss the profitable opportunities to be found in writing for the theatre, the larger part of his analysis was devoted to a craft he knew much better – 'well paid' reviewing. As he explained, 'Reviewing is not an unpleasant task' and after a decade of contributing to periodicals he was an old hand:

> Carlisle introduced me to the *Critical* in 1798, and I wrote some years for it at the low rate of three guineas per sheet. My work was not worth more. It brought me from 50 to 100£ yearly, a very acceptable addition to my very straightened income. It made me look for my opinions upon many subjects which had not occupied much of my attention before, and it made me acquire more knowledge of contemporary Literature than I should else have possessed. For the *Annual* I received four guineas, as much as the concern could afford, but greatly below the value of my work, for the former apprenticeship had made me a skilful workman.[2]

After such relatively humble beginnings, by the late 1800s Southey was in demand by the reviews and (or so he claimed) even able to choose which ones he wrote for. In 1807 he 'refused ten guineas per sheet' from the *Edinburgh* on 'the grounds of my total dissent from all its principles of morals and politics as well as taste'.[3] Within less than two years, he did, however, accept the offer of work from another periodical – the *Quarterly* – and by 1810 noted that the money it brought in was 'a great help ... They pay ten guineas a sheet, and for the life of Nelson ... twenty'. Indeed the income generated by the *Quarterly* was such that, in 1811, Southey rejected Thomas Norton Longman's request to be the 'prop and pillar' of another new periodical, partly on the grounds that he was only offered a flat 'ten-guinea price' for his labours.[4]

Southey's entanglement with the *Quarterly* was to prove by some margin the longest lasting of all his engagements with the reviews, running from 1809 until 1839, from the middle to the effective end of his working life. Moreover, his ninety attributed contributions form a substantial body of work.[5] They constitute at one and the same time his 'most important reviewing and a seriously neglected body of his [mature] prose writings'. They were also 'the chief medium through which he publicly expressed his political, social, literary, and moral opinions'.[6]

## Reviewing for the *Quarterly Review*

There is no doubt that Southey's association with the *Quarterly* was a productive one. As well as generating several hundred pages of critical prose, it also led to a variety of spin offs from and elaborations on individual essays. For example, an article on 'Bell and Lancaster's *Systems of Education*', first published in the *Quarterly* in August 1811, was 'altered and extended ... to form a little volume called the Origin Nature & Object of the New System of Education'.[7] In turn this led, eventually, to Southey being commissioned by Bell's executors to write a life of the educationalist.[8] What turned out to be his most successful and enduring prose work – the *Life of Nelson* (1813) – also had its origins in Southey's labours for the *Quarterly*, an 1809 review essay on the nascent industry of Nelsonian biography.[9] Other articles, including controversial writings on the poor and parliamentary reform, were revised and republished as a two-volume collection of his *Essays, Moral and Political*, which appeared in 1832, the year of the Great Reform Act.[10] The timing of this publication was in turn an indication of the seriousness with which the Poet Laureate regarded his interventions in public debates about the nation's future prosperity, its political, social and moral health.

Southey owed to John Murray the idea to expand into book length his essay on other peoples' 'Lives of Nelson'; Southey repaid Murray with interest, introducing possible new reviewers to the publisher.[11] Other forms of collaboration marked his written contributions to the *Quarterly*. For example, he consulted with John Rickman over the contents of individual essays, such as 'Capt. Pasley on the Military Policy of Great Britain'.[12] At times, though, such collaboration was, at best, reluctant and enforced, with essays being rewritten or censored by the review's editors. For example, his articles on Pasley and 'On the Corn Laws' contained contributions by John Wilson Croker.[13] From the very outset, Southey objected violently to such intervention. As early as 1809 he noted that his work for the very first volume of the *Quarterly* had '... suffered grievously from mutilation, partly inflicted to shorten what is still the longest article in the book, more frequently for the sake of weeding out whatever savoured of heresy, political or religious, no very easy operation to perform upon a man who weaves it in the very warp of his discourse'.[14] On this occasion, he took his revenge by inscribing the sections William Gifford had cut out of the published essay into his own personal copy of the *Quarterly*, in an attempt to reassert control (privately at least) over his own words.[15] His anger at what he thought to be unjustified and unjustifiable censorship was to become something of a refrain and, indeed, also carried over into fury regarding the political censorship of his earliest poems as Poet Laureate.[16] Of course in both cases (as reviewer and poet) his ability to actually do anything about it was markedly circumscribed. Complaining to anyone who would listen was, though, a useful means of venting personal dislike of hate figures such as Gifford, whose editing Southey described as akin to 'emasculation' and 'castration', and also a means of differentiating the efforts of such men from his own. As he explained, Gifford's inelegant interventions turned sense into nonsense: 'If there be a logical arrangement he is sure to dislocate it … If there be a felicitous phrase, he is sure to gouge the sentence'.[17] At times the impact of his alterations was so extreme that Southey declared himself to be alienated from his own 'mutilated prose', hardly able to 'recognize my own writing and … unable to defend it' if occasion required.[18]

## Southey Reviewed

Southey's laments are a reminder of both his own status as a writer and his dual (and dualistic) relationship with the *Quarterly*. Unlike most other contributors, he both wrote for and was written about in its pages. Essays on his works appeared with reasonable regularity, although, significantly, the *Quarterly* avoided reviewing the Poet Laureate's more controversial poems, in particular his odes and the *Vision of Judgement* (1821).[19] The convention of anonymous reviewing – which he protested against – ensured that, whilst he was reviewed by name, his own review essays were always nameless.[20] This complex relationship between 'Southey' the author and 'Southey' the critic explains some of his ambivalence to the *Quarterly* and its practices. From the outset, he expressed disquiet with the verbal ferocity employed by some of his fellow contributors. In 1809 (just after the appearance of the first issue) he complained to Walter Scott that the '… *Quarterly* is a little too much in the temper of the *Edinburgh* to please me. No man dips his pen deeper in the very gall of bitterness than I can do … but I do not like to see scorn and indignation wasted on trivial objects – they should be reserved, like the arrows of Hercules for occasions worthy of such weapons.'[21] His concerns persisted. Although he acknowledged the importance of the *Quarterly* in 'fighting the battles of the country and of the Government'[22] he was not always satisfied with the ways in which this end was accomplished. In 1818 he urged Murray to

... give all the praise in your review that can honestly be given ... The cursed system of acrimonious criticism has prevailed too generally and too long ... any gratuitous attack, any wound wantonly inflicted makes a man your enemy, when he might as well have been your friend.[23]

Southey's anxiety to differentiate the *Quarterly* from the *Edinburgh* is understandable given his own (and his associates') treatment at the hands of Francis Jeffrey and his colleagues. His doubts might also appear hypocritical when set against his own use of invective. Yet what Southey was asking for was criticism that was well-judged, appropriate, and therefore effective: the use of the reviewer's critical lash when the occasion demanded but not otherwise.

In his work for the *Quarterly* Southey was attempting to tread a fine line. He was aware, as an author-critic, of the difficulties of both trades and keen to differentiate himself from ill-judged and ill-informed practitioners of the latter one, from men such as Gifford and Jeffrey. His contemporaries were not convinced. As author and reviewer the Poet Laureate was an extremely controversial figure. The author of the *Quarterly*'s review of *Roderick, the Last of the Goths* (1814) was stating the obvious when he noted in his first sentence, 'No poet in our language, or perhaps in any other, has been more the object of contemporary criticism than Mr. Southey'.[24] To opponents such as Byron and Hazlitt, the Poet Laureate's two careers (as poet and reviewer) were proof of his lack of political, moral and cultural integrity. They demonstrated his inability to stick to either one coherent identity or one set of opinions. Byron relished the irony that 'as a poet the Laureate' had been 'the butt of the *Anti-Jacobin*' and now as a reviewer 'he is the prop of the *Quarterly Review*'.[25] Hazlitt, too, was impressed by this incongruence, noting how Southey was the only person who could have written both the Jacobin play *Wat Tyler* and 'the article on Parliamentary Reform' in the *Quarterly*.[26] For him, Southey was best summed up as a 'prose-poet' a phrase that contained as 'many contradictions', ambiguities and instabilities of identity as the Poet Laureate himself.[27]

If Southey's work as a hireling of the *Quarterly* promoted the idea of his mobility and damaged him fatally in the eyes of political and cultural enemies, it had an impact in another equally significant way on his contemporary and longer-term reputations.[28] Although as his career developed he had moved progressively from writing unprofitable poetry to producing more-profitable prose, Southey never entirely abandoned his poetic career. He continued to publish new poems – and new editions of old ones – well into the 1830s. Moreover, in his role as a critic, Southey was careful to distinguish himself and fellow poet-reviewers from mere 'criticasters'.[29] In 1811, for example, the *Quarterly* reviewed his oriental romance *The Curse of Kehama* (1810).[30] The article was by Walter Scott, whose position as poet-critic was analogous to Southey's own.[31] Southey perspicuously noted that the review was not merely 'very friendly' but that 'the analysis of the story is given *in the language of a poet*.[32] He did indeed have much to be pleased with. Scott had lauded *Kehama* as a most 'extraordinary poem', a work of 'moral agency' that accomplished 'one of the chief objects of poetry – the elevation of the human mind'. In turn Southey was praised 'as a poet and a man' and described as peerless: 'no bard of modern days possesses a more abundant share of imagination, the highest of poetic qualities'. Southey also took note of Scott's juxtaposition of poetic licence with critical authority, his comparison between the poet who 'allows too little to the general principles of taste' and the critic who 'rests too much upon usage and authority', and his eventual championing of the former.[33] As he later explained to Scott, 'If we poets did but always enjoy the privilege of being tried by our peers, how much injustice and injury should we escape!'[34] Southey's sense of the superiority of the critic who was also a poet in the reviewing of poetry offers a rebuke to unpoetic reviewing contemporaries such as Francis Jeffrey.

Yet whilst the guise of poet-critic was one Southey was willing (through financial exigency if nothing else) to adopt, it was also one that concerned some of his poetry-writing associates. Indeed, resistance came from two of those to whom Southey was assumed by contemporaries to be closest: William Wordsworth and Samuel Taylor Coleridge. Southey's work as a reviewer had long made Wordsworth anxious. As early as 1799 he had dismissed Southey as a 'professional critic', adding that he 'care[d] little for the praise' of such men.[35] Wordsworth's comments were a response to the most controversial of Southey's early reviews, his appraisal of *Lyrical Ballads* (1798).[36] The product of more than just an angry moment, they established a pattern for what was to follow. Throughout his career, Wordsworth was, in fact, reluctant to think of Southey as a poet, or at least to think of him as being a poet that in anyway resembled or was akin to Wordsworth himself. He dismissed *Madoc*, published in 1805, as failing 'in the highest gifts of the poet's mind Imagination in the true sense of the word, and knowledge of human Nature and the human heart'.[37] (It is, of course, important to remember that these were Wordsworthian definitions of what made a 'great Master' and that other contemporary critics saw much to admire in Southey's poem, one of them comparing it favourably with *Paradise Lost*.[38]) Southey's move into other literary fields – biography, history and criticism (especially the latter) – gave Wordsworth further proof of what he perceived as a lack of commitment to the serious tasks of writing poetry and being a poet. Whilst Southey was not quite one of the 'Scribblers in Pamphlets and Periodical publications', he was also not exclusively devoted to a poetic career.[39] He was, as Wordsworth noted in 1822, capable of 'making regular progress in *many works* – his history of the Peninsular War, a Book on the Church in England, two Poems, with regular communications in the Quar^ly Review into the bargain'.[40] This lack of concentration on being a poet was a theme he returned to after Southey's death in March 1843. The inscription Wordsworth supplied for the monument to the Poet Laureate in Crosthwaite Church used the word 'poet' (and the lack of initial capitalization is signifi-cant) just once.[41] In a letter to Isabella Fenwick, he implied very strongly that Southey's ability to 'lay down his [poetic] work at pleasure and turn to any-thing else' meant that his poetry would not 'live [long] in the hearts of his Fellow creatures', that his posthumous fame would be negligible.[42]

Wordsworth's unease with Southey's combination of the roles of poet and critic was shared by Coleridge. The latter's doubts about Southey's poetry dated back into the mid 1790s, when the two ambitious young writers had met in Oxford, and did not allay with the passing of time.[43] They were expressed in letters and (characteristically) conversation. In 1811, for example, Henry Crabb Robinson reported Coleridge saying that he 'considered neither ... [Southey or Scott] as poets'.[44] Even Coleridge's public defences were marked by ambivalence. In the *Biographia Literaria* (1817) he inveighed against modern critics, men who 'degraded [books] into culprits' and judged 'the merits of a poet ... by accidental failures'.[45] Although he defended Southey against reviews conducted on the principles of 'arbitrary dictation and petulant sneers' and praised the 'versatility of his talents', he was lukewarm on the subject of his poetry,[46] noting that 'When future critics shall weigh out his guerdon of praise and censure, it will be Southey *the poet* only, that will supply them with the scanty materials for the latter'.[47]

Coleridge's words, of course, helped supply ammunition with which those critics he was purportedly defending Southey against could attack him. They have also had a more insidious long-term effect. The image of Southey as a sec-ond-rate poet, an image sedulously promoted by Coleridge and Wordsworth, has proven to be an enduring one. Only recently has this received opinion come in for revision by scholars keen to revise the canon and decentre Romanticism.

## Southey as a Literary Reviewer

Looking at what Southey wrote – rather than what was written about him by Coleridge and Wordsworth – brings home that fact that his work for the *Quar-terly* attempts to combine his two roles, staking his claim to be a poet-critic on his *own* terms. This emerges most clearly in the articles he wrote on literary topics – as opposed to overtly social and political subjects. The remainder of this essay will focus on a segment of his *Quarterly* reviewing largely overlooked in previous accounts: his essays on literature, in particular on poems and poets.[48] Southey's 'literary' essays for the *Quarterly* demonstrate the eclecticism of his concerns, as well as his interest in comparative literature. They range from reviews of newly-published poems and plays, through essays on literature in translation (especially from Spanish and Portuguese, two languages Southey was fluent in), biographies of writers and literary histories, to publications dealing with contemporary issues such as copyright law.[49] The essays respond to the wide range of books rolling off the presses in the early nineteenth century and act as a reminder to students buried in Austen and Wordsworth that Romantic period literary production was far from being the exclusive preserve of novelists and poets. In the context of Southey's own writing life and of his reluctance to write theoretical justifications of his works – his refusal to follow the example of Wordsworth's 'Prefaces' to *Lyrical Ballads* or Coleridge's *Biographia Literaria* – the essays also form his most extended engagement in literary analysis and extensive commentary on what it was to be a writer.

Southey's reviews frequently expose the incestuous nature of literary culture in early nineteenth-century Britain. Being personally acquainted with the author of a volume was no bar to appraising it in a journal and, indeed, a reviewer's anonymity could mask their connections to their subject. In January 1813, for example, Southey asked Murray if he might review Coleridge's drama *Remorse* 'while the play is a novelty, and criticism may contribute to assist it'.[50] His offer of extending his notice into 'a sketch of the history, or rather the degradation and decline of our drama' was not taken up, and the task of writing on *Remorse* fell to John Taylor Coleridge (the nephew – as opposed to the brother-in-law – of its author).[51] On other occasions, though, his attempts to puff the works of friends and acquaintances were more successful. For example, Charles Lloyd's translation of Alfieri (a work dedicated to Southey) was noticed by the Poet Laureate in the *Quarterly* for January 1816 and Thomas Southey's *Chronological History of the West Indies* given a 'hearty shove' in July 1828.[52]

At times Southey's personal knowledge of a writer assumed a ludic quality. In September 1812 the *Quarterly* published his assessment of *Count Julian: a Tragedy*.[53] Praising the beauty of some passages and noting the 'obscurity' of others, Southey (himself in the guise of unnamed reviewer) speculated about the identity of the drama's anonymous author:

> We should have no hesitation in ascribing ... [it] to the author of a narrative poem of which the story is strange and unprepossessing, and the diction obscure, but in which the higher requisites of poetry are incidentally displayed in an eminent degree ... but when an author has not thought proper to affix his name, the critic who gives it publicity assumes an authority to which neither the laws of courtesy nor of his profession entitle him.[54]

The essay's toying with ideas of anonymity (the chain of namelessness runs from author, to earlier 'narrative' poem and finally reviewer) is an elaborate game, one played out strictly in the public sphere. Southey later joked that he had been asked if he were the writer of *Count Julian*, 'a great compliment to me, and little discernment in those who proposed it'.[55] In fact he knew very well whom its anonymous author was – Walter Savage Landor, a poet he had long admired and a good friend for some years. His first acquaintance with Landor's work went back to 1798 when he read *Gebir* – the 'narrative' poem he refused to name in his review of *Count Julian*.[56] Southey's admiration for it was such that it was one of a handful books of contemporary poetry he took with him on his second visit to Portugal in 1800 – the others were Coleridge's poems (probably his 1797 collection), a volume of Robert Burns and the second edition of *Lyrical Ballads*.[57] However, he did not come face to face with *Gebir*'s author until 1808 when he met Landor during a trip to Bristol. Southey was immediately smitten, describing his fellow poet as 'one of the most extraordinary men whom I have ever seen, and certainly one of the ablest'.[58] In the following decade, Landor had a major impact on Southey's poetic career. Poor sales, especially of *Madoc* (1805), had discouraged the latter from publishing any new long poems and led him to abandon work on a long-planned and partially written romance centred upon Hindu mythology.[59] Landor encouraged him to return to it, offering (though his offer was rejected) to finance publication. The completed oriental poem – *The Curse of Kehama* – was published in 1810 and dedicated to Landor, but for whom 'it would never have been finished'.[60]

Southey reciprocated the favour by involving himself in Landor's *Count Julian* before its publication. The drama was on a Spanish subject: the story of the Spanish nobleman Julian who, after the rape of his daughter by the Visigothic King Rodrigo, supported a Moorish invasion of Spain. It was a subject that interested Southey too, and that formed the basis of his monodrama 'Florinda' and his fifth and final long poem *Roderick*.[61] The two poets swapped ideas for their respective works and compared notes over a third poem that dealt with the same subject, Walter Scott's *The Vision of Don Roderick* (1811).[62] In addition, Southey recommended *Count Julian* to John Murray, promising that if Murray published it he would 'review it, [and] make it the subject of as good an article upon the Drama as I am capable of producing'.[63] Murray accepted the offer and the scene was set for one of his publications (*Count Julian*) being reviewed in another (the *Quarterly*). Southey did not produce the large-scale essay on national drama that he had promised, but there is no doubt that he saw the tragedy as emerging at a crucial moment for British culture. It was, he told Landor on receiving a presentation copy of *Count Julian*,

> ... a work *sui generis*. No drama to which it can be compared has ever yet been written, and none ever will be, except it be by the same hand. You are the only poet whom it seems to me impossible to imitate ... What will be the reception of this drama? ... Being what we are, and living in an age when public criticism is upon

works of fine literature at the very point of *pessimism*, I can only guess that it will pass silently ...[64]

The *Quarterly* provided the vehicle by which Southey ensured that *Count Julian* – unlike so many other pieces of 'fine literature' – escaped the worst excesses of contemporary criticism and did not 'pass silently'.

Other essays for the *Quarterly*, also reviews of the writings of friends and acquaintances, displayed Southey's own refusal to be silent, allowing him to air his views on the debased nature of much contemporary 'public criticism', criticism, of course, from which he had suffered and continued to suffer. For example, in an 1811 article on James Montgomery's *West Indies* and *Wanderer in Switzerland* he offered a detailed analysis of the state of literature and literary criticism.[65] Contrary to the claims of some contemporary 'reasoner[s]', poets and poetry were, he noted, of use and value. Poets, even those of 'indifferent' ability, were not tricksters and no harm was done to society by 'the publication of [even] common-place verses'. Indeed most books of poetry were beneficial to the economy, sustaining trade and creating wealth:

> They defraud no person of his money, no one being compelled to purchase them; and they rob no one of his time, for no one is bound to read them, except the professional critic, who has no right to complain, because they furnish him with employment in his profession. On the other hand, even the reasoner, whose dim scope of vision never looks beyond the wealth of nations, will not assert that no good is done by it; for the letter-founder, the paper-maker, the printer, the bookseller, and all their dependents, confute such an assertion. The most humble volume that ever stole into oblivion from the press, has been useful to them.[66]

As well as reminding 'professional critics' that they owed their jobs to the writers whose works they reviewed, Southey attacked the 'less excusable feelings' and 'pure malice' that (he believed) actuated much contemporary criticism. The behaviour of a 'new school of critics', men who sought to destroy rather than foster the productions of 'meritorious individuals', had created an 'England' in which the poet 'has no honour'.[67] It was a situation that the poet-critic Southey was determined to combat – and the pages of the *Quarterly* provided him with a suitable arena. His choice of the phrase 'new school' is significant. It echoes the *Anti-Jacobin*'s earlier singling out of a dangerous 'New School' of poets, subversive writers whose work threatened national integrity and safety at a time of crisis (the French war and invasion scares of the late 1790s).[68] In his 1811 essay, Southey – identified by many as the leader of those Jacobin poets – appropriates and makes the phrase his own, a weapon in his own critical armoury rather than an insult to be used against him. He redeploys it to label the writings of what he as poet and critic perceived to be a much greater threat to English culture, a group of antagonistic, wrong-headed, contemporary critics, led by a vicious 'master'.

Unnamed in the actual review, the 'master' critic (and the term is deeply ironic) Southey had in mind was Francis Jeffrey, editor of the *Edinburgh* and author of a number of withering attacks on him and his associates.[69] Jeffrey's treatment of one of Montgomery's earlier publications was, so Southey affirmed, evidence of both his dodgy methods and his suspect morality.[70] To prove this case, he quoted at length from and paraphrased Jeffrey's offending article: with its description of Montgomery as 'very weakly, very finical, and very affected', 'burlesque description' of the poems, and playing off of the poet-victim against other contemporaries. Instead of passing over Montgomery's poems 'in silence', as he should have done if they were 'in reality as worthless as here represented', Jeffrey had resorted to indecent and heartless personal abuse, thus dragging criticism into the gutter.

Dangerous and immoral though the 'new school of criticism' was, Southey went further, portraying it as being out of step with public (national) taste and feeling.[71] This was a case he had been arguing for some time. In his 1810 review of James Grahame's *British Georgics* (1809) he had observed that, whilst 'the criticasters of his own country were pronouncing sentence of condemnation upon it', the same poet's previous work, *The Sabbath* (1804), 'had found its way from one end of Great Britain to the other; – it was in the mouths of the young, and in the hearts of the aged'.[72] This sense of what Jeffrey and his ilk had condemned being taken up by the reading nation (regardless of age or geographical location) was to be reiterated in Southey's 1811 essay on Montgomery. Rather than being consigned to oblivion by critical opprobrium, Montgomery's poems had endured and were 'still heard of, still read, and admired, and purchased, and re-edited'. The pronouncements of 'the careful guardian of public taste', Jeffrey, had been further confounded by the fact that – in response to public demand – 'a second volume [of Montgomery's poems] had been published'. The 'new school of criticism', then, imperilled both individual poets (the writers it victimized) and society as a whole – to read and believe the words of men like Jeffrey was to subscribe to false, dangerous doctrines and potentially to imperil the nation's well-being. In its place, Southey advocated a more humane, civilized way of conducting critical discourse, an approach that valued 'what is beautiful in thought, feeling, and expression'.[73] As his 1811 attack on Jeffrey shows, Southey's *Quarterly* essays provide an index of his extensive – and combative – engagement with contemporary culture. His own prescription for a more moderate form of criticism was not, however, one that he himself followed consistently. Indeed, more personal (possibly named) attacks on Jeffrey were excised from the 1811 essay by Gifford.[74]

## Southey Misattributed

What Southey produced for the *Quarterly* was controversial enough, but articles he did *not* write for the journal – or rather what he was wrongly accused by contemporaries of having written – were to prove equally important and controversial. Misattribution was an inevitable by-product of the early nineteenth-century culture of anonymous reviewing. Whilst anonymity (or the fiction of anonymity) could have an entertaining side, giving pleasure to the possessors of secret knowledge, as when Southey told a friend how he longed to see the *British Critic*'s review of *Roderick*, 'because it is written by John Taylor Coleridge (which, I believe is a secret; mind you that, Mr. Bedford!)', it could also have damaging consequences.[75] Anonymity that led to misattribution had the potential to do great harm within what was essentially a small literary community, fostering ill-feeling, antagonism and paranoia. Being accused of writing articles which he had not written was not unique to Southey, but the willingness of his contemporaries to *think* he was the author of something he was not is evidence of how closely some of them (especially those who did not share his politics) were prepared to identify him – or attempt to identify him – with the politics of the *Quarterly* and to use him 'as a convenient whipping boy in their own attacks' upon it.[76] Southey himself was very aware of this and hated it. As he explained to the Quaker poet Bernard Barton, his connection with the *Quarterly* meant that he had to 'endure a large portion of the grossest abuse and calumny for opinions which I do not hold, *and articles which I have not written*'.[77]

Misattribution caused particular problems in Southey's already troubled public and private relationships with a generation of younger poets, writers who, influenced as they may have been by his early works, found it hard to see the radical poet of the 1790s in the conservative Poet Laureate of the 1810s. For example, a review of Leigh Hunt's *Foliage*, published in the *Quarterly* for January 1818, attracted the attention of Byron and Shelley.[78] Though the review's author was John Taylor Coleridge, the two younger poets were convinced that it was by Southey. Byron, already incensed with the Laureate for spreading a story that he was involved in a 'league of incest', vented his fury in the (suppressed) prefatory materials to his new poem *Don Juan*. A 'Dedication' attacked Southey as a renegade ('my Tory ultra-Julian') and sexual inadequate ('quite adry, Bob!'), whilst a 'Preface' invited readers to presume that the 'Dedication' was the product of 'one who may have a cause of aversion from the said Southey'.[79] The Laureate, it added, was one who

> ... feeds the cravings of his wretched vanity – disappointed in its nobler hopes, and reduced to prey upon such snatches of fame as his contributions to the *Quarterly Review* (and the consequent praise with which a powerful journal repays its assistants)

can afford him – by the abuse of whosoever may be more consistent, or more successful, than himself – and the provincial gang of scribblers gathered round him.[80]

Byron's anger was also expressed in more indirect form. The Hispanic context
the reader was asked to imagine for *Don Juan* – the possibility that the poem's
narrator was 'either an Englishman settled in Spain – or a Spaniard who had
travelled in England' – represents his occupation of territory that Southey (one
of the most prominent Hispanists of the time) had long regarded as his own.[81]

  Shelley, who shared Byron's conviction, had even more reason to be enraged.
His own association with Hunt had been affirmed both by *Foliage*, which addressed
two sonnets to him, and by the author of the *Quarterly* article, who, although he
did not name Shelley, had referred to his expulsion from Oxford, marital break-
up and the 'atheist' inscription he had reportedly written in a visitor's book in
Chamonix.[82] Convinced that the article was by Southey and proof of his 'dreadful hatred', even Hunt's reassurances to the contrary failed to placate Shelley or
prevent him from committing precisely the same mistake just under a year later.[83]
The *Quarterly* for April 1819 contained a review of Shelley's *The Revolt of Islam*,
attacking it as the work of a 'friend' and disciple of Hunt, the 'least pernicious' of
a dangerous school of poets, but one who nevertheless the reader needed to be
cautioned against.[84] Revealing details of Shelley's time at Oxford and his private
life, the essay portrayed him as a would-be reformer who was, in fact, 'too young,
too ignorant, too inexperienced, and too vicious to undertake the task of reform-
ing any world, but the little world within his own breast'. Although the review's
unnamed author was once again John Taylor Coleridge, its subject – and victim
– became certain Southey was responsible. So strong was Shelley's conviction that
he wrote to Hunt (as he had done with the notice of *Foliage*) and began a letter to
the *Quarterly* 'which was apparently intended as an attack' on the Laureate.[85] He
also decided to confront Southey directly and in 1820 wrote to him.[86] His letter
ignited a brief correspondence, letters illustrating the political and religious chasm
that separated the two writers.[87]

  The reasons behind Shelley's willingness to misattribute hostile reviews to
Southey have been the cause of scholarly enquiry.[88] Yet, although the differences
between the older and younger writer have been well documented, their similarities have been underplayed. In October 1819, at the height of his fury over the
Laureate's supposed authorship of the review of the *Revolt*, Shelley wrote to the
publisher Charles Ollier. Asserting that 'Southey wrote the article in question',
he added that the 'only other remark worth notice in this piece is the assertion
that I imitate Wordsworth'.[89] The section of the *Quarterly* essay Shelley was referring to had described him as:

   ... an unsparing imitator ... he draws largely on the rich stores of another mountain
   poet [Wordsworth], to whose religious mind it must be a matter, we think, of perpet-

ual sorrow to see the philosophy which comes pure and holy from his pen, degraded and perverted, as it continually is, by this miserable crew of atheists or pantheists, who have just sense enough to abuse its terms, but neither heart nor principle to comprehend its import, or follow its application.[90]

Shelley defended himself to Ollier, noting that he had dealt with imitation in the preface to the *Revolt*. Citing the examples of Byron and Wordsworth, he asserted that it was inevitable that all writers 'of any particular age' were 'marked with' a 'certain similarity'.[91] What is notable about his observations is not their private responsiveness to a public critique, but their selectivity. They completely ignore a second writer whom the reviewer had accused him of imitating. Immediately before the section comparing Shelley and Wordsworth, the reviewer, spying another literary indebtedness, saw a kinship between the *Revolt* and the later works of Southey, though the tone of the former was 'less subdued, and the copy altogether more luxuriant and ornate than the original'.[92] Shelley's silence cannot be attributed to reluctance to being publicly linked with a writer of opposing political views. If this had been the case he would have also ignored the comparison drawn between himself and Wordsworth. His passing over of Southey reveals both unwillingness to acknowledge poetic indebtedness and a refusal to give credence to a similarity that other contemporaries had detected.

The Shelley-Southey relationship was, indeed, characterized by a vocabulary of likeness (as well as dissimilarity). On meeting the younger poet for the first time in late 1811, Southey had been struck by a strange kinship to himself. Shelley was, he told, friends, 'the very ghost of what I was at his age [20; Southey's age in 1794] poet, philosopher, & jacobin, & moralist & enthusiast'.[93] Shelley, whilst unwilling to be Southey's 'proselyte', had in turn expressed admiration for the older 'poet', 'claim[ing] to know large parts of *Thalaba* and *Kehama* by heart from his schooldays'.[94] Southey had, he observed in 1811, 'all that characterises the poet – great eloquence tho' obstinacy in opinion which arguments are the last things that can shake'.[95] (These features, of course, also characterized Shelley.[96]) Indeed his willingness to see 'the poet' in Southey (something Wordsworth was significantly more reluctant to do) both indicates his youthful regard for (and indebtedness to) the older man's writing and creates an implicit kinship between them. The definition of the 'poet' Shelley applied to Southey was, after all, was one that was equally applicable to Shelley himself.

Southey's poetic influence on Shelley was detectable in *Queen Mab, Alastor* and the *Revolt* (the oriental settings of the latter two echoing *Thalaba* and *Kehama*).[97] Even though his feelings towards the Laureate became increasingly fierce and his comments more 'abusive', this did not stop others associating them. The connection did not even have to be literary. In November 1817 Henry Crabb Robinson met Shelley for the first time at William Godwin's house.[98] Immediately he was struck by the poet's 'resemblance to Southey, particularly in his voice'.⁹⁹ By the time the *Quarterly*'s review of the *Revolt* appeared, in 1819, Shelley's determination to differentiate himself from Southey was complete – and resulted in his refusal to verbalize (let alone vocalize) about any possible kinship. Instead he expressed his opposition to the Laureate and his real – and imagined – *Quarterly* reviews in letters and (in more coded but nonetheless polemical form) in the preface to *Adonais*.

## Conclusion

In February 1823 Gifford, on the hunt for someone to review a volume of poems, admitted to Scott that there was no point approaching Southey because he 'declines Poetry – and has from the first' (*QR* Letter 237).¹⁰⁰ In fact, as this essay has shown, this was not quite the truth. Southey had from the very earliest days of his association with the *Quarterly* reviewed the occasional volume of poetry and had used his 'literary' essays to advance his view of the role of the poet-critic. Yet his 'literary' work for the *Quarterly* was increasingly dominated by his sense of being out-of-step with his contemporaries. As he explained to Bernard Barton in 1820:

> ... though I bear a part in the Quarterly review ... I have long since found it necessary, for reasons which you may easily apprehend, to form a resolution of reviewing no poems whatever. My principles of criticism, indeed, are altogether opposite to those of the age. I would treat everything with indulgence, except what was mischievous; and most heartily do I disapprove of the prevailing fashion of criticism, the direct tendency of which is to call bad passions into full play.¹⁰¹

Southey did not quite stick to his 'resolution' – continuing (occasionally) to review poems for the *Quarterly* until the early 1830s. Yet so high-profile and controversial was his reputation that it was, ironically, the *Quarterly* articles on the contemporary poems he did *not* review – the essays that were misattributed to him – that were most influential. These misattributed reviews – and the private and public ire they provoked – added fuel to an already large fire. They helped (especially when read alongside Southey's political essays) to confirm his opponents' worst opinions of him and gave added impetus – and literary-political edge – to other poetic, anti-Southeyan products such as the preface to Shelley's *Adonais* and the dedication to Byron's *Don Juan*.¹⁰²

# 8 ROBERT SOUTHEY'S CONTRIBUTION TO THE *QUARTERLY REVIEW*

## W. A. Speck

The *Quarterly Review* was launched by George Canning in 1808 as an antidote to the *Edinburgh Review*, which he considered to be defeatist in its attitude towards Napoleon. Southey's views on the Spanish uprising against Bonaparte, which had begun earlier that year, and the need for Britain to support it, coincided with Canning's. The editor of the new journal, William Gifford, therefore approached him through Grosvenor Bedford, a mutual friend, asking him to contribute to it. It was ironic that Canning and Gifford had previously lambasted the poet in the *Anti-Jacobin* in the 1790s, when they singled his verse out as specimens of 'Jacobin' poetry. But his politics had become much more conservative since then. His former pacifism, for instance, had been transformed into a vigorous call to arms against the threat from France. Now Southey agreed to write for the periodical, but with conditions. While he welcomed the opportunity to back the war effort, he was not prepared to become a government hack and support all its policies. As he put it to Bedford he wanted it to be made clear to Gifford that

> I despise all parties too much to be attached to any. I believe that this country must continue the war while Bonaparte is at the head of France, and while the system which he has perfected remains in force. I therefore from my heart and soul execrate and abominate the peace mongers.

Nevertheless he was 'an enemy to any further concessions to the Catholics'.[1] If the ministry introduced Catholic Emancipation, therefore, and required the *Quarterly* to support it, he would stop contributing to it.

Southey preferred to write reviews of books rather than overtly political essays. He had reviewed an eclectic range of titles in the *Annual Review*, to which he had contributed since 1802, only ending his contributions when the *Quarterly* was launched. The *Annual* was divided into several sections, such as 'Voyages and Travels', 'Theology', 'History, Politics and Statistics', 'Geography',

'Poetry' and 'Biography'. Southey's reviews appeared in most of them.[2] He was to display a similar eclecticism in the *Quarterly*. Between 1809 and 1839 he wrote nearly one hundred articles for the journal, establishing himself as one of its major contributors.[3] To comment on each of them would fill a volume. What this examination of them therefore focuses on is how far he managed to steer a course between supporting the policies of the ministry of which he approved, and defending his own views where they differed from the official line taken by the periodical.

His very first review, which appeared in Number 1 of the *Quarterly* (dated February 1809 but published on the first day of March), was on 'Periodical Accounts relative to the Baptist Missionary Society'. It opened with a sweeping passage on the early Church which implicitly repudiated Gibbon:

> The rapid progress of Christianity during the first ages of the Church, and its victory over the established forms of classical superstition, the schools of ancient philosophy, and the barbarous mythologies of the northern nations, were the united produce of the ardent piety and indefatigable zeal of the first preachers of the Gospel, and the blessing and assistance of heaven.

Southey's conviction that providence intervened in mundane affairs was crucial to his view of history. He referred to it when he managed to drag a reference to Napoleon into what was primarily a critique of the Particular Baptists' mission to India:

> India is perpetually in danger – not from Buonaparte – that would be the last object of his ambition – he is not idiot enough to believe that England is to be conquered there, nor is it for Asia that Providence seems to have appointed him its executioner upon worn out dynasties and degraded nations ...[4]

Another article on missionary activity, this time in the South Sea Islands, gave him the opportunity to expatiate on the state of nature. It betrays an intrinsic conservatism with its assertion that 'those savages have been found the happiest and least deteriorated in their moral nature, among whom society most nearly resembles the patriarchal system'. Some residual radicalism, however, can be detected behind his insistence that this system 'in contradiction to the sophistry of the Filmer school, has nothing in common with despotism, and however monarchy may end it always begins in violence and injustice'.[5]

An aspect of the *Quarterly* which Southey found unappealing was a tendency to be disparaging about the United States of America. Although he was increasingly disturbed by the development of democracy there, he nevertheless admired the American experiment and took every opportunity to extol it. One came up early when he was asked to review Abiel Holmes's *American Annals; or, A Chronological History of America from its Discovery in 1492 to 1806*. 'The

Americans have acquired a distinct national character', he claimed, 'the family likeness has been lost'. Nevertheless he concluded that 'there is a bond between us of blood and of language which no circumstance can break ... Nations are too ready to admit that they have natural enemies, why should they be less willing to believe that they have natural friends?'[6]

Early in 1810 Southey reviewed four works on Admiral Nelson which he dismissed with lofty disdain in five pages. He then proceeded to take up another forty narrating Nelson's career which became the basis of his most celebrated work, his biography of the admiral which appeared in 1813.[7] It can be said that Southey invented the image of Nelson as the supreme English hero. As Mike Barker put it recently, 'it is Southey who is responsible to a large extent for the common concept we have today of Nelson as the quintessential heroic figure'.[8] It also gave Southey another opportunity to extol the success of British arms against the French, one he took whenever he could in fulfillment of his accepting the invitation to contribute to the *Quarterly*. Thus later in 1810, in a review of *The Portuguese Observer*, he condemned the French occupation of Portugal following the flight of the royal family to Brazil in 1807. The concluding paragraph excoriated Napoleon and had a sting in the tail for his British admirers:

> Such has been the career of that imperial barbarian, that he obtains an amnesty for his old crimes by perpetrating new ones; and his perjuries and assassinations have ceased to excite astonishment in Europe because they are now looked upon as regular parts of his political system. Even in this country there are men who, when they are reminded of his guilt, think it a sufficient reply to tell us of his greatness; and would have us fall down and worship the golden image at the very time when the Spaniards are walking through the burning fiery furnace ... They are never weary of exaggerating the wisdom and the power of Bonaparte; – according to them it is still the English who disturb the peace of the continent ... Callous and cowardly sophists![9]

In his reviews of missionary activities he had contrived to get a dig in at Methodism, maintaining that 'of all forms of Christianity that of the Methodists is the least attractive and the most irrational'.[10] 'There are materials before me for another set-to at the Evangelicals', he wrote in January 1810; 'my intention is not to be angry with them, but only to dissect them alive'.[11] The review, of *Hints to the Public and the Legislator on the Nature and Effect of Evangelical Preaching* 'by a barrister' (James Sedgwick), appeared in November 1810. Unexpectedly it began by attacking Sedgwick's tract as 'a farrago of folly and falsehood'. Southey even defended the Methodists from his claim that they were antinomians, and credited them with evangelizing the poorer classes who had been alienated from the established Church. Yet it went on to attack the Evangelicals' and Methodists' magazines. 'Of these publications we have no hesitation in saying that they produce evil – great evil, nothing but evil.'[12] There may have been even more outspoken criticism, for Gifford 'cut out several passages from the article as first written'.[13] Southey took exception to Gifford's exercise of the editorial scissors, calling them 'castrations'.

He was even more offended when the editor commissioned John Wilson Croker, the First Secretary to the Admiralty, to tone down his next review, which was of *An Essay on the Military Policy and Institutions of the British Empire* by Charles Pasley. Croker took his job so seriously that he ended up writing all but the last four pages himself. Southey's conclusion to the article reinforced the basic message of the journal:

> Woe will be to us, and to Europe whose deliverance must come from us, and to lib-
> erty, and knowledge, and pure morals and true religion, which with us must stand or
> fall, if the government of this mighty country, in these momentous times, should be
> entrusted to men 'who talk of danger which they fear, And honour which they do
> not understand!'[14]

Despite Southey's complaints Gifford made substantial cuts to his very next review, of 'Bell and Lancaster's *System of Education*'. In 1806 he had praised Lancaster's system in the *Annual Review*, but now came down heavily in favour of Bell's, in direct opposition to the advocacy of his rivals in the *Edinburgh Review*. He had come to prefer Lancaster's system because Bell was Church of England whereas Lancaster was a Dissenter. 'The system of English policy consists of church and state', he asserted;

> they must stand together or fall together; and the fall of either would draw after it the
> ruin of the finest fabric ever yet created by human wisdom under divine favour. Now
> to propose a system of national education, of which it is the avowed and distinguish-
> ing principle that the children shall not be instructed in the national religion, is to
> propose what is palpably absurd.[15]

Southey was outraged with Gifford's cuts to his review, complaining that it 'would have been the heaviest blow the Edinburgh has ever received if all the shot of my heavy artillery had not been drawn before the guns were fired'.[16] He therefore proceeded to expand it to a pamphlet twice its length, *The Origin, Nature and Object of the New System of Education*.

Southey's willingness to review an astonishing range of books, and his ability to gear almost any topic to the *Quarterly*'s commitment to supporting the government, were both displayed in an article he contributed in 1812 on two books dealing with Iceland. He merely used their titles as hooks on which to hang rambling remarks on Iceland. These he concluded with the observation that the historian who recorded Britain's 'struggles and her triumphs should be destined to relate that, while she stood forward alone against the most formidable tyranny which ever yet assailed the liberties of mankind, her rulers found leisure to think of the distresses of a forlorn and suffering people' – the Icelanders![17]

His next review, of *Biographie Moderne*, was more directly relevant to the *Quarterly's* political stance. It appeared with the title 'Lives of Remarkable Characters who have Distinguished Themselves from the Commencement of the French Revolution to the Present Time'. 'To those readers who do not remember the beginning of the French Revolution it would be difficult or impossible to convey the feelings which they have excited in us', Southey remarked. He insisted that the first age of the Revolution, which he called 'the age of reformers', had been salutary, for 'many things in France required reform'. Unfortunately 'the intrigues of Orleans and his party, the patriotism of the reformers, and the mistaken philosophy of the republicans, ended in delivering up the country to the vilest wretches that ever disgraced humanity'. According to Southey, 'the chief cause' of the Revolution was that the French Court 'suffered (during the first heats) a set of journalists to abuse the liberty of the press – an abuse which must overthrow any government that permits it ... The government that suffers itself to be insulted with impunity is from that moment in danger'.[18] This was one of the lessons of that era which were relevant to Britain in 1812, especially following the assassination of the Prime Minister, Spencer Perceval. Southey wrote to John Murray, the publisher of the *Quarterly*, to say that the review was on

> a subject most mournfully well-timed. The direful state of the populace which this late deplorable event has disclosed, tho it may have surprised me less than it has done most people, has alarmed me more deeply, because I have long distinctly seen the causes which were at work to produce it ... I feel certain that unless the most vigorous measures be speedily taken against those who by their speeches and writings are instigating the mob to rebellion, it will be too late ... This danger I will show in the *Quarterly*. (QR Letter 125)

Later in 1812 he submitted one of his more celebrated essays, 'On the state of the poor'. 'It is an attack upon Malthus, upon the manufacturing system and upon the Cobbetts and the Hunts who have produced this Luddite feeling in the mob', and he informed a friend,

> the conclusion is to recommend modes of employment for those who want to work – further education upon a national establishment, military and naval schools to receive as many children as may be offered, extensive colonization, and those means of improving our own stock at home and advancing the human race of which the operation would be without contingent evil or inconvenience and the effect certain.[19]

This was to advocate state intervention on a scale few contemporaries envisaged. The article was scathing about Adam Smith's *Wealth of Nations*, which Southey dismissed as 'a tedious and hard-hearted book'. So far from endorsing the doctrine of laisser-faire, Southey proposed public works to alleviate unemployment: 'Better would it be for the state to build pyramids in honour of our Nelsons and

Wellingtons than that men who have hands and are willing to work should hunger for want of employment'.[20]

Where he was surprisingly 'progressive' in his economic notions, he was markedly backward-looking in his religious views. This became clear in his review of three books on 'The History of Dissenters'. 'Of all the blessings which have been vouchsafed to England', he maintained,

> the Reformation is the greatest. It rid us of Catholic idolatry, Catholic polytheism, the celibacy of the clergy and the abomination of auricular confession – an evil compared with which the monstrous fables and other anti-Christian institutions of the Romish church shrink into insignificance. The price we paid for the deliverance was a religious struggle which after more than a century broke out into a civil war, which the termination of that war mitigated, but could not quell, and which has continued to the present day.[21]

So Southey perpetuated the religious battles of the seventeenth century into the nineteenth.

In 1815 Southey made a pilgrimage to the battlefield of Waterloo. On his way through London he visited John Murray in Albemarle Street and left with him the proofs of a review of an article on the Duke of Wellington. In it he had sung his grace's praises: 'The personal behaviour of this great captain has been, on all occasions, as perfect as his conduct as a general; – to say that he is brave is to give him praise which he shares with all his army; but that for which, above all other officers, he is distinguished, is that wonderful union of the coolest patience with the hottest courage'.[22] When Southey returned from the Continent late in October he called again on Murray, expecting that the July issue would have been published and, with it, his article on Wellington. He was surprised to find that it was still in proof, but thought it could be because Murray wanted to include new material from his visit to the battlefield. But when three weeks later he received copy of half of the article, he was appalled to discover that changes had been made to it, some of which altered the sense of what he had written. Thus his assertion that Wellington had been surprised by the French had been dropped, and the claim inserted that there had been no surprise, while his acknowledgement that the Prussians deserved some of the credit for the allied victory had also been expunged. Southey protested to Gifford and to Murray, who informed him that the alterations had been made by Croker at the instigation of the Duke of Wellington himself. This came as a complete surprise, causing him to complain that 'I had been chosen as a fit mouthpiece for conveying falsehood to the public through an accredited channel'.[23] 'I will expunge all mention which I have made of the Duke's having been surprised', he conceded to Murray, 'but as to affirming there was *no* surprise and detracting from the Prussians, refusing them the praise which is their due, this I will never do, nor suffer myself in any way to be made instrumental in doing'.[24]

In 1816 Southey published another article on the poor, which was in many respects a sequel to the one he had contributed to the *Quarterly* four years earlier. He acknowledged that there had been an overall improvement in the standard of living, but denied that the lower classes had benefited from the general improvement. On the contrary, they were not only relatively but absolutely poorer than they had been two centuries earlier. Unless their condition also improved the outlook for society was perilous. Education of the masses was essential: 'The cost of national education is rendered so trifling by Dr Bell's intellectual steam-engine that the expense would present no obstacle'. The essay ended with another attack on Malthus.

> The better the people are instructed, the happier and the better they will become; the happier they are, the more they will multiply; the more they multiply the greater will be the wealth, and strength, and security of the state; and these maxims are as certain as the laws of nature and of God.[25]

Southey's contributions to the *Quarterly* became more overtly political. The one he published on 'Parliamentary Reform' in the October 1816 issue, which appeared early in the following year, revealed his growing conservatism. Thus Burke, whom he had previously reviled, was now extolled as 'this great statesman', while he dismissed the advocates of electoral reform as 'some weak men, some mistaken or insane ones, and other very wicked ones'.[26] Although reviews in the journal were unsigned, and therefore meant to be anonymous, those by Southey were well known to be his. Thomas Love Peacock satirized the tone of this article in his novel *Melincourt*, in which Southey appears as 'Feathernest', as asserting that 'we, and those who think with us, are the only wise and good men'.[27]

Despite the furore caused by his article on parliamentary reform, Southey continued to write political reviews. In 'The Rise and Progress of Popular Disaffection', which appeared in 1817, he insisted that there was a conspiracy to overthrow the government. The following year the *Quarterly* published his essay 'On the Means of Improving the People', in which Southey attributed pauperism to 'misfortune in one instance, misconduct in fifty'.[28]

How far his youthful radicalism had progressed towards conservatism can to some extent be traced by his changing attitude towards the Duke of Marlborough. In 'The Battle of Blenheim' he had published one of the more celebrated pacifist poems in the English language. The lines 'it was the English fought the French, / and put the French to rout; / but what they fought each other for / we never did find out',[29] sum up his view that the battle was meaningless. In 1820 he reviewed William Coxe's *Life of Marlborough* for the *Quarterly*. In the review he claimed that 'the battle of Blenheim ... is one of those few actions which have produced a change in the fortunes of Europe'. He lambasted the Tories of Anne's reign, whose opposition to the Duke of Marlborough played into the hands of Louis XIV, and applied their example to his own times: 'The effect produced in our own days by a more decisive victory upon a viler faction shows us that in all times party-spirit is the same and that it utterly destroys all true English feeling'.[30] This essay was reprinted in 1822 by Rivington and the Society for Promoting Christianity as the *Life of John, Duke of Marlborough, Abridged from the Quarterly Review*!

Another article which was reprinted separately, though not until after Southey's death, was on Oliver Cromwell, which appeared in the issue for July 1821. In it he professed his belief in providential intervention in history: 'The defeat of Charles [II] at Worcester is one of those events which most strikingly exemplify how much better events are disposed of by Providence than they would be if the direction were left to the choice even of the best and the wisest of men'. He concluded that Cromwell was 'the most fortunate and least flagitious of usurpers'.[31]

'Flagitious' was one of Southey's favourite adjectives. He used it again in a review of 'Gregoire – History of Religious Sects' when he attacked the Catholic Church for publishing legends as authentic biographies.

> This very romance of St Patrick (there is not a more flagrant one in the whole Acta Sanctorum, though there are many more flagitious) was published ... with an insolent appeal to its miracles and its authenticity against the Protestants. The Protestant, therefore, on his part, is justified in appealing to it as proof of the practices of the Romish church.[32]

The adjective occurred again in his 'Progress of Infidelity' in which he animadverted on the newly-coined word 'Liberal': 'we are thankful for the word – it is well that we should have one which will at once express whatever is detestable in principle, and flagitious in conduct'. The review admirably condenses Southey's views on the erosion of traditional beliefs in the eighteenth century. He blamed four writers in particular – Voltaire, Rousseau, Hume and Gibbon – for 'sapping the foundations of civil order and individual happiness'. 'The progress of irreligion in this country before the French Revolution was more extensive than it appeared to be', he observed.

> Still the unbelievers, compared with the population of the country, were not numerous, and public opinion was strongly against them. It was not till the standard of hell was triumphantly displayed in France, that they assumed the character of a party in the kingdom, avowed the whole extent of their opinions and the end at which they aimed, and began to corrupt the populace, as the revolutionists had done, whose example they were endeavouring to follow in all points. Clubs were formed, not in the metropolis only, but in small provincial towns, of deists and of atheists; debating societies were instituted for the propagation of their opinions, and the works of

Paine, Volney and Mirabeau were circulated in a form which put them within the reach of the lowest orders who could read.

Since then there had been a reaction among the higher ranks of society, who, Southey thought, were more religious than at any time since the Restoration of Charles II. The press, however, was continuing to subvert the beliefs of the lower orders. 'In what will these things end?' he asked, and answered:[33]

Not in the subversion of the throne and altar! Not in the irremediable ruin and indelible disgrace of this great, this glorious, this happy Kingdom! – but in enabling us to meet the danger by showing us where our weakness lies; in rousing the friends of the Constitution; in increasing the zeal and thereby the influence of the clergy; in causing a more vigilant execution of the laws; and in strengthening the bulwarks of the state; – in the exposure and shame and punishment of those whose machinations are directed against the institutions under which and through which England has risen and flourished, the punishment of those who carry on their attempts openly, and the confusion and perpetual infamy of those who proceed with more cunning but not with less guilt.

This was a message which the readers of the *Quarterly* were apparently eager to hear.

Southey had submitted this article for the January 1823 issue of the *Quarterly*. Unfortunately, late in 1822 Gifford's health deteriorated to the extent of serious thought being given to his successor as editor of the *Quarterly*. Southey recommended John Taylor Coleridge, the nephew of the poet, to John Murray. Because of Gifford's continuing health problems 'The Progress of Infidelity' did not appear until July. When it appeared it offended Southey's old friend Charles Lamb, who had published his *Essays of Elia* in January. Southey referred to them in his article, observing, in a draft, that Lamb's book 'only wanted a saner religious feeling to be as delightful as it was original'. On reflection he concluded that the adjective 'saner' was insensitive, given Lamb's mental illness, and changed it to 'sounder'. He later insisted that he intended 'to re-model the sentence when it should come to me in the proof; and that proof never came'.[34] Yet on 22 March he recorded that 'I have to-day received the proofs of my paper upon ... the Rise and Progress of Infidelity'.[35] Moreover when he wrote to Gifford in April he asked him not to cut the 'praise which is bestowed upon Elia ... It is written in kindness, and carries with it a monition, which may be felt as it is intended'.[36] Still, Lamb took offence at the comment on his religious feelings and launched a savage attack upon Southey, entitled 'A Letter from Elia', in *The London Magazine* that October. Southey felt so guilty about the unfortunate adjective that he replied offering to forgive Lamb if he would in turn forgive him for using it. The gesture was reciprocated. When Southey visited Lamb in his house in Islington that November they were emotionally reconciled.

As it happened Gifford's health improved, so Coleridge's appointment was delayed until 1824. That December, Gifford finally terminated his editorship of the *Quarterly* and Murray accepted Southey's recommendation of John Coleridge as his successor.

Southey had stirred up a hornet's nest with his *Book of the Church*, in which he had defended the Church of England as the bulwark of the Constitution against threats from Catholics and Dissenters. His scathing remarks about Catholicism had prompted some angry ripostes, which he responded to in turn in the *Vindiciae Ecclesiae Anglicana*. In it he drew attention to works which to him vindicated his strictures on the superstitions of the Roman Catholic Church. One, *La Vie et Revelations de la Soeur Nativite*, instead of incorporating in the book he decided to review for the *Quarterly*, since 'it will appear sooner, get into wider circulation, and have more effect'.[37] Sister Nativity, a French nun, died in 1798 after giving an account of her visions to an abbé. 'She was as ignorant as Joanna Southcott', Southey asserted, 'and very probably as diseased both in body and mind'. Her account was one of 'a series of impostures' by which 'the corruptions of the papal church have constantly been supported'.[38]

When it was published, in 1826, the editorship of the *Quarterly* had changed again. Murray had replaced John Taylor Coleridge with John Gibson Lockhart. Southey was aghast when he learned of this, writing to Sir Walter Scott, Lockhart's father-in-law, to protest about it. He felt angry on John Coleridge's behalf, having recommended him for the editorship. 'Murray probably thinks that I am bound by necessity to his *Review* and may be transferred with it, like a serf who is attached to the soil', Southey told Scott. 'He is mistaken.'[39] He informed John Coleridge that his replacement was due to Murray's 'double dealing'.[40] 'I lose by the change an editor whom I knew, and on whom I could rely', he observed, 'but I am released from any motive for continuing to work at that occupation longer than my own convenience may render necessary'.[41]

Southey thought that the political changes of 1827 would have an adverse effect on the *Quarterly*. Lord Liverpool, the Prime Minister, had a stroke on 17 February and had to resign. He was succeeded by George Canning, who, though a Tory, showed his willingness to ally with Whigs, which led four Tories to quit the Cabinet. Southey suspected that Canning was less in sympathy with the *Quarterly* than with the *Edinburgh Review*, which could well become the ministerial organ. He had himself been reconciled to Lockhart's editorship of the *Quarterly*, especially when he learned that John Coleridge had taken up the cause of Catholic Emancipation, so that if he had continued to edit the *Quarterly* Southey would have ended his contributions to it. Suspecting that Murray would fall into line with Canning and pursue a liberal policy, he wrote to warn him that 'if the *Quarterly* abandons those constitutional principles of Church and State which it has maintained another journal will be started upon them'.[42]

Lockhart, however, assured him that the journal would not change its political stance despite the accession to power of Canning and a coalition ministry.

Southey bolstered the *Quarterly's* Toryism with a critique of Henry Hallam's *Constitutional History of England*, which he dismissed as 'a sort of Whig's Bible'.[43] When John Murray asked him to tone down some of the severer passages in the review, Southey undertook 'to strike out any passage ... which bears the slightest appearance of angry feeling or of personal incivility'. He nevertheless thought that Hallam's book displayed 'the worst and sourest spirit of Whiggery throughout' and therefore deserved to be censured. 'My dear Murray, do not think me *prejudiced* because I hold clear opinions and have a strong sense of their importance', he insisted. 'This neither renders me unjust or uncharitable.'[44] When it appeared in the *Quarterly* for January 1828, Southey's review of Hallam's *Constitutional History* concluded that it displayed 'the spirit and the feeling of the party to which he has attached himself, its acrimony and its arrogance, its injustice and its ill temper'.[45]

Southey's main contributions to the political debates stirred up by Catholic Emancipation and parliamentary reform both appeared in the *Quarterly's* issue of January 1831. The first merits Southey's own judgement of it as 'one of the best political papers which I have ever written'.[46] He originally entitled it 'Letter to the People', preferring it to 'To the Lower Orders' because, as he explained to Murray 'though mainly intended for them it will allow of my addressing high and low'.[47] When it appeared it carried the heading 'The Moral and Political State of the British Empire'. It surveyed the course of events during the previous decade, providing Southey's judgements on its leading politicians. For the first time in the *Quarterly* the issue of Catholic Emancipation was openly addressed, for Canning and Gifford had suppressed it. Southey criticized Wellington and Peel for surrendering to those who advocated it, and sympathized with those who had resisted and felt 'disappointed by those in whom they trusted ... disappointed we say, preferring to use an inadequate rather than an offensive word, because we write in sorrow, not in resentment'.[48] Clearly he himself felt betrayed by Wellington, and especially by Peel. His main attack was on his now familiar targets of the ignorance of the masses and its exploitation by revolutionary demagogues.

The other article was a review of Dymond, 'On the Principles of Morality'.[49] Dymond had claimed that the middle classes were the most moral. At a time when this view was used to reinforce the agitation for their enfranchisement, Southey took issue with it. Against it he advanced the proposition that the upper class held the moral high ground: 'Possibly it might be found that more and greater temptations befall the man who is struggling for fortune than him who has always been in possession of it'. He proceeded to argue that the merchants and manufacturers had benefited at the expense of the lower class. Dymond's assertion that 'political power is rightly possessed only when it is possessed by the consent of the community' was also challenged.

> It would indeed conveniently dispose of all troublesome questions concerning kings *de jure* and *de facto*, and invest with clear right any ephemeral idol of a populace or of a nation ... but it would divest them also as easily for such a right, instead of being fixed upon the strong foundation of principles and laws, veers with the weathercock of public opinion.

Southey would have confined political power to those who had inherited it from their ancestors. Government by consent would produce 'instability, insecurity, disorder – an age of convulsions, anarchy and misery'.

Lest he be taken to have no sympathy for the plight of the poor, Southey went on to insist:

> Let us not be misunderstood. Inequality in the excess wherein it now exists in most European countries, and nowhere more than in our own, is a great and crying evil; and would be intolerable if it were irremediable; and will and must become so, if it be not remedied. The physical and moral condition of the populace must be greatly and essentially improved ... What must be done is to provide, not merely that none shall perish for want of necessaries, but that none, except through their own misconduct, shall be without the decent comforts of civilized life. The humblest occupations of honest labour ought to procure these.

He repeated his concern for the poor in the *Quarterly* for March 1832: 'During more than twenty years, it has been the constant doctrine of this journal, that the condition of our working classes must be physically and morally improved, if we would avert the horrors of a *bellum servile*'.[50] Indeed, Southey started to be repetitive about this as he had become about so many themes in his long service to the *Quarterly*. 'This Journal will bear us witness', he wrote a year later,

> that, for more than twenty years, we have insisted that ... unless the condition of the poor be improved ... (and till it be physically improved, it is in vain to look for moral improvement,) nothing can save this nation from a more tremendous subversion than history has yet recorded as a warning to mankind![51]

Southey's long stint effectively came to an end in 1834, though he contributed four more articles to the *Quarterly* between 1836 and 1839. He had always said that when he could afford it he would drop the hack work which had been essential for his 'ways and means' in order to concentrate on works he hoped would last. Thus he gradually phased out reviewing for the *Quarterly*, which he had been inclined to do anyway following several disagreements with John Murray. The last arose from an article which Southey had written on the Corn Laws, which had included a passage on Ebenezer Elliott, the 'Corn Law Poet'. Lockhart had taken the decision as editor to cut it. Southey was not particularly offended by this, but he was outraged when Murray paid him only £70 rather than the £100 he had been promised, on the grounds that his article was shorter than it should have been. Southey put it down to Murray's 'incoherent transactions', his euphemism for the publisher's drinking habit.[52]

Although Southey continued to contribute to the *Quarterly* as long as he needed the money, he did not sell out to it. He kept to his resolve to write only in support of those government policies of which he approved, and expressed opinions on others of which they disapproved. 'Feathernest', Peacock's pseudonym for him, was thus very far off the mark.

# APPENDIX A: LIST OF LETTERS

The editor supplied the essay contributors with his unpublished edition of the following letters. Throughout the volume, the letters are referred to as 'QR Letter', followed by the serial number supplied below. Acronyms employed in the list are defined in the key to abbreviations on pp. ix–x.

| Letter No. | Correspondents | Date | Source |
|---|---|---|---|
| 1 | John Murray to George Canning | 25 September 1807 | JM |
| 2 | John Murray to Anne Murray | 5 October 1808 | JM |
| 3 | William Gifford to George Canning | 12 October 1808 | Leeds WYL250 8 66a |
| 4 | Walter Scott to William Gifford | [25 October 1808] | JM |
| 4A | Walter Scott to William Gifford | [25 October 1808] | Morgan MA 426, ff. 59, 58 |
| 5 | Walter Scott to George Ellis | 2 November 1808 | Morgan MA 426, ff. 54–5 |
| 6 | William Gifford to Walter Scott | 9 November 1808 | NLS 3877, ff. 191–4 |
| 7 | George Ellis to Walter Scott | 11 November 1808 | NLS 3877, ff. 195–6 |
| 8 | John Murray to Walter Scott | 15 November 1808 | NLS 3877, ff. 200–3 |
| 9 | John Murray to Walter Scott | 17 November 1808 | NLS 3877, ff. 204–5 |
| 10 | George Ellis to Walter Scott | 22 November 1808 | NLS 3877, ff. 211–12 |
| 11 | George Ellis to Walter Scott | 29 November 1808 | NLS 3877, ff. 213–14 |
| 12 | John Murray to Walter Scott | 1 December 1808 | NLS 3877, ff. 215–16 |
| 13 | John Murray to Walter Scott | 6 December 1808 | NLS 3877, ff. 219–20 |
| 14 | George Ellis to Walter Scott | [18 December 1808] | NLS 3877, ff. 223–5 |
| 15 | William Gifford to Walter Scott | 20 January 1809 | NLS 3878, ff. 6–7 |
| 16 | William Gifford to Walter Scott | 20 February 1809 | NLS 3878, ff. 25–6 |
| 17 | John Murray to James Ballantyne | 27 February 1809 | JM |
| 18 | James Ballantyne to John Murray | 13 March 1809 | JM |
| 19 | William Gifford to George Canning | 15 March 1809 | Leeds WYL250 8 66a |
| 20 | William Gifford to Walter Scott | [c. 20 March 1809] | NLS 3878, ff. 239–42 |
| 21 | William Gifford to John Ireland | [May 1809] | JM |
| 22 | James Stephen to John Murray | 2 May 1809 | JM |
| 23 | John Murray to William Gifford | 12 May 1809 | JM |
| 24 | John B. Morritt to Walter Scott | 17 July [1809] | NLS 3878, ff. 90–1 |
| 25 | John Murray to William Erskine | 21 July 1809 | NLS 11000, f. 138 |

| Letter No. | Correspondents | Date | Source |
|---|---|---|---|
| 26 | William Gifford to William Erskine | 10 August 1809 | NLS 11000, ff. 61–2 |
| 27 | William Gifford to Walter Scott | 22 August 1809 | NLS 3878, ff. 121–2 |
| 28 | George Ellis to John Murray | 5 November [1809] | JM |
| 29 | William Gifford to Walter Scott | 20 November 1809 | NLS 3878, ff. 211–12 |
| 30 | William Gifford to Edward Copleston | 8 December 1809 | Devon 1149M, f. 74 |
| 31 | George Ellis to Walter Scott | 22 December 1809 | NLS 3878, ff. 232–3 |
| 32 | William Gifford to George Canning | 30 December 1809 | Leeds WYL250 8 66a |
| 33 | William Gifford to Walter Scott | 30 December 1809 | NLS 3878, ff. 236–8 |
| 34 | William Gifford to Edward Copleston | 3 January 1810 | Devon 1149M, f. 75 |
| 35 | William Gifford to Edward Copleston | [9 February 1810] | Devon 1149M, f. 114 |
| 36 | William Gifford to Edward Copleston | 17 February 1810 | Devon 1149M, f. 76 |
| 37 | William Gifford to Walter Scott | 17 February 1810 | NLS 3879, ff. 24–6 |
| 38 | William Gifford to Edward Copleston | [23 February 1810] | Devon 1149M (no folio no.) |
| 39 | William Gifford to Edward Copleston | [c. March 1810] | Devon 1149M, f. 113 |
| 40 | George Ellis to Walter Scott | 8 March 1810 | NLS 3879, ff. 29–30 |
| 41 | William Gifford to Walter Scott | 28 March 1810 | NLS 3879, ff. 50–2 |
| 42 | John Murray to John W. Croker | [c. 2 April 1810] | Iowa, f. 110 |
| 43 | William Gifford to George Ellis | 6 April 1810 | BL Add. MSS 28099, ff. 71–2 |
| 44 | William Gifford to Robert Southey | 18 April 1810 | NLS 2528, f. 7 |
| 45 | William Gifford to Edward Copleston | 21 April 1810 | Devon 1149M, f. 78 |
| 46 | Robert Southey to John Murray | 22 April 1810 | JM |
| 47 | William Gifford to Walter Scott | 30 April 1810 | NLS 3879, ff. 60–3 |
| 48 | William Gifford to Walter Scott | 9 May 1810 | NLS 3879, ff. 74–5 |
| 49 | William Gifford to George Ellis | 21 May 1810 | BL Add. MSS 28099, ff. 73–4 |
| 50 | William Gifford to Walter Scott | 24 May 1810 | NLS 3879, ff. 116–17 |
| 51 | John Murray to John Bristed | 8 June 1810 | JM |
| 52 | William Gifford to George Ellis | 12 July 1810 | BL Add. MSS 28099, ff. 75–6 |
| 53 | John Murray to Walter Scott | 28 August 1810 | NLS 3879, ff. 171–2 |
| 54 | William Gifford to George Ellis | 31 August 1810 | BL Add. MSS 28099, ff. 77–8 |

| Letter No. | Correspondents | Date | Source |
|------------|----------------|------|--------|
| 55 | William Gifford to George Ellis | 3 September 1810 | BL Add. MSS 28099, ff. 79–80 |
| 56 | William Gifford to George Ellis | 7 September 1810 | BL Add. MSS 28099, ff. 81–2 |
| 57 | William Gifford to Walter Scott | 22 September 1810 | NLS 3879, ff. 197–9 |
| 58 | William Gifford to John Murray | [24 September 1810] | JM |
| 59 | John Murray to William Gifford | 25 September 1810 | JM |
| 60 | William Gifford to George Ellis | 1 October 1810 | BL Add. MSS 28099, ff. 83–4 |
| 61 | John Murray to George Ellis | 2 October 1810 | Morgan MA 1441 |
| 62 | William Gifford to George Ellis | 16 October 1810 | BL Add. MSS 28099, ff. 67–8 |
| 63 | William Gifford to John Murray | [17 October 1810] | JM |
| 64 | William Gifford to Edward Copleston | 18 October 1810 | Devon 1149M, f. 79 |
| 65 | William Gifford to Walter Scott | 27 October 1810 | NLS 3879, ff. 227–9 |
| 66 | George Ellis to John Murray | 3 November [1810] | JM |
| 67 | William Gifford to George D'Oyly | 9 November 1810 | Wellcome S/11/1810/20 68126 |
| 68 | William Gifford to George Ellis | 15 November 1810 | BL Add. MSS 28099, ff. 85–6 |
| 69 | William Gifford to Walter Scott | 22 November 1810 | NLS 3879, ff. 262–3 |
| 70 | William Gifford to George Ellis | 26 November [1810] | BL Add. MSS 28099, ff. 65–6 |
| 71 | George Ellis to George Canning | [5] December 1810 | Leeds WYL250 8 62 |
| 72 | George Canning to William Gifford | 9 December 1810 | JM |
| 73 | William Gifford to George Ellis | 21 December 1810 | BL Add. MSS 28099, f. 87 |
| 74 | John Murray to Sharon Turner | [*c.* 24 December 1810] | JM |
| 75 | William Gifford to Walter Scott | 29 December 1810 | NLS 3879, ff. 289–92 |
| 76 | William Gifford to George Ellis | 31 December 1810 | BL Add. MSS 28099, ff. 88–90 |
| 77 | George Ellis to Walter Scott | 9 January 1811 | NLS 3880, ff. 1–2 |
| 78 | William Gifford to Edward Copleston | 9 January 1811 | Devon 1149M, f. 80 |
| 79 | William Gifford to George Ellis | 2 February 1811 | BL Add. MSS 28099, ff. 91–2 |
| 80 | William Gifford to Edward Copleston | 11 February 1811 | Devon 1149M, f. 81 |
| 81 | William Gifford to Edward Copleston | 17 February 1811 | Devon 1149M, f. 82 |

| Letter No. | Correspondents | Date | Source |
|---|---|---|---|
| 82 | William Gifford to James H. Monk | 25 February 1811 | Trinity C 11 1, f. 131 |
| 83 | William Gifford to Edward Copleston | 26 February 1811 | Devon 1149M, f. 83 |
| 84 | William Gifford to Edward Copleston | 9 March 1811 | Devon 1149M, f. 84 |
| 85 | William Gifford to Edward Copleston | 11 March 1811 | Devon 1149M, f. 85 |
| 86 | William Gifford to Edward Copleston | 12 March 1811 | Devon 1149M, f. 86 |
| 87 | William Gifford to Edward Copleston | 18 March 1811 | Devon 1149M, f. 87 |
| 88 | William Gifford to Edward Copleston | 11 April 1811 | Devon 1149M (no folio no.) |
| 89 | William Gifford to Edward Copleston | 13 April 1811 | Devon 1149M, f. 88 |
| 90 | William Gifford to Walter Scott | 17 April 1811 | NLS 3880, ff. 91–2 |
| 91 | William Gifford to George Ellis | 19 April 1811 | BL Add. MSS 28099, ff. 95–6 |
| 92 | William Gifford to Edward Copleston | 29 April 1811 | Devon 1149M, f. 90 |
| 93 | John Murray to John W. Croker | [3 May 1811] | Iowa, f. 40 |
| 94 | William Gifford to Edward Copleston | 31 May 1811 | Devon 1149M, f. 91 |
| 95 | John Murray to John W. Croker | 3 June [1811] | Iowa, f. 209 |
| 96 | William Gifford to Edward Copleston | 4 June 1811 | Devon 1149M, f. 92 |
| 97 | William Gifford to Walter Scott | 6 July 1811 | NLS 3880, ff. 151–4 |
| 98 | George Ellis to Walter Scott | 28 July 1811 | NLS 3880, ff. 209–11 |
| 99 | William Gifford to Edward Copleston | 4 August 1811 | Devon 1149M, f. 93 |
| 100 | William Gifford to Edward Copleston | 26 August 1811 | Devon 1149M, f. 94 |
| 101 | William Gifford to Edward Copleston | 3 September 1811 | Devon 1149M, f. 95 |
| 102 | William Gifford to Edward Copleston | 14 September 1811 | Devon 1149M (no folio no.) |
| 103 | William Gifford to Edward Copleston | 19 September 1811 | Devon 1149M, f. 98 |
| 104 | John Murray to John W. Croker | [c. late September 1811] | Iowa, f. 251 |
| 105 | George Ellis to John Murray | [c. late September 1811] | Iowa, f. 132 |
| 106 | William Gifford to Walter Scott | 6 October 1811 | NLS 3881, ff. 75–7 |

| Letter No. | Correspondents | Date | Source |
|---|---|---|---|
| 107 | William Gifford to Edward Copleston | 12 October 1811 | Devon 1149M, f. 99 |
| 108 | John Murray to William Gifford | 25 October 1811 | JM |
| 109 | William Gifford to Edward Copleston | 27 October 1811 | Devon 1149M, f. 100 |
| 110 | William Gifford to Edward Copleston | 29 October 1811 | Devon 1149M, f. 101 |
| 111 | William Gifford to Walter Scott | 30 October 1811 | NLS 3881, ff. 95–7 |
| 112 | John Murray to John W. Croker | [c. October 1811] | Iowa, f. 117 |
| 113 | William Gifford to Edward Copleston | 7 December 1811 | Devon 1149M, f. 102 |
| 114 | William Gifford to George Ellis | 12 December 1811 | BL Add. MSS 28099, ff. 97–8 |
| 115 | Robert Southey to John Murray | 13 December 1811 | JM |
| 116 | Peter Elmsley to William Gifford | 18 December 1811 | Westminster |
| 117 | George Ellis to George Canning | 21 December 1811 | Leeds WYL250 8 66a |
| 118 | William Gifford to Walter Scott | 24 January 1812 | NLS 3882, ff. 35–6 |
| 119 | William Gifford to Edward Copleston | 4 February 1812 | Devon 1149M, f. 105 |
| 120 | William Gifford to Edward Copleston | 12 February 1812 | Devon 1149M, ff. 103–4 |
| 121 | William Gifford to Walter Scott | 28 February 1812 | NLS 3882, ff. 87–8 |
| 122 | William Gifford to George Ellis | 3 March 1812 | BL Add. MSS 28099, ff. 99–100 |
| 123 | William Gifford to Edward Copleston | 3 March 1812 | Devon 1149M, f. 106 |
| 124 | William Gifford to Walter Scott | 14 April 1812 | NLS 3882, ff. 136–7 |
| 125 | Robert Southey to John Murray | 19 May 1812 | JM |
| 126 | William Gifford to Edward Copleston | 23 May 1812 | Devon 1149M, ff. 107–8 |
| 127 | William Gifford to Walter Scott | 29 May 1812 | NLS 3882, ff. 173–4 |
| 128 | John Murray to John W. Croker | [c. June 1812] | Iowa, f. 103 |
| 129 | John Murray to John W. Croker | [c. June 1812] | Iowa, f. 289 |
| 130 | William Gifford to Edward Copleston | 3 June 1812 | Devon 1149M, f. 109 |
| 131 | John Murray to John W. Croker | [c. July 1812] | Iowa, f. 249 |
| 132 | William Gifford to Walter Scott | 7 July 1812 | NLS 3883, ff. 41–2 |
| 133 | William Gifford to George Ellis | 15 July 1812 | BL Add. MSS 28099, ff. 101–4 |
| 134 | William Gifford to George Ellis | 20 July 1812 | BL Add. MSS 28099, ff. 107–8 |
| 135 | William Gifford to George Ellis | 3 August 1812 | BL Add. MSS 28099, ff. 109–10 |
| 136 | William Gifford to Walter Scott | [c. 4 October 1812] | NLS 3653, ff. 31–2 |

| Letter No. | Correspondents | Date | Source |
|---|---|---|---|
| 137 | William Gifford to Edward Copleston | 5 October 1812 | Devon 1149M, f. 111 |
| 138 | William Gifford to Robert W. Horton | 28 October 1812 | Derbyshire D 3155 M C 5925 |
| 139 | William Gifford to Edward Copleston | 28 October 1812 | Devon 1149M, f. 112 |
| 140 | William Gifford to Walter Scott | 9 November 1812 | NLS 3883, ff. 122–5 |
| 141 | William Gifford to Robert W. Horton | 10 December 1812 | Derbyshire D 3155 M C 5927 |
| 142 | William Gifford to George Ellis | 7 January 1813 | BL Add. MSS 28099, ff. 111–12 |
| 143 | William Gifford to John Murray | [*c.* February 1813] | JM |
| 144 | William Gifford to George Ellis | 16 March 1813 | BL Add. MSS 28099, ff. 113–14 |
| 145 | John Barrow to John Murray | 4 May 1813 | JM |
| 146 | John Barrow to John Murray | 24 May 1813 | JM |
| 147 | William Gifford to Robert W. Horton | 21 June 1813 | Derbyshire D 3155 M C 5932 |
| 148 | William Gifford to George Ellis | 30 June 1813 | BL Add. MSS 28099, ff. 115–16 |
| 149 | John Murray to Peter Elmsley | 7 July 1813 | JM |
| 150 | John Murray to John W. Croker | [*c.* August 1813] | Iowa, f. 67 |
| 151 | William Gifford to George Ellis | 1 November 1813 | BL Add. MSS 28099, ff. 117–18 |
| 152 | William Gifford to George Ellis | 13 December 1813 | BL Add. MSS 28099, ff. 119–20 |
| 153 | G. Leveson-Gower to Robert W. Horton | 19 January 1814 | Derbyshire D 3155 M C 5938 |
| 154 | William Gifford to George Ellis | 8 February 1814 | BL Add. MSS 28099, ff. 121–2 |
| 155 | John Murray to John W. Croker | [*c.* March 1814] | Iowa, f. 191 |
| 156 | John Murray to John W. Croker | 25 March [1814] | Iowa, f. 192 |
| 157 | William Gifford to John Murray | 25 March [1814] | Iowa, f. 97 |
| 158 | William Gifford to George Ellis | 14 May 1814 | BL Add. MSS 28099, ff. 123–4 |
| 159 | William Gifford to John Murray | [*c.* August] 1814 | JM |
| 160 | William Gifford to Francis Freeling | 22 November 1814 | Private |
| 161 | William Gifford to George Ellis | 2 December 1814 | BL Add. MSS 28099, ff. 125–6 |
| 162 | William Gifford to William Huskisson | 9 February 1815 | BL Add. MSS 38740, ff. 71–3 |
| 163 | John Murray to John W. Croker | [*c.* June 1815] | Iowa, f. 55 |
| 164 | John Murray to John W. Croker | 20 October 1815 | Iowa, f. 104 |

| Letter No. | Correspondents | Date | Source |
|---|---|---|---|
| 165 | John Murray to John W. Croker | 2 November 1815 | Iowa, f. 106 |
| 166 | John Murray to John W. Croker | 9 November [1815] | Iowa, ff. 222–3 |
| 167 | William Gifford to John Taylor | 12 December 1815 | Morgan PML 52349 |
| 168 | William Gifford to George Canning | 16 February 1816 | Leeds WYL250 8 66a |
| 169 | John Murray to John W. Croker | [February 1816] | Iowa, f. 206 |
| 170 | John Murray to John W. Croker | [February 1816] | Iowa, f. 276 |
| 171 | William Gifford to Walter Scott | 6 March 1816 | NLS 3887, ff. 17–18 |
| 172 | John Murray to John W. Croker | [c. April 1816] | Iowa, f. 129 |
| 173 | John Murray to John W. Croker | 18 August 1816 | Iowa, f. 131 |
| 174 | John Murray to John W. Croker | [c. December 1816] | Iowa, f. 66 |
| 175 | Robert Southey to John Murray | 13 December 1816 | JM |
| 176 | William Gifford to John Backhouse | 10 January 1817 | NLS 584, f. 175 |
| 177 | John Murray to John W. Croker | [c. 18 April 1817] | Iowa, f. 135 |
| 178 | John Murray to John W. Croker | [21 May 1817] | Iowa, f. 290 |
| 179 | John Murray to John W. Croker | [c. July 1817] | Iowa, f. 102 |
| 180 | William Gifford to John Murray | [16 August 1817] | Iowa, f. 94 |
| 181 | John Murray to John W. Croker | [18 August 1817] | Iowa, f. 246 |
| 182 | William Gifford to Walter Scott | 11 September 1817 | NLS 886, ff. 149–50 |
| 183 | William Gifford to George Canning | 17 September 1817 | Leeds WYL250 8 66a |
| 184 | John Murray to John W. Croker | [c. October 1817] | Iowa, f. 59 |
| 185 | John Murray to John W. Croker | 30 December 1817 | Iowa, f. 245 |
| 186 | John Murray to John W. Croker | [c. December 1817] | Iowa, f. 11 |
| 187 | George Canning to William Gifford | 26 April 1818 | Beinecke Osborn 2701 |
| 188 | William Gifford to Walter Scott | 30 April 1818 | NLS 3889, ff. 79–80 |
| 189 | John Murray to John W. Croker | [c. May 1818] | Iowa, f. 342 |
| 190 | John Murray to John W. Croker | [c. May 1818] | Iowa, f. 9 |
| 191 | John Murray to John W. Croker | 28 July [1818] | Iowa, f. 220 |
| 192 | John W. Croker to John Murray | 29 July [1818] | JM |
| 193 | John Murray to John W. Croker | 30 July [1818] | Iowa, f. 8 |
| 194 | William Gifford to John Murray | 6 August 1818 | JM |
| 195 | William Gifford to James H. Monk | October 1818 | Trinity C 11 1, ff. 134–5 |
| 196 | Robert Southey to John Murray | 7 October 1818 | JM |
| 197 | William Gifford to James H. Monk | 5 January 1819 | Trinity C 11 1, ff. 135–6 |
| 198 | William Gifford to James H. Monk | 6 January 1819 | Trinity C 11 1, ff. 137–8 |
| 199 | William Gifford to James H. Monk | 16 January 1819 | Trinity C 11 1, ff. 139–41 |

| Letter No. | Correspondents | Date | Source |
|---|---|---|---|
| 200 | William Gifford to John Backhouse | 28 January 1819 | Perkins |
| 201 | John Murray to John W. Croker | [29 January 1819] | Iowa, f. 244 |
| 202 | William Gifford to John Murray | [29 January 1819] | Iowa, f. 93 |
| 203 | William Gifford to John Murray | [c. 30 January 1819] | Iowa, f. 96 |
| 204 | William Gifford to James H. Monk | 30 January 1819 | Trinity C 11 1, ff. 141–3 |
| 205 | John W. Croker to William Gifford | 30 January 1819 | Clements Croker Letter book 8 |
| 206 | James H. Monk to Jane S. Hughes | 10 February 1819 | Trinity C 9 2, f. 1 |
| 207 | William Gifford to Edward Copleston | [c. 16 February 1819] | Northumberland ZAN/ M12/D5/ 138 |
| 208 | William Gifford to James H. Monk | [20 February 1819] | Trinity C 11 1, ff. 143–6 |
| 209 | James H. Monk to Jane S. Hughes | 28 February 1819 | Trinity C 9 2, f. 2 |
| 210 | William Gifford to James H. Monk | 4 March 1819 | Trinity C 11 1, ff. 146–7 |
| 211 | William Gifford to John Backhouse | 11 March 1819 | Perkins |
| 212 | James H. Monk to Jane S. Hughes | 12 March 1819 | Trinity C 9 2, ff. 3–4 |
| 213 | William Gifford to James H. Monk | April 1819 | Trinity C 11 1, f. 147 |
| 214 | James H. Monk to Jane S. Hughes | 15 April 1819 | Trinity C 9 2, f. 4 |
| 215 | James H. Monk to Jane S. Hughes | 23 April 1819 | Trinity C 9 2, f. 5 |
| 216 | John Murray to Thomas D. Whitaker | 10 May 1819 | JM |
| 217 | William Gifford to John Murray | [23 July 1819] | Iowa, f. 95 |
| 218 | George Colman to John Murray | [25 December 1819?] | JM |
| 219 | John Murray to John W. Croker | [c. April 1820] | Iowa, f. 275 |
| 220 | William Gifford to John G. Lockhart | 6 April 1820 | NLS 934, ff. 188–9 |
| 221 | William Gifford to Walter Scott | 18 April [1820] | NLS 142, ff. 28–9 |
| 222 | James Glassford to John Murray | 19 April 1820 | JM |
| 223 | John W. Croker to John Murray | 13 July 1820 | JM |
| 224 | John Murray to John W. Croker | [15 July 1820] | Iowa, ff. 227–8 |
| 225 | John Murray to John W. Croker | 1 September 1820 | JM |
| 226 | William Gifford to George Canning | 3 October [1820] | Perkins |
| 227 | William Gifford to George Canning | 13 January 1821 | Perkins |
| 228 | John Murray to John W. Croker | [May 1821] | Iowa, f. 65 |
| 229 | John Murray to John W. Croker | [c. May 1821] | Iowa, f. 98 |
| 230 | William Gifford to John Murray | [28 December 1821] | JM |

| Letter No. | Correspondents | Date | Source |
|---|---|---|---|
| 231 | John Murray to John W. Croker | [*c.* 1822] | Iowa, f. 77 |
| 232 | William Gifford to Edward Copleston | 4 January 1822 | NLW 21743C 17 4 |
| 233 | John Murray to John W. Croker | [*c.* April 1822] | Iowa, f. 56 |
| 234 | William Gifford to Edward Copleston | 27 June [1822] | NLW 21743C 17 1 |
| 235 | Francis Cohen to John Murray | 13 November 1822 | JM |
| 236 | William Gifford to George Canning | 19 December 1822 | Leeds WYL250 8 66a |
| 237 | William Gifford to Walter Scott | 13 February 1823 | NLS 3896, ff. 44–5 |
| 238 | Hudson Lowe to Gideon Gorrequer | 16 February 1823 | PRO J 76 7 1, f. 5 |
| 239 | Gideon Gorrequer to John Murray | 20 February 1823 | PRO J 76 7 1, f. 20 |
| 240 | Gideon Gorrequer to Comte de Montholon | 26 February 1823 | PRO J 76 7 1, f. 26 |
| 241 | John Murray to Gideon Gorrequer | [1 March 1823] | PRO J 76 7 1, f. 30 |
| 242 | Gideon Gorrequer to John Murray | 5 March 1823 | PRO J 76 7 1, f. 35 |
| 243 | Walter Scott to William Gifford | 23 March 1823 | Houghton S 59M–4 |
| 244 | John Murray to John W. Croker | [March 1823] | Iowa, f. 280 |
| 245 | John Murray to John W. Croker | [March 1823] | Iowa, f. 279 |
| 246 | John Murray to John W. Croker | 28 March 1823 | Iowa, f. 100 |
| 247 | John Murray to John W. Croker | [31 March 1823] | Iowa, f. 340 |
| 248 | John T. Coleridge to John Murray | 6 May 1823 | JM |
| 249 | John Murray to John T. Coleridge | 6 May 1823 | JM |
| 250 | William Haygarth to John Murray | 22 June 1823 | JM |
| 251 | William Gifford to Edward Copleston | [*c.* 10 July 1823] | NLW 21743C / 17 2 17 3 |
| 252 | John Barrow to John Murray | 18 August 1823 | JM |
| 253 | William Gifford to John Murray | [September 1823] | JM |
| 254 | John Barrow to John Murray | 12 October 1823 | JM |
| 255 | John Murray to William Haygarth | 10 December 1823 | JM |
| 256 | Reginald Heber to [Unidentified] | [*c.* late 1823] | Liverpool |
| 257 | William Gifford to George Canning | 23 April 1824 | Leeds WYL250 8 66a |
| 258 | William Gifford to Walter Scott | 29 August 1824 | NLS 3898, ff. 92–3 |
| 259 | John Murray to William Gifford | 16 September 1824 | JM |
| 260 | John W. Croker to John Murray | 12 October 1824 | JM |
| 261 | John T. Coleridge to John Murray | 21 September 1825 | JM |
| 262 | John. G. Lockhart to John W. Croker | 16 November [1825] | Clements Croker Letter book 1 |
| 263 | John T. Coleridge to John Murray | 12 December 1825 | JM |
| 264 | John T. Coleridge to John Murray | 21 December 1825 | JM |
| 265 | John T. Coleridge to John Murray | late December 1826 | JM |
| 266 | John T. Coleridge to John Murray | 9 February 1826 | JM |

| Letter No. | Correspondents | Date | Source |
|---|---|---|---|
| 267 | Robert Gooch to John Murray | May 1826 | JM |
| 268 | John Murray III to Charles J. Monk | 29 March [1875] | JM |

# APPENDIX B: TRANSCRIPTION
## OF KEY LETTERS

This appendix consists of the editor's transcription of a number of letters that are often quoted and cited in the present volume. The transcribed letters are, by serial number, *QR* Letters 1, 2, 3, 4, 6, 7, 8, 28, 29, 40, 51, 58, 59 and 66. (Concerning the serial numbers, see Appendix A.)

## 1. John Murray to George Canning[1]

Bookseller – / 32 Fleet Street / London / 25 September 1807

SIR

I venture to address you upon a subject that is not perhaps undeserving of one moment of your attention.

There is a work entitled the Edinburgh Review, written with such unquestionable talent that it has already obtained an extent of circulation not equalled by any similar publication. The principles of this work are however so radically bad, that I have been led to consider the effect which such sentiments so generally diffused, are likely to produce; and to think that some means equally popular ought to be adopted to counteract their dangerous tendency. But the publication in question is conducted with such high and decisive authority by *the Party* of whose opinions it is the organ, that there is little hope of producing against it any effectual opposition, unless it arise from you Sir, and your friends – Should you Sir think the idea worthy of encouragement I should with equal pride and willingness engage my arduous exertions to promote its success, but as my object is nothing short of producing a work of the greatest talent and importance, I shall entertain it no longer if it be not so fortunate as to obtain the high patronage which I have thus Sir taken the liberty to solicit.

Permit me sir to add that the person who thus addresses you is no adventurer, but a man of some property inheriting a business that has been established for nearly a century. I therefore trust that my application will be attributed to its proper motives, and that your goodness will at least pardon its intrusion.

I have the honour to be Sir / Your most humble and most obedient servant
John Murray[2]

## 2. John Murray to Anne Murray[3]

Edinburgh. 5 October 1808 / Wednesday Evening 6 o'clock

My dearest Annie

I returned today about 3 o'clock from my visit to Mr Scott and had the pleasure of finding your letter which would have been more agreeable perhaps if you had said something about your own health and my sons and if you had told me what you had been about and where visiting – but I presume that you continue well and are content.

Upon reading your letter I really began to feel that I had been rather dilatory of late in writing to my dearest girl but it is as she supposes my time has been completely engrossed by business and engagements. I wrote you a few hasty lines on Monday from Ashiestiel[4] when I had arrived on Sunday intending to leave it the next day but Mr Scott was pressing for my remaining longer and I was too happy in the opportunity of improving my acquaintance with him not to remain. A very rich literary man who lives not far from Hawkestone in Shropshire Mr Heber was on a visit to Mr Scott also. On the Monday Mr S. took us along that most interesting walk to Newark Tower – the Braes of Yarrow and other places celebrated in his poem[5] made even more interesting to us by being shewn there by the poet himself. We set out immediately after my short letter to you for which they waited and we did not return until 5 o'clock – it was a truly delightful walk – the evening was passed in most charming conversation in which both Mr Scott and Mr Heber excel – yesterday Mr S. took Mr Heber and myself in his carriage and Mr Ballantyne rode on the Dickey – to Holy Melrose which he took us over and shewed us all these beauties even the hasty look of it which I took upon a former yet more interesting occasion, had not allowed me to remark.[6] In our way we passed Mr Bruces who happened to be standing in the Park (the father I mean). Mr Scott knew and bowed to him and I did the like but he could not have recollected me, as I never saw him but the day he dined at Mr Allens when you were there. We passed also Lord Somervilles where Mr and Mrs Somerville are now staying – but to my great regret I could not call upon either. When Mr Ballantyne and I left Mr Scott and Mr Heber at Melrose and traveled to Kelso – my first attention was to secure the room where my dearest love and I rested once before and I did not sleep she will believe me without a thousand thoughts of her whom I now love a thousand times more dearly than when we were there together. We passed the day tolerably agreeably as the Mrs Ballantynes whom you know came to see us; and this morning at Six we set out for Edinburgh. I am truly happy in being able to assure you of the most complete satisfaction which I derive from my visit to Mr Scott and it has now realized or [is] likely to do so, all that had been agitating in my mind for this last Twelve months and of which you shall know the particulars when we meet. I arrived so late today that I can not set out tomorrow, but positively I will quit Edinburgh for Bridgenorth on Friday and I will hope to embrace my dearest wife and kiss my dearest boy on Monday at the latest –[7]

My most dear Girl / your faithful husband / John Murray

## 3. William Gifford to George Canning[8]

12 October 1808 / James Street

MY DEAR CANNING

I perfectly agree with the Lord Advocate as to the pernicious tendency of the Edinburgh Review not only in this country, but in Germany where the scoundrel Professors are not yet cured of their Jacobinism.

– I think too that a better plan cannot be proposed than to set Scotchmen against Scotchmen, and that if good and true men can be found, very favourable effects will be produced. As to our Reviews, they are worse than ever. The Critical is fallen into the hands of a set of mischievous and hot headed boys, the Hodgsons and Drurys, &c, who are emulating the worst parts of the Edinburgh Review. The Monthly is coolly malignant and those that should be serviceable, the British Critick and the Anti-J[acobin] are conducted by time serving mawkish drivellers. So much for the necessity of something better.[9]

Now as to what I can do. I am, like Othello, declined into the vale of years,[10] and from nature and habit, very inert. Yet, such is my anxiety to further the cause I love, that if no more be wanted than an Editor who would arrange and overlook the various articles, and carry them through the press, I will, while you continue in Office, rouse myself in my elbow chair, and undertake it. I do this, because I know of no other whom you could securely trust – with me, you are perfectly safe.

If, then, this be what is wanted by these gentlemen, and my services are accepted; it must be understood that for the sake of consistency and many other urgent causes, I must be endowed with a sort of Dictatorial power over what comes before me. I will use it with lenity, but with the strictest vigilance.

If, however, an Editor be wanted to take a leading part in the composition, I must then reluctantly decline it on the score of inability. The business of revising, altering, occasionally adding, and finally carrying a work of this kind through the press will occupy fully as much time as I can ever promise myself.

I may add here, en passant, that I have declined, several times, very advantageous offers that have been made me for this very occupation: but I did not like the men, nor, altogether, the objects in view. – Frankly, the present is the most promising plan that has been presented to me. I do not know the strength of Walter Scott in criticism; but have no doubt that a competent body of young *aspirants* may be found at Glasgow and Edinburgh, to produce a very respectable and serviceable work.

Perhaps I have given you all this trouble in vain – When you hear more you will let me know; meanwhile, I shall preserve the secret.[11]

I hope you have ordered the Capt. that carries out Lord and Lady Holland to bore a hole in the bottom of the ship a few leagues from the land. I hate those opposition Riders: Buonaparte has an agent in every one of them. N. B. Perhaps it may be sufficient to drown the lady.

I ought to thank you for thinking of Belgrave Hoppner.[12] You have made him and his friends very happy, and I hope the young man will do his part to prove his sense of your kindness. Ever most truly yours

Wm Gifford

## 4. Walter Scott to William Gifford[13]

[25 October 1808]

SIR

By a letter from the Lord Advocate of Scotland in consequence of a communication between his Lordship and Mr Canning on the subject of a new Review to be attempted in London I have the pleasure to understand that you have consented to become the editor a point which in my opinion goes no small way to insure success to the undertaking. In offering a few observations on the details of such a plan I only obey the commands of our distinguished friends without having the vanity to hope I can point out any thing of consequence which must not have readily occurred to a person of Mr. Giffords literary experience and eminence. The task however having been so imposed on me I beg permission to offer my sentiments in the miscellaneous way in which they occur to me.

The extensive reputation and circulation of the Edinburgh Review is chiefly owing to two circumstances. First that it is entirely uninfluenced by the Booksellers who have contrived to make most of the other reviews mere vehicles for advertising and puffing off their own publications or running down those of their rivals. Secondly the very handsome recompense which the Editor not only holds forth to his regular assistants but actually forces upon those whose rank and fortune make it a matter of indifference to them. The Editor to my knowledge acts on the principle that even Czar Peter working in the trenches must accept the pay of a common soldier. This general rule removes all scruple of delicacy and fixes in his service a number of contributors who might otherwise have felt reluctance to accept of compensation for their labours even the more because that compensation was a matter of convenience to them. There are many young men of talent and enterprize who are extremely glad of a handsome apology to work for fifteen or twenty guineas, upon whose gratuitous contributions no reliance could be placed and who nevertheless would not degrade themselves by being paid labourers in a work where others ~~only laboured~~ <wrote> for honour <alone>. From this I deduce two points of doctrine first that the projected work must be considerd as independent of all bookselling influence secondly that the contributors must be handsomely recompensed and that it be a rule that each shall accept of the price of his labour. Mr. John Murray of Fleetstreet a young bookseller of capital and enterprize and who has more good sense and propriety of sentiment than fall to the share of most of his brethren paid me a visit some time ago at Ashiestiel and as I found he had held some communication with Mr. Canning (altho indirectly) I did not hesitate to give him my sentiments on these points of the plan and I found his ideas most liberal and satisfactory.

The Office of Editor supposing all preliminaries arranged is of such consequence that had you not been pleased to undertake it I fear the project might have fallen wholly to the ground. He must be invested with the unlimited power of controul for the purpose of selecting curtailing and correcting the contributions; and as the person immediately responsible to the Public and to the Bookseller that each Number shall be published in its due time it will be the Editors duty to consider and settle the articles of which ~~each~~ it shall consist and to take early measures for procuring them from the persons best qualified to write upon the several subjects of criticism. And this you will find so difficult if entirely entrusted to auxiliaries that I foresee with pleasure you will be soon compelled to appear yourself (occasionally at least) in the field. At the same time if you think my services worth acceptance as a sort of Jackal or Lions provider I will do all in my power to assist in this troublesome department of Editorial duty. But there is another point of consequence besides the task of providing and arranging materials for each number. One very successful expedient of the Edinr. Editor and on which his popularity has in some measure risen is the art of giving life and interest even to the duller articles of his Review. He receives for example a criticism upon a work of deep research from a person who has studied the book and understands the subject and if it happens to be written which may often be the case in a tone of stupefying mediocrity he renders it palatable by a few lively paragraphs or entertaining illustrations of his own or perhaps by generalising and systematising the knowledge which it contains. By this sort of *fineering*[14] he converts without loss of time or hindrance of business an unmarketable commodity into one which from its general effect and spirit is not likely to disgrace those among which it is placed. Such exertions on the part of an Editor are indispensable to a well conducted review for those who possess the knowledge necessary to review books of research or of abstruse disquisition are sometimes unable to put their criticisms however just into a readable far less a pleasant or captivating shape and as their science can not be obtained 'for the nonce' by one capable of writing well the only remedy is that a man of talent for composition should revise their lucubrations. And I should hope many friends and well wishers to the undertaking would be disposed to assist in this part of the task and altho they might not have leisure to write themselves might yet revise and correct such articles.

Permit me to add that you Sir possess in a peculiar degree a facility of the greatest consequence to the undertaking in having access to the best sources of political information. It would not certainly be advisable that the work should in its outset assume exclusively a political character. On the contrary the articles upon science and miscellaneous literature ought to be such as may challenge comparison with the best of contemporary reviews. But as the real reason of instituting the publication is the disgusting and deleterious doctrine with which the most popular of these periodical works disgraces its pages it is essential to consider how opposite and sounder principles can be most advantageously brought forward. On this ground I hope it is not too much to expect from those who have the power of befriending us in this respect that they should upon topics of national interest furnish the Reviewer confidentially and through the medium of the Editor with accurate views of points of fact so far as they are fit to be made public. This is the most delicate yet most essential part of our scheme. On the one hand it is certainly not to be understood that we are to be tied down to advocate upon all occasions and as matter of course the cause of administration. Such indiscriminate support and dereliction of independence would prejudice both ourselves and our cause in the eye of the public. On the other hand the work will obtain a decided ascendance over all competition so soon as the public shall learn (not from any vaunt of the conductors but from their own observation) that upon political subjects the new critics are possessed of early and of accurate information. The opposition have regularly furnished the Edinburgh review with this command of facts so far as they themselves possessed them and surely you bring dear Sir enjoying the confidence of Mr. Canning and other persons in power and in defence of whose principles we are buckling our armour may safely expect to be intrusted with the political information necessary to give credit to the work and with the task of communicating it to those whom you may chuse to employ in laying it before the public.

Concerning the mode and time of publishing the Review perhaps you will judge a quarterly publication most advisable. It is difficult to support one of more frequent recurrence both on account of the want of important books and the time necessary to collect valuable materials. The name is of some consequence at least in Mr. Murrays estimation, for myself I think any one which has little pretension might serve the turn. The English Review for example once conducted by Gilbert Stewart[15] might be revived under your auspices. The search after regular correspondents whose contributions can be relied upon ought to be begun but should not stop the publication of the first Number. I am not afraid of finding many such when the reputation of the work has been decidedly established by three or four numbers of the very first order. Besides hunting about for those persons would make the design public which should if possible be confined to persons worthy of trust for it will have a double effect if the first Number comes on the public by surprize without being prejudiced either by the unreasonable expectation of friends or the artifices and misrepresentations of the enemy. The first Number should be out in January if possible and might contain the following <political> articles Foxes history Grattans Speeches and any book or pamphlet which could give occasion for a distinct and enlightened view of Spanish affairs. This last alone would establish the character of the work. The lucubrations of the Edinburgh Review on that topic have done the work great injury with the public and I think the sale of the publication might be reduced at least one half by the appearance of a rival review which with pretensions to the same height of literary talent and independence of character should speak a political language more familiar to the British ear than that of subjugation to France. After all the matter is become very serious. From eight to nine thousand copies of that review are quarterly dispersed and with all deference to the information and high talents of the Editor (which nobody can think of more highly than I do) much of this popularity is owing to their <its> being the only respectable and independant publication of the kind. In Edinburgh or I may say in Scotland there is not one out of twenty who reads the work that agrees in political opinion with the Editor, but it is ably conducted and how long the generality of readers will continue to dislike the strain of politics so artfully mingled with topics of information and amusement is worthy of deep consideration. But I am convinced it is not too late to stand in the breach. The first Number of our proposed Review if conducted with ability if it can be compiled without any the plan taking wind and if executed with the talent which may reasonably [be] expected will burst among the Whigs (as they call themselves) like a bomb. From the little observation I have made I think they suffer peculiarly under cool sarcastic ridicule accompanied by dispassionate argument. Having long had a sort of exclusive occupation of the press owing to the negligence of all literary assistance on the part of those who thought their good cause should fight its own battle they seem to feel with great acuteness any appeal to the reading public like champions who having been long accustomed to push have lost the art of parrying. Now suppose that upon a foe of this humour our projected work steals out only drawing the attention of the public by the accuracy of its facts and the stile of its execution without giving them the satisfaction of bidding a public defiance I conceive that that their indignation expressd probably through the Edinr. Review will soon give us an opportunity of coming to close quarters with that publication should it be thought advisable and that with a much better grace than were we to announce a previous determination of hostility. In the mean while I am for gliding into a state of hostility without a formal declaration of war and if our forces for one or two numbers be composed of volunteers and amateurs we will find it easy when our arms have acquired reputation to hire troops of condottieri and to raise and discipline regular forces of the line. You are a much better Judge than I can be who are fit to be put into the van of the battle – You have the Ellis's the Roses cum plurimis aliis – we have lost a host in Mr. Frere and can only hope he is serving the common cause more effectually in another capacity. You can never want scholars while Oxford stands where it did. Richard Heber was with me during Murrays visit and knowing his zeal for the good cause I availd myself of his advice: His brother Reginald would be a most excellent coadjutor and I doubt not to get his assistance. I believe I can command some respectable assistance here but I rely much on that of Mr. William Erskine the Advocates brother in law and my most intimate friend. I think we can get you both some scientific articles and some Scotch metaphysics which you know are fashionable however deservedly or otherwise. My own studies have been rather limited but I understand in some sort literary antiquities and history and have been reckoned a respectable tirailleur in the quizzing department of the Edinr. Review <in which I wrote occasionally> untill these last two years when its tone of politics became so violent; I only mention this lest you should either estimate my talents by my zeal (which would occasion great disappointment) or think me like many good folks more ready to offer advice than assistance. Mr. Murray seems to count upon Malthus for the department of political œconomy and if you approve I could when I come to town sound Matthias[16] whose study of foreign classics has been proceeding extensively. It [is certain some][17] push must be made at first for if we fail we shall disgrace ourselves and do great injury to our cause. I would not willingly be like my namesake, Walter the pennyless, at the head of a crusade consisting of a disorderly rabble and I judge of your feelings by my own. But 'screw your courage to the sticking place and we'll *not fail*.'[18] Supposing the work conducted with spirit the only ground from which it can be assaild with a prospect of success would be a charge of its being conducted intirely under ministerial influence. But this may be parried first by labouring the literary articles with as much pains as the political and so giving to the review a decided character independant of the latter department further the respect of the public may be maintained by the impartiality of our criticism. I would not willingly

## 6. William Gifford to Walter Scott[19]

James Street / Buckingham Gate / 9 November 1808

DEAR SIR,

As I wished to have some conversation with Mr Canning previously to answering your most friendly letter,[20] it became necessary to wait for the lucky opportunity; and such was the pressure of publick business, and what is equally grievous, publick dinners, that he could not spare me an hour till Friday evening. He had read your remarks with great satisfaction, and with a perfect conviction of their propriety and justness in every instance. All this and more, he desired me to say; and to express his hope that your arrival in town would be earlier than you seem to intimate, as it will <make> him very happy to see you. All necessary information will be given; and I know of nothing that can be reasonably required, which will be denied.

I have also seen Lord Hawkesbury,[21] but, as it was before I had talked with Mr Canning, I said very little; that little, however, appeared to meet his wishes. Mr Long[22] and Mr Huskisson I will call on speedily, and I have no doubt but that we shall obtain their support.

So far there is nothing to discourage; but I have many and serious fears of myself. From habit, feebleness of constitution (for I never yet knew what health was) and, perhaps, from years, there is come upon me, in the language of Bottom such an *exposition* of dullness,[23] that, if my friends did not sometimes stick pins in my cushion, and set me in motion, you would certainly read among the casualties of this or the following year, 'Died, of an elbow chair. Wm Gifford'. The natural and unfortunate consequence of this, is a dread of society, and an estrangement from many valuable acquaintances, who might <now>, do 'yeoman's service'.[24]

With all this, however, I was not without strong feelings of indignation at the base dereliction of national honour, which we have lately witnessed; but as I saw no practicable means of correcting it, I was but the more confirmed in my lethargy. Still, when Mr Canning transmitted to me the Lord Advocate's letter, together with his own earnest wishes on the subject, I was so charmed with seeing the light break upon us from <the only> quarter whence it could possibly come with advantage, that I, too adventurously, it is to be feared, engaged to occupy a station which would task to the uttermost infinitely more vigour and ability than I ever possessed.

Such, my dear Sir, is the picture of my mind – and now to something more like business.

You will not suppose that I mean to flatter when I say that I should utterly despair but for the powerful assistance of your Northern friends: They have activity, energy, habits of deep thinking and a shrewdness which peculiarly fits them for criticism. In some of these things we are, as my old acquaintance ——[25] says, 'but swine to them'.[26] On Scotland, therefore, rest all our hopes; and, for some time, at least, we can only aspire to the name of weak auxiliaries. Thereafter, perhaps, we may come 'to fill a pit as well as better men';[27] but at present we go for 'little in count', and less in efficacy.

Mr Canning has undertaken to see Geo. Ellis. He will be a treasure, if we can enlist him. I will endeavour to find out Mr W. Rose: – But who can do more with these gentlemen than yourself? If we are fortunate enough to acquire a tangible form, I will get Lord Hawkesbury to enquire of Dr. Jackson of Christ Church[28] for some good and true men at Oxford: and if that hotbed of malignity, Cambridge, from which spring your Critical Reviews, and other deleterious funguses, conceal a prophet that has not bowed the knee to Baal, I think it possible to ferret him out. But all this is *in posse*,[29] and we want immediate succour.

But what, you will say, are your thoughts of my letter?[30] After what is said of it by the Lord Advocate, (for he has read it) and Mr. Canning, I may very properly withhold my opinion: – but the truth is, that I cordially and conscientiously approve of it in every particular. Your regulations must be followed, your suggestions adopted, and made the Canon law of the Undertaking. Every word that you have written, convinces me that you have declined (I know not for what reason) a department for which you are so much better qualified than the person whom your partial judgment has recommended to it, that I wonder at my own temerity (to give it no worse a name) in retaining it a moment; which, after all, I can only do, by your kindly condescension to be 'viceroy over me'.[31]

Fox's Hist[ory]. should certainly be in the first number. It is hourly losing ground, and neither friendship nor party spirit can long preserve it from total neglect: still, matter of high import may be introduced in a review of it. It is pleasant to see how his followers criticise it.[32] The man was a great man, ergo his work &c. It puts me in mind of a sarcasm of one of the Fathers (Tertullian, I think) who retorts upon a critic of this kind; Ex *persona* probas fidem, or ex fide personam?[33] – With respect to Spanish affairs, I believe Southey is well qualified to speak of them; and, in this particular point, his heart is as it should be. I understand that he is an honourable man, and perhaps it may not be improper to sound him. I suppose there must be some poetry. Hodgson's Juvenal[34] would not be a bad article, but I have no one to take it up. Since I heard from you, I stumbled upon a translation of Persius;[35] this, if necessary, might be got ready. Perhaps it would not be amiss to admit a greater number of articles than the Edinburgh Review. It would be favourable to variety; and inter nos, more than one Number of that work has been tolerably dull for want of it.

But all this only serves to bring me round to the old exclamation, What can I do? I am not acquainted with the particular bent of your friends' studies on whom our infant efforts must depend for success, nor can I hope for immediate assistance here. Your next letter, I hope, will be consolatory; but I look forward to your arrival for the quieting of my apprehensions.

I have seen Mr Murray, and am much pleased with him. We are fortunate, I think, in our publisher. He is very sanguine, and will hear of no doubts nor difficulties.

I am ashamed to look back on the chaos of this letter; if you can shake the elements of it into a little intelligible order, it is more than I expect: but I [have] been interrupted a dozen times [since] I first sat down, by Lottery business, which brightens the faculties like a page of Crantz or Jacob Behmen.[36]

Whatever may be the fate of our proposed scheme I shall at least derive one solid satisfaction from it: it has given me an opportunity of expressing my esteem and respect for you, and of adding that

I am, with perfect sincerity / your ever obliged and faithful servant / Wm. Gifford

P.S. I believe it was Mr Stratford Canning who had some communication with Mr Murray, and not our friend.[37]

## 7. George Ellis to Walter Scott[38]

Claremont 11 November 1808

MY DEAR SCOTT

Ashiestiel is not, most certainly, in Nova Zembla, nor is it even at Teskant or St Petersburg, or at Berlin, or Vienna; how comes it then that our letters are so long on the road? They stop not to drink, neither do they sleep;[39] and yet your letter of the 2d of this month only reached me here on the 9th. Albeit, you will not, I trust, be very impatient, because a visit from my friend Dr Young, to whom, thank heaven, I owe the excellent health I now enjoy, has during two whole days prevented me from answering your four most excellent quarto pages. I might indeed have found time to say to you 'I sympathize in all your feelings, and partake of all your opinions, and am ready to undertake any part of the task which you may chuse to propose to me' – but this would not have been an answer, because you must have known it before; and besides, it would have left you embarrassed by the necessity of first asking of your own mind, and then explaining to me, all the details of a plan which you have not yet perhaps drawn out with rule and compass and so forth, although you may have ascertained with sufficient precision the proportions of all the essential parts of the building. – But having now sufficient leisure to put questions, I ask, in the first place, how soon you propose to begin, and what works you would select as a date for the commencement of our labours? Should the first number embrace all, or at least the principal publications of the present year, or of its last six, or last three months? Should the plan exactly resemble that of the Edinburgh Reviewers as far as relates to the *selection* of the objects of its criticism, and, if so, ought it to be at all retrospective, and to what degree? Should it extend, as the Edinburgh review has done, to *foreign* articles, many of which have appeared to me extremely uninteresting? – You may say that all these and many similar questions must remain for future discussions when we meet; and this is very true; but it may be essential, with a view to gaining time, that some two or three of us should have thought over and suggested an answer to them beforehand. My own idea is that the Edinburgh Reviewers have most shamefully departed from their original professions by passing over without notice some works of great value (for example Malthus's book, and some others) whilst they have frequently, in their eagerness to produce a premeditated essay of their own on some popular subject, selected, as an excuse for the introduction of that subject, any paltry pamphlet that without their notice might have been lost or mislaid in the printers' warehouse; – and yet that it may be perhaps quite necessary for us, in some cases, to follow their example. It would therefore follow that, if we mean to act by the public with perfect good faith we ought, in limine,[40] – to promise one of two things, viz either a candid though short review of every volume that issues from the press, or a selection grounded not solely on the intrinsic merit of the work published, but, not unfrequently[41] on our own opinion of the importance of the subject which it professes to treat, and sometimes on our estimation of its popularity only. I am quite persuaded that a truly excellent review might become, merely as a vehicle of *instruction*, the most valuable volume of every year, because in almost every other book there is a great deal of *verbiage*; but in addition to this, it is certainly capable of becoming highly important in a moral and political light, without the sacrifice of much of its literary utility; and, bad as the world is by some supposed, and by others wished to be, it is still easier to obtain popularity for such a work by good-natured pleasantry and plain sense, than even by that ribaldry to which the Edinburgh Reviewers have so successfully employed against authors who, if they possessed equally extensive means of circulating their satire, would have often been an overmatch for their critics. Under this persuasion I have no doubt of our ultimate success; and indeed I consider the high fortune of our rivals as one principal ground of hope; because, as those who have perused the morning-post are anxious to read the morning-chronicle, so, when the Edinburgh Review shall have a professed rival, will all its readers be eager to compare the antidote with the poison. Certainly, the Monthly review first established and gave currency to the British Critic; a work from the beginning most wretchedly conducted, and which could never have found a reader had not a large portion of the public determined to devote a certain period of time to hopeless dullness, rather than be disgusted by eternal Jacobinism. – So let the trumpet sound whenever our levies shall be completed! –

Canning put into my hands some weeks ago a letter from your Lord Advocate in which your suggestion was mentioned, but I did not then suppose that you were likely to have leisure to take any efficient part in setting on foot an undertaking which must, however easy it may ultimately become, require considerable exertions in the first instance. I rejoice to find that my fears were groundless, and where you are concerned, shall 'feel confident against the world in arms'.[42] Canning himself cannot, I fear, give us any assistance beyond an occasional hint, because he really does at present carry the world on his shoulders. Frere too, though not likely to be in want of some occasional moments of leisure, has so much business as to afford an excellent plea for idleness; and that plea he will certainly urge, so that we cannot reckon on any material assistance from him. But though these are two of the very best nonsense-mongers I know, there must be some more very good ones in the world, and on the right side of the world too, since some of the best pieces in the Antijacobin, though hitherto unclaimed, must have been the productions of some British (I suspect North-British) pen: and the hand which directed it will, I trust, administer its occasional assistance.

Heavens! what a long letter! – well! I have done – Best love from all. I *did suspect* you of assisting Captain Carlton[43] and mentioned my suspicion to Canning. –

Ever affectionately yours G. E.

## 8. John Murray to Walter Scott[44]

London 15 November 1808 / Tuesday

DEAR SIR

I have been desirous of writing to you for nearly a week past, but I never felt more the want of a personal conversation. I will endeavour, however, to explain myself to you, and will <rely> on your confidence and indulgence for secrecy and attention in[45] what I have to communicate.

I have before told you that the idea of a new Review has been revolving in my mind for nearly two years, and that more than twelve months ago I addressed Mr Canning upon the subject. The propriety, if not the necessity, of establishing a journal upon principles opposite to those of the Edinburgh Review has occurred to many <men> more enlightened ~~men~~ than myself and I believe the same reason has prevented others as it has done myself from attempting it – namely the immense difficulty of obtaining talent of sufficient magnitude to render success even *doubtful*. By degrees my plan has gradually floated up to this height, – but there exists at least an equal difficulty yet – that peculiar talent ~~in the hand~~ <in an editor> of rendering our other great sources advantageous to their best possible degree. This I think may be accomplished, but it must be effected by your arduous assistance, for a little time at least. Our friend Mr G[ifford] whose writings shew him to be both a man of learning and wit – has lived too little in the world lately – to have obtained that delicacy of tact whereby he can feel at one instant, and habitually, what ever may gratify public desire or excite public attention and curiosity. – But this you know to be a leading feature in the talents of Mr Jeffray and his friends and that without the most happy choice of subjects as well as of the ability to treat them well – without catching 'the manners living as they rise'[46] – the Edinburgh Review would not have obtained the success which it has done, and that no other review, however preponderating in solid merit, will obtain attention without it. Entering the field too as we shall do against an army commanded by the most skilful generals, it will not do for us to leave any of our best officers behind as a reserve, for they would be of no use if we are defeated at first – but We must enter with our most able commanders at once and we shall then acquire confidence if not reputation, and increase in numbers as we proceed. Our first numbers must contain the most valuable and *striking* information in politics and the most interesting articles of general literature and science – written by our most able friends. If our plan appears <so> likely of being advantageous to the ministers, whose measures, to a certain extent, we intend to justify to support or to recommend and assist, that they have promised their support – when *can* that support be so advantageously given, either for their own interests or ours own as at the commencement, when we are most weak – have the most arduous onset to make, and when we do and must stand most in need of help. If our first numbers are not written with the greatest ability, upon the most interesting topics – it will not excite public attention – no man, even the friend of the principles we adopt, will leave the sprightly pages of the Edinburgh Review to read a dull detail of stail morality up or dissertations upon subjects whose interest has long fled. I do not say this from any [even] the smallest doubt, of our having all that we desire in these respects in our power – but because I am apprehensive that without your assistance it will not be drawn into action. And my reason for this fear I will thus submit to you. You mentioned in your Letter to Mr Gifford that our Review should open with a grand Article upon Spain[47] – meaning a display of the politic<al> feelings of the people – and the probable end of the results of this important contest – and I suggested to Mr G— that Mr Frere should be written to, which he said was easy, and that he thought that he would do it – for Frere could not only give better facts upon this subject, but could write them better than any other person. But having in my project given the name of Southey as a person who might assist occasionally, in a number or two hence – I found at our next interview that Mr G— who does not know Mr S— had spoken to a friend to ask Mr S. to write *the* article upon Spain.[48] It is true that Mr S— knows a great deal about Spain, and upon another occasion would have given a good article upon this subject – but at present – *his* is not the kind of knowledge upon which we want, and it is, moreover, trusting our secret to a stranger who has, by the way, a directly opposite bias in politics. Mr G also told me with very great stress that among the articles he had submitted to you was *Hodgson's Translation of Juvenal,* which at no time was a very interesting article for us, and having been published more than 6 months ago, it would be now a stupid one – and you must observe in this also that it would necessarily involve a comparison with Mr Giffords own translation, which must of course be praised – and it thus shows an *individual* feeling – the least spark of which in our early numbers must both betray and ruin us. He talks of reviewing, *himself*, a late translation of *Persius* for *entre nous* a similar reason. He has himself nearly completed a translation, which will be published in a few months.

In what I have said upon this most exceedingly delicate point, and which I again submit to your most honourable confidence, there is no other object than just to shew you without reserve how we stand, and to exemplify what I set out with, that without skilful management and judicious instructions we shall totally mistake the road to the accomplishment of the arduous task which we have undertaken, and involve the cause and every individual in not merely a defeat, but also disgrace. I must observe also that Mr Gifford is the most obliging and well meaning man alive and that he is perfectly ready to be instructed in those points, of which his seclusion renders him ignorant, and all that I wish and mean is, that we should struggle to open clearly to him the view which is so obvious to us. That our first number must be a most brilliant one in every respect, and to effect this we must avail ourselves of every valuable political information we can command, and that those persons who have the real interest in supporting the concern must be called upon immediately for their strenuous personal help. The fact must be obvious to you that if Mr Canning, Mr Frere, Mr Scott, Mr Ellis and Mr Gifford with their immediate and true friends will exert themselves heartily in every respect, so as to produce, with *secrecy*, only *one* – remarkable attractive number – their further *Labour* will be[49] <light> for with such a first number in our hands, we may solicit and obtain any other help that we require – and then the persons above named will only be called on for their information, facts, hints, advice and *occasional* articles. But without this, without producing a number that shall at least vibrate on the scale of excellence with the best of the Edinburgh Review it were better not attempted. We should do more harm to our cause by an unsuccessful attempt to upend it, than we should do by leaving it to chance and the increasing reputation of the Edinburgh Review – will most certainly be inversely to our *unsuccessful* opposition.

In the first number we should as much as possible exhibit an aspect of the most sincere independence – political and literary – for <if> we can once fix ourselves upon public attention, honnied drops of party sentiment may be delicately insinuated into the unsuspecting ear, and the public shall be what the good and prudent minister desires, without themselves perceiving their change of sentiment. If our first number be independent, the rest may venture to the defensive[50] – giving opinions opposite to those of the Edinburgh Review without appearing to notice them and when we are strong indeed we shall gradually

advance to partial attacks upon their weakest points. The Sardonic Grin however will be our best weapon. – But after all the department which will be our
ultimate and only solid resort – is Literature – this therefore ~~our~~ demands our
best care and cultivation – let us espouse[51] the feelings of literary men – and ~~if~~
<when> we <must> chastise them – let it be with the gentle hand of a parent
rather than with the scourge of a slave master. – It would be very desirable also, I
conceive, to introduce *foreign* literature, of which we are, at this time, so very little informed and from which it would appear that we are almost excluded. And
yet *we* shall not be so if our ministerial friends are really desirous to promote
~~their in~~ our interest and *their own*. Mr Canning or even Mr Gifford, who knows
Mr Frere may write to him and beg him to send over any interesting performance
in Spain – to give us some articles that will exhibit the state of literature in that
country – from Sweden – Italy – Germany – particularly the latter, and even
from france we might through envoys – their secretaries – or even messengers
– procure Books if Mr Canning would tell who to address to and, allowing us to
write to them, merely say it was his desire[52] that our request should be attended
[to] – I contend that the more, from any solid course, our Review is rendered
interesting and popular – the more effectually any view or interest of the ministers in it, will be answered – and that, if they desire the thing to be done at all
– they should do it *effectually* – and this is one source of information which, at
this time particularly, would give our work a decided superiority over any other.
– Mr Gifford appears to think that we should not be so very dissertative as the
Edinburgh Review and that we should admit more articles, ~~and~~ this is perhaps
desirable as it will enable us to give really a review of the literature of the three
months. – When I had the pleasure of conversing with you upon the subject, I
attached a greater importance to the *Title* of the Review than I think, with you,
it merits, and the London Quarterly Review, if you approve of it, would perhaps
be sufficiently simple and might therefore do.

    With respect to bookselling-interference with the Review, I am equally con-
vinced as yourself ~~with~~ <of> its total incompatibility with a really respectable
and valuable critical journal such as I trust the projected one ever will be, and I
assure you nothing can be more distant from my views, which ~~as in~~ are confined
to the ardour which I feel for the cause and principles which it will be our object
to support, and the honour, and professional reputation which would obviously
result to the publisher of so important a work – to which, it were silly to suppress
that I shall not be *sorry* to derive from it as much profit as I can satisfactorily
enjoy, consistent with the liberal scale upon which it is my first desire to act,
towards, every writer and friend concerned in it. Respecting the terms upon
which the Editor shall be placed, at first, I have proposed and it appears to be
satisfactory to Mr Gifford that he shall receive either previous to or immediately
after the publication of each Number the sum of One Hundred and Sixty Guin-

eas (w[hi]ch is 10 – 10 – p[er] sh[ee]t), which he is to distribute as he thinks proper without any question or interference on my part, and that in addition to this he shall receive from me the sum of Two Hundred Pounds annually merely as the Editor. This Sir is much more than I can flatter myself with the return of, for the first year at least, but it is my intention that his salary shall ever increase proportionately to the success of the work under his management. The Editor has a most arduous office to perform and the success of the work must depend in a great measure upon his activity.

On the other side I have made out a list of ~~art~~ Publications that are new and interesting, adding also such as have been announced and may be expected in time for being reviewed for our first numbers – I have also submitted a list of Literary ~~mem~~ men whom we may both now and hereafter more or less engage as contributors. From the list you will select such articles of *durable* interest as might be begun upon immediately and upon the subject of them you will perhaps have the kindness to write to Mr Gifford – and if you approve of any of the plans which I have thus tediously submitted to you – it is only requisite to point them out to Mr Gifford and he will immediately get them executed from Mr Canning, Mr Frere – Lord Hawkesbury – Mr Long – and all our first *political* literary characters he can command, from long intimacy and by their well bestowed friendship for him – of Mr Ellis too we must elicit great exertions for the first number – he has been already enlisted by Mr Canning himself, who you know is very intimate with him, and I do really believe that if it were expressly engaged Mr Canning might be induced to write an article himself, for he is very earnest in the plan.

My letter has run into such unexpected lengths [that][53] I am obliged to defer the list of books &c un[til] tomorrow and I shall only add once more that no person can be more agreeable to me than Mr Gifford or more desirous in every respect of attending to recommendations, and I have stated what I have done in the most confidential manner to you in order to show how necessary it will be for us to insinuate into him the right tone of feeling and spirit and activity.

Tomorrow also I will write upon the subject of the Novels.[54] I sent by the coach yesterday Richardsons Correspondence and Pamela the last edition w[hi]ch contains curious additions – and Hassan the Arabian Nights[55] – you will find the Index to the Monthly Review – a very good Catalogue of Novels – I have several catalogues which I will send also – the Novels and the Review actually occupy all of my time and thoughts – I trust that [you] will be in town early in December – I beg you to [give] my best compliments to Mrs Scott and to all our[56]

Dear Sir / your obliged and faithful Servant / John Murray

## 28. George Ellis to John Murray[57]

Sunning Hill 5 November [1809]

DEAR SIR

I hasten to reply to your long and excellent letter of yesterday, and perfectly coincide with you in opinion as to the following main points viz, 1° – That our third number was, perhaps, very *profound*, but most notoriously and unequivocally *dull*, so dull indeed that I have not been able, after much enquiry, to discover any *one* person who has been able or willing to read *at all* the ponderous essay on the Greek Article, or who has cared <much> about the disquisition on Gothic Architecture; or who has not been disappointed by the critique on Miss Edgeworth,[58] or – but this is enough, quite enough, and it is obvious that our vessel cannot much longer keep afloat when thus over-ballasted.

2° – That we ought to do better, and might do better, and should do much better, if Gifford were *less patient and laborious*. For, if he employed, in making annotations on *printed* works one tenth part of the time which he consumes in correcting the bad language, and in attempting to elicit a rational meaning from the shapeless lumps of criticism which are sent to him in *MS*, we should be sure of surpassing the Edinburgh Review. At least in point of wit and variety.

3° That *novelty* is essential to our success, and that consequently it is a duty which we owe to ourselves and to the publick to put our collective *veto* upon any learned *trash* which our editor, from motives of good nature, and from a fear of offending the zealous contributors to our undertaking, may, from time to time have amassed.

But, after saying that *I* perfectly agree with you on all these points, I must add my full and firm conviction that Gifford equally admits them; and I am consequently at a loss to understand your fear of 'harassing' him by expostulation, or of engaging in litigation with him on the subject of '*first principles*'. He, I am persuaded, would admit the dullness of the last number, but he would say to you – 'It is dull because W Scott, the first instigator of our enterprize, contributed *nothing*; because <Turner and> Erskine, on whom we founded some expectations, contributed *nothing*; because Southey's critique on Lord Valentia's travels was not equal to what we hoped from his pen;[59] because having a large number of pages to supply, and such as I could not have filled up by my own efforts to my own satisfaction, I was compelled to make a selection from the materials in my hands'. And is not this answer, as far as he is concerned, satisfactory? or, can you or I assert that he rejected what was new and lively, and selected what was old and dull?

The publick, probably, has been disappointed, you and I, all of us have certainly been disappointed. But why? Simply, in my opinion, from want of *variety*; from the want of two or three spirited and playful articles, of articles which might have been supplied in a few hours, but which, merely because it was so easy to do it, none of us thought of supplying. Let us consider the principal articles of the last number. *I* have heard, from a variety of quarters, and from many where I should least have expected it, a very high, and as I think a very just commendation of the article on *Insanity*. That on *Paley* also, as far as I can judge, has been very generally approved. That on the Missionary travels also is assuredly excellent, and I believe very popular. The colonial article has, I understand, met with very great success amongst the small class of readers who are interested in that subject, and has, I know, attracted a few and may perhaps attract hereafter some <more> subscribers to whom our review would otherwise have been unknown. The review of Moore's campaign has, as you tell me, been very generally read. Now, I would ask, whether any one number of the Edinburgh review, or any other work of similar extent has done better? A little playful nonsense in lieu of those ponderous articles to which I have already alluded would, I am persuaded, have rendered our last number far superior to that which preceded it, or to that of the rival review in the estimation of the publick.

Do not think, therefore, that you are at issue with Gifford or with any of us upon *first principles*. The difference between us, if there be any difference, can only be about the *quickest* mode of attracting customers to our shop. Some of us perhaps may be too solicitous to draw in chance-comers, and others to secure the supply of regular families, but in the mean time our rivals have the steady advantage of a long-established house, and can vend vapid liquors with more ~~advant~~ certainty than we can sell that which is sound and wholesome, but we shall establish the reputation of our tap by degrees, whether the sign of our ale-house be a fool's jacket or a Doctor's wig, if we can once get our cellar well-stored, and avoid the necessity of forcing the same draught on different palates.

Now this last seems to me to be our great desideratum. You are certainly entitled to protest against any articles in our bill of fare, and to suggest any others in their place, but whilst there is a practicable difficulty of filling the table; the means of overcoming this difficulty must be first devised, and of this you say nothing. To select from all the *newest* publications those which are most interesting, and to send them to Southey, Scott, Turner, &c is easy, but if ill health, necessary occupation, amusement, or any other cause prevents all or any of them from executing the task, or if they happen to execute it carelessly, where is our resource, unless Gifford employs the coarser materials which happen to be within his reach? I am convinced that we are, at present, too few; that the persons on whom we principally depend *could* not, conveniently to themselves, and therefore *would not* undertake to fill four reviews in a year. I am in great doubt whether we shall soon produce a number containing as much *intrinsic solid* merit as the last, dull as it unquestionably was. But, as I have already said, it is very easy to avoid that dullness which arises only from uniformity, since, for this purpose, nothing more is necessary than to select, in each number, three or four articles which are capable of being treated with pleasantry, and to allot *them* to the persons best able to treat them in such manner. If, to come at once to the point, you can suggest at present one or two such articles to me, I will undertake them, and will readily employ my influence, if I possess any, with Gifford and W Scott, to do the same with two or three more. This will at least render the tone and colouring of our next number sufficiently different from the last.

I am at present occupied on a critique which I have promised Sir Francis D'Ivernois[60] on his little work 'Effets du Blocus Continental' &c and I wish also to write a criticism on Canning's 'Letter to Lord Camden';[61] but excepting these two articles which probably will not occupy more than ten pages each, I shall not feel disposed to do any thing for the next Number unless you should be able to suggest to me something of a lighter kind. Canning has given me an Italian work relative to the affairs of the Pope containing the official correspondence between the Papal ministers and the French Generals in Italy, which might perhaps furnish an interesting article, but <which> must be serious, and would require more labour and time than I could at present conveniently employ upon it; and the 'Etat de la Russie' which I had also intended to undertake, is liable to the same objection.[62]

Ever yours faithfully / G Ellis

## 29. William Gifford to Walter Scott[63]

James Street / 20 November 1809

MY DEAR SIR,

The unaccountable silence of Murray during his long absence, will throw us somewhat out of our regular period of appearance. I was in earnest expectation of receiving something from you, before now; and I yet hope a little proof[64] will arrive for our hungry devils.

If you desert us, I do not think we can stand, and my hopes, which were once pretty sanguine, begin to fail me.

Murray cries like the horse leach incessantly,[65] not for more men! but for novelty.[66] If this could be found, it would be well, but when he shuts up his books for two months out of the three, it is rather to be wished than expected.

You will hear I suppose from G[eorge] Ellis in a post or two. He is every thing that I could hope or desire: – but he seems to think that the editorship of a review is rather more of a sinecure than I find it. I certainly want energy and industry and health – but more than all I want assistance. Oxford does not nothing – except, like Antient Pistol at his leek – that it *eats and swears*[67] – for it is angry at the insults of the Edinburgh Reviewers and yet puts them up. Cambridge is <but> little better. Both promise, and both think that sufficient.

Our friend C[anning]. has written a most admirable précis of his late conduct &c. It will be printed, and you of course will have an early copy. It is not
intended for publication, but as it will necessarily get into circulation, we shall
have an article on it, which may <even now> be set down as interesting. Of all
this, perhaps, you will be better informed by G. E.

Canning is much pleased with your letter. He must soon be in power again;
for he is not only the best speaker now in Parliament, but the ablest and most
spirited Politician either in or out of it – and further, this deponent sayeth
not.[68]

But pray take our case into your pitiful consideration. This is now the second
Number, which, as my acquaintance at Cam[bridge]. says, has *desiderated* you
– *non hoc pollicitus tuæ*![69] Vale, my excellent friend, and believe me, in spite of my
flippancy, your ever faithful and obliged.

Wm. Gifford

## 40. George Ellis to Walter Scott[70]

Sunning Hill 8 March 1810

MY DEAR SCOTT,

...

Let me now say a few words on the subject of our review which, so far as any
literary purpose is concerned, I consider as now fairly afloat. The last Number
appeared to me to be excellent, and all that I have seen of that which is shortly to
appear is, I think, worthy of it.[71] I trust that you will have sent something as good
as the truly eloquent little morsel on the Battle of Talavera, which was a perfect
jewel.[72] But I much wish to have your opinion as to the choice of subjects which,
from what you see and hear, you think it would be most important to discuss.
G[ifford]. writes me word 'if we do not lead the opinions of the publick it must
be our fault, for they evince the greatest possible disposition to be led'; and I
believe he is right. The detestation of our rivals which has been long rumbling in
the breasts of many ingenious men has already procured us some very powerful
literary support, as you will have seen by the critique on Dr Parr in our last, and
as you will see by an article on S. S's sermon (*not* by the same hand) in our next,[73]
and I have little doubt that we shall soon decidedly out-write the Edinburgh
Review on most subjects; but it is as a political engine that their work is seriously
formidable; and it must be by trying to encourage and keep together and direct
those who think rightly in politics that we must render ourselves really useful.
We have, here, a more extensive horizon than you, but you see and hear much
which we do not, and it would, I think, be very important that some part of our
work should be particularly directed towards your part of the empire where our
rivals have the advantage of being guided in their topics by a more minute and

correct knowledge of the country. Many of your prophecies respecting our plan, or rather *yours*, for you were our father, have been fulfilled. The work is established; assistants worth acquiring have been acquired; and, without injuring the sale of our adversaries, which we cannot perhaps expect, we have already gained access to about half of their subscribers, and are likely in a short time to accompany them every where as the Courier accompanies the Morning Chronicle. It is particularly *now*, and henceforward, that it will be necessary to 'hoist more pendants and fix more broadsides' than we have been accustomed to do, and to prove that we are 'King's ships', and it is on this subject that I shall be very anxious when we meet (I hope we shall soon meet?) to concert some regular plan of operations. I am afraid that the number now coming out will be very deficient in this respect, as I know of only one article (and that is of Sunning Hill manufacture) which can properly be called political.[74] The next, of course, will be much more abundant both on home and foreign politics; but I want to have some contrivance for doing these things more frequently through the medium of articles of literature – but it will be easier to discuss the minutiae of our manoeuvres in conversation than in writing.

As I have scribbled over so much paper I will send this to Charles to be franked, for it is not at all worth the postage; but it will tell you that I am alive, and that I often think of you and that I have a pleasure in writing to you, and that my little helpmate and her niece, and myself unite in love to Mrs S. to whom we beg you to present our joint congratulations on the vrai successes, literary and pugilistic, of the young Laird – Ever affectionately

Yours, G. Ellis

### 51. John Murray to John Bristed[75]

8 June 1810

SIR

I had the pleasure of receiving safely your obliging Letter dated 6th March, together with the inclosed copy of a Letter to Messrs Longman. I have to regret that a pressure of particular business requiring often my absence from home, has prevented me until this day from giving the attention due to the subject of your communication. I have however this day had a conversation with Mr Butterworth, and I write to acquaint you that there is little doubt but that I shall have the satisfaction of complying with your request of Publishing the 'Hints' &c. in the way you propose, at our joint expense and propose for one edition, after which the copyright will remain entirely your own. Mr Butterworth had lent his copy of the 'Hints' &c to Mr [James] Stephen who had left it at his country house so that I could not see it to day but it will be given for my perusal tomorrow or the day following after which I will write to you more decisively upon the subject.[76]

I do not profess to be, nor am I willing to become a *political* Publisher – but I am so anxiously and firmly attached to the government that I am always disposed to publish any thing decidedly able and respectable that may be written in their favor. It is indeed by this course alone that I shall be enabled to prove in the least degree serviceable. In support of this system I have commenced a work entitled the 'Quarterly Review' which I flatter myself you have seen. It has risen to high reputation and has already extended to a circulation of 5,000 copies – the writers are all gentlemen of the first rank and talents and indeed nothing but the greatest ability will enable a man to write a review which is to compress the information of a folio in the compass of a few pages and to render them interesting. Should you happen either not to know of this Journal or not to receive it regularly, I could wish for the favor of your pointing out the means by which I could have the pleasure of sending it, upon its publication both to yourself and Mr Jackson. *William* Gifford[77] the author of the Baviad and the Maviad and the translator of Juvenal is its editor and – Southey – Walter Scott – Mr Ellis – and other gentlemen equally eminent and respectable are its contributors. Perhaps you and some of your most able friends may be induced to try your skill at a Critique, taking care to select works which are either in themselves or in their Subjects generally interesting – for instance a review sent over instantly on the publication in America of Mr Walsh's Pamphlet on the 'Genius and disposition of the French Government'[78] would have been interesting and valuable. If there were any work that would give us a view of the present State of Literature in America, they must be written with great care and ability, without coarseness or violence, taking care to put the reader completely in possession of the points you wish to establish, and making him if possible so insensibly to feel your opinions as to adopt them, believing them to be his own, arising from his own conviction. Barlow's Poem, though excessively dull, would have been made an acceptable review, as the only attempt at the Epic in America.[79] If there be any thing curious either political or literary whether ingenious or remarkably absurd which you had no time or disposition to review yourself, I would gladly pay the expense of its immediate transportation. I trust you will do me the favor to pardon the intrusion of this Subject upon you – nothing whatever can be received gratuitously; whoever writes must receive at the ratio of *Ten Guineas* for every sheet – no consideration can admit of our dispensing with this stipulation.

The Articles should be compressed within the compass of sixteen pages if possible.[80]

I am, Sir / Your Most obedient Servant / J. M.

## 58. William Gifford to John Murray[81]

Monday night [24 September 1810]

DEAR SIR

I thought that there was something wrong, by the Printer's not sending anything, and by your not waiting as you *promised*.

I cannot say that I am much gratified by your note, or by your conduct; the latter wants openness, and the former has an unnecessary air of intimidation. There is no necessity for you to pursue a losing speculation, which I should be the last person on earth to encourage; and there is yet time, I presume, to recover a considerable part of that 5000 £ which you have so unwisely put in hazard. That you want openness is apparent; because you never inform me what you intend to do; but suffer me to blunder on to my own disgrace. You say you have no advisers: how can I credit this, when with two or three better things in your hand, you print the Eton Article which we had agreed should not be printed in this Number?[82] It was certainly not by my advice that Huet was made to follow Wordsworth, when either the Cam[bridge] verses or Field's article, which is lively and amusing should have come before it – But I wish not to prolong this strain – a little more will make me quite weary of a part which is far enough from a pleasant one. – To come to the chief purport of your letter, I will send to Mr C[opleston]. if you agree to abide by his answer: on no other condition will I consent to violate my feelings by affronting a gentleman of character and reputation, for such Mr Davison is. He probably came to town on purpose to see his Article. He has seen it. He has revised it, and is returned in the full expectation of its appearance. After all, I do not quite enter into your opinion of it. It is clear, sensible and intelligent. I wish, indeed, it had more spirit and interest: so I do of many other articles which yet pass muster very well. Nor do I find any great fault with its sober tone: there is enough in this Number to provoke the scurril language of our opponents, without calling down more of it on Mr Copleston.

Pitt, I am informed I shall have tomorrow. One sheet of Crabbe is come, and is every thing that I expected:[83] it is in vain, however, to set it up till the rest arrives. I am promised two sheets more directly – whether these will be the whole, I cannot tell: if so, the Article will make a full sheet.

Ever yours, &c. / W Gifford

P.S. I must have the revise to send to Oxford. I ought to have had it last night.

## 59. John Murray to William Gifford[84]

25 September 1810 / Tuesday

DEAR SIR

I regret exceedingly that you were not well pleased with my note but I will believe from the very obliging manner in which you have answered it that you are not *very* much offended with its author. – I entreat you to be assured that the term intimidation can never be applied to any part of my conduct towards you for whom I entertain the highest esteem and regard both as a writer and as a friend. – If I am over-anxious it is because I have let my hopes of fame as a bookseller rest upon the establishment and celebrity of this journal. – My character, as well with my professional brethren, as with the public is at stake upon it – for I would not be thought silly by the one or a mere speculator by the other. – I have a very large business as you may conclude, the only reason for my mentioning it before, by the capital I have been able to throw into this one publication – and yet my mind is so entirely engrossed, my honour is so completely involved in this one thing, that I neither eat drink nor sleep upon anything else. I would rather it excelled all other Journals and I gained nothing by it than gain £300 a year by it without trouble if it were thought inferior to any other. – This Sir is true – when you hear how my mind harbours scarce any other thought but of this Journal you then will the more easily believe me when I assure you again that I advise with no friend of mine upon it – whatever I say to you or do in it is entirely from myself – and it is perhaps from the fear that you do not attend to me, because you imagine I do not solely depend upon you or because my remarks are not judicious – that I may appear to you not quite as open – Respecting the Eton Article for instance[85] – Mr [Sharon] Turner told me the Book was written by a friend of his a Mr Green – I thought the Book a good literary subject for a Review and sent it with Hariots Travels[86] as you told me to Mr Sumner – he liked it and reviewed it – I took it into my head that it would have been a very ingenious and interesting article and I was very anxious about its appearance but I was disappointed when I saw it in print and on reading the Book – which I find is very dull and such as many hundred classical minds could have put together – But I had no adviser in this. Turner has not the most distant notion that it was to be received – This is so I assure you –

I withheld Herrick[87] until we should be in active need of something to make up because I had taken it into my head that the writer does not possess sufficient talent to balance against our admitting such a person to write in such a Review – remember Twiss told every one that he wrote an Article in the Edinburgh Review[88] – every one said the article was bad and these people go up and down boasting of their communications to such a Journal as ours – I could enjoy an hundred such – I thought too, if it were desirable to notice Herrick that no one could have done it so well as Mr Ellis – ~~I don't think you or Mr E or Mr C.~~ Greek Articles are not read generally even by those who are capable of understanding them – I don't think you or Mr E[llis] or Mr C[anning] would read them in any other Journal – they should therefore be refused. I can concede to very important Works such as Herculanensia Wyttenbach[89] Jonston &c &c the review by the very first classical scholars. I asked Mr Doyly what he thought of the Review of Burgesses Euripidies[90] – he said it was supposed to be written by an Under Graduate and they did not think much of it – A Greek article should be very able indeed so as to excite attention at the Universities where almost alone it is read – If provided too – *one* good religious article in each number would render us more service than two or three – but we should always have one.

As soon as I had read your obliging note this morning I sent over the Cambridge verses and Fields article which can both follow the Diary which I would have taken out but the first form of it is worked.[91]

Respecting the Oxford Article,[92] I assure you you mistake me – either as to this or any other article believe me I am not so silly as to venture that my opinion can balance you and yours – all I *presume* is to lay my own poor unadvised sentiments before you – and all I ask is the favor of their hearing – if you think with me that upon the whole we would be better without this article – then I shall feel obliged if you put the matter delicately to Mr C[opleston] – but if you think that although we and Mr C would not be served by it – but that *you* by which I always mean *we* – can not just omit it and that the refusing it may be inconvenient and hazardous let it go in at once – I have hurried the corrections of it and you will have a revise of the first pages at any rate –.[93]

## 66. George Ellis to John Murray[94]

3 November [1810]

Dear Sir

I am only able to answer, very shortly, the variety of matter contained in your long letter.

To begin with the Quarterly –

I cannot, of course, doubt your correctness of statement in a confidential ~~statement~~ letter to me, and, if I feel surprised at the information that 'no one number has, hitherto, paid its own expenses' it is only because I had conceived that the extent of circulation which you mention as necessary to replace those expenses, (4000 copies) though inferior to that which, from some of your former communications, I supposed you to have long since attained, was greater than any man at the commencement of a new undertaking could anticipate with much confidence, until the work should have continued for a much longer period than ours has yet done, to fulfil the promises held out at its commencement. Be this however as it may, I do not feel the less confident that your most sanguine expectations will ultimately be realised.

As to the cause of our advance in respect to circulation being less rapid than you expected, I do not concur in the opinions to which you seem to attach the most weight. There are, I think, in the progress of a periodical work, certain periods by which they are all affected. The *expectations* excited in a *part* of the public, generally gives a considerable impulse to its incipient effort; but, after this, there are always occasional alternations of popularity, acting most capriciously, and by fits and starts, which accelerate or retard its progress, until, its *mass* begins to give it a more regular and uniform momentum, with which it continues for a very considerable time, and then, beginning to relax, is, by that very mass more and more retarded, and ultimately stops. Such will, I am persuaded, be our destiny. To our *extensive* success there is at present, very obviously, only *one* intelligible obstacle, which is a degree of *irregularity* which must of necessity induce, in the public mind, a doubt of our ultimate perseverance. Those who perceive that we are, from quarter to quarter, progressively less and less punctual, *must* infer from it that we feel progressively more and more the difficulty of fulfilling our engagements, and are likely, in a short time to abandon the enterprise in despair. No opinion of the *merit* of our review will or can support us against this supposition. The effect of it will and must operate on readers of *all* tastes. That a popular topic is sometimes deferred; that a dull subject is sometimes unnecessarily treated; and that G[ifford]. who, though able and active is neither infallible, <nor indefatigable, may be> sometimes induced by friendship to prefer, as compelled by want of materials to tolerate a heavy article, I admit, and regret; but I *know*, by experience, that many articles which I have extremely disapproved, have found numerous admirers; and I am quite sure that most of our late numbers have been, in point of intrinsic merit, as good as the world have a right to expect, and much better than the corresponding numbers of our rivals. Hence I infer that *punctuality* is, in our present situation, our great and only desideratum. This we must attain. Whether we proceed or follow our rivals is immaterial: but, the days of publication once *fixed* we ought to adhere to them; which will be much easier for us than for the Edinburgh Review, because we publish in London. If we can get out our next Number by the *first* of December, it would, I think, be best to allow ourselves in future exactly three months for each, and invariably adhere to the 1st of March, June, September and December – if another fortnight be indispensable, we may adopt the 15th instead of the 1st of the same months; which may perhaps do nearly as well.

...

Ever yours &c / G. E.

# NOTES

## Cutmore, 'Introduction'

1.  A recent volume edited by Kim Wheatley, *Romantic Periodicals and Print Culture* (London: Frank Cass, 2003), specifically undertakes to refocus debate on the nature and impact of nineteenth-century journals. The present collection continues that effort and illustrates the value of anchoring theoretical discussion in primary sources. Since the 1940s only one monograph has been published on the *Quarterly*, Joanne Shattock's *Politics and Reviewers: The Edinburgh and the Quarterly in the Early Victorian Age* (Leicester: Leicester University Press, 1989). Shattock covers the period of John Gibson Lockhart's editorship, which for the most part is outside the scope of the essays in this volume. Chapters or substantial discussion of the *Quarterly* appeared in the 1980s and 1990s in books by Peter Morgan, Jon Klancher and Kim Wheatley. Their works depend mostly on secondary sources. Earlier twentieth-century work on the *Quarterly* was undertaken by Roy Benjamin Clark, by Walter Graham and by Hill Shine and Helen Chadwick Shine. Clark's 1930 biography of William Gifford depends on Samuel Smiles's nineteenth-century biography of John Murray and on John Lockhart's memoir of Sir Walter Scott. Graham's 1920s work on conservatism in the *Quarterly* is ill-informed and now of limited value. The Shines transcribed and to a limited extent supplemented an unpublished manuscript in the John Murray Archive that purports to identify contributors to the *Quarterly Review*. As I demonstrated in an article in *Victorian Periodicals Review*, the Shines' methodology was faulty and their work has had to be redone ('*Wellesley Index* I's *Quarterly Review* Identifications: Was the Murray Register a Reliable Source?', *Victorian Periodicals Review*, 27:4 (1994), pp. 294–9). While there are many references in scholarly articles to individual *Quarterly Review* essays, and while a number of useful articles on the journal have appeared in the past fifty years, including articles by Shattock, Wheatley and Thomas, none are based, as the essays in this volume are, on a survey of all known primary sources.
2.  The *Quarterly Review* materials consist of manuscript letters, letter books, financial accounts, publisher's memoranda, warehouse inventories and subscription lists. For an overview of critical theory as it relates to Romantic-period journals, see Wheatley's Introduction to Wheatley (ed.), *Romantic Periodicals and Print Culture*, pp. 1–18.
3.  Scott, too, was a frequent contributor. However, he corresponded mainly with Gifford and his association with the *Quarterly* virtually terminated in 1811.
4.  Coleridge reviewed Hunt in Number 36 (article #456) and Shelley in Number 42 (article #510). Gifford sent him Hazlitt's *Round Table* to review, but whether it was Coleridge

who reviewed it in Number 33 (article #425) is unknown. Here and throughout this volume, article serial numbers are keyed to the index pages in the *Quarterly Review Archive*, ed. J. Cutmore: <www.rc.umd.edu>. For *QR* articles published after 1825 and for *ER* articles, reference numbers are to *WI* throughout the volume.

5. The Gifford-Copleston correspondence, Devon 1149M, is published on the *Quarterly Review Archive*.

6. John Murray letters, MsL M9826c, Iowa.

7. Article #492, in the July 1818 number, published in February 1819.

8. In the period 1809–25, no women were associated with the *Quarterly Review*, except as objects of critical attention.

9. I use the term 'conservative' not to designate adherence to a party or a platform, but more loosely, to describe an evolving constituency that, fearful of Jacobin revolution, venerated national institutions and established forms, and entertained an attitude or bias that was generally in favour of the status quo. It can be argued, as Boyd Hilton does in his essay in the present volume, that the *Quarterly*, by pitting itself against the *Edinburgh* and by representing the Canningite party, helped highlight the conservative-liberal dichotomy and contributed to the need to articulate 'conservatism' in the abstract.

10. Throughout this volume, the notation '*QR* Letter' refers to the editor's unpublished edition of *Quarterly Review*-related correspondence. For a list of these letters and their sources, see Appendix A, pp. 179–88. For a selection of transcribed letters particularly relevant to this volume, see Appendix B, pp. 189–215.

11. Gifford and Scott spoke of 'the cause' and the King with affection and conviction: 'such is my anxiety to further the cause I love' (*QR* Letter 3, Gifford to Canning); the journal's 'purpose should be to offer to those who love their country and to those whom we would wish to love it a periodical work of criticism conducted with equal talent but upon sounder principle' from that of the *Edinburgh Review* (*QR* Letter 5, Scott to Ellis); 'But if I were one of the present men, I would loudly and decidedly, take up the cause of the good old king' (*QR* Letter 75, Gifford to Scott); 'Let us, however, adhere to ... the old sentiment of love and veneration for the king' (*QR* Letter 76, Gifford to Ellis).

12. On the development of British nationalism, see especially L. Colley, *Britons: Forging the Nation 1707–1837* (New Haven, CT: Yale University Press, 1992). On British nationalists' use of literature, see L. Lipking, *Ordering of the Arts in Eighteenth-Century England* (Princeton, NJ: Princeton University Press, 1970); G. Newman, *The Rise of English Nationalism: A Cultural History 1740–1830* (New York: St Martin's Press, 1987); and J. Sorenson, *The Grammar of Empire* (Cambridge: Cambridge University Press, 2000). On canon formation and nationalism, see, for a start, J. B. Kramnick, *Making the English Canon: Print-Capitalism and the Cultural Past, 1700–70* (Cambridge: Cambridge University Press, 1998); and M. Gamer, *Romanticism and the Gothic: Genre, Reception, and Canon Formation* (Cambridge: Cambridge University Press, 2000). See also Kevin Gilmartin's recently-published *Writing Against Revolution: Literary Conservatism in Britain, 1790–1832* (Cambridge: Cambridge University Press, 2007). Gilmartin argues that at this time conservative journals such as the *Quarterly Review* were engaged in a campaign to preserve the nation's core values by advocating the organic transformation of its cultural and social establishments.

13. At this time the recipient paid the postage. This was a problem for Gifford and Murray, as they did not wish to impose upon their contributors and collaborators.

14. Franks on letters received by Gifford and Murray include those of Sir John Barrow, John Wilson Croker, George Canning, George Longman, Lord Byron, Sir Granville Leveson

Gower, William Hamilton and Lord Gambier. Murray looked to Croker and Barrow for franks; Gifford drew upon a much wider field.

15. Gifford did ask Canning for secret service money to cover the costs of postage, but I have found no evidence that he received any (*QR* Letter 19).

16. Already by 1812 the *Antijacobin Review, and True Churchman's Magazine* was taking the *Quarterly* to task for allying itself with the Canningites in Parliament. 'The *Quarterly Review*, established in avowed opposition to the baleful meteor of the north [the *Edinburgh Review*], and conducted on better principles ... has, unhappily, degenerated into a mere party engine.' The writer's evidence was the journal's silence on the question of '*Catholic Claims*' ('Reviewers Reviewed', *Antijacobin Review*, 43 (September 1812), p. 114).

17. At the close of his tenure, Gifford reaffirmed that his primary reason for serving as editor was his desire to protect Canning's interests (*QR* Letter 257). There is no reason to doubt Gifford's sincerity. The two men met and corresponded often, and Canning patently entertained a genuine affection for Gifford.

18. References to the *Quarterly* occupy four columns in Corson's notes to Grierson's edition of *SL*, thereby marking it as a major topic in Scott's life, but frequent references to the journal do not extend much beyond 1812. See J. C. Corson, *Notes and Index to Sir Herbert Grierson's Edition of the Letters of Sir Walter Scott* (Oxford: Clarendon Press, 1979).

19. James Hogg to John Murray, 7 May 1815, quoted in Smiles, *Memoir*, vol. 1, p. 349.

20. Shattock, *Politics and Reviewers*, p. 96.

21. Murray's rate in 1810 for most of his other contributors was the same as Constable's at the *Edinburgh Review*, ten guineas per sheet (*QR* Letters 8, 51, 216). To judge from Murray's cash day books, at that time the usual payment was between £15 and £25 per article.

22. Bedford-Southey correspondence, Bodleian Library, Eng. MS. Lett. d. 52, ff. 117–18, f. 124; d. 53, ff. 96–7.

23. T. F. Dibdin, *The Library Companion; or, The Young Man's Guide, and the Old Man's Comfort, in the Choice of Library*, 2 vols (London: Harding, 1824), vol. 1, p. xvii. Some of the ellipses appear in the original.

24. For instance, Anne Cleaver, the wife of the Bishop of St Asaph, in her old age presented her complete run of the journal, one hundred volumes, to Sir Thomas Henry Browne, Felicia Hemans's brother. It is notable in passing that Cleaver, evidently conscious of the permanent historical value of these issues of the *Quarterly Review*, recorded the date when she received her copy, a practice that has proved useful in establishing the journal's real publication dates.

25. Editor's collection.

26. Heber, then on a 'flying visit from Craven', attended the seminal meeting at Scott's Ashiestiel in early October 1808 during which the *Quarterly* was first set on foot (*QR* Letters 2, 5).

27. Shattock, *Politics and Reviewers*, p. 15.

28. Croker to Murray, 29 March 1823, quoted in Smiles, *Memoir*, vol. 2, pp. 57–8.

29. Article #492.

30. W. Hazlitt, *Letter to William Gifford* (London: John Miller, 1819), p. 41.

31. Such as the lucrative contracts to publish the Navy List and the official Admiralty accounts of polar exploration (*QR* Letter 229). Not all of Murray's efforts to gain government commissions succeeded (*QR* Letter 93).

32. Hazlitt, *Letter to William Gifford*, p. 5.
33. Though more so if one could demonstrate that periodical reviewing was an avocation, not a vocation, a demonstration of one's intellectual muscle, not an exhibition of one's need for cash.
34. The patronage system saw William Gifford draw £1,000 from a double commissioner-ship of the national lottery, £200 as clerk of the foreign estreats and £300 as paymaster of gentlemen pensioners. Even in death Gifford was honoured for his services to the state as editor of the *Quarterly Review* – surely not for the *Baviad*. He is buried in the poets' corner in Westminster Abbey. It helped that his best friend and executor was the Dean of Westminster. The mechanics of patronage are well exampled by another *Quarterly* reviewer, Croker. See C. Hamilton, 'John Wilson Croker: Patronage and Clientage at the Admiralty, 1809–57', *Historical Journal*, 58:1 (2000), pp. 49–77.
35. Distinct from cronyism and nepotism, patronage was, by definition, a reward for loyalty and service to the Crown. Even in this period, radicals could gain executive office, if, like James Mill, they demonstrated innate talent or had connections.
36. The highest dignity the founder of the *British Critic* attained – the Reverend Robert Nares – was a prebend of St Paul's Cathedral. The patronage reward to John Gifford for his editorship of the *Antijacobin* was a police magistracy. J. B. S. Morritt warned that should the *Quarterly* fail to confront the *Edinburgh* directly, it might descend to the 'solemn nothinglyness' of the *British Critic* (*QR* Letter 24; cf. Letter 7). William Gifford declared that the *British Critic* and the *Antijacobin* were 'conducted by time serving mawkish drivellers' (*QR* Letter 3).
37. Liverpool Papers, BL Add. MSS 38269.

## 1 Wheatley, 'Plotting the Success of the *Quarterly Review*'

1. W. Graham, *Tory Criticism in the Quarterly Review 1809–53* (New York: Columbia University Press, 1921; rpt 1970), p. 5.
2. Wheatley (ed.), *Romantic Periodicals and Print Culture*, p. 10. See also my *Shelley and His Readers: Beyond Paranoid Politics* (Columbia, MO: University of Missouri Press, 1999), pp. 45–8, 128–9, 134–7.
3. W. Wordsworth, *The Thirteen-Book 'Prelude'*, ed. M. L. Reed (Ithaca, NY: Cornell University Press, 1991), p. 109 (VI.620). On the open-endedness of periodical literature in general, see M. Beetham, 'Open and Closed: The Periodical as a Publishing Genre', *Victorian Periodicals Review*, 22:3 (Fall 1989), pp. 96–100.
4. W. St Clair, *The Reading Nation in the Romantic Period* (Cambridge: Cambridge University Press, 2004); J. P. Klancher, *The Making of English Reading Audiences 1790–1832* (Madison, WI: University of Wisconsin Press, 1987).
5. Ibid., p. 52.
6. D. Latané, 'The Birth of the Author in the Victorian Archive', *Victorian Periodicals Review* 22:3 (Fall 1989), pp. 110–17, on pp. 114–15.
7. St Clair, *The Reading Nation in the Romantic Period*, p. 284. St Clair sees the *Quarterly* as a 'source for building our understanding of horizons of expectations' (p. 284) concern-ing 'the mainstream official ideology' and therefore at odds with the 'emerging romantic aesthetic' (p. 286).
8. M. Parker, *Literary Magazines and British Romanticism* (Cambridge: Cambridge University Press, 2000); N. Sweet, 'The *New Monthly Magazine* and the Liberalism of the 1820s', in Wheatley (ed.), *Romantic Periodicals and Print Culture*, pp. 147–62.

9.  Formally named, that is. The idea of the *Quarterly*, and its name, had previously been concocted by Stratford Canning and others; as Cutmore points out in his forthcoming *Contributors to the Quarterly Review: A History 1809–25* (London: Pickering & Chatto, 2008), the journal resulted from 'a confluence of events and personalities'.

10. J. Sutherland, *The Life of Walter Scott: A Critical Biography* (Oxford: Blackwell, 1995), p. 139.

11. Invited two years previously by Scott to contribute to the *Edinburgh*, Robert Southey had written to Scott: 'The emolument to be derived from writing at ten guineas a sheet … instead of seven pounds for the *Annual* [*Register*], would be considerable; the pecuniary advantage resulting from the different manner in which my future works would be handled [by the *Edinburgh Review*] probably still more so. But my moral feelings must not be compromised' (June 1807); quoted in Smiles, *Memoir*, vol. 1, p. 95. While Murray's comment suggests that the *Edinburgh* was capable or at least thought capable of 'puffing' the works of its own reviewers, it was generally admitted that its publisher, Archibald Constable, did not pressure Jeffrey to notice the books that proceeded from his press. It is this sort of restraint that Scott was calling for from Murray.

12. [J. Mill], 'Periodical Literature. Art IX. *The Quarterly Review*', *Westminster Review*, 2 (October 1824), pp. 463–503, on p. 463. On the other hand, the fact that Leigh Hunt's *The Story of Rimini* (1816), for example, was published by Murray did not prevent it from being attacked by the *Quarterly*. But Mill's slur illustrates perception rather than practice.

13. Shattock, *Politics and Reviewers*, p. 13. Henry Crabb Robinson, for instance, though perhaps not a typical purchaser, regularly read both from cover to cover. See H. C. Robinson, *Henry Crabb Robinson on Books and their Writers*, ed. E. J. Morley, 3 vols (London: J. M. Dent and Sons, 1938). By Cutmore's count, of the 266 *Quarterly Review* subscribers recorded by John Murray in his 1809–12 subscription book, 26 also purchased the *Edinburgh Review*.

14. Cf. a remark made by Robert Southey to his brother about the *Quarterly*: 'In plain English, the Ministers set it up. But they wish it not to wear a party appearance'. Quoted by S. Jones, *Hazlitt: A Life* (Oxford: Clarendon Press, 1989), p. 248. Cf. also Hazlitt's reference to the *Quarterly* in his essay, 'Mr. Jeffrey', in *The Spirit of the Age* (1825) as 'stick[ing] at nothing to serve the turn of a party', in W. Hazlitt, *The Complete Works of William Hazlitt*, ed. P. P. Howe, 21 vols (London: J. M. Dent and Sons, 1930–4), vol. 11, p. 127.

15. Similarly, Murray's 15 November 1808 letter to Scott stresses the need for political 'independence' yet anticipates using 'every valuable political information we can command' (*QR* Letter 8).

16. Cf. J. Stoddart, 'Cultures of Print: Mass Markets and Theories of the Liberal Public Sphere', in E. J. Clery, C. Franklin and P. Garside (eds.), *Authorship, Commerce and the Public: Scenes of Writing, 1750–1850* (Basingstoke: Palgrave Macmillan, 2002), pp. 171–85. Stoddart discusses 'the aristocratic model of polite skimming of topics' (p. 175).

17. As indeed turned out to be the case; Cutmore notes in his Introduction to the present volume that Gifford relied upon an army of sub-editors.

18. This is not the only passage in which Scott asserts that a high-quality beginning will lead to the recruitment of 'regular contributors', if 'we are once set agoing by a few dashing numbers' (*QR* Letter 5). In his 2 November 1808 letter to Ellis, Scott refers to 'our formidable competitors who after all are much better at cutting than parrying and whom

uninterrupted triumph ~~have~~ has as much unfitted for resisting a serious attack as it has done Buonaparte for the Spanish war'. The 'triumph' of the *Edinburgh*, that is to say, actually makes it vulnerable to 'attack'. In the same letter Scott told Ellis to 'hang your birding piece on its hooks take down your old anti Jacobin armour and remember your swashing blow' (*QR* Letter 5). So much for avoiding the *Edinburgh*'s 'violent' political tone (*QR* Letter 4A).

19.   Scott had already assured Ellis that 'in point of learning you Englishmen have ten times our scholarship' (*QR* Letter 5) and Gifford would later tell Scott that, due to English cowardice, 'all our chance of a respectable first appearance depended upon Scotland' (*QR* Letter 15). Picking up on Scott's earlier warfare imagery, Ellis later reiterated a sense of the weakness of the group as well as their supposed leader: 'But we Southerners are, after all, such inefficient troops that, unless your Scottish army forms our corps de reserve, and establishes magazines for our support, our commander fears that we shall soon be starved out of the field' (*QR* Letter 14). Apparently the constant replenishment of 'troops' will be necessary: the *Quarterly* will be a hungry maw.

20.   *SL*, vol. 2, pp. 127–30; vol. 12, pp. 305–7.

21.   *SL*, vol. 2, p. 129.

22.   *SL*, vol. 2, p. 128.

23.   *SL*, vol. 2, pp. 128–9.

24.   Shifting terms, Scott insists that such asceticism will pay off in the form of plain sailing: 'Let us but once get afloat, and our labour is not worth talking of; but, till then, all hands must work hard' (*SL*, vol. 2, p. 128). Canning, it seems, will be the *Quarterly*'s equivalent of Czar Peter, enlisted to work alongside commoners in the trenches.

25.   Quoted from Smiles, *Memoir*, vol. 1, p. 153. Smiles dates this letter 12 March 1809.

26.   Article #15.

27.   Quoted from Smiles, *Memoir*, vol. 1, p. 146; *SL*, vol. 2, pp. 157, 158.

28.   Article #66.

29.   Quoted from Smiles, *Memoir*, vol. 1, p. 155.

30.   Articles #15, 34.

31.   Article #579.

32.   Ellis offered another explanation for the *Quarterly*'s precarious state: its tendency to lag behind the expected date of publication. Ellis insists that '*extensive* success' is endangered by 'irregularity' (*QR* Letter 66). Apropos of the eighth number, he claims that 'punctuality … will redeem our character … because it was apprehended that our troops, being all volunteers, began to be disgusted with the constantly accruing toils of a regular campaign, and that we were incapable of being mustered at the established hour of putting the dishes upon the table' (*QR* Letter 77). The blending of the ongoing images of 'bills of fare', 'cookery' and warfare hint that the *Quarterly*'s hostility towards the *Edinburgh* may be veiled but also diluted by shows of hospitality.

33.   Quoted from Smiles *Memoir*, vol. 1, p. 165. Smiles dates this letter 12 September 1809.

34.   M. Butler, 'Culture's Medium: The Role of the Review', in *The Cambridge Companion to British Romanticism*, ed. S. Curran (Cambridge: Cambridge University Press, 1993), pp. 120–47, on p. 123.

## 2 Hilton, "'Sardonic Grins" and "Paranoid Politics"'

1.  More than anything it was Francis Jeffrey's 1807 review of Cobbett, in which he 'enunciated the classic Whig doctrine of the balance of the Constitution', that 'irrevocably stamped the *Edinburgh Review*'s character as a political publication'. J. Clive, *Scotch Reviewers: The Edinburgh Review, 1802–15* (London: Faber and Faber, 1957), p. 104, citing H. R. Vassall, third Lord Holland, *Further Memoirs of the Whig Party, 1807–21*, ed. Lord Stavordale (London: John Murray, 1905), p. 387.

2.  My use of 'conservative' and 'conservatism' in this chapter is anachronistic, though a case has been made for crediting the *Quarterly Review* with bringing those terms into play. See J. J. Sack, 'The *Quarterly Review* and the Baptism of the "Conservative Party" – A Conundrum Resolved', *Victorian Periodicals Review*, 24 (1991), pp. 170–2. I have also used the anachronistic term 'liberal Toryism' because of its pedigree in the historiography. Otherwise I have followed Gifford and his correspondents in *not* using 'Tory' or 'Toryism', which were still mainly terms of abuse, though they were sometimes used in a neutral sense after about 1815, and then increasingly in a positive sense from the late 1820s onwards. See B. Hilton, *A Mad, Bad, and Dangerous People?: England 1783–1846* (Oxford: Oxford University Press, 2006), pp. 195–7.

3.  Whitbread was an advanced Whig and a member of 'the Mountain', so named after Robespierre, Danton, Marat and Saint-Just in the Revolutionary Convention.

4.  K. Wheatley, 'Paranoid Politics: The *Quarterly* and *Edinburgh* Reviews', *Prose Studies*, 15 (1992), pp. 319–43.

5.  See also Gifford to Ellis, 26 November 1810 (*QR* Letter 70); and Murray to Croker, 1 September 1820 (*QR* Letter 225).

6.  K. Feiling, *Sketches in Nineteenth Century Biography* (London: Longmans, Green, 1930), p. 59.

7.  H. Ben-Israel, *English Historians on the French Revolution* (Cambridge: Cambridge University Press, 1968), p. 180–1.

8.  [J. W. Croker], 'Faber's *Internal State of France*', *QR*, 11 (1811), p. 238 (article #167).

9.  Feiling, *Sketches in Nineteenth Century Biography*, p. 61.

10. W. Thomas, *The Quarrel of Macaulay and Croker: Politics and History in the Age of Reform* (Oxford: Oxford University Press, 2000), pp. 202–3; [J. W. Croker], 'Robespierre', *QR*, 108 (1835), pp. 517–80 (*WI* #464).

11. E. Burke, *A Letter to a Noble Lord on the Attacks made upon Him and His Pension* (1796), in *The Writings and Speeches of Edmund Burke Volume 9: The Revolutionary War, 1794–7*, ed. R. B. McDowell (Oxford: Oxford University Press, 1991), p. 176.

12. [G. Ellis], 'Mr Canning's Letters to Earl Camden', *QR*, 4 (1809), pp. 413–14 (article #62).

13. R. G. Thorne, *History of Parliament: The Commons 1790–1820*, 5 vols (London: Secker and Warburg, 1986), vol. 3, p. 399.

14. Though for a possibly grudging acknowledgement of Castlereagh's merits, see Gifford to Canning, 16 February 1816, *QR* Letter 168.

15. Croker to Vesey Fitzgerald, 20 December 1821, in *The Croker Papers: The Correspondence and Diaries of John Wilson Croker*, ed. L. J. Jennings, 2 vols (New York: Charles Scribner's Sons, 1884), vol. 1, p. 219.

16. For Canning's influence on the development of Conservatism, see Hilton, *A Mad, Bad, and Dangerous People?*, pp. 286–328, 372–97; for the different ways in which 'Canningism' (loosely defined as an appreciation of, and ability to work, 'public opinion')

anticipated the development of Whig-Liberalism, see J. Parry, *The Rise and Fall of Liberal Government in Britain* (New Haven, CY: Yale University Press, 1983), pp. 27–52.

17. [J. Davison, H. H. Drummond and E. Copleston], 'Replies to the Calumnies against Oxford', *QR*, 7 (1810), pp. 177–206 (article #113).

18. P. B. Nockles, *The Oxford Movement in Context: Anglican High Churchmanship, 1760–1857* (Cambridge: Cambridge University Press, 1994), pp. 270–4; M. G. Brock, 'The Oxford of Peel and Gladstone, 1800–40', and R. Brent, 'The Oriel Noetics', in *The History of the University of Oxford: Volume VI, Nineteenth-Century Oxford, Part 1*, ed. M. G. Brock and M. C. Curthoys (Oxford: Oxford University Press, 1997), pp. 49–53, 72–6.

19. Its mouthpiece was the *British Critic* (1793–1843), which was relaunched on Hackney lines in 1813.

20. J. J. Sack, 'The Memory of Burke and the Memory of Pitt: English Conservatism Confronts its Past, 1806–29', *Historical Journal*, 30 (1987), pp. 623–40.

21. B. Jenkins, *Henry Goulburn 1784–1856: A Political Biography* (Montreal and Kingston: McGill-Queens Press, 1996), p. 22.

22. Note to article #106 in *Quarterly Review Archive*, ed. Cutmore.

23. S. Andrews, *Unitarian Radicalism: Political Rhetoric, 1770–1814* (Houndmills: Palgrave, 2003), pp. 149–60.

24. *Christian Observer*, 29 (1829), p. 432.

25. [W. Roberts], 'Dr Copleston on Necessity and Predestination', *British Review*, 18 (1821), p. 361.

26. [W. Roberts], 'More's Practical Piety', *British Review*, 1 (1811), p. 348. Roberts later became More's first biographer.

27. More to James Stephen, 1816, in W. Roberts, *The Life, Letters, and Opinions of William Roberts*, ed. A. Roberts (London: Seeley, 1850), p. 65.

28. [W. Roberts], 'Reports on the Poor Laws', *British Review*, 10 (1817), p. 384.

29. [W. Roberts], 'Chalmers's Astronomical Discourses', *British Review*, 10 (1817), pp. 9, 29–30; *The Life, Letters, and Opinions of William Roberts*, pp. 58–61.

30. B. Hilton, *The Age of Atonement: The Influence of Evangelicalism on Social and Economic Thought, 1795–1865* (Oxford: Oxford University Press, 1988), pp. 56–8.

31. 'Canning goes and all the world are *mad* to hear him.' Murray to Croker, 21 May 1817, *QR* Letter 178.

32. T. Gisborne, *The Testimony of Natural Theology to Christianity* (London: T. Cadell and W. Davies, 1818), pp. 64–5.

33. [T. Dunham Whitaker], 'Gisborne's *Natural Theology*', *QR*, 41 (1819), p. 41 (article #495).

34. Gifford to Murray, July and September 1823, in H. Shine and H. Chadwick Shine, *The Quarterly Review under Gifford: Identification of Contributors 1809–24* (Chapel Hill, NC: University of North Carolina Press, 1949), p. 84.

35. [E. Copleston], 'Buckland – *Reliquiae Diluvianae*', *QR*, 57 (1823), p. 165 (article #680).

36. At one point Perceval teed up Croker to try to persuade Gifford to take the government's line on the currency issue rather than Canning's and Huskisson's. 'This put me in a "towering passion," and I told [Croker] to remind Mr Perceval, that his attention to the *Quarterly* was rather late: that I had never yet received the slightest intimation that he knew of its existence'. Gifford to Ellis, 26 November 1810, *QR* Letter 70.

37. See D. M. Craig, 'Republicanism becoming Conservative: Robert Southey and Political Argument in Britain, 1789–1817' (PhD dissertation, University of Cambridge, 2000), the most significant study to date.

38. [R. Southey], 'The Poor', *QR*, 29 (1816), p. 235 (article #385).

39. P. James, *Population Malthus: His Life and Times* (London: Routledge and Kegan Paul, 1979), p. 348.

40. Southey continued to review for the *Quarterly*, but not often on mainstream social and economic issues.

41. That is to say, sinful.

42. [J. B. Sumner], 'Malthus *on Population*', *QR*, 34 (1817), pp. 402–3 (article #434).

43. Malthus first wrote for the *Quarterly* in 1823. In 1824 he reviewed McCulloch's *Encyclopaedia Britannica* article on political economy, and made the significant complaint that it ignored the impact of supply and demand on the determination of value.

44. Even so, it was *Fraser's Magazine* (1830–82) that would eventually express conservative evangelical attitudes best.

45. Croker to Sir George Sinclair, August 1840, in *Memoirs of the Life and Works of Sir George Sinclair*, ed. J. Sinclair (Edinburgh: William Blackwood; London: T. Cadell, 1837), pp. 223–4.

46. 'On Spain and Portugal we stand on high ground; this, too, is our rival's weak side.' Gifford to Scott, 17 April 1811, *QR* Letter 90.

47. Holland, *Further Memoirs of the Whig Party*, p. 15.

48. *Parliamentary Debates*, 1st series, 27:150 (17 November 1813).

49. E. Halévy, *The Liberal Awakening (1815–30)*, rev. edn, trans. E. I. Watkin (New York: Barnes and Noble, 1961), pp. ix–x.

50. Feiling, *Sketches in Nineteenth Century Biography*, p. 55.

51. Ibid., p. 66. In fact Croker was not as wedded to every aspect of the ancien régime as Feiling's words imply. An Irishman, he supported Roman Catholic emancipation, for example, one reason why he backed Canning.

52. Ben-Israel, *English Historians on the French Revolution*, pp. 177–8.

53. Holland to Grey, 21 December 1826, in K. Feiling, *The Second Tory Party 1714–1832* (New York: St Martin's Press, 1951), pp. 401–2.

54. I am grateful for the advice and suggestions of Jonathan Cutmore. The opinions expressed are of course my own.

# 3 Cutmore, 'A Plurality of Voices in the *Quarterly Review*'

1. Gifford was the *Quarterly's* first editor. In the early nineteenth century, presenting or requesting a lock of hair was a common social gesture. Virginia Murray told me that there were 'bales of hair in the vault' of the John Murray Archive at 50 Albemarle Street.

2. JM MS, JM II's *Quarterly Review* planning notes. For the names in Murray's notebook, see Cutmore, *Contributors to the Quarterly Review*.

3. Elsewhere in his notebook, Murray records assignments for two other publishers, Cadell and Longman, and for Scott's printer, Ballantyne. Though James Ballantyne was actively involved in the production of the journal's first two numbers, there is no evidence that the other two men took part. Thomas Cadell became Scott's publisher after 1825.

4. The meeting took place over three days beginning on 2 October. Sutherland in his *The Life of Walter Scott* (p. 139) notes that Ballantyne was present at the meeting; other

historians have missed that important detail; cf. Smiles, *Memoir*, vol. 1, p. 400; and E. Johnson, *Sir Walter Scott*, 2 vols (London: Hamish Hamilton, 1970), vol. 1, p. 232.

5.  'Tory' and 'conservative' are used in this essay for the sake of convenience: at the founding of the *Quarterly Review* 'Tory' was at best a facetious term, not a label accepted by any faction or party; as a party label, 'conservative' was not used at all. Following Corson, I have regularized the spelling of Scott's country residence as 'Ashiestiel'. See Corson, *Notes and Index to Sir Herbert Grierson's Edition*.

6.  Murray's early *Quarterly Review* subscription list is preserved in the John Murray Archive.

7.  In the Introduction to the present volume, I argue that the founders of the *Quarterly Review* were British nationalists.

8.  L. Brake, *Subjugated Knowledges: Journalism, Gender, and Literature in the Nineteenth Century* (Basingstoke: Macmillan, 1994), p. 121.

9.  Kim Wheatley in her essay in the present volume explores Murray's profit motive in conducting the *Quarterly Review*.

10. Shattock, *Politics and Reviewers* thus nicely describes the two great literary-political journals of the period.

11. The first version of the advertisement appeared in various London newspapers at the beginning of January 1809. A revised version appeared at the end of the month. These are the variants between the first and second versions: ᵃ Gentlemen] Authors; ᵇ they would] would; ᶜ of the] to their; ᵈ the] their; ᵉ the] their; ᶠ Literature, with ... conducted.] Literature.

12. We know the decision against a prospectus was taken at Ashiestiel because, without having any further communication with each other, direct or indirect, following the meeting both Scott and Murray refer to it in letters (Scott to Gifford, 25 October 1808, *QR* Letter 4; Murray to Scott, 15 November 1808, *QR* Letter 8).

13. Baffled by the decision to work in secret, Smiles concluded that Murray and his coadjutors wished to guard an escape route lest the project fail, surely a poor compliment to the principals' courage and determination. Smiles, *Memoir*, vol. 1, p. 124.

14. JM MS. Stanley Lane Poole, the author of a *The Life of ... Stratford Canning*, 2 vols (London: Longmans, Green, 1888), evidently saw the letter, but in digesting it he left out the detail that, crucially, dates to the late spring or early summer of 1807 the walk along Pall Mall when Stratford Canning and his friends Gally Knight and Richard Wellesley thought up the idea of the *Quarterly Review*. There was a notable connection between Murray and the Pall Mall friends, for the three men were indebted to him: he had rescued them some years before from complications over their Etonian literary publication, 'The Miniature'. It was undoubtedly out of a sense of obligation to the young publisher that Stratford Canning brought Murray and Gifford together in January 1808 to discuss his, Stratford's, *Quarterly Review* project. Despite the coincidence of these two men who knew each other having had the same idea at about the same time and directing it to the same person, George Canning, prior to September 1807 they did not coordinate their efforts.

15. In November 1797, George Canning, George Ellis and John Hookham Frere hired Gifford to edit their Pittite journal *The Anti-Jacobin; or, Weekly Examiner*. That newspaper should not be confused with the Protestant Constitutionalist *Antijacobin Review, and True Churchman's Magazine* (1798–1821).

16. So far as can be determined, the first Scott heard about Stratford Canning's part was when Gifford told him that it was Stratford, not George, Canning, with whom Murray

had discussed starting a new journal. See Gifford to Scott, 9 November 1808, *QR* Letter 6.

17. The evidence in this essay demonstrates Murray's aggressive management of his gentlemen, but his countervailing timidity is also well attested to. Byron called him 'the most timorous of God's booksellers'; 'a reed shaken in the wind' was Scott's verdict; 'all sail and no ballast' is how Rose saw him. Croker exactly described Murray's usual way of making a decision: 'like other weak people, he *commits* himself on such or such a point and then goes round the circle of his acquaintance until he can find someone whose advice may countenance the source to which he had already pledged himself'. These quotations are in Shattock, *Politics and Reviewers*, p. 51.

18. Indeed, Gifford excluded Murray from his 'little band'; it consisted of Scott, Ellis and himself.

19. Scott to Gifford, 'our scheme', 'our proposed Review' (*QR* Letter 4); Gifford to Scott, 'our proposed scheme' (*QR* Letter 6); Gifford to Ellis, 'our Review' (*QR* Letter 158); Murray to Scott, 'our Review' (*QR* Letter 8); Ellis to Scott, 'our Review' (*QR* Letter 11); Murray to Croker, Barrow, and others, 'my Review' (*QR* Letters 164, 170, 179, 190, 237); Stephen, Barrow and Southey to Murray refer to the *Quarterly* as 'your review' (*QR* Letters 22, 146, 196); Gifford to Canning, 'the Review' (*QR* Letter 257). On at least one occasion, in December 1808, Scott, writing to Murray, magnanimously referred to 'your Review'. See *SL*, vol. 2, pp. 178–9. Scott, who was asking a favour of Murray, knew how to appeal to the publisher's ego. He was also acknowledging Murray's legal proprietorship.

20. In his letter he invites the statesman to endorse a journal to offset the 'radically bad' principles of the liberal *Edinburgh Review*.

21. Dictionary definitions of 'merchant adventurer' and 'noblesse oblige' exactly describe the motivation Murray was denying and the one he was laying claim to. Adventurer: 'one that engages or shares in commercial enterprises of considerable risk for profit'. Noblesse oblige: 'the obligation of honourable, generous, and responsible behaviour that is a concomitant of high rank or birth'. *Merriam-Webster* subscription dictionary: <http://unabridged.merriam-webster.com>. The reader may object that Murray's correspondent was not an aristocrat. True, but the system Canning upheld was a vestige of the ancien régime.

22. The Number was dated 'February 1809' but it appeared on 1 March. 'Tomorrow, the first of March, will be published ... the First Number of / the Quarterly Review by John Murray ...' (*Courier*, 28 February 1809).

23. J. O. Hayden, *The Romantic Reviewers, 1802–24* (Chicago, IL: Chicago University Press, 1968), p. 23, 23n., catalogues the plans of various groups to combat the *Edinburgh Review*.

24. Gifford was an acquaintance of James Stephen and a friend of one of the leading Saints, Lord Teignmouth. Thornton, Stephen and Macaulay, despite their good intentions, did not in the end contribute except as subeditors of other men's reviews; but it was with their encouragement that the second-generation Saints Henry Stephen and Robert Grant became involved as contributors. Barrow called Teignmouth one of Gifford's 'patrons' in the conduct of the *Quarterly Review* (*QR* Letter 146).

25. Ellis to Scott, 22 October 1810, NLS MS 3879, ff. 222–3.

26. A letter Grosvenor Bedford sent to Peter Elmsley on 26 January 1809 confirms that Scott told others that the idea started with him. In summarizing the origins of the soon-to-be published *Quarterly*, Bedford states that the 'idea originated with Walter Scott about

three months ago'. Bedford's information came from Scott via Southey (Westminster MS; my thanks to Chris Stray for pointing me to this letter). That Scott claimed to be the originator is also confirmed in *QR* Letter 7.

27. Graham, *Tory Criticism in the Quarterly Review*, p. 6.

28. In a number of cogently argued letters to Scott and Gifford, Ellis developed a marketing strategy for the journal, a political agenda and an editorial plan. Canning, Ellis and Gifford also held a series of editorial conferences in November and December 1808. See *QR* Letters 7, 10, 11, 14, 29.

29. Scott wrote to Murray on 30 November (see *SL*, vol. 2, pp. 114–15). Murray anticipated him by writing on 26 November. See Murray to Scott, 26 November 1808, JM MS, and Smiles, *Memoir*, vol. 1, pp. 98–9.

30. 'Canning put into my hands some weeks ago a letter from your Lord Advocate in which your suggestion was mentioned ...'. Ellis to Scott, 11 November 1808, *QR* Letter 7.

31. Ellis's 11 November 1808 reply is *QR* Letter 7.

32. So much so that he felt compelled to apologize to Scott for his lack of progress; see Murray to Scott, 26 November 1808, JM MS.

33. He refers to the *Quarterly Review* project in one sentence as 'my plan' but in another sentence as 'our plan'.

34. Emphasis added. By 'two years' Murray may be reminding Scott that in 1806 they (Scott and Murray) had agreed to support Thomas Campbell's plan for a new literary magazine (*SL*, vol. 2, pp. 45–6; Campbell to Murray, 3 March 1806, in Smiles, *Memoir*, vol. 1, p. 324).

35. [S. Turner], 'Austrian State Papers' (article #35).

36. JM MS, Murray to Annie Murray, 8 August 1809; cf. JM MS, same, 19 July 1809.

37. That it was in Murray's character to interfere is confirmed in his continuing to meddle with the editor's conduct of his duties when Coleridge took over from Gifford and when Lockhart took over from Coleridge.

38. 'I know not what to do to facilitate your labour', he wrote to Gifford early on, 'for the articles which you have long had lie scattered without attention, and those which I ventured to send to the printer undergo such retarding corrections, that even by this mode we do not advance' (Murray to Gifford, 11 May 1809, quoted in Smiles, *Memoir*, vol. 1, p. 156). In 1823, Barrow expressed, too harshly, his negative conclusion about the utility of Gifford's 'retarding corrections', but his condemnation contained a grain of truth: 'You know, as well as myself, what little alteration or addition he makes – in fact it is mere twaddling, and admits not of any excuse whatever' (Barrow to Murray, 18 August 1823, *QR* Letter 252).

39. The most egregious instances when Murray interfered with Gifford's editorial prerogatives involved the contributors Conybeare, Pillans, Tuner, Kidd, Glassford, Sumner, Thomson and Monk.

40. Smiles, *Memoir*, vol. 1, p.184.

41. The record is unclear about whether Scott declined the editorship during the discussions at Ashiestiel.

42. Murray to Scott, 26 November 1808, JM MS; Erskine to Campbell-Colquhoun (*SL*, vol. 2, pp. 101–2, 102n.).

43. JM MS.

44. See note 34 above.

45. The Saints were a group of evangelical philanthropists dedicated to slave-trade abolition and to the 'reformation of manners'. Their impact on British society was broad and deep. The best work on the Saints' influence is Hilton, *The Age of Atonement*. For background,

see D. W. Bebbington, *Evangelicalism in Modern Britain: A History from the 1830s to the 1980s* (London: Routledge, 1989); I. Bradley, *The Call to Seriousness: The Evangelical Impact on the Victorians* (London: Cass, 1976); R. J. Hind, 'William Wilberforce and the Perceptions of the British People', *Historical Research*, 60 (October 1987), pp. 321–35; E. M. House, *Saints in Politics: The Saints and the Growth of Freedom* (London: George, Allen, and Unwin, 1953); and M. Jaeger, *Before Victoria: Changing Standards and Behaviour, 1787–1837* (London: Chatto and Windus, 1956).

46. On 27 October 1810, Gifford told Scott that Grant's article was 'our manifesto, our political creed, which we must contend for' (*QR* Letter 65).

47. A version of this narrative of the Saints' role in the founding of the *Quarterly Review* is a chapter in my 1991 University of Toronto PhD dissertation, 'Saints, Prophets, and Paternalists'.

48. 'Ingram on Methodism' in the January 1808 number (*WI* #388) and 'Indian Missions' in the April 1808 number (*WI* #406). After the formation of the *Quarterly*, Smith continued the series in the April 1809 number with 'Styles on Methodists and Missions' (*WI* #455).

49. Southey to H. H. Southey, 7 December 1808, in *Selections from the Letters of Robert Southey*, ed. J. W. Warter, 4 vols (London: Longman, Brown, Green, and Longmans, 1856), vol. 2, p. 114.

50. Smiles, *Memoir*, vol. 1, pp. 116–17.

51. *SL*, vol. 2, pp. 136–7.

52. In Elton's review of the evangelical poet Worgan in Number 6, for instance (article #96).

53. Articles #244, #688.

54. Articles #594, #772.

55. Although Church parties existed in the 1810s and 1820s, the differences between them were more muddled than they would become in the 1830s and later. See Nockles, *The Oxford Movement in Context*, pp. 25n., 25ff.

56. On 'moderate' and 'extreme' evangelicals, see Hilton, *The Age of Atonement*, pp. 10–15. Moderate evangelicals, such as the Saints, optimistically believed that humankind and the Holy Spirit, in a kind of joint-stock venture, could establish God's kingdom before Christ's Second Coming; many extreme evangelicals pessimistically believed that God would bring about his kingdom without our help, but that he would wait until after the Second Coming. Moderate, not extreme, evangelicals were more or less welcome in the *Quarterly Review* under Gifford. On the Church parties, see Nockles, *The Oxford Movement in Context*, and A. Burns, *The Diocesan Revival in the Church of England c. 1800–70* (New York: Oxford University Press, 1999). Gifford was probably a 'high and dry' Church-and-State man who valued the Church in part because it was a component of the establishment.

57. A name given to the *Edinburgh* in the Midlands. See H. Pearson, *Memoirs of the Life and Writings of the Rev. Claudius Buchanan*, 2 vols (Oxford: Oxford University Press, 1817), pp. 191–2.

58. If proof were needed of the sincerity of Brougham's commitment to abolition, he wrote twenty-three articles on this single subject during Jeffrey's tenure, an extraordinary concentration of effort.

59. Celestial metaphors were common in contemporary nicknames for the *Edinburgh*, such as this example, 'the aurora-*borealis* (great *Northern* light)', from the *Satirist*, 1 (December 1807), p. 318.

60. *WI* #163. For the episode, see H. Atkinson and G. A. Jackson (eds.), *Brougham and His Early Friends*, 2 vols (London: privately printed, 1908), vol. 2, pp. 130, 143–6, 150.

61. *WI* #439.

62. Before 1809, in their letters Coleridge, Southey and Scott, and William and Dorothy Wordsworth, specifically complained about the following reviews of poets: 'Southey's *Thalaba*', 1 (October 1802); 'Thelwall's *Poems*', 2 (April 1803); 'Southey's *Madoc*', 7 (October 1805); 'Poems by W. Wordsworth', 11 (October 1807); and 'Scott's *Marmion*', 12 (April 1808). Jeffrey wrote all of these reviews.

63. The Montgomery review is *WI* #332; the Cowper review is (part 1) *WI* #57, (part 2) *WI* #160. In addition to these articles and Sydney Smith's articles on Methodism and missions, religious readers were offended by: a review of the sermons of Sir Henry Moncreiff, the leader of the Scottish evangelical party (*WI* #218); a review of Hoyle's religious poem 'Exodus' (*WI* #249); a review by Sir William Drummond of the evangelical matriarch Hannah More's *Hints to a Princess* (*WI* #294); and an article on the Curates' Salaries Bill (*WI* #427).

64. *ER* #364, #422, #439.

65. Southey to Coleridge, 9 December 1807, quoted in E. L. Griggs, 'Robert Southey and the *Edinburgh Review*', *Modern Philology*, 30 (August 1932), pp. 100–3, on p. 100.

66. See Southey to Scott, 8 December 1807, in *Life and Correspondence of Robert Southey*, ed. C. C. Southey, 6 vols (London: Longman, Brown, Green and Longmans, 1849–50), vol. 3, pp. 124–5, 127; and Southey to Grosvenor Bedford, 11 November 1808, in *NL*, vol. 1, p. 492.

67. See note 48 above.

68. J. Conder, *Reviewers Reviewed* (Oxford: Reid, 1811), p. 23.

69. The religious world's reaction to Smith's articles was in the tradition of the long-running 'decorum of religious ridicule' debate, a cultural carry-over from the seventeenth and eighteenth centuries. On this debate, see R. Anselment, '*Betwixt Jest and Earnest*': *Marprelate, Milton, Marvell, Swift and the Decorum of Religious Ridicule* (Toronto: University of Toronto Press, 1979), pp. 1–32; and E. Bloom and L. D. Bloom, *Satire's Persuasive Voice* (London: Cornell University Press, 1979), esp. ch. 4: '*Sacramentum Militiae*: Religious Satire', pp. 160–201.

70. Brougham to Macvey Napier, 9 March 1825, BL Add. MSS 34617, f. 54.

71. H. Brougham, *The Life and Times of Henry Brougham, Written by Himself*, 3 vols (Edinburgh: William Blackwood, 1871), vol. 1, p. 262. Evangelicals generally were sensitive about this distinction, as we see in a January 1805 *Courier* notice: a condemned murderer about to be executed wanted it known that he died as a devout communicant of the Church of England, not as a Methodist!

72. The Church of England evangelical leadership sponsored Claudius Buchanan (1766–1815): the evangelical patriarch John Newton converted him, Henry Thornton supported him while he was at Cambridge, and Charles Grant helped bring about his 1796 appointment as a chaplain to the East India Company. He eventually made a modest fortune as Vice-Provost of the Company's college at Fort William. See Pearson, *Memoirs of ... the Rev. Claudius Buchanan*, and, for other relevant sources, the *ODNB* entry.

73. Examples of the extensive public reaction include: *Critical Review*, 3rd ser., 8 (May 1806), pp. 49–60, in which the reviewer, though otherwise negative, declared the subject to be 'of the very highest importance'; *Monthly Review*, 53 (May 1807), pp. 40–5; *British Critic*, 26 (September 1805), pp. 254–60, and 27 (March 1806), pp. 217–60; *Eclectic Review*, 1 (April 1805), pp. 378–86, and 1 (September 1805), pp. 668–73; *Monthly Repository*, 1 (September 1806), pp. 444–5.

74. M. Knutsford, *Life and Letters of Zachary Macaulay* (London: Edward Arnold, 1900), p. 297; C. H. Philips, *The East India Company, 1784–1834* (Manchester: Manchester University Press, 1961), pp. 188–9.

75. *The Times*, 9 January 1807, p. 3.

76. On the Vellore mutiny and the anti-missions reaction, see Philips, *The East India Company*, pp. 160–2, 168–9; and A. T. Embree, *Charles Grant and British Rule in India* (New York: Columbia University Press, 1962), pp. 237–49. Historians have vindicated the missionaries: see S. Neill, *History of Christianity in India, 1707–1858* (Cambridge: Cambridge University Press, 1985), pp. 149–50. These and other historians, though, have taken little note of Buchanan's role in shaping public reaction to the incident or to Smith's use of it.

77. On the meaning and importance of these factions to the history of the Company, see Philips, *The East India Company*, pp. 23–4. For the opposition to Grant and Parry, see ibid., pp. 161, n., 164, n.

78. Scott-Waring to Warren Hastings, 21 March 1808, BL Add. MSS 29183, f. 203, 'There is a most excellent Critique in the Edinburgh Review, not on the Pamphlets written but on the general subject of Indian Missions'.

79. Smith had a demonstrable influence on the debate. Although in January 1808 only the *Monthly Review*, the *Eclectic* and the *Evangelical Magazine* reviewed a couple of pamphlets on the question, after Smith's 'Ingram on Methodism' appeared, all of the main reviews (excepting the *British Critic*) stepped into the fray with extensive articles pitched at a high level of urgency. See also Farington's long diary entry for 3 February 1808 in which he relates the mistaken impression that Grant and Thornton, 'inclined to Methodism', had chosen irresponsible enthusiasts as missionaries to be sent out to India. If the missionaries were not recalled, he wrote, 'India wd. soon be lost to us'. *The Diary of Joseph Farington*, ed. K. Garlick and A. Macintyre, 16 vols (New Haven, CT: Yale University Press, 1978–84), vol. 9, ed. K. Cave, pp. 3213–14.

80. R. Wilberforce and S. Wilberforce, *The Life of William Wilberforce*, 5 vols (London: John Murray, 1838), vol. 3, p. 364; H. Morris, *The Life of Charles Grant* (London: John Murray, 1904), p. 302.

81. Thomas Creevy, Speech on the Stipendiary Curates Salaries Bill (8 June 1808; Commons), *Parliamentary Debates*, 11, col. 834.

82. *WI* #427. Smith improved upon a passage in Lord Milton's 8 June 1808 speech on the Curates Salaries Bill: 'Poverty had hitherto been the badge of honour of our religious; but opinions had changed, and it was now necessary alone that the clergy should be respectable, but they must also be rich'. *Parliamentary Debates*, 11, col. 836.

83. Jeffrey blamed the commencement of the *Quarterly Review* on his own mischievousness in not reining in Drummond and Brougham. See F. Horner, *Memoirs and Correspondence*, ed. L. Horner, 2 vols (London: John Murray, 1852), vol. 1, p. 465, and cf. vol. 1, p. 212. For complaints about the *Edinburgh*'s skepticism, see Brougham, *The Life and Times*, vol. 1, p. 262. Jeffrey warned Sir William Drummond, who was responsible for a number of articles offensive to orthodox Christian readers, to avoid controversy: Jeffrey to Drummond, [November 1806], in G. Festing, *John Hookham Frere and His Friends* (London: Nisbet, 1899), pp. 144–5.

84. *NL*, vol. 2, p. 271.

85. The difficulty of defining what 'High Church' means in this period is discussed by James J. Sack in his *From Jacobite to Conservative: Reaction and Orthodoxy in Britain, c. 1760–1832* (Cambridge: Cambridge University Press, 1993), pp. 194–8. In the present essay, I draw a distinction between Erastian Orthodox Churchmen (also called 'old high church') and pre-Tractarian, anti-Erastian High Churchmen.

86. Christopher Hibbert and Amanda Foreman (whom Hibbert cites) highlight the Whigs' social and linguistic separateness. See, respectively, *Queen Victoria: A Personal History* (Cambridge: Da Capo Press, 2001), p. 65; and *Georgiana, Duchess of Devonshire* (New York: Random House, 1998), pp. 30, 45–6.

87. Gifford to Murray, 17 May 1811, quoted in Smiles, *Memoir*, vol. 1, p. 193.

88. The Orthodox are also known as 'high and dry' or 'old high church'. These are the so-called 'two bottle orthodox' – Erastian Church-and-State men – that Ollard contrasts with the 'spiritual orthodox', the men I refer to as the pre-Tractarian High Churchmen. See S. L. Ollard, *A Short History of the Oxford Movement* (London: Mowbray, 1935), pp. 21–5.

89. As Hilton puts it in his essay in the present volume, 'by 1800 this third species of Churchmanship, while retaining an undogmatic and relativist approach to scriptural truth, was also becoming more fervent in its approach to worship, the outcome being referred to sometimes as liberal Anglicanism, and in an Oxford context known then as Noeticism'.

90. Sack, in *From Jacobite to Conservative*, develops the thesis that in this period conservative periodicals generally were driven by a desire to defend Christianity and the prerogatives of the established Church.

91. Lockhart purged the journal of at least one constituency that played an important role during Gifford's tenure, the Noetics, whom he considered to be 'a set of d—d idiots' (quoted in Shattock, *Politics and Reviewers*, p. 55). A High Churchman himself, though he distrusted the Anglo-Catholic tendencies of the Tractarians, in his coverage of religion Lockhart tended to exclude the Erastian Orthodox in favour of the anti-Erastian High Church. As for the *Quarterly* espousing High Tory views under Lockhart, the situation is complicated. Although the *Quarterly* took the High Tories' position on two defining topics – Catholic Emancipation and the reform of parliament – Lockhart's chief political writer, Croker, wrote in support of the Maynooth grant and he backed Peel's Corn Law policy.

92. 'I once thought of Robert Grant [for the editorship] but he proved timid, and indeed his saintly propensities would render him suspected'. Gifford to Canning, 8 September 1824, quoted in Smiles, *Memoir*, vol. 2, p. 163.

93. For the transition of the editorship from Coleridge to Lockhart, see Shattock, *Politics and Reviewers*; Thomas, *The Quarrel of Macaulay and Croker*; and Cutmore, *Contributors to the Quarterly Review*.

94. As Shattock points out, Murray now became 'in many respects his own editor ... Lockhart was tentative in his suggestions, deferred to his judgement, made diplomatic reference to "your Review" and assumed that the final decisions were his'. Shattock, *Politics and Reviewers*, p. 56.

95. On the shift in cultural momentum from the liberal to the High Tories, see Hilton, *The Age of Atonement*, *passim*.

96. Article #440, p. 532.

97. My thanks to Christopher Stray and Sylvia Jones Cutmore for reading and commenting on drafts of this essay.

## 4 Stray, 'Politics, Culture and Scholarship'

1. Virgil, *Georgics*, II.401. His remarks were doubly apt: in December 1810 he was not only moving towards a new issue, but beginning a new (third) annual cycle of four quarterly issues.

2. Classical phrases and references, some in Greek but most in Latin, occur in many of Gifford's letters.

3. J. Boswell, *Life of Johnson*, 2 vols (London: Oxford University Press, 1927), vol. 1, p. 484. Not all members of polite society could be assumed to understand such phrases: Johnson complained of David Garrick that 'He has not Latin enough. He finds out the Latin by the meaning, and not the meaning by the Latin' (ibid., vol. 1, p. 603).

4. C. A. Stray, *Classics Transformed: Schools, Universities, and Society in England 1830–1960* (Oxford: Clarendon Press, 1998), pp. 7–29; F. Waquet, *Latin, or the Empire of a Sign* (London: Verson, 2001); Stray, 'Scholars, Gentlemen and Schoolboys: The Authority of Latin in Nineteenth and Twentieth-Century England', in C. Burnett and N. Mann (eds), *Britannia Latina: Latin in the Culture of Great Britain from the Middle Ages to the Twentieth Century* (London: Warburg Institute, 2005), pp. 194–208.

5. It did not enter the Oxford curriculum until the 1890s; at Cambridge it had to wait until the 1910s.

6. *The Antiquities of Athens, Measured and Delineated by James Stuart and Nicholas Revett*, 2 vols (London: John Haberkorn, 1762–87). A three-volume edition appeared in 1794, a fourth volume in 1816 and a fifth in 1830.

7. See article #377.

8. Articles #110, #242, #426.

9. T. De Quincey, 'The Antigone of Sophocles as Represented on the Edinburgh Stage in December 1845. Part 1', *Tait's Edinburgh Magazine*, 17 (February 1846), pp. 111–16, on p. 111; reprinted in D. Masson (ed.), *The Collected Writings of Thomas De Quincey*, 14 vols (Edinburgh: Adam and Charles Black, 1897), vol. 10, pp. 360–1.

10. W. R. Ward, *Georgian Oxford: University Politics in the Eighteenth Century* (Oxford: Clarendon Press, 1965), pp. 13–14.

11. J. Gascoigne, *Cambridge in the Age of the Enlightenment* (Cambridge: Cambridge University Press, 1989), pp. 270–99; A. Warwick, *Masters of Theory: Cambridge and the Rise of Mathematical Physics* (Chicago, IL: University of Chicago Press, 2003). For a recent discussion of the contrasts between the two universities, see C. A. Stray, 'Non-Identical Twins: Classics in Nineteenth-Century Oxford and Cambridge', in C. A. Stray (ed.), *Oxford Classics: Teaching and Learning 1800–2000* (London: Duckworth Publishers, 2007), pp. 1–13.

12. These were pioneered by St John's in 1765, followed in 1790 by Trinity.

13. See in general C. A. Stray, 'From one Museum to another: The *Museum Criticum* (1813–26) and the *Philological Museum* (1831–3)', *Victorian Periodicals Review*, 37 (2004), pp. 289–314.

14. Monk to Blomfield, 8 February 1813, Trinity Monk A2/7. Quoted by permission of the Master and Fellows of Trinity College, Cambridge.

15. They were thus 'Greek play bishops': see Stray, *Classics Transformed*, pp. 39, 41, 61. It should be stressed that political and religious opinions were also relevant to the appointment of such men, as was pointed out by John William Donaldson in *Classical Scholarship and Classical Learning* (Cambridge: Deighton, Bell, 1856), p. 183.

16. '[W]hy should his [Porson's] disciples ... admit nothing to have the least claim to attention which is not of the Porsonian School?' S. Butler, *A Letter to the Rev. C. J. Blomfield, A.B., Containing Remarks on the Edinburgh Review of the Cambridge Aeschylus, and Incidental Observations on that of the Oxford Strabo* (Shrewsbury: W. Eddowes, 1810), p. 14. On the Porsonians, see M. L. Clarke, *Greek Scholarship in England from 1700 to 1830* (Cambridge: Cambridge University Press, 1945), pp. 85–101; C. O. Brink, *English Classical Scholarship: Historical Reflections on Bentley, Porson, and Housman* (New York: Oxford University Press, 1986), p. 99–113. On the Porsonian cult, see C. A. Stray, 'The Rise and Fall of Porsoniasm', *Cambridge Classical Journal*, 53 (2007), pp. 40–71.

17. See *Gentleman's Magazine* (November 1812), pp. 444–5, 517–20; (April 1813), pp. 351–4, 633–6; 'Graeculus' (January 1813), p. 33, that many thought 'J. H. M.' was in fact Barker. Graeculus himself was Peter Elmsley, as he admitted to Blomfield: Blomfield to Elmsley, 24 February 1813, Elmsley papers, Westminster. These papers are quoted in this chapter by permission of the Headmaster of Westminster School.

18. Articles #138 and #381.

19. Monk to Blomfield, 15 July 1813, Trinity Monk A2/10. The target of the proposed satire was Edmund Barker.

20. Article #571. Valpy printed a sixteen-page reply to Blomfield which was attached to his current advertisements for books. These were bound up with the *Quarterly Review*; he thus managed to have his response distributed by the enemy. Few of such bound-in items have survived, but Valpy's text is preserved as a separate item: BL, shelfmark 816. l.47(76.).

21. See Cutmore, *Contributors to the Quarterly Review*; article #571, pp. 377, 294.

22. Article #492.

23. P. Knight, 'The Oxford Edition of Strabo', *ER*, 14 (July 1809), pp. 429–41 (*WI* #478); S. Smith, 'Edgeworth's *Professional Education*', *ER*, 15 (October 1809), pp. 40–53 (*WI* #484).

24. E. Copleston, *A Reply to the Calumnies of the Edinburgh Review against Oxford* (Oxford: J. Cooke and J. Parker, 1810); *A Second Reply* (Oxford, 1810); *A Third Reply* (Oxford, 1811). Payne Knight, Smith and John Playfair replied with 'Calumnies against Oxford', *ER*, 16 (April 1810), pp. 158–87 (*WI* #517). Copleston's pamphlets were reviewed (favourably) in the *Quarterly* (article #113), but the article was the subject of a serious conflict between Gifford and Murray (see the note to article #113 in *Quarterly Review Archive*, ed. Cutmore).

25. Article #113.

26. The article in question must be the August 1813 *Edinburgh* review of Hermann's edition of Photius (*WI* #573). The tentative attribution in *WI* is therefore confirmed. Ironically, *WI* made its attribution on the ground that Blomfield was a regular contributor. In fact, the refusal of Jeffrey to return this article to its author was, together with religious differences, the cause of Blomfield's *ceasing* to be a regular contributor.

27. A. T. Grafton, 'Polyhistor into Philolog: Notes on the Transformation of German Classical Scholarship 1780–1850', *History of Universities*, 3 (1983), pp. 159–92.

28. For an example, see article #381, discussed below.

29. Bedford to Elmsley, 26 January 1809, Elmsley papers, Westminster. The three men had been fellow-pupils at Westminster School.

30. The balance between minority interests could itself be a subject of negotiation: Elmsley reported to Butler on 14 November 1811 that he had promised Jeffrey an article on

Catholics, 'as the price of his inserting a long paper of mine on the Preface to the Hecuba', BL Add. MSS 34583/342. The reference is to *ER* #579 and 595.

31. 'The Alcestis of Euripides' (article #381), on p. 125. The 'minute criticisms' occupy pp. 117–25. The theme was taken up by John Symmons of Oxford, reviewing Blomfield's *Agamemnon* in 1820 (article #597, p. 529): 'We are afraid we have tired the general reader by the minuteness of our philological remarks'.

32. Blomfield to Elmsley, 6 May 1812, Elmsley papers, Westminster.

33. Elmsley to [Blomfield], 8 February 1813, Bodleian Library MS Autogr. d 24, ff. 150r.–1v. Blomfield is not addressed by name, but he is clearly the recipient. Compare A. Blomfield, *A Memoir of Charles James Blomfield*, 2 vols (London: John Murray, 1863), vol. 1, p. 12, who quotes from the letter.

34. Article #6, p. 69.

35. In 1809, Oxford had two classical prizes or scholarships, while Cambridge had seven; by 1824 the totals had risen to three and ten respectively.

36. Article #121.

37. It is interesting that the book was published by Valpy, who in the same year brought out the first issue of the *Classical Journal*, soon to become the rival of Monk and Blomfield's *Museum Criticum* and the stamping ground of their bête noire, the irritating E. H. Barker.

38. M. L. Clarke, *Richard Porson: A Biographical Essay* (Cambridge: Cambridge University Press, 1937), p. 104.

39. *ER* article #617.

40. Article #227, p. 402. The mistaken attribution to Robert Southey in *DNB* is taken over by *ODNB*. The article is not included in the definitive list in K. Curry and R. Dedmon, 'Southey's Contributions to *The Quarterly Review*', *Wordsworth Circle*, 6 (1974), pp. 261–72. In the *Quarterly Review Archive* Cutmore introduces evidence that may point to Scott, but Scott was hardly competent to review a book of Latin compositions, as Sharon Ragaz notes in the present volume: 'That the reviewer himself shows an extensive and intensive knowledge of the language and prosody might cast doubt on Scott's authorship of this review: his knowledge of Latin was serviceable at best'. In 1812, when the Cambridge classicist James Bailey wrote to Scott congratulating him on his *Border Minstrelsy* and enclosing some Latin verses, Scott replied that 'Upon the point of Latinity the approbation of a Scotsman is not worth having ...'. Scott to Bailey, 12 March 1812, *SL*, vol. 3, p. 192. The most likely candidate is Gifford. The reviewer, though finding much to criticize, was careful to include a meed of praise; it can hardly be called 'savage', as Pillans's *ODNB* article has it.

41. These 'epics' were named after two notorious poetasters of the late Roman Republic, Bavius and Maevius (Virgil, *Eclogues*, III.90–1; Horace, *Epodes*, X).

42. C. A. Bristed, *Five Years in an English University*, 2nd edn (New York: G. P. Putnam, 1852), p. 136.

43. Article #207 on Persius, and articles #209, #305 on Juvenal.

44. Article #305.

45. Unless, that is, he knew about Badham's signed reply, 'Dr Badham's Defence against the *Quarterly Review*', *New Review*, 1 (1813), pp. 351–4. *Specimens* is rare: the only copies I have located are at the Bodleian Library, Oxford; University of Texas; and University of Virginia. Charles Badham is a famous name among classicists; but this is not the celebrated Greek scholar (1813–84) who ended up as professor of classics in Sydney, nor his brother the naturalist Charles David Badham (1805–57), author of *Prose Halieutics*, but

their father (1780–1845), professor of physic at Glasgow. (The article on Badham père in *ODNB* mentions his authorship, but without evidence.)

46. His textbooks included a Latin grammar of 1781, published anonymously. It can be shown to be Seyer's by comparison with the second edition of 1804. Both editions survive in single copies: the first is BL, shelfmark 12935.bb.40, the second is an unrecorded copy in the author's possession.

47. Articles #6, #22, #61.

48. *ER* article #400.

49. H. F. Clinton, *Fasti Hellenici*, 3 vols (Oxford: Clarendon Press, 1827–30), and *Fasti Romani*, 2 vols (Oxford: Oxford University Press, 1845–50).

50. C. J. F. Clinton (ed.), *Literary Remains of Henry Fynes Clinton* (London: Longman, Brown, Green, and Longmans, 1854). Like Elmsley, Clinton was enabled by an inheritance to devote much of his time to scholarship. In his case, this was reinforced by the express wish of his benefactor that he should not be ordained; though this was offset by being plunged into parliamentary politics by his patron the Duke of Newcastle.

51. Articles #3, #218, #309. The latter attribution is confirmed by Blomfield's remark in a letter of 7 October 1814 to Peter Elmsley: 'I have sent to Gifford a long article on the Romaic language for the next Quarterly, in which several persons are decently abused'. Elmsley papers, Westminster.

52. Blomfield to Elmsley, 13 December 1814: 'You see I have been dabbling in modern Greek, which I have found rather interesting, but, I think, quite useless to a critical scholar. I used formerly to entertain a different opinion'. Elmsley papers, Westminster.

53. Article #539. Murray later thought Blomfield might have been involved; he may have been misled by the memory of his authorship of article #309.

54. Cf. article #141.

55. Clarke, *Richard Porson*, pp. 15–16.

56. 'The Cambridge edition of Aeschylus', *ER*, 15 (October 1809), pp. 152–63 (*WI* #491); (January 1810), pp. 315–22 (*WI* #499). Butler responded to the review with a pamphlet in the form of a letter to Blomfield, of whose authorship of the review he affected to be ignorant: *A Letter to the Rev. C. J. Blomfield*.

57. Trinity College, Cambridge, Conclusion Book 1646–1811, p. 626.

58. R. Porson, *Adversaria: notæ et emendationes in poetas Græcos quas ex schedis manuscriptis Porsoni deprompserunt et ordinarunt nec non indicibus instruxerunt Jacobus Henricus Monk A.M., Carolus Jacobus Blomfield A.M.* (Cambridge, 1812).

59. Including articles #80, #138, #206, #220, #597.

60. Elizabeth Barrett to Hugh Boyd, [December 1835], in E. B. Browning, *The Barretts at Hope End: The Early Diary of Elizabeth Barrett Browning*, ed. E. Berridge (London: John Murray, 1974), p. 54. I am grateful to Scott Lewis for confirming the text of Barrett's letter.

61. Review of LP set in *Daily Telegraph*, 11 November 1961.

62. Elmsley to Butler, 17 August 1811, BL Add. MSS 34583, f. 334.

63. Article #138.

64. Article #220, p. 216.

65. Monk to Murray, 25 August 1818, JM MS.

66. Article #206.

67. Article #220.

68. Elmsley papers, Westminster. The friend in Cambridge was presumably George D'Oyly. Grosvenor Bedford wrote to Elmsley,

I hear that the Edinburgh Review is about to close in consequence of the great luminaries, Jeffery, Brougham & Horner all finding themselves too much employed in the law to spare time for conducting it. If so, the Quarterly will get an immense start, for the British appears to me as orthodox and as dull as the British Critic. (n.d. [1812], Elmsley papers, Westminster)

69. On 24 July 1812 Blomfield wrote to Elmsley, 'I had some thoughts of giving a summary account of your Oedipus, but I can get no answer from Jeffrey. I believe he is about to get rid of the concern altogether.' Elmsley papers, Westminster.

70. *ER* articles #542, #579.

71. *ER* article #595.

72. W. R. Ward, *Victorian Oxford* (London: Cass, 1965), pp. 37–8; M. G. Brock, 'The Oxford of Peel and Gladstone', pp. 51–2.

73. The year of election is not easy to establish. The *Historical Register of the University of Oxford* (Oxford: Clarendon Press, 1888), p. 49, dates the appointment to 1811, followed by M. G. Brock, 'The Oxford of Peel and Gladstone', p. 55; the *Gentleman's Magazine* reported the appointment to the chair in its issue of March 1812 (p. 287), but in its obituary of Gaisford (July 1855, pp. 99–100) stated that he was elected in 1811. Boase's *Modern English Biography* (I.1115) dates the appointment firmly, but without a source, to 29 February 1812. His source was probably the *London Gazette*, no. 16578 (25–9 February 1812), p. 381, where the appointment is announced.

74. E. A. Varley, *The Last of the Prince Bishops: William Van Mildert and the High Church Movement in the Early Nineteenth Century* (Cambridge: Cambridge University Press, 2002), p. 49. In 1815, his niece married Thomas Gaisford.

75. S. Butler, *The Life and Letters of Dr. Samuel Butler*, 2 vols (London: John Murray, 1896), vol. 1, p.88.

76. See Murray to Elmsley, 7 July 1813 (*QR* Letter 149); and Elmsley to Murray, 25 June and 11 July 1813, JM MS.

77. Monk to Murray, 13 November 1813, JM MS. Elmsley's article, 'Notes on the Ajax of Sophocles', duly appeared in the third issue of *Museum Criticum*, pp. 351–69, and continued in the fourth issue, pp. 469–88; both issues were published in 1814.

78. C. Collard, 'Peter Elmsley', in R. B. Todd (ed.), *Dictionary of British Classicists*, 3 vols (Bristol: Thoemmes Continuum, 2004), vol. 1, pp. 286–8, on p. 287.

79. Article #250. The letter incidentally confirms a suggested attribution to Blomfield, since the 'Trans Tweedian' piece he is referring to is surely *ER* #637, the review of Hermann's Photius in the *Edinburgh Review* in July 1813 (see *WI*).

80. *ER* article #542; *QR* article #138.

81. Gaisford to Elmsley, 12 February 1811, 21 January 1815, Elmsley papers, Westminster. Apart from a review of a collection of Greek comic fragments, Gaisford is not known to have contributed to periodicals at all.

82. The author of articles #584, #638, #672.

83. W. Haygarth, *Greece: a Poem, in Three Parts; with Notes, Classical Illustrations, and Sketches of the Scenery* (London: W. Bulmer, 1814).

84. Unpublished biographical sketch by Stella G. Miller.

85. Compare the opinion of the Oxford chronologist Henry Fynes Clinton in 1821: '... defective styles are seldom improved. The practice of forty years, and of ten octavo volumes, has not purified the style of Mr Mitford.' Clinton (ed.), *Literary Remains of Henry Fynes Clinton*, p. 170.

86. Their *Herculanensia* appeared in 1810. Almost a decade later, in 1819, Peter Elmsley and Humphry Davy were sent out to unroll and decipher the papyri, but the project foundered on the intractability of both the papyri and their local guardians.

87. Articles #110, #242, #426.

88. *ER* articles #524, #629. See Gifford's reference to it in his letter to Scott of 27 October 1810 (*QR* Letter 65): 'You are right – the enemy feels us – tant mieux. There is more than one thing which he will not like in this Number. George's sly sneer at the "perfumes of Astrachan" is excellent.'

89. Among those taking this view was Richard Payne Knight. On the whole affair, see W. St Clair, *Lord Elgin and the Marbles* (Oxford: Oxford University Press, 1998); T. Webb, 'Appropriating the Stones: The 'Elgin Marbles' and the English National Taste', in E. Barkan and R. Bush (eds), *Cleaning the Stones/Naming the Bones: Cultural Property and the Negotiation of National and Ethnic Identity* (Los Angeles, CA: Getty Research Institute, 2002), pp. 51–6; M. Beard, *The Parthenon* (London: Profile, 2002), pp. 18–20, 155–73.

90. *QR* article #377; *ER* article #732.

91. Articles #363, #365.

92. Blomfield suggests (article #363, p. 232) that 'Dr Spurzheim would infallibly discover in Mr Tweddell's occiput a new organ – that of *annotativeness*'.

93. A. E. Housman, *M. Manilii Astronomicon, Liber Primus* (London: Grant Richards, 1903), p. xlii. The two deaths occurred in 1825, Blomfield's elevation in the previous year.

94. For the contrasting styles of the two universities, see C. A. Stray, 'Curriculum and Style in the Collegiate University: Classics in Nineteenth-Century Oxbridge', *History of Universities*, 16 (2001), pp. 183–218.

95. My thanks for help of various kinds go to Eileen Curran, Jonathan Cutmore, Patrick Finglass, Bob Kaster, Virginia Murray, Eddie Smith and Jonathan Smith. I should like to dedicate this chapter to Martin Lowther Clarke, a pioneer historian of classical scholarship, and at 96 still a constructive critic of those who follow in his footsteps.

# 5 Ragaz, 'Walter Scott and the *Quarterly Review*'

1. Peter Garside's 'Essay on the Text' in his edition of *Waverley* (forthcoming, Edinburgh: Edinburgh University Press, 2007) discusses the dating of the early fragments of Scott's first novel. For information on Scott's work on *Queenhoo Hall*, see <www.british-fic­tion.cardiff.ac.uk>. In the present article, all bibliographical information about Scott is from W. B. Todd and A. Bowden, *Sir Walter Scott: A Bibliographical History 1796–1832* (New Castle, DE: Oak Knoll Press, 1998).

2. J. G. Lockhart, *Memoirs of the Life of Sir Walter Scott*, 7 vols (London: Macmillan, 1837), vol. 2, pp. 200–1.

3. Constable had a half share in *Marmion*. The other London publisher of *Marmion*, with a quarter share, was William Miller, whose premises at 50 Albemarle Street Murray was later to purchase. See Smiles, *Memoir*, vol. 1, pp. 76–7. Murray's wish to become Scott's publisher was realized only with *Tales of My Landlord* in 1816 during another cooling of the Scott-Constable relationship. *Tales* was co-published with William Blackwood. For a complete publishing history of this novel, see S. Ragaz, J. Belanger and P. Garside, 'Walter Scott, *Tales of My Landlord*: A Publishing Record', *Cardiff Corvey: Reading the Romantic Text*, <www.cf.ac.uk/encap/corvey/articles/database/landlord.html>.

4. As Jonathan Cutmore points out in *Contributors to the Quarterly Review*, the journal resulted from 'a confluence of events and personalities'.

5. Lockhart, *Memoirs of ... Scott*, vol. 2, p. 195, accounts for the rupture. Lockhart notes that Scott blamed Alexander Hunter but Lockhart, who was hostile to John Ballantyne, held Ballantyne responsible. Hunter's 'warm temper' was also to cause Constable problems in his relationship with Longman and Company. See T. Constable, *Archibald Constable and his Literary Correspondents*, 3 vols (Edinburgh: Edmonston and Douglas, 1873), vol. 2, p. 339. Scott described him as 'a sort of Whig run mad'; see Scott to George Ellis, 13 December 1808, in *SL*, vol. 2, p. 135. For John Ballantyne, see S, Ragaz, 'Ballantyne, John (1774–1821)', *ODNB*.

6. Scott denied being upset by the review, and in any event would have seen the author, Francis Jeffrey, as the appropriate target for his anger. In letters of April 1808 to Anna Seward and Robert Surtees, Scott mentions good-humouredly discussing the review with Jeffrey over dinner; see *SL*, vol. 2, pp. 51, 54. To Mrs Scott of Harden in May 1808 he expounded more fully on the review but again in conciliatory and judicious terms; see *SL*, vol. 2, p. 66. For the view that it had hurt Scott and would predispose him to put his energies behind the *Quarterly*, see, for example, William Erskine's letter of 23 October 1808 to Archibald Campbell-Colquhoun, in *SL*, vol. 2, pp. 101–2, n. The review of *Marmion* is [F. Jeffrey], 'Scott's *Marmion: a Poem*', *ER*, 12 (April 1809), pp. 1–35 (*WI* #398).

7. Scott to John Murray, 15 November 1808, in *SL*, vol. 2, pp. 124–7. The Cevallos article is [H. Brougham and F. Jeffrey], 'Don Pedro Cevallos on the French Usurpation of Spain', *ER*, 13 (October 1808), pp. 215–34 (*WI* #439).

8. Scott's growing dissatisfaction with the *Edinburgh* can be traced in his late 1807 correspondence with Robert Southey. In November 1807, he wrote proposing that Southey contribute to the review, in view of Southey's urgent need for steady income. In a letter of 8 December, Southey declined on the basis of irreconcilable political differences (see *SL*, vol. 1, pp. 386, 389). On 15 December, Scott admitted to his own increasing distaste for views expressed by the *Edinburgh* (*SL*, vol. 1, p. 400). If only informally at this stage, an alliance against the Whig review was clearly in the process of being formed.

9. See Scott to George Ellis, 18 November 1808, in *SL*, vol. 2, pp. 128–9. '[W]e have to trust ... that decent, lively, and reflecting criticism, teaching men not to abuse books only, but to read and to judge them, will have the effect of novelty upon a public wearied with universal efforts at blackguard and indiscriminating satire'.

10. This was an important qualifier. For example, Murray suggested asking Thomas Moore to be a contributor; see *QR* Letter 13. Scott mentioned his name to Charles Kirkpatrick Sharpe, who raised objections likely on the basis not of Moore's satiric bent but of lingering uncertainties about where his Irish-inflected political allegiances would fall. See Scott to Sharpe, *SL*, vol. 2, pp. 143, 149.

11. For the series of novels, see Lockhart, *Memoirs of ... Scott*, vol. 2, p. 173; and Scott's letter of 30 October 1808 to Murray (*SL*, vol. 2, pp. 114–15). See also Smiles, *Memoir*, vol. 1, pp. 86–9. The plans came to nothing when the series was pre-empted by Longman's very successful set on the same model, edited by Anna Barbauld.

12. See *QR* Letter 2 and Smiles, *Memoir*, vol. 2, pp. 96–7.

13. The meeting's dates can be established from letters Murray wrote to his wife. See *QR* Letter 2.

14. The letter survives in these two slightly different versions. That in the John Murray Archive (*QR* Letter 4) is the copy Scott sent to Gifford and it is incomplete: the final leaf

is missing. The other version (*QR* Letter 4A), in the Pierpont Morgan Library, is a draft that Scott sent to George Ellis. In his unpublished edition, Cutmore indicates variants and Grierson has a note on some of the differences between the two versions (*SL*, vol. 2, pp. 100–1).

15. *SL*, vol. 2, pp. 101–2, n.

16. That this was not the case with the *Edinburgh* is proven by an example close to hand: Constable published *Marmion* and also the *Edinburgh* in which Jeffrey's hostile review was printed.

17. *SL*, vol. 2, pp. 114–15.

18. *SL*, vol. 2, pp. 123–4. *SL*, following Smiles, makes it seem as if Scott wrote two separate letters to Murray on the same date; it prints the other part in vol. 2, pp. 119–20. See Millgate ref. #399, where it is established that the two parts refer to one letter of 2 November.

19. The most significant of these letters is that of 15 November 1808, where Murray seems to attempt to regain control of the project, asserting that the idea of a new periodical originated with him. He also reasserts the urgent need for Scott's assistance because of apprehensions about Gifford: 'without skilful management and judicious instructions we shall totally mistake the road to the accomplishment of the arduous task which we have undertaken' (*QR* Letter 8). For Gifford on Murray, see his letter to Edward Copleston of 8 December 1809, where he laments Murray's interference which is 'owing to the preposterous mode in which the Rev. was established: a publisher being appointed, and some progress made, before an Editor was fixed on' (*QR* Letter 30). Clearly, Murray and Gifford disagreed on the sequence of events in the review's founding, and Scott was appealed to from both sides.

20. Lockhart, *Memoirs of ... Scott*, vol. 1, p. 247, states that Scott was in London when the first number appeared. This was not the case: Scott and his wife set out for London only on 5 April (see the postscript to his letter to Murray of 27 March in *SL*, vol. 2, p. 186). Lockhart also takes the occasion for another swipe at John Ballantyne, implying that it was owing to his incompetence in managing the Scottish sales of the periodical that the relationship between Scott and Murray did not develop as envisaged by the latter.

21. Scott to Murray, 19 March 1809, in *SL*, vol. 2, pp. 182–3.

22. *SL*, vol. 2, pp. 141–4, 148–9.

23. When Gifford said that it had been received too late for the first number, Sharpe commented to Scott in a letter of 5 March 1809 that he had 'a shrewd suspicion that it never will [be printed]' (*SL*, vol. 2, p. 173, n.). For Scott's endorsement, see his letter to Sharpe of 17 February 1809 (*SL*, vol. 2, pp. 166–7). In Scott's letter of 13 January he says that he will 'stand bail' for the kindly reception of any article by Sharpe; he must have been deeply embarrassed by Gifford's behaviour in this instance.

24. Scott to Morritt, in *SL*, vol. 2, pp. 152–4.

25. Articles #17, #9.

26. See Scott to Murray, 10 March 1809, in *SL*, vol. 2, pp. 178–9 and ff. Greenfield's article is '*Amelie Mansfield*', *QR*, 2 (article #23).

27. His article on Robert Monteath's *Forester's Guide and Profitable Planter* was published in the *Quarterly* for October 1827 (*WI* #144) and the review of Sir Henry Steuart's *Planter's Guide* in the *Quarterly* for March 1828 (*WI* #153). A review of Sir Humphry Davy's *Salmonia, or Days of Fly-Fishing* appeared in the October 1828 *Quarterly* (*WI* #182). For the article on military bridges (#460), Scott received the assistance of 'a scientific friend' (Smiles, *Memoir*, vol. 2, p. 9).

28. Scott to Ellis, 18 November 1808, in *SL*, vol. 2, p. 129.
29. Entry for 17 January 1827, in *The Journal of Sir Walter Scott*, ed. W. E. K. Anderson (Oxford: Clarendon Press, 1998), p. 301.
30. *SL*, vol. 2, pp. 284–5. The review of *Ida* is by Gifford (article #4).
31. Article #25.
32. In the postscript to a letter of 25 February 1809 to Murray (*SL*, vol. 2, p. 170), Scott describes Cumberland as being 'beneath contempt'. The reference may be to Cumberland's plans to establish a review where all contributions were to be signed; Scott mentions this in his letter to Sharpe of 30 December 1808 (*SL*, vol. 2, p. 143).
33. Scott may be being disingenuous in the Lady Abercorn letter. Cromek possibly visited Scott during his 1808 tour of Scotland and it was at this point that the undesired flattery was expressed. However, it was not until 1810 when Cromek published *Select Scottish Songs* that the 'abuse' occurred – and at that date Cromek was responding to the article in the *Quarterly*, having heard rumours of Scott's authorship. See R. H. Cromek, *Select Scottish Songs, Ancient and Modern* (London: T. Cadell and W. Davies, 1810), pp. 252–3. The review of *Reliques* is article #2.
34. To Murray on 3 December 1810 Scott described Cromek as a 'perfect Brain-sucker living upon the labours of others'. See *SL*, vol. 2, p. 409.
35. Cromek's editorial work on Burns is now recognized to be of more importance than previously thought; see J. W. Egerer, *A Bibliography of Robert Burns* (Edinburgh: Oliver and Boyd, 1964), p. 115.
36. Proceeds from the first collected edition of Burns by Dr James Currie had been to benefit the poet's family. See M. DeLacy, 'Currie, James (1756–1805)', *ODNB*.
37. Article #361.
38. Articles #407 and #475. For Byron's reaction to article #407, see his letter to Murray of 3 March 1817, in *Byron's Letters and Journals*, ed. L. A. Marchand, 13 vols (London: John Murray, 1973–94), vol. 5, p. 178, and his letter to Thomas Moore of 10 March 1817, in vol. 5, p. 185.
39. Article #87. For Scott's assistance to Maturin, see S. Ragaz, 'Maturin, Archibald Constable, and the Publication of *Melmoth the Wanderer*', *Review of English Studies*, 57 (2006), pp. 359–73.
40. Erskine probably sub-edited the article (see Cutmore's note to article #417 in *Quarterly Review Archive*). Lockhart's editorial note in *The Miscellaneous Prose Works of Sir Walter Scott*, 28 vols (Edinburgh: Cadell, 1835), vol. 19, p. 1, states that the entire manuscript is in Scott's hand, but writers often submitted a fair copy to Gifford.
41. *SL*, vol. 2, p. 157.
42. Ibid.
43. *SL*, vol. 2, p. 182.
44. Ibid.
45. According to Millgate, of the 113 letters exchanged between Scott and Murray, 85 date from before 1820. Correspondence is sporadic in the 1820s, and increases again in 1830. Scott recommended Lockhart to the position of editor, although he also cautioned his son-in-law that he must be sure not to continue writing the kind of sharply satiric material that characterized Lockhart's contributions to *Blackwood's Edinburgh Magazine*. See his letter of 15 October 1825, in *SL*, vol. 9, pp. 251–4.
46. Having been sent a copy of *Frankenstein* by Percy Bysshe Shelley, Scott assumed he was the author. His review in *Blackwood's Edinburgh Magazine* of March 1818 opposes

Croker's harsh criticisms by bestowing considerable praise and identifying the novel as a singularly interesting work.

47. Article #2.
48. Article #13.
49. Article #15.
50. Article #16.
51. *SL*, vol. 2, p. 157.
52. *SL*, vol. 2, p. 158.
53. Article #19.
54. Article #25.
55. Article #36.
56. Article #71.
57. Article #87.
58. Article #90.
59. Article #100.
60. Article #131.
61. Article #227.
62. Article #261.
63. Article #361.
64. Article #366.
65. Article #369.
66. Article #407.
67. Article #417.
68. Article #460.
69. Article #466.
70. Article #470.
71. Article #475.
72. Article #718.

## 6 Cameron, 'John Barrow, the *Quarterly*'s Imperial Reviewer'

1. L. C. de Guignes, *Voyage à Pèkin, Manille, et l'île de France*, 3 vols (Paris: Imprimerie Impériale, 1808).
2. See J. Barrow, *An Auto-Biographical Memoir of Sir John Barrow, Bart., Late of the Admiralty* (London: John Murray, 1847), pp. 499–501; see also Barrow to Macvey Napier, 22 February 1843, BL Add. MSS 34623, ff. 433–44; and Barrow to John Murray, 22 February 1843, JM MS.
3. G. T. Staunton, *Memoirs of the Chief Incidents of the Public Life of Sir George Thomas Staunton* (London: L. Booth, 1852), pp. 41–4.
4. [Barrow], 'De Guignes – *Voyages à Peking, &c*', *QR*, 4 (article #48).
5. Staunton to Grant, 20 November 1809, Staunton Papers, Perkins; Staunton, *Memoirs*, pp. 41–4.
6. Articles #68, #82.
7. [Barrow], 'The Laws of China', *QR*, 6 (article #85), esp. pp. 275–7.
8. Barrow's negotiations connected with what became the Amherst Embassy to China are contained in the BL India Office Records, G/12/196, ff. 1–32, and G/12/197, ff. 1–8. A summary is contained in PRO Foreign Office Records, FO17/1l 54, ff. 2–5. See also

Barrow to Banks, 3 October 1815, British Museum of Natural History, Dawson Turner Collection, 19, ff. 196–7.

9. Article #333.

10. On the shipping interest, see articles #208, #260, #280, #297; on conflict with the United States, see articles #180, #219.

11. For example, George Fletcher Moore to Joseph Moore, 29 November 1832, Original Letters and Diaries of G. F. Moore, BL263, J. S. Battye Library of Western Australian History.

12. *QR*, 78 (article *WI* #192).

13. 'The Cape of Good Hope', *QR*, 43 (article #522).

14. Barrow, *An Auto-Biographical Memoir*, p. 504.

15. J. L. Cranmer-Byng, *An Embassy to China: Being the Journal Kept by Lord Macartney during his Embassy to the Emperor Ch'ien Lung, 1793–94* (London: Longmans, 1962), pp. 308–9; A. Peyrefitte, *The Collision of Two Civilisations: The British Expedition to China in 1792–4* (London: Harvill, 1993), p. 555; F. Fleming, *Barrow's Boys* (New York: Atlantic Monthly Press, 1998), pp. 3–8.

16. D. H. Varley, 'Mr Chronometer: Some Footnotes on Sir John Barrow', in J. G. Kesting, S. I. Malan, A. B. Smith and L. E. Taylor (eds), *Libraries and People* (Cape Town: C. Struik, 1970), pp. 141–9; D. H. Varley, 'Sir John Barrow', in W. J. Kock and D. W. Kruger (eds), *Dictionary of South African Biography*, 5 vols (Cape Town: Tafelberg Publishers, 1968–87), vol. 2, pp. 34–6.

17. J. Barrow, *Description of Pocket and Magazine Cases of Mathematical Drawing Instruments* (London: J. and W. Watkins, 1792).

18. G. L. Staunton, *An Authentic Account of an Embassy from the King of Great Britain to the Emperor of China*, 2 vols (London: George Nicol, 1797); H. Robbins, *Our First Ambassador to China. An Account of George, Earl of Macartney* (London: John Murray, 1908); Cranmer-Byng, *An Embassy to China*.

19. Staunton, *An Authentic Account*, vol. 2, p. 408.

20. G. M. Theal, *Records of the Cape Colony*, 5 vols (London: Clowes, 1897–9), vol. 2, pp. 110–11.

21. These are outlined in M. Boucher and N. Penn (eds), *Britain at the Cape, 1795 to 1803* (Houghton: Brenthurst, 1992), pp. 91–124.

22. V. S. Forbes, *Pioneer Travellers in South Africa, 1750–1800* (Cape Town: A. A. Balkema, 1965), p. 135.

23. N. Mostert, *Frontiers. The Epic of South Africa's Creation and the Tragedy of the Xhosa People* (New York: Knopf, 1992), esp. pp. 289–303.

24. Published as J. Barrow, *An Account of Travels into the Interior of Southern Africa in the Years 1797 and 1798*, 2 vols (London: T. Cadell and W. Davies, 1801–4).

25. Boucher and Penn (eds), *Britain at the Cape*, pp. 132–3.

26. J. Barrow, *Travels in China* (London: T. Cadell and W. Davies, 1804), reprinted in 1806.

27. Barrow, *An Auto-Biographical Memoir*, pp. 251–5.

28. See note 24 above.

29. [F. Jeffrey], 'Barrow's Travels in China', *ER*, 5 (January 1805), pp. 259–88 (*WI* #192); [Jeffrey], 'Barrow's Travels in Southern Africa', *ER*, 4 (July 1804), pp. 443–57 (*WI* #173), esp. pp. 452–7; [Jeffrey], 'Barrow's Voyage to Cochin China', *ER*, 9 (October 1806), pp. 1–18 (article *WI* #311), on pp. 1, 18.

30. For example, 'Barrow's Travels in China', *British Critic*, 25 (February 1805), p. 119; 'Barrow's Travels in China', *Antijacobin Review and Magazine*, 18 (December 1804), pp. 337–8.

31. M. Streak, *The Afrikaner as Viewed by the English* (Cape Town: C. Struik, 1974), p. 22; M. Adas, *Machines as the Measure of Men: Science, Technology, and Ideologies of Western Dominance* (Ithaca, NY: Cornell University Press, 1989), pp. 177–83.

32. Z. Shunhong, 'British Views on China during the Time of the Embassies of Lord Macartney and Lord Amherst (1790–1820)' (PhD dissertation, Birkbeck College, London, 1990), p. 127.

33. See article #208 on ship design, article #514 on dockyards and articles #208, #320, #704 on dry rot.

34. Barrow worked with Seppings on article #328, the Brunels on article #519, the Rennies on articles #514, #519 and Watt on article #514.

35. Barrow discusses Mauritius in article #139 and the retention of possessions in, for example, articles #178, #353.

36. See articles #659, *WI* #105, *WI* #188.

37. Bathurst's undated minute in PRO, Colonial Office Series, CO 324/75, f. 266; see also J. J. Eddy, *Britain and the Australian Colonies, 1818–1831* (Oxford: Clarendon Press, 1969), p. 235.

38. On Malta, see article #383; the Ionian Islands, article #678; Zanzibar, article #657; Western Port, articles #104, #311, *WI* #51, *WI* #145; Melville Island, articles *WI* #51, *WI* #145; New Zealand, articles #722, *WI* #145, *WI* #681; Ceylon, articles #139, #228, #353, #406; Hawaii, article s#402, *WI* #122; the Ryukyu Islands, article #438; and Port Essington, article *WI* #681.

39. See articles #337, #368, #373, *WI* #188.

40. For Stamford Raffles, see articles #422, *WI* #230; and for Mountstuart Elphinstone, see article #360

41. For Malcolm, see articles #258, #688; Pottinger, article #308; and Kinneir and Morier, article #327.

42. See articles #457, #472, #486.

43. See articles #544, #609.

44. See Liverpool to Castlereagh, 21 July 1815, quoted in M. J. Thornton, *Napoleon after Waterloo. England and the St. Helena Decision* (Stanford, CA: Stanford University Press, 1968), p. 62.

45. For example, W. H. Smyth, *The Royal Geographical Society and its Labours* (London: Royal Geographical Society, 1846); C. R. Markham, *The Fifty Years Work of the Royal Geographical Society* (London: John Murray, 1881); H. R. Mill, *The Record of the Royal Geographical Society, 1830–1930* (London: Royal Geographical Society, 1930).

46. D. Mackay, *In the Wake of Cook. Exploration, Science and Empire, 1780–1801* (London: Croom Helm, 1985).

47. H. B. Carter, *Sir Joseph Banks* (London: British Museum, 1988), pp. 498–503.

48. A. G. E. Jones, 'Sir John Ross and Sir John Barrow', in A. G. E. Jones, *Polar Portraits: Collected Papers* (Whitby: Caedmon, 1992), pp. 219–28.

49. W. H. Smyth, *Sketch of the Rise and Progress of the Royal Society Club* (London: J.B. Nichols, 1860), p. 69. See also M. Hall, *All Scientists Now: The Royal Society in the Nineteenth Century* (Cambridge: Cambridge University Press, 2002), p. 4.

50. See articles #602, #657, *WI* #105, *WI* # 473.

51. [J. Barrow], 'Sir Rufane Donkin and the Niger', *QR*, 81 (article *WI* #206).

52. [J. Barrow], 'Rodney's Battle of 12th April', *QR*, 83 (article *WI* #219). The dispute is outlined in the Lockhart–Murray correspondence and Barrow–Murray correspondence in the John Murray archive, January–August 1830.

53. Article #245. Barrow to Macvey Napier, Admiralty, 22 December 1814, BL Add. MSS 34611, ff. 143–4.

54. Hall to Napier, 23 January 1841, encl. Barrow to Hall, Admiralty, 21 January 1841, BL Add. MSS 34621, ff. 477–9.

55. Barrow–Murray correspondence, July–August, 1840, JM MS.

56. See articles *WI* #1758, *WI* #1844, *WI* #1859, *WI* #1809, *WI* #1868.

57. Barrow to Napier, 11 July 1817, BL Add. MSS 34612, ff. 121–2.

58. [J. Barrow], 'The Australian Colonies', *QR*, 135 (article *WI* #481).

59. G. T. Staunton, *Memoir of Sir John Barrow, Bart. and Description of the Barrow Monument* (privately printed, 1852), pp. 11–12.

60. J. M. R. Cameron, 'The Northern Settlements: Outposts of Empire', in P. Statham (ed.), *The Origins of Australia's Capital Cities* (Cambridge: Cambridge University Press, 1989), pp. 279–91.

61. [H. Brougham], 'Park's Last Journey and Life', *ER*, 24 (February 1815), pp. 471–90 (*WI* #719).

62. [J. Barrow], 'Park's *Journal of a Mission to the Interior of Africa*', *QR*, 25 (article #337).

63. Goulburn to Barrow, 28 July 1815, PRO, Admiralty Records, ADM1/2167 (T34), and Goulburn to Barrow, August 1815, ADM1/4234.

64. Barrow to Melville, 9 August 1815, PRO, Admiralty Records, ADM1/2167 (T34).

65. Carter, *Sir Joseph Banks*, pp. 500–2.

66. [J. Barrow], 'On the Polar Ice and the Northern Passage into the Pacific', *QR*, 35 (article #451), published on 21 February 1818. The apparent inconsistency between stated and actual publication date is explained by most issues of the *Quarterly* under Gifford's editorship, and particularly the later issues, having been published late.

67. J. Barrow, *A Chronological History of Voyages into the Arctic Region* (London: John Murray, 1818).

68. T. Stamp and C. Stamp, *William Scoresby, Arctic Scientist* (Whitby: Caedmon, 1975), pp. 62–72; T. H. Levere, *Science and the Canadian Arctic. A Century of Exploration, 1818–1918* (Cambridge: Cambridge University Press, 1993), esp. pp. 36–50; A. Savours, *The Search for the North West Passage* (New York: St Martin's Press, 1999), pp. 39–55.

69. [J. Barrow], 'Ross's Voyage of Discovery', *QR*, 41 (article #503), published on 4 June 1819.

70. Smiles, *Memoir*, vol. 2, pp. 30–2.

71. [J. Barrow], 'De Humboldt's Travels', *QR*, 28 (article #368), esp. p. 402, 'Humboldt's American Researches', *QR*, 30 (article #394), 'De Humboldt's Travels', *QR*, 42 (article #505), and 'Peron – Voyages de Decouvertes. Tome II', *QR*, 33 (article #428). See also Barrow's 'De Humboldt's Travels. – Part II', *QR*, 35 (article #446), which adopts a much less critical tone and approach.

72. [J. Barrow], 'The Royal Geographical Society', *QR*, 46 (*WI* #282), esp. p. 78.

73. Barrow to Murray, 2 September 1817, JM MS.

74. [J. Barrow], 'Embassy to China', *QR*, 34 (article #438), and 'Hall's *Account of the Loo-Choo Islands*', *QR*, 36 (article #455).

75. A. J. S[mith], 'South African Water-Colours by Lady Barrow', *Africana Notes and News*, 11:9 (1955), pp. 331–7.

76. *The Diaries of Sylvester Douglas (Lord Glenbervie)*, ed. F. Bickley 2 vols (London: Constable; Boston, MA: Houghton Mifflin, 1928), vol. 2, p. 300.

77.  Quoted in H. J. Anderson, *South Africa a Century Ago (1797–1801)* (Cape Town: Miller, 1924), p. 160.

## 7 Pratt, 'Hung, Drawn and Quarterlyed'

1.  Robert Southey to Hugh Chudleigh Standert, 14 December 1809, in *NL*, vol. 1, p. 523.
2.  Ibid. Carlisle is the surgeon Anthony Carlisle (1768–1840). For Southey's work for the *Critical*, see J. Zeitlin, 'Southey's Contributions to *The Critical Review*', *Notes and Queries*, 136 (1918), pp. 35–6, 66–7, 94–7, 122–4, supplemented by *NL*, vol. 1, pp. 158–9, n. 5. His contributions to the *Annual* are listed in J. Raimond, *Robert Southey. L'homme et son temps, L'oeuvre, Le rôle* (Paris: Didier, 1968), pp. 594–7. He had previously contributed poetry and the occasional essay to the *Monthly Magazine*, see K. Curry, 'Robert Southey's Contributions to *The Monthly Magazine* and *The Athenaeum*', *Wordsworth Circle*, 11 (1980), pp. 215–18.
3.  *NL*, vol. 1, p. 523. Southey expressed similar sentiments in a letter to Mary Barker, 21 December 1807, quoted in R. G. Kirkpatrick Jr, 'The Letters of Robert Southey to Mary Barker from 1800–26' (PhD dissertation, Harvard University, 1967), p. 259.
4.  See Southey to Joseph Cottle, 9 February 1810, in *NL*, vol. 1, p. 527; and Southey to Grosvenor Charles Bedford, 14 January 1811, in *NL*, vol. 2, p. 4.
5.  For attributions to Southey and also an account of essays misattributed to him, see Curry and Dedmon, 'Southey's Contributions to *The Quarterly Review*'.
6.  Ibid., p. 261.
7.  Southey to Mary Barker, 8 January 1812, in Kirkpatrick, 'The Letters of Robert Southey to Mary Barker', p. 376. This eventually became a pamphlet of the same title. See G. Carnall, *Robert Southey and His Age: The Development of a Conservative Mind* (Oxford: Clarendon Press, 1960), pp. 135–6.
8.  This was incomplete at the time of the onset of Southey's final illness. It was finished by his second wife Caroline Bowles Southey and his son Charles Cuthbert Southey, and published as *The Life of the Rev. Andrew Bell: Comprising the History of the Rise and Progress of the System of Mutual Tuition*, 3 vols (London: John Murray, 1844). For an account of the quarrels that bedevilled the work's completion, see L. Pratt, 'Family Misfortunes? The Posthumous Editing of Robert Southey', in L. Pratt (ed.), *Robert Southey and the Contexts of English Romanticism* (Aldershot: Ashgate, 2006), pp. 219–38.
9.  Published in Number 5 (article #84) and republished, with additions and adjustments, as *The Life of Nelson*, 2 vols (London: John Murray, 1813). For Gifford's praise of the essay, see his letter to Southey of 18 April 1810, *QR* Letter 44.
10. Published as *Essays, Moral and Political*, 2 vols (London: John Murray, 1832). The volumes included 'On the State of the Poor, the Principles of Mr. Malthus's Essay on Population, and the Manufacturing System, 1812', *QR*, 16 (article #224); 'The Poor', *QR*, 29 (article #385); and 'Parliamentary Reform', *QR*, 31 (article #409). For a complete listing, see Curry and Dedmon, 'Southey's Contributions to *The Quarterly Review*', pp. 263–5.
11. For an example, see Southey to Caroline Bowles, 5 April 1827, in *The Correspondence of Robert Southey with Caroline Bowles*, ed. E. Dowden (Dublin: Hodges, Figgis, 1881), pp. 116–17. Murray also facilitated Southey's work by borrowing books on his behalf and

by sending him cartloads of books, many of which he permitted him to keep. Southey to John Rickman, 1 August 1810, in *NL*, vol. 1, p. 538; JM MS, book loans register.

12. See O. Williams, *Lamb's Friend the Census-Taker: Life and Letters of John Rickman* (London: Constable, 1912), pp. 154–5. Southey had earlier tried to persuade Rickman to write for the *Quarterly*, noting that 'no man living' was his 'equal ... upon the subject of political economy'. Ibid., p. 148.

13. 'Capt. Pasley', *QR*, 10 (article #148); 'On the Corn Laws', *QR*, 101 (*WI* #388). For the attribution of co-authorship see Curry and Dedmon, 'Southey's Contributions to *The Quarterly Review*', pp. 263, 268.

14. 14 March 1809, in *NL*, vol. 1, p. 503.

15. For Gifford's alternative view see his observations to Walter Scott, 28 March 1810: 'we have also a very well written Article by Southey – indeed, excellent. It has cost me an infinity of pains, merely, however, to reduce it, for it originally filled four sheets!' (*QR* Letter 41). See also his caution to George Ellis, 6 April 1810: 'Southey requires to be watched ... But I perfectly agree with you in all you say of him: there is an irresistible charm, at times, in his style, and a pathos that is truly touching' (*QR* Letter 43). In a letter to Ellis of 3 September 1810 Gifford claimed that Southey included sections censored from the *Quarterly* 'as of a dangerous or doubtful tendency' in his work for the *Edinburgh Annual Register* (*QR* Letter 55).

16. Southey's first Laureate poem, the ode *Carmen Triumphale* (published in newspapers on 1 January 1814), had a troubled genesis. On the advice of John Wilson Croker and John Rickman, Southey toned down its politics, removing five stanzas from the original draft. The excised stanzas were later incorporated (along with three new ones) in a second 'ode invective, and devoratory' (Southey to Rickman, 11 January 1814, in *NL*, vol. 2, p. 93) – the 'Ode written during the negotiations with Buonaparte' published in the *Courier* on 3 February 1814. Although he was able to recycle these unused parts, Southey remained deeply dissatisfied with the *Carmen Triumphale*, referring to it as the '*Carmen Castratum*': 'this unhappy poem' which 'has cost me ten times the time and trouble that it is worth'. Southey to Mary Barker, December 1813, in Kirkpatrick, 'The Letters of Robert Southey to Mary Barker', pp. 424–5.

17. Southey to Grosvenor Charles Bedford, 14 January 1815, in *Selections from the Letters of Robert Southey*, vol. 2, p. 393. Examples of essays altered by Gifford are listed in Curry and Dedmon, 'Southey's Contributions to *The Quarterly Review*', pp. 263, 267; and also Carnall, *Robert Southey and His Age*, pp. 221–3. For Gifford's description of prolixity as Southey's 'besetting sin', see his letter to Edward Copleston, 23 May 1812 (*QR* Letter 126).

18. Southey to John Murray, 10 November 1819, in *NL*, vol. 2, p. 204.

19. The *Quarterly* did, however, review *The Curse of Kehama* (1810) (Scott in Number 9, article #131), *Roderick, the Last of the Goths* (1814) (Bedford in Number 25, article #335) and *A Tale of Paraguay* (1825) (Coleridge in Number 64, article #791). Southey's prose works reviewed included *The Life of Wesley* (1820) (Heber in Number 47, article #558).

20. See, for example, *NL*, vol. 2, p. 204.

21. 11 March 1809, in *NL*, vol. 1, p. 501.

22. Southey to John Murray, 3 April 1818, in *NL*, vol. 2, p. 181.

23. 8 April 1818, in *NL*, vol. 2, p. 184.

24. [G. Bedford], 'Southey's *Roderick*', *QR*, 25 (article #335).

25. Byron, 'Some Observations upon an Article in *Blackwood's Magazine*, no. xxix, August, 1819', in L. Madden, *Southey: the Critical Heritage* (New York: Routledge and Kegan Paul, 1972), p. 267.
26. 'Parliamentary Reform' (article #409).
27. William Hazlitt, unsigned review, *Examiner* (9 March 1817), in Madden, *Southey*, pp. 233–5.
28. For Southey's mobility – and Byron's complex responses to it see – J. J. McGann, 'The Book of Byron and the Book of the World', in J. J. McGann, *The Beauty of Inflections: Literary Investigations in Historical Method and Theory* (Oxford: Clarendon Press, 1985), pp. 255–93.
29. For Southey's condemnation of 'criticasters' see his review of James Grahame's *British Georgics* in *QR*, 6 (article #98), p. 457.
30. [W. Scott], 'Southey's *Kehama*', *QR*, 9 (article #131). In a letter of 22 September 1810 (*QR* Letter 69), Gifford asked Scott to review *Kehama*, 'a most strange thing of Southey's, which in your hands might do wonders, as it might lead to a view of Southeys poetical excellencies and defects – and he would not take anything wrong from you'. See also *QR* Letter 73, Gifford to Ellis, 21 December 1810; and *QR* Letter 75, Gifford to Scott, 29 December 1810, in which he characterized Southey as having 'such woeful deliquiums of taste and sense, such talents and such genius, that he is altogether the most singular creature imaginable'. Scott's review was delayed by one issue because of concern that it would appear before *Kehama* was published (*QR* Letter 77, Ellis to Scott, 9 January 1811).
31. Ellis claimed that he saw no resemblance between Southey and Scott (Ellis to Scott, 9 January 1811, *QR* Letter 77).
32. Southey to Mary Barker, 4 June 1811, in Kirkpatrick, 'The Letters of Robert Southey to Mary Barker', p. 363 (emphasis added).
33. 'Southey's *Kehama*' (article #131).
34. 18 February 1812, in *NL*, vol. 2, p. 31.
35. William Wordsworth to Joseph Cottle, May 1799, in J. A. Butler, 'Wordsworth, Cottle and the *Lyrical Ballads*: Five Letters, 1797–1800', *Journal of English and Germanic Philology*, 77 (1976), pp. 139–53, on p. 145.
36. *Critical Review*, n.s. 24 (1798), pp. 197–204.
37. Wordsworth to Sir George Beaumont, 3 June 1805, in Madden, *Southey*, p. 100.
38. See the *Imperial Review*, 5 (November 1805), pp. 465–73, in Madden, *Southey*, p. 105. See also D. Chandler, 'Wordsworthian Southey: The Fashioning of a Literary Reputation', *Wordsworth Circle*, 34 (2003), pp. 14–19.
39. Wordsworth to James Losh, 4 December 1821, in *The Letters of William and Dorothy Wordsworth: The Later Years. Part I. 1821–8*, ed. E. de Selincourt, 2nd rev. edn, ed. A. G. Hill (Oxford: Clarendon Press, 1978), p. 96 (emphasis added).
40. Wordsworth to Walter Savage Landor, 20 April 1822, in *Wordsworth, The Later Years. Part I*, p. 123 (emphasis added).
41. Reprinted in Madden, *Southey*, p. 416.
42. 5 October 1844, in Madden, *Southey*, p. 418.
43. For early examples, see S. T. Coleridge, *The Collected Letters*, ed. E. L. Griggs, 6 vols (Oxford: Clarendon Press, 1956–71), vol. 1, pp. 103–4, 116.
44. Robinson, *On Books and Their Writers*, vol. 1, p. 48.
45. S. T. Coleridge, *The Collected Works*, Bollingen Series 75, gen. ed. K. Coburn, 16 vols (London: Routledge and Kegan Paul, 1969–2001), 7: *Biographia Literaria*, ed. J. Engell and W. J. Bate, 2 vols (1983), vol. 1, pp. 57, 61.

46. Ibid. vol. 1, pp. 62–3. Coleridge's description of Southey's 'talents' is itself an indication of his ambivalence. For his distinction between 'mere *talent* (or the faculty of appropriating and applying the knowledge of others)' and 'the creative and self-sufficing power of absolute Genius', see ibid., vol. 1, pp. 31–2.

47. Ibid., vol. 1, p. 67 (emphasis added).

48. Critics have preferred to concentrate on Southey's reviews connected to politics and to social and imperial issues. A notable exception is D. Fairer, 'Southey's Literary History', in Pratt (ed.), *Robert Southey and the Contexts of English Romanticism*, pp. 1–17.

49. For examples not discussed in this essay, see Southey, 'Lord Holland's Life and Writings of Lope de Vega', *QR*, 35 (article #441); 'Life and Writings of Camoëns', *QR*, 53 (article #627); 'Hayley's Life and Writings', *QR*, 62 (article #734), 'Chalmers's English Poets', *QR*, 22 (article #310), and *QR*, 23 (article #313); and 'Inquiry into the Copyright Act', *QR*, 41 (article #502).

50. *NL*, vol. 2, p. 47.

51. *NL*, vol. 2, p. 47, n. 2. Coleridge, 'Coleridge's *Remorse*', *QR*, 21 (article #294).

52. Southey to Murray, 10 November 1819, in *NL*, vol. 2, p. 205. 'Alfieri's Life and Writings', *QR*, 28 (article #367); '*Chronological History*', *QR*, 75 (*WI* #172). Southey asked to review Lloyd's book, informing Bedford that 'The necessity of my doing it, as it imports Lloyd's feeling, you will very well understand', 14 January 1815, in *Selections from the Letters of Robert Southey*, vol. 2, p. 394. Southey was heavily involved in his brother Thomas's book, arranging for Longman to publish it by subscription and writing 'certain connecting parts' himself (*NL*, vol. 2, p. 205). In addition, he noticed his niece Sara Coleridge's translation of Dobrizhoffer, 'Account of the Abipones', *QR*, 52 (article #612); his correspondent James Montgomery's *West Indies*, *Wanderer in Switzerland* and *World Before the Flood*, 'Montgomery's *West Indies*', *QR*, 12 (article #172), and 'Montgomery's *World*', *QR*, 21 (article #288); his friend William Taylor's edition of the works of Frank Sayers (who in his turn was a major influence on Southey's early poetry), 'Sayers's *Works*', *QR*, 69 (*WI* #113); and a book on Devonshire by another friend, Anna Eliza Bray, 'Bray's *Letters*', *QR*, 118 (*WI* #1837).

53. [R. Southey], 'Landor's *Count Julian*', *QR*, 15 (article #211).

54. Ibid.

55. *Selections from the Letters of Robert Southey*, vol. 2, p. 335.

56. Southey reviewed *Gebir* in the *Critical Review*, 27 (1799), pp. 29–39.

57. Southey to Samuel Taylor Coleridge, 1 April 1800, in *Life and Correspondence of Robert Southey*, vol. 2, p. 56. On 14 October [1802] Southey informed John Rickman of the appearance of 'more Geberish [Landor's anonymously published *Poetry by the Author of Gebir* (1802)] ... The man talks treason safely, because he uses such hard language and wraps up his meaning so that nobody will find it out. Yet there is very admirable stuff in him' (*NL*, vol. 1, p. 292).

58. Southey to Rickman, 15 April 1808, in *Selections from the Letters of Robert Southey*, vol. 2, p. 55.

59. Southey did occasionally hint at some of his own pet poetic projects in reviews. See for example the allusion to his own long-abandoned poem 'The Kalendar' in his review of Grahame's 1809 volume, *British Georgics* (article #98): 'The English kalendar ... is not less rich in subjects for poetry than the Fasti of the Romans; and some poet of purer faith and better taste ... may one day build his fame upon it'. The most detailed account of the 'Kalendar' is P. Jarman, 'Feasts and Fasts: Robert Southey and the Politics of Calendar', in Pratt (ed.), *Robert Southey and the Contexts of English Romanticism*, pp. 49–67.

60. Southey to Landor, 27 September 1810, in *Selections from the Letters of Robert Southey*, vol. 2, p. 203.

61. For 'Florinda', see R. Southey, *Poetical Works, 1793–1819*, gen. ed. L. Pratt, 5 vols (London: Pickering & Chatto, 2004), vol. 5: Selected Shorter Poems, 1793–1810, ed. L. Pratt, pp. 423–6. For *Roderick*, see D. Saglia, *Poetic Castles in Spain: British Romanticism and Figurations of Iberia* (Amsterdam: Rodopi, 2000), pp. 82–98.

62. For examples, see *Selections from the Letters of Robert Southey*, vol. 2, pp. 204, 216–17; for Scott, see ibid., vol. 2, p. 225.

63. *NL*, vol. 2, p. 10.

64. Southey to Landor, 9 February 1812, in *Selections from the Letters of Robert Southey*, vol. 2, pp. 252–3.

65. 'Montgomery's *West Indies*' (article #172). Although they were on good terms, Montgomery did not reciprocate the favour and Southey later complained about his 'very injudicious' appraisal of *Roderick*, published in the *Eclectic Review*. Southey to Grosvenor Bedford, 28 June 1815, in *Selections from the Letters of Robert Southey*, vol. 2, p. 414.

66. 'Montgomery's *West Indies*' (article #172).

67. Ibid.

68. See *Anti-Jacobin, or Weekly Examiner*, 1 (20 November 1797), pp. 6–7. For examples of *Anti-Jacobin* parodies of Southey, see Madden, *Southey*, pp. 55–60.

69. For confirmation of this identification, see Southey's observation to Charles Wynn, 'The new "Quarterly" has two articles of mine, the "Inquisition," and "Montgomery's Poems:" the latter ought to have some bitter remarks upon Jeffrey, but I know not whether they have past the censor's office', 4 February 1812, in *Selections from the Letters of Robert Southey*, vol. 2, p. 251.

70. [F. Jeffrey], 'Montgomery's Poems', *Edinburgh Review*, 9 (January 1807), pp. 347–55 (*WI* #332).

71. 'Montgomery's *West Indies*' (article #172).

72. 'Grahame's *British Georgics*' (article #98). Southey's public praise of Grahame was in stark contrast with his private opinion of the *British Georgics*; see Southey to John Murray, 22 April 1810 (*QR* Letter 46), promising Murray 'an article about Grahames dismal book – in which I will endeavour to amuse the reader, keep his attention upon the subject and yet lead it from the author, – for sorry am I to say that his Georgics are literally good for nothing'. Gifford shared Southey's low opinion; see Gifford to Walter Scott, 17 February 1810, *QR* Letter 37. Southey was offended by Jeffrey's negative review of Grahame's *The Sabbath* in *ER*, 5 (January 1805), pp. 437–42 (*WI* #205).

73. 'Montgomery's *West Indies*' (article #172).

74. See Gifford to Edward Copleston, 29 October 1811, *QR* Letter 110.

75. Southey to Bedford, 28 June 1815, in *Selections from the Letters of Robert Southey*, vol. 2, p. 415.

76. Curry and Dedmon, 'Southey's Contributions to *The Quarterly Review*', p. 268.

77. Southey to Barton, 21 January 1820, in *Life and Correspondence of Robert Southey*, vol. 5, p. 15 (emphasis added).

78. [J. T. Coleridge], 'Hunt's *Foliage*', *QR*, 36 (article #456). As early as 28 August 1810 Murray had described Hunt to Scott (*QR* Letter 53) as: 'most vilely wrongheaded in politics which he has allowed to turn him away from the ~~pursuit of~~ path of elegant criticism which might have led him to eminence and respectability'. On 8 April 1818, Southey complained to Murray that Croker's review of *Rimini*, published in the *Quar-*

*terly* in 1816, had done 'less than justice' to Hunt, 'a conceited writer, and a man of the most villainous principles, but of no inconsiderable powers' (*NL*, vol. 2, p. 184). See [J. W. Croker], 'Hunt's *Rimini*', *QR*, 28 (article #374). For the Hunt circle and the 'Lake School' see J. N. Cox, 'Leigh Hunt's Cockney School: The Lakers' "Other"', *Romanticism on the Net*, 14 (May 1999), <www.ron.umontreal.ca>.

79. G. Gordon, Lord Byron, *The Complete Poetical Works*, ed. J. J. McGann, 7 vols (Oxford: Clarendon Press, 1980–6), vol. 5, 'Dedication', ll 136, 24, pp. 8, [3]; and 'Preface', p. 84.

80. Ibid., p. 85.

81. Ibid., p. 83. Southey himself had travelled in Spain and published an account of his journey, *Letters Written During a Short Residence in Spain and Portugal* (Bristol: Joseph Cottle, 1797). He was also the creator of 'Espriella', the fictitious 'Spanish' narrator of *Letters from England*, 3 vols (London: Longman, Hurst, Rees and Orme, 1807). The dispute between Byron and Southey continued into the 1820s. For a detailed recent account, see T. Fulford, 'Poetic Hells and Pacific Edens', *Romanticism on the Net*, 32–3 (November 2003–February 2004), <www.ron.umontreal.ca>.

82. [J. T. Coleridge], 'Hunt's *Foliage*' (article #456). The sonnets were 'To Percy Shelley, on the degrading notions of Deity' and 'To the Same'. The volume also contained a sonnet 'To John Keats'.

83. Shelley to Hunt, [20?] December 1818, in P. B. Shelley, *The Letters*, ed. F. L. Jones, 2 vols (Oxford: Clarendon Press, 1964), vol. 2, p. 66.

84. [J. T. Coleridge], 'Shelley's *Revolt of Islam*', *QR*, 42 (article #510). On or close to 31 December 1817 Murray had dispatched the suppressed *Laon and Cythna* (1817) to John Wilson Croker, warning him: 'I send you a most extraordinary Poem by Godwin's new Son-in-Law – pray keep it under Lock and Key – it is an avowed defence of *Incest* – the author is the vilest wretch in existence – living with Leigh Hunt – the Book was published and he is now endeavouring to suppress it –' (*QR* Letter 186).

85. See K. N. Cameron, 'Shelley vs. Southey: New Light on an Old Quarrel', *Publications of the Modern Language Association of America*, 57 (1942), pp. 489–512, on p. 491.

86. Shelley had 'thought of writing to Southey' during the earlier controversy over the review of *Foliage*. See Shelley, *The Letters*, vol. 2, p. 66.

87. The correspondence is printed in *The Correspondence of Robert Southey with Caroline Bowles*, pp. 357–66; and Shelley, *The Letters*, vol. 2, pp. 203–5, 230–2.

88. See Cameron, 'Shelley vs. Southey'.

89. Shelley, *The Letters*, vol. 2, p. 127.

90. 'Hunt's *Foliage*' (article #456).

91. Shelley, *The Letters*, vol. 2, p. 127.

92. 'Hunt's *Foliage*' (article #456).

93. Southey to Mary Barker, 8 January 1812, in Kirkpatrick, 'The Letters of Robert Southey to Mary Barker', p. 375. For the accounts Southey sent to other correspondents, see his letters to John Rickman, 6 January 1812, in Williams, *Lamb's Friend the Census-Taker*, pp. 158–9; Charles Danvers, 13 January 1812, in *NL*, vol. 2, pp. 19–20; and Grosvenor Bedford, 4 January 1812, in *Life and Correspondence of Robert Southey*, vol. 3, pp. 325–6, a passage censored from this is published in *NL*, vol. 2, p. 20, n. 3.

94. Shelley to William Godwin, 16 January 1812, printed in Madden, *Southey*, p. 155; M. Butler, 'Repossessing the Past: The Case for an Open Literary History', in M. Levinson, M. Butler, J. McGann and P. Hamilton (eds), *Rethinking Historicism: Critical Readings in Romantic History* (Oxford: Blackwell, 1989), pp. 64–84, on p. 79.

95. Shelley to Elizabeth Hitchener, 26 December 1811, reprinted in Madden, *Southey*, p. 154.

96. Compare with Henry Crabb Robinson's 1817 description of Shelley's conversation as 'vehement and arrogant and intolerant'. Robinson, *On Books and Their Writers*, vol. 1, p. 212.

97. On 7 March 1816 Shelley sent Southey a copy of *Alastor* as evidence of his 'admiration [for him] as a poet', *The Correspondence of Robert Southey with Caroline Bowles*, p. 357. For contemporary recognition of the connections between Southey and Shelley's poetry, see J. E. Barcus (ed.), *Shelley: The Critical Heritage* (London: Routledge, 1975), pp. 75, 396. For a discussion of *Thalaba's* influence on Shelley, see the Introduction to Southey, *Poetical Works*, vol. 3: *Thalaba the Destroyer*, ed. T. Fulford; and Butler, 'Repossessing the Past', pp. 79–80. For *Thalaba* and the *Revolt*, see N. Leask, *British Romantic Writers and the East: Anxieties of Empire* (Cambridge: Cambridge University Press, 1992), p. 110.

98. Robinson, *On Books and Their Writers*, vol. 1, p. 212. Cameron, 'Shelley vs. Southey', provides the fullest account of Shelley's increasing hostility to Southey.

99. Robinson, *On Books and Their Writers*, vol. 1, p. 212.

100. Gifford to Scott, 13 February 1823 (*QR* Letter 239).

101. Southey to Barton, 21 January 1820, in *Life and Correspondence of Robert Southey*, vol. 5, p. 15.

102. I am grateful to Carol Bolton, Jonathan Cutmore, Ian Packer and Bill Speck for their comments on an earlier version of this essay and to Mary Dawson and the Arts Team of the Hallward Library, University of Nottingham, for all their assistance.

## 8 Speck, 'Robert Southey's Contribution to the *Quarterly Review*'

1. Robert Southey to Grosvenor Bedford, 9 November 1808, Bodleian MS Eng. Lett. c. 24, f. 82.

2. K. Curry, 'Southey's Contributions to the *Annual Review*', *Bulletin of Bibliography*, 16 (1941), pp. 196–7.

3. Curry and Dedmon, 'Southey's Contributions to *The Quarterly Review*'.

4. *QR*, 1 (article #17), pp. 193, 210.

5. *QR*, 3 (article #37), p. 32.

6. *QR*, 4 (article #55), pp. 331, 337.

7. *QR*, 5 (article #84), pp. 218–62.

8. M. Barker, 'Robert Southey, his Biography of Nelson and the "deplorable transaction"', *Mariner's Mirror*, 91 (2005), pp. 324–8, on p. 324.

9. *QR*, 7 (article #102), p. 24.

10. *QR*, 3 (article #37), p. 54.

11. Southey to Mary Barker, 29 January 1810, in *Selections from the Letters of Robert Southey*, vol. 2, p. 191.

12. *QR*, 8 (article #127), p. 508.

13. Curry and Dedmon, 'Southey's Contributions to *The Quarterly Review*', p. 263.

14. *QR*, 10 (article #148), p. 436.

15. *QR*, 11 (article #168), p. 289.

16. Southey to John May, 2 November 1811, in *Life and Correspondence of Robert Southey*, vol. 3, p. 319.

17. *QR*, 13 (article #182), pp. 91–2.

18.  *QR*, 14 (article #204), pp. 414–15, 437.
19.  Southey to Charles Danvers, 5 January 1813, BL Add. MSS 30928, f. 127.
20.  *QR*, 16 (article #224), pp. 337, 352–3.
21.  *QR*, 19 (article #264), pp. 92–3.
22.  *QR*, 26 (article #352), p. 470.
23.  Southey to Charles Watkin Williams Wynn, 15 December 1815, in *NL*, vol. 1, p. 523; vol. 2, p. 126.
24.  Southey to John Murray, 'Wednesday 3 o'clock' [November 1815], JM MS.
25.  *QR*, 29 (article #385), p. 227.
26.  *QR*, 31 (article #409), pp. 248, 271.
27.  T. L. Peacock, *Melincourt* (London: T. Hookham, and Baldwin, Cradock, and Joy, 1817; London: Macmillan, 1896), p. 290.
28.  *QR*, 32 (article #419), pp. 81, 86.
29.  R. Southey, 'The Battle of Blenheim' (1798), ll. 31–4, in Southey, *Poetical Works*, vol. 5, pp. 226–8.
30.  *QR*, 45 (article #534), pp. 19, 29–30.
31.  *QR*, 50 (article #588), pp. 335, 347.
32.  *QR*, 55 (article #649), p. 22.
33.  *QR*, 56 (article #673), pp. 516, 520–1, 523.
34.  Southey to Moxon, 2 February 1836, in *Life and Correspondence of Robert Southey*, vol. 6, p. 288.
35.  Southey to Bedford, 22 March 1823, in *Selections from the Letters of Robert Southey*, vol. 3, p. 383.
36.  *NL*, vol. 2, p. 245.
37.  Southey to Herbert Hill, 4 September 1825, in *Selections from the Letters of Robert Southey*, vol. 3, p. 504.
38.  *QR*, 33 (*WI* #75), p. 410.
39.  Southey to Walter Scott, 25 November 1825, *NL*, vol. 2, pp. 288–90.
40.  Southey to John Coleridge, 11 December 1825 (copy), Harry Ransome Humanities Research Center, University of Texas.
41.  Southey to John Rickman, 4 December 1825, in *Selections from the Letters of Robert Southey*, vol. 3, p. 514.
42.  Southey to John Murray, 16 June 1827, in *NL*, vol. 2, p. 313.
43.  Southey to Thomas Southey, 24 July 1827, BL Add. MSS 47890, f. 133.
44.  Southey to John Murray, 17 December 1827, JM MS.
45.  *QR*, 37 (*WI* #151), p. 260.
46.  Southey to Grosvenor Bedford, 29 January 1831, in *NL*, vol. 2, p. 361.
47.  Southey to John Murray, 26 December 1830, JM MS.
48.  *QR*, 44 (*WI* #257), p. 265.
49.  *QR*, 44 (*WI* #253), pp. 83–120.
50.  *QR*, 47 (*WI* #300), p. 99.
51.  *QR*, 49 , (*WI* #338) p. 80.
52.  Southey to Edith May, 3 April 1834, in *NL*, vol. 2, p. 406.

# Appendix B: Transcription of Key Letters

1. Source: JM MS, letterbook copy in John Murray II's hand. The Murray archive also preserves a secretary's copy that contains minor variants. The version in Smiles, *Memoir*, vol. 1, p. 93, is closer to the secretary's than to John Murray II's copy.

2. The letter appears to position Murray as the originator of the idea of the *Quarterly*. That distinction, however, properly belongs to Stratford Canning. It was he who, over a period of twelve months beginning in the late spring of 1807, contacted Murray, George Canning and William Gifford to advance an inspiration that he had had with some of his Cambridge friends. Stratford Canning presented a prospectus to George Canning, who approved it; he brought Murray and Gifford together; and he introduced Murray to a body of political sponsors and potential contributors, the *Anti-Jacobin* group. We discover Stratford Canning's role alluded to in the postscript to *QR* Letter 6, but there is no better evidence of his importance than a letter dated Hastings, 20 March 1875, in which he unambiguously stakes his claim to be the journal's *primum mobile*. (The letter is hitherto unpublished.)

   Shall I tell you how it first came into thought? Three college youths, Richard Wellesley, Gally Knight and myself, were walking one day in Pall Mall, when the 8th year of the century was passing out of spring into summer. The conversation happened to turn upon the Edinburgh Review, then little more than a novelty. One of us, I have forgotten which, exclaimed, why should not we have a counter review *here*? The idea took roots – we talked it over seriously – the name was settled, the *present* name, among us. I wrote the sketch of a prospectus, and submitted our notion to Canning then in office. He referred me to Gifford, who approved the plan, and received your father on my introduction as its publisher *in petto*. It was my lot to go abroad on public service two or three months afterwards meaning to return at the end of the year. Providence ruled otherwise, and I was absent more than four years ... (Stratford Canning to John Murray III, JM MS)

   Relying upon the vaguer account published in Lane-Poole's *The Life of ... Stratford Canning*, historians have misdated Canning's activities to 1808. This letter permits us to understand that, with the walk along Pall Mall having taken place in May or June, 1807 ('the 8th year of the century' – counting from 1800, as Stratford Canning does), the origins of the *Quarterly* had a significant history prior to Murray sending his letter to George Canning.

3. Source: JM MS. Postmark: 8 OC 1808. See note 7 below.

4. In the holograph, 'Ashestiel', I have followed Corson in regularizing the spelling of Scott's residence as 'Ashiestiel'.

5. Newark tower is a ruin on the banks of the Yarrow, three miles from Selkirk. From the 'Introduction' to Scott's *Lay of the Last Minstrel*: 'He pass'd where Newark's stately tower / Looks out from Yarrow's birchen bower'.

6. Melrose Abbey, in reference to an earlier visit there with his wife.

7. The balance of the letter concerns domestic matters. The postscript reads:

   Dear Love Oct 7

   I most unfortunately carried this letter in my pocket and forgot to send it yesterday. I am in doubt if I shall not arrive before it can reach you. I set out today at 2 o'clock to Preston where I will sleep (please God) tomorrow night and the next day I will hope to be with my most dear wife or early on Monday – yours faithfully / J.M.

8. Source: Leeds WYL250 / 8 (bundle 66a).

9.  Henry Drury (1778–1841) and Francis Hodgson (1781–1852), members of Byron's wider circle, contributed to but did not conduct the *Critical* and the *Monthly*. Both journals supported liberal positions on matters of the day. *The Antijacobin Review, and Magazine; or, Monthly, Political, and Literary Censor* was edited by John Gifford. (He was not related to William Gifford.) Except for the name, strategically adapted from George Canning and Gifford's *Anti-Jacobin; or, Weekly Examiner*, this hyper-Tory journal bore little relation to its predecessor.

10. *Othello*, III.iii.266.

11. Gifford waits upon Scott to accept or decline the editorship or upon the outcome of negotiations that will decide if the projected journal will go forward.

12. (Richard) Belgrave Hoppner (1786–1872), at this time a clerk in the Foreign Office, was the second son of the portrait artist John Hoppner, one of Gifford's closest friends. At Venice he became an acquaintance of Lord Byron.

13. Source: JM MS. *QR* Letter 4 is transcribed from the holograph Walter Scott sent to Gifford. Evidently, Gifford, conscious of the historic nature of the letter, presented it to Murray. *SL*, vol. 2, pp. 100–9, and Smiles, *Memoir*, vol. 1, pp. 104–7, published imperfect transcriptions. I indicate where *SL* substantively deviates from the holograph. *QR* Letter 4A is a transcription of Scott's draft of *QR* Letter 4. *QR* Letter 4 establishes why no prospectus was written – to maintain surprise; it demonstrates that from the outset Gifford was under the watchful eyes of Scott and Murray; that in his pruning and enlivening articles Gifford was obeying a principle set down by Scott; and that reviews of science and literature were by design enlisted in the service of the Crown as a distraction from the propaganda purposes of the journal. Scott showed this letter to Archibald Campbell-Colquhoun, the Lord Advocate, and to William Erskine. He asked Campbell-Colquhoun to show it to George Canning, who was then to pass it on to Gifford.

14. So in the holograph. *SL*, transcribing the JM MS, has 'finessing'. Lockhart, transcribing the Morgan MS, has 'veneering'. Each is incorrect. The letter groupings 'fin' and 'ring' are unmistakable in both manuscripts; 'ee' is unmistakable in the Morgan MS. 'Fineering' is applying an inlay or a veneer' (*OED*: 'obs'). Smollett uses the word: 'The Italians call it *pietre commesse*, a sort of inlaying with stones, analogous to the fineering of cabinets in wood' (*Travels through France and Italy*, 2 vols (London: R. Baldwin, 1766), letter 28.

15. Lockhart's note: 'The *English Review* was started in January, 1783, under the auspices of the elder Mr. John Murray of Fleet Street. It had Dr G. Stuart for editor, and ranked among its contributors Whittaker the historian of Manchester, Dr William Thomson, etc., etc.'

16. *SL* has 'Malthus'. Thomas James Mathias (1753/4–1835), Italian scholar.

17. Some words are obscured by wear and tear at a fold in the MS. The words in brackets are *SL*'s conjectural reading.

18. *Macbeth*, I.vii.60.

19. Source: NLS 3877, ff. 191–4. Millgate ref. 11135. Frank: 'Geo. Longman / London Ninth November 1808 / Address: Walter Scott Esq / North Castle St / Edinburgh'. Longman (*c.* 1773–1822), scion of the publishing family, was a Whig MP.

20. *QR* Letter 4.

21. Robert Banks Jenkinson, the future Prime Minister, went by the courtesy title Lord Hawkesbury until he succeeded his father, in December 1808, as the second Earl of Liverpool.

22. Charles Long (1760–1838), from 1826 Baron Farnborough, a Pittite politician.
23. *A Midsummer Night's Dream*, IV.i.39.
24. *Hamlet*, V.ii.36.
25. An illegible name appears here in the holograph.
26. I have supplied the closing quotation mark.
27. *1 Henry IV*, IV.iii.66.
28. Cyril Jackson (1746–1819), the politically powerful Dean of Christ Church, Oxford, did not become a reviewer.
29. In the realm of possibility.
30. *QR* Letter 4.
31. Cf. *1 Henry VI*, V.iv.131.
32. No review appeared in the *Quarterly* of Fox's *A History of the Early Part of the Reign of James the Second* (London: William Miller, 1808). Francis Jeffrey reviewed it in *ER* #412.
33. 'Do you judge the faith by the man, or the man by the faith?'
34. No review of Hodgson's *Juvenal* (1807) appeared in the *Quarterly*. James Pillans, who became a contributor to the *Quarterly*, reviewed it in *ER* #400. On Hodgson, see *QR* Letter 3.
35. See article #27.
36. English variants for Albert Krantz (1448–1517), German ecclesiastical historian, and Jacob Böhme (1575–1624), the German mystic. Gaps in this sentence are caused by a tear in the manuscript.
37. An important confirmation of Stratford Canning's seminal role in the formation of the *Quarterly* (see note 2 above). The 'friend' is George Canning.
38. Source: NLS 3877, ff. 195–6. Millgate ref. 11136.
39. Cf. Matthew 6:26–8.
40. 'At the outset'.
41. So in the holograph.
42. *1 Henry IV*, V.i.115–17.
43. [W. Scott], 'Preface to Carleton's Memoirs, Containing Biographical Notices of the Earl of Peterborough', in [D. Defoe], *Memoirs of Capt. George Carleton, An English Officer: Including Anecdotes of the War in Spain Under the Earl of Peterborough* (Edinburgh, 1809), pp. i–xv.
44. Source: NLS 3877, ff. 200–3. Millgate ref.: 11138. Postmarks: 15 NOV [1]808; 18 NOV 1808. Published in Smiles, *Memoir*, vol. 1, pp. 109–12, without the final paragraph and the paragraph beginning, 'In the first Number'.
45. In the holograph; the word 'in' is written over the word 'to'.
46. Pope, *Essay on Man* (1732), I.11.
47. Ellis wrote the article on Spain in *QR*, 1, article #1.
48. The friend is Grosvenor Bedford (fl. 1792–1838), chief clerk of the Audit Office. One of Southey's regular correspondents, he was also a frequent visitor at Murray's.
49. Murray has struck out a word here.
50. So in the holograph, but surely intending 'offensive'.
51. So in the holograph, though perhaps intending 'respect'.
52. Murray has struck out a word here.
53. Removal of the wafer has damaged parts of this paragraph.
54. Scott, Murray and the Ballantynes projected a uniform series of novels, mostly British, a few foreign. Had the series seen the light of day, it would have run to as many as two hundred volumes. In the end, Murray backed out of the risky venture.
55. *The Story of Abou Hassan, or The Sleeper Awakened* (1807).

56. A tear in the manuscript obscures some words in this sentence, including the final word, which is missing.
57. Source: JM MS. Date: year from docket and contents. Docket: '1809 / G. E. / respecting third Number / Sir F. D'Ivernois'. Under the docket, in Smiles's hand: 'Novr 5th 1809'. Published in part in Smiles, *Memoir*, vol. 1, p.163.
58. Sayers on the 'Doctrine of the Greek Article', article #45; Whitaker on 'Gothic Architecture', article #40; Stephen on Edgeworth's *Tales*, article #42.
59. *QR*, 3, article #40.
60. A learned Genevan, François D'Ivernois (1757–1842) was one of a number of continental conservatives that Gifford, Ellis, Canning and Croker were in active contact with. Some, including D'Ivernois and Jean-Gabriel Peltier, were in exile in London. Others, such as Friedrich von Gentz, who translated the economic writings of D'Ivernois, were still actively at work in Europe. D'Ivernois became a British citizen and was knighted for his sometimes clandestine services to the Crown.
61. Ellis reviewed D'Ivernois in *QR*, 5, article #70, and Canning's '*QR* Letter' in *QR*, 4, article #62.
62. Ellis reviewed *Empire de Russie* in *QR*, 5, article #72.
63. Source: NLS 3878 (ff. 211–12). Millgate ref. 11240. A three-sentence extract is published in *Familiar Letters of Sir Walter Scott*, ed. D. Douglas, 2 vols (Edinburgh: Douglas, 1894).
64. The word 'proof' is an uncertain reading.
65. Proverbs 30:15.
66. See *QR* Letter 28.
67. *Henry V*, V.ii.47–8.
68. A stock legal phrase.
69. 'This is not what you promised', Horace, *Odes*, I.15.
70. Source: NLS 3879, ff. 29–30. Millgate ref. 11264.
71. Number 4 was published on 23 December 1809. Number 5 was published on 31 March 1810.
72. Scott reviewed Croker's *Battles of Talavera* in *QR*, 4, article #63.
73. Grant reviewed Parr's *Fox* in *QR*, 4, article #60. Dudley reviewed Sydney Smith in *QR*, 5, article #81.
74. Ellis reviewed 'Ld. Grenville and Dr. Duigenan on Catholic Claims' in *QR*, 5, article #79.
75. Source: JM MS, letterbook copy in a secretary's hand. Address: 'J. Bristed Esq (John Bristed Esqr, Jas. Eastburn's Esq, Merchant, New York)'.
76. John Bristed, *Hints on the National Bankruptcy of Britain: and on Her Resources to Maintain the Present Contest with France* (New York, 1809). Murray did not publish an edition.
77. That is, as distinct from John Gifford, editor of the *Antijacobin Review*.
78. Ellis reviewed that work in *QR*, 6, article #86.
79. Joel Barlow, *The Columbiad* (Philadelphia, 1807).
80. Bristed submitted a review of *The American Review* but, as it was 'incompatible with' the *Quarterly's* 'plan to notice any periodical works', Gifford rejected it. Murray to Bristed, 12 December 1811, copy JM MS, letterbook. It is possible that some of Bristed's material was used in *QR*, 13, article #180.
81. Source: JM MS. Date: month and year from the docket; dated in relation to *QR* Letter 59 (Murray's draft reply) and with reference to 'Monday night', in Gifford's hand above

the salutation. Docket: in John Murray II's hand, '1810 Sept / Gifford, W'. Quoted in Smiles, *Memoir*, vol. 1, pp. 182–3.

82. Mentioned in the letter, from Number 7: 'Eton', article #111; 'Huet', article #109; 'Wordsworth', article #108; 'Field's', article #112; 'Davison', article #113; 'Pitt', article #114.

83. Grant reviewed Crabbe's *Borough* in *QR*, 8, article #115.

84. Source: JM MS, copy in John Murray II's hand. The passage, 'I entreat you to be assured … This Sir is true', is published, with modifications, in Smiles, *Memoir*, vol. 1, p. 185. The letter is a response to *QR* Letter 58.

85. Sumner reviewed *Diary of a Lover of Literature* in *QR*, 7, article #111.

86. John Harriott, *Struggles through Life: Exemplified in the Various Travels and Adventures in Europe, Asia, Africa, and America, of Lieut. John Harriott* … (London, 1807).

87. Field reviewed *Select Poems from Herrick, Carew* in *QR*, 7, article #112.

88. In the holograph, some of the words in the first two sentences of this paragraph are unclear.

89. Young reviewed *Herculanensia* in *QR*, 5, article #67. No review appeared in the *Quarterly* of Daniel Albert Wyttenbach, *Bibliotheca Critica* (Amsterdam, 1808). I have not identified Jonston (or variant).

90. I have not positively identified the author of *QR*, 5, article #80.

91. Falconer reviewed 'Cambridge verses' in *QR*, 8, article #121.

92. Davison reviewed *Replies to Calumnies Against Oxford* in *QR*, 7, article #113.

93. In the holograph, some words in the final sentence are illegible. The sentence reads in part, 'before … tomorrow the correction upon it – cost … 15 s/ of reprinting two whole sheets'.

94. Source: JM MS. Date: year from the letter's contents. One paragraph is published in Smiles, *Memoir*, vol. 1, p. 188.

# WORKS CITED

## Primary Sources

Anon., 'Barrow's Travels in China', *Antijacobin Review and Magazine*, 18 (December 1804), pp. 337–8.

—, 'Barrow's Travels in China', *British Critic*, 25 (February 1805), p. 119.

—, 'Reviewers Reviewed', *Antijacobin Review*, 43 (September 1812), p. 114.

Badham, C., 'Dr Badham's Defence against the *Quarterly Review*', *New Review*, 1 (1813), pp. 351–4.

Barlow, J., *The Columbiad* (Philadelphia, 1807).

Barrow, J., *Description of Pocket and Magazine Cases of Mathematical Drawing Instruments* (London: J. and W. Watkins, 1792).

—, *An Account of Travels into the Interior of Southern Africa in the Years 1797 and 1798*, 2 vols (London: T. Cadell and W. Davies, 1801–4).

—, *Travels in China* (London: T. Cadell and W. Davies, 1804).

—, *A Chronological History of Voyages into the Arctic Region* (London: John Murray, 1818).

—, *An Auto-Biographical Memoir of Sir John Barrow, Bart., Late of the Admiralty* (London: John Murray, 1847).

Blomfield, A., *A Memoir of Charles James Blomfield*, 2 vols (London: John Murray, 1863).

Boswell, J., *Life of Johnson*, 2 vols (London: Oxford University Press, 1927).

Bristed, C. A., *Five Years in an English University*, 2nd edn (New York: G. P. Putnam, 1852).

Bristed, J., *Hints on the National Bankruptcy of Britain: and on Her Resources to Maintain the Present Contest with France* (New York, 1809).

Brougham, H., *The Life and Times of Henry Brougham, Written by Himself*, 3 vols (Edinburgh: William Blackwood, 1871).

Browning, E. B., *The Barretts at Hope End: The Early Diary of Elizabeth Barrett Browning*, ed. E. Berridge (London: John Murray, 1974).

Burke, E., *The Writings and Speeches of Edmund Burke Volume 9: The Revolutionary War, 1794–7*, ed. R. B. McDowell (Oxford: Oxford University Press, 1991).

Butler, S., *A Letter to the Rev. C. J. Blomfield, A.B., Containing Remarks on the Edinburgh Review of the Cambridge Aeschylus, and Incidental Observations on that of the Oxford Strabo* (Shrewsbury: W. Eddowes, 1810).

—, *The Life and Letters of Dr. Samuel Butler*, 2 vols (London: John Murray, 1896).

Byron, G. Gordon, Lord, *Byron's Letters and Journals*, ed. L. A. Marchand, 13 vols (London: John Murray, 1973–94).

—, *The Complete Poetical Works*, ed. J. J. McGann, 7 vols (Oxford: Clarendon Press, 1980–6).

Clinton, C. J. F. (ed.), *Literary Remains of Henry Fynes Clinton* (London: Longman, Brown, Green, and Longmans, 1854).

Clinton, H. F., *Fasti Hellenici*, 3 vols (Oxford: Clarendon Press, 1827–30).

—, *Fasti Romani*, 2 vols (Oxford: Oxford University Press, 1845–50).

Coleridge, S. T., *The Collected Letters*, ed. E. L. Griggs, 6 vols (Oxford: Clarendon Press, 1956–71).

—, *The Collected Works*, Bollingen Series 75, gen. ed. K. Coburn, 16 vols (London: Routledge and Kegan Paul, 1969–2001), 7: *Biographia Literaria*, ed. J. Engell and W. J. Bate, 2 vols (1983).

Conder, J., *Reviewers Reviewed* (Oxford: Reid, 1811).

Constable, T., *Archibald Constable and his Literary Correspondents*, 3 vols (Edinburgh: Edmonston and Douglas, 1873).

Copleston, E., *A Reply to the Calumnies of the Edinburgh Review against Oxford* (Oxford: J. Cooke and J. Parker, 1810).

—, *A Second Reply* (Oxford, 1810).

—, *A Third Reply* (Oxford, 1811).

Croker, J. W., *The Croker Papers: The Correspondence and Diaries of John Wilson Croker*, ed. L. J. Jennings, 2 vols (New York: Charles Scribner's Sons, 1884).

Cromek, R. H., *Select Scottish Songs, Ancient and Modern* (London: T. Cadell and W. Davies, 1810).

De Quincey, T., 'The Antigone of Sophocles as Represented on the Edinburgh Stage in December 1845. Part 1', *Tait's Edinburgh Magazine*, 17 (February 1846), pp. 111–16, on p.111, in D. Masson (ed.), *The Collected Writings of Thomas De Quincey*, 14 vols (Edinburgh: Adam and Charles Black, 1897), vol. 10, pp. 360–1.

Dibdin, T. F., *The Library Companion; or, The Young Man's Guide, and the Old Man's Comfort, in the Choice of Library*, 2 vols (London: Harding, 1824).

Donaldson, J. W., *Classical Scholarship and Classical Learning* (Cambridge: Deighton, Bell, 1856).

Douglas, S., *The Diaries of Sylvester Douglas (Lord Glenbervie)*, ed. F. Bickley, 2 vols (London: Constable; Boston, MA: Houghton Mifflin, 1928).

Farington, J., *The Diary of Joseph Farington*, ed. K. Garlick and A. Macintyre, 16 vols (New Haven, CT: Yale University Press, 1978–84).

Fox, C. J., *A History of the Early Part of the Reign of James the Second* (London: William Miller, 1808).

Gisborne, T., *The Testimony of Natural Theology to Christianity* (London: T. Cadell and W. Davies, 1818).

Guignes, L. C. de, *Voyage à Pèkin, Manille, et l'île de France*, 3 vols (Paris: Imprimerie Impériale, 1808).

Harriott, J., *Struggles through Life: Exemplified in the Various Travels and Adventures in Europe, Asia, Africa, and America, of Lieut. John Harriott ...* (London, 1807).

Haygarth, W., *Greece: a Poem, in Three Parts; with Notes, Classical Illustrations, and Sketches of the Scenery* (London: W. Bulmer, 1814).

Hazlitt, W., *Letter to William Gifford* (London: John Miller, 1819).

—, *The Complete Works of William Hazlitt*, ed. P. P. Howe, 21 vols (London: J. M. Dent and Sons, 1930–4).

Holland, H. R. Vassall, third Lord, *Further Memoirs of the Whig Party, 1807–21*, ed. Lord Stavordale (London: John Murray, 1905).

Horner, F., *Memoirs and Correspondence*, ed. L. Horner, 2 vols (London: John Murray, 1852).

Lane Poole, S., *The Life of ... Stratford Canning*, 2 vols (London: Longmans, Green, 1888).

Lockhart, J. G., *Memoirs of the Life of Sir Walter Scott*, 7 vols (London: Macmillan, 1837).

Markham, C. R., *The Fifty Years Work of the Royal Geographical Society* (London: John Murray, 1881).

Mill, H. R., *The Record of the Royal Geographical Society, 1830–1930* (London: Royal Geographical Society, 1930).

[Mill, J.], 'Periodical Literature. Art IX. *The Quarterly Review*', *Westminster Review*, 2 (October 1824), pp. 463–503.

Peacock, T. L., *Melincourt* (London: T. Hookham, and Baldwin, Cradock, and Joy, 1817; London: Macmillan, 1896).

Pearson, H., *Memoirs of the Life and Writings of the Rev. Claudius Buchanan*, 2 vols (Oxford: Oxford University Press, 1817).

Porson, R., *Adversaria: notæ et emendationes in poetas Græcos quas ex schedis manuscriptis Porsoni deprompserunt et ordinarunt nec non indicibus instruxerunt Jacobus Henricus Monk A.M., Carolus Jacobus Blomfield A.M.* (Cambridge, 1812).

Roberts, W., *The Life, Letters, and Opinions of William Roberts*, ed. A. Roberts (London: Seeley, 1850).

[Roberts, W.], 'More's Practical Piety', *British Review*, 1 (1811), p. 348.

—, 'Chalmers's Astronomical Discourses', *British Review*, 10 (1817), pp. 9, 29–30.

—, 'Reports on the Poor Laws', *British Review*, 10 (1817), p. 384.

—, 'Dr Copleston on Necessity and Predestination', *British Review*, 18 (1821), p. 361.

Robinson, H. C., *Henry Crabb Robinson on Books and their Writers*, ed. E. J. Morley, 3 vols (London: J. M. Dent and Sons, 1938).

Scott, W., *The Miscellaneous Prose Works of Sir Walter Scott*, 28 vols (Edinburgh: Cadell, 1835).

—, *Familiar Letters of Sir Walter Scott*, ed. D. Douglas, 2 vols (Edinburgh: Douglas, 1894).

—, *The Letters of Sir Walter Scott*, ed. H. Grierson, et al., 12 vols (London: Constable, 1932–7).

—, *The Journal of Sir Walter Scott*, ed. W. E. K. Anderson (Oxford: Clarendon Press, 1998).

[Scott, W.], 'Preface to Carleton's Memoirs, Containing Biographical Notices of the Earl of Peterborough', in [D. Defoe], *Memoirs of Capt. George Carleton, An English Officer: Including Anecdotes of the War in Spain Under the Earl of Peterborough* (Edinburgh, 1809), pp. i–xv.

Shelley, P. B., *The Letters*, ed. F. L. Jones, 2 vols (Oxford: Clarendon Press, 1964).

Sinclair, G., *Memoirs of the Life and Works of Sir George Sinclair*, ed. J. Sinclair (Edinburgh: William Blackwood; London: T. Cadell, 1837).

Smiles, S., *A Publisher and his Friends: Memoir and Correspondence of the Late John Murray*, 2nd edn, 2 vols (London: John Murray, 1891).

Smollett, T., *Travels through France and Italy*, 2 vols (London: R. Baldwin, 1766).

Smyth, W. H., *The Royal Geographical Society and its Labours* (London: Royal Geographical Society, 1846).

—, *Sketch of the Rise and Progress of the Royal Society Club* (London: J.B. Nichols, 1860).

Southey, R., *Letters Written During a Short Residence in Spain and Portugal* (Bristol: Joseph Cottle, 1797).

—, *Letters from England*, 3 vols (London: Longman, Hurst, Rees and Orme, 1807).

—, *The Life of Nelson*, 2 vols (London: John Murray, 1813).

—, *Essays, Moral and Political*, 2 vols (London: John Murray, 1832).

—, *The Life of the Rev. Andrew Bell: Comprising the History of the Rise and Progress of the System of Mutual Tuition*, 3 vols (London: John Murray, 1844).

—, *Life and Correspondence of Robert Southey*, ed. C. C. Southey, 6 vols (London: Longman, Brown, Green and Longmans, 1849–50).

—, *Selections from the Letters of Robert Southey*, ed. J. W. Warter, 4 vols (London: Longman, Brown, Green, and Longmans, 1856).

—, *The Correspondence of Robert Southey with Caroline Bowles*, ed. E. Dowden (Dublin: Hodges, Figgis, 1881).

—, *New Letters of Robert Southey*, ed. K. Curry, 2 vols (New York: Columbia University Press, 1965).

—, *Poetical Works, 1793–1819*, gen. ed. L. Pratt, 5 vols (London: Pickering & Chatto, 2004).

Staunton, G. L., *An Authentic Account of an Embassy from the King of Great Britain to the Emperor of China*, 2 vols (London: George Nicol, 1797).

Staunton, G. T., *Memoir of Sir John Barrow, Bart. and Description of the Barrow Monument* (privately printed, 1852).

—, *Memoirs of the Chief Incidents of the Public Life of Sir George Thomas Staunton* (London: L. Booth, 1852).

Theal, G. M., *Records of the Cape Colony*, 5 vols (London: Clowes, 1897–9).

Wilberforce, R., and S. Wilberforce, *The Life of William Wilberforce*, 5 vols (London: John Murray, 1838.

Wordsworth, W., *The Thirteen-Book 'Prelude'*, ed. M. L. Reed (Ithaca, NY: Cornell University Press, 1991).

Wordsworth, W., and D. Wordsworth, *The Letters of William and Dorothy Wordsworth: The Later Years. Part I. 1821–8*, ed. E. de Selincourt, 2nd rev. edn, ed. A. G. Hill (Oxford: Clarendon Press, 1978).

Wyttenbach, D. A., *Bibliotheca Critica* (Amsterdam, 1808).

## Secondary Sources

Adas, M., *Machines as the Measure of Men: Science, Technology, and Ideologies of Western Dominance* (Ithaca, NY: Cornell University Press, 1989).

Anderson, H. J., *South Africa a Century Ago (1797–1801)* (Cape Town: Miller, 1924).

Andrews, S., *Unitarian Radicalism: Political Rhetoric, 1770–1814* (Houndmills: Palgrave, 2003).

Anon., *Historical Register of the University of Oxford* (Oxford: Clarendon Press, 1888).

Anselment, R., *'Betwixt Jest and Earnest': Marprelate, Milton, Marvell, Swift and the Decorum of Religious Ridicule* (Toronto: University of Toronto Press, 1979).

Atkinson, H., and G. A. Jackson (eds.), *Brougham and His Early Friends*, 2 vols (London: privately printed, 1908).

Barcus, J. E. (ed.), *Shelley: The Critical Heritage* (London: Routledge, 1975).

Barker, M., 'Robert Southey, his Biography of Nelson and the "deplorable transaction"', *Mariner's Mirror*, 91 (2005), pp. 324–8.

Beard, M., *The Parthenon* (London: Profile, 2002).

Bebbington, D. W., *Evangelicalism in Modern Britain: A History from the 1830s to the 1980s* (London: Routledge, 1989).

Beetham, M., 'Open and Closed: The Periodical as a Publishing Genre', *Victorian Periodicals Review*, 22:3 (Fall 1989), pp. 96–100.

Ben-Israel, H., *English Historians on the French Revolution* (Cambridge: Cambridge University Press, 1968).

Bloom, E., and L. D. Bloom, *Satire's Persuasive Voice* (London: Cornell University Press, 1979).

Boucher, M., and N. Penn (eds), *Britain at the Cape, 1795 to 1803* (Houghton: Brenthurst, 1992).

Bradley, I., *The Call to Seriousness: The Evangelical Impact on the Victorians* (London: Cass, 1976).

Brake, L., *Subjugated Knowledges: Journalism, Gender, and Literature in the Nineteenth Century* (Basingstoke: Macmillan, 1994).

Brent, R., 'The Oriel Noetics', in M. G. Brock and M. C. Curthoys (eds), *The History of the University of Oxford: Volume VI, Nineteenth-Century Oxford, Part 1* (Oxford: Oxford University Press, 1997), pp. 72–6.

Brink, C. O., *English Classical Scholarship: Historical Reflections on Bentley, Porson, and Housman* (New York: Oxford University Press, 1986).

Brock, M. G., 'The Oxford of Peel and Gladstone, 1800–40', in M. G. Brock and M. C. Curthoys (eds), *The History of the University of Oxford: Volume VI, Nineteenth-Century Oxford, Part 1* (Oxford: Oxford University Press, 1997), pp. 49–53.

Burns, A., *The Diocesan Revival in the Church of England c. 1800–70* (New York: Oxford University Press, 1999).

Butler, J. A., 'Wordsworth, Cottle and the *Lyrical Ballads*: Five Letters, 1797–1800', *Journal of English and Germanic Philology*, 77 (1976), pp. 139–53.

Butler, M., 'Repossessing the Past: The Case for an Open Literary History', in M. Levinson, M. Butler, J. McGann and P. Hamilton (eds), *Rethinking Historicism: Critical Readings in Romantic History* (Oxford: Blackwell, 1989), pp. 64–84.

—, 'Culture's Medium: The Role of the Review', in *The Cambridge Companion to British Romanticism*, ed. S. Curran (Cambridge: Cambridge University Press, 1993), pp. 120–47.

Cameron, J. M. R., 'The Northern Settlements: Outposts of Empire', in P. Statham (ed.), *The Origins of Australia's Capital Cities* (Cambridge: Cambridge University Press, 1989), pp. 279–91.

Cameron, K. N., 'Shelley vs. Southey: New Light on an Old Quarrel', *Publications of the Modern Language Association of America*, 57 (1942), pp. 489–512.

Carnall, G., *Robert Southey and His Age: The Development of a Conservative Mind* (Oxford: Clarendon Press, 1960).

Carter, H. B., *Sir Joseph Banks* (London: British Museum, 1988).

Chandler, D., 'Wordsworthian Southey: The Fashioning of a Literary Reputation', *Wordsworth Circle*, 34 (2003), pp. 14–19.

Clarke, M. L., *Richard Porson: A Biographical Essay* (Cambridge: Cambridge University Press, 1937).

—, *Greek Scholarship in England from 1700 to 1830* (Cambridge: Cambridge University Press, 1945).

Clive, J., *Scotch Reviewers: The Edinburgh Review, 1802–15* (London: Faber and Faber, 1957).

Collard, C., 'Peter Elmsley', in R. B. Todd (ed.), *Dictionary of British Classicists*, 3 vols (Bristol: Thoemmes Continuum, 2004), vol. 1, pp. 286–8.

Colley, L., *Britons: Forging the Nation 1707–1837* (New Haven, CT: Yale University Press, 1992).

Corson, J. C., *Notes and Index to Sir Herbert Grierson's Edition of the Letters of Sir Walter Scott* (Oxford: Clarendon Press, 1979).

Cox, J. N., 'Leigh Hunt's Cockney School: The Lakers' "Other"', *Romanticism on the Net*, 14 (May 1999), <www.ron.umontreal.ca>.

Craig, D. M., 'Republicanism becoming Conservative: Robert Southey and Political Argument in Britain, 1789–1817' (PhD dissertation, University of Cambridge, 2000).

Cranmer-Byng, J. L., *An Embassy to China: Being the Journal Kept by Lord Macartney during his Embassy to the Emperor Ch'ien Lung, 1793–94* (London: Longmans, 1962).

Curry, K., 'Southey's Contributions to the *Annual Review*', *Bulletin of Bibliography*, 16 (1941), pp. 196–7.

—, 'Robert Southey's Contributions to *The Monthly Magazine* and *The Athenaeum*', *Wordsworth Circle*, 11 (1980), pp. 215–18.

Curry, K., and R. Dedmon, 'Southey's Contributions to *The Quarterly Review*', *Wordsworth Circle*, 6 (1974), pp. 261–72.

Cutmore, J. (ed.), *The Quarterly Review Archive*, <www.rc.umd.edu>.

—, 'Saints, Prophets, and Paternalists' (PhD dissertation, University of Toronto, 1991).

—, '*Wellesley Index* I's *Quarterly Review* Identifications: Was the Murray Register a Reliable Source?', *Victorian Periodicals Review*, 27:4 (1994), pp. 294–9.

—, *Contributors to the Quarterly Review: A History 1809–25* (forthcoming, London: Pickering & Chatto, 2008).

Eddy, J. J., *Britain and the Australian Colonies, 1818–1831* (Oxford: Clarendon Press, 1969).

Egerer, J. W., *A Bibliography of Robert Burns* (Edinburgh: Oliver and Boyd, 1964).

Embree, A. T., *Charles Grant and British Rule in India* (New York: Columbia University Press, 1962).

Fairer, D., 'Southey's Literary History', in L. Pratt (ed.), *Robert Southey and the Contexts of English Romanticism* (Aldershot: Ashgate, 2006), pp. 1–17.

Feiling, K., *Sketches in Nineteenth Century Biography* (London: Longmans, Green, 1930).

—, *The Second Tory Party 1714–1832* (New York: St Martin's Press, 1951).

Festing, G., *John Hookham Frere and His Friends* (London: Nisbet, 1899).

Fleming, F., *Barrow's Boys* (New York: Atlantic Monthly Press, 1998).

Forbes, V. S., *Pioneer Travellers in South Africa, 1750–1800* (Cape Town: A. A. Balkema, 1965).

Foreman, A., *Georgiana, Duchess of Devonshire* (New York: Random House, 1998).

Fulford, T., 'Poetic Hells and Pacific Edens', *Romanticism on the Net*, 32–3 (November 2003–February 2004), <www.ron.umontreal.ca>.

Gamer, M., *Romanticism and the Gothic: Genre, Reception, and Canon Formation* (Cambridge: Cambridge University Press, 2000).

Garside, P., 'Essay on the Text', in W. Scott, *Waverley*, ed. P. Garside (forthcoming, Edinburgh: Edinburgh University Press, 2007).

Gascoigne, J., *Cambridge in the Age of the Enlightenment* (Cambridge: Cambridge University Press, 1989).

Gilmartin, K., *Writing Against Revolution: Literary Conservatism in Britain, 1790–1832* (Cambridge: Cambridge University Press, 2007).

Grafton, A. T., 'Polyhistor into Philolog: Notes on the Transformation of German Classical Scholarship 1780–1850', *History of Universities*, 3 (1983), pp. 159–92.

Graham, W., *Tory Criticism in the Quarterly Review 1809–53* (New York: Columbia University Press, 1921; rpt 1970).

Griggs, E. L., 'Robert Southey and the *Edinburgh Review*', *Modern Philology*, 30 (August 1932), pp. 100–3.

Halévy, E., *The Liberal Awakening (1815–30)*, rev. edn, trans. E. I. Watkin (New York: Barnes and Noble, 1961).

Hall, M., *All Scientists Now: The Royal Society in the Nineteenth Century* (Cambridge: Cambridge University Press, 2002).

Hamilton, C., 'John Wilson Croker: Patronage and Clientage at the Admiralty, 1809–57', *Historical Journal*, 58:1 (2000), pp. 49–77.

Hayden, J. O., *The Romantic Reviewers, 1802–24* (Chicago, IL: Chicago University Press, 1968).

Hibbert, C., *Queen Victoria: A Personal History* (Cambridge: Da Capo Press, 2001).

Hilton, B., *The Age of Atonement: The Influence of Evangelicalism on Social and Economic Thought, 1795–1865* (Oxford: Oxford University Press, 1988).

—, *A Mad, Bad, and Dangerous People?: England 1783–1846* (Oxford: Oxford University Press, 2006).

Hind, R. J., 'William Wilberforce and the Perceptions of the British People', *Historical Research*, 60 (October 1987), pp. 321–35.

House, E. M., *Saints in Politics: The Saints and the Growth of Freedom* (London: George, Allen, and Unwin, 1953).

Housman, A. E., *M. Manilii Astronomicon, Liber Primus* (London: Grant Richards, 1903).

Jaeger, M., *Before Victoria: Changing Standards and Behaviour, 1787–1837* (London: Chatto and Windus, 1956).

James, P., *Population Malthus: His Life and Times* (London: Routledge and Kegan Paul, 1979).

Jarman, P., 'Feasts and Fasts: Robert Southey and the Politics of Calendar', in L. Pratt (ed.), *Robert Southey and the Contexts of English Romanticism* (Aldershot: Ashgate, 2006), pp. 49–67.

Jenkins, B., *Henry Goulburn 1784–1856: A Political Biography* (Montreal and Kingston: McGill-Queens Press, 1996).

Johnson, E., *Sir Walter Scott*, 2 vols (London: Hamish Hamilton, 1970).

Jones, A. G. E., 'Sir John Ross and Sir John Barrow', in A. G. E. Jones, *Polar Portraits: Collected Papers* (Whitby: Caedmon, 1992), pp. 219–28.

Jones, S., *Hazlitt: A Life* (Oxford: Clarendon Press, 1989).

Kirkpatrick, R. G., Jr, 'The Letters of Robert Southey to Mary Barker from 1800–26' (PhD dissertation, Harvard University, 1967).

Klancher, J. P., *The Making of English Reading Audiences 1790–1832* (Madison, WI: University of Wisconsin Press, 1987).

Knutsford, M., *Life and Letters of Zachary Macaulay* (London: Edward Arnold, 1900).

Kramnick, J. B., *Making the English Canon: Print-Capitalism and the Cultural Past, 1700–70* (Cambridge: Cambridge University Press, 1998).

Latané, D., 'The Birth of the Author in the Victorian Archive', *Victorian Periodicals Review* 22:3 (Fall 1989), pp. 110–17.

Leask, N., *British Romantic Writers and the East: Anxieties of Empire* (Cambridge: Cambridge University Press, 1992).

Levere, T. H., *Science and the Canadian Arctic. A Century of Exploration, 1818–1918* (Cambridge: Cambridge University Press, 1993).

Lipking, L., *Ordering of the Arts in Eighteenth-Century England* (Princeton, NJ: Princeton University Press, 1970).

McGann, J. J., 'The Book of Byron and the Book of the World', in J. J. McGann, *The Beauty of Inflections: Literary Investigations in Historical Method and Theory* (Oxford: Clarendon Press, 1985), pp. 255–93.

Mackay, D., *In the Wake of Cook. Exploration, Science and Empire, 1780–1801* (London: Croom Helm, 1985).

Madden, L., *Southey: the Critical Heritage* (New York: Routledge and Kegan Paul, 1972).

Morris, H., *The Life of Charles Grant* (London: John Murray, 1904).

Mostert, N., *Frontiers. The Epic of South Africa's Creation and the Tragedy of the Xhosa People* (New York: Knopf, 1992).

Neill, S., *History of Christianity in India, 1707–1858* (Cambridge: Cambridge University Press, 1985).

Newman, G., *The Rise of English Nationalism: A Cultural History 1740–1830* (New York: St Martin's Press, 1987).

Nockles, P. B., *The Oxford Movement in Context: Anglican High Churchmanship, 1760–1857* (Cambridge: Cambridge University Press, 1994).

Ollard, S. L., *A Short History of the Oxford Movement* (London: Mowbray, 1935).

Parker, M., *Literary Magazines and British Romanticism* (Cambridge: Cambridge University Press, 2000).

Parry, J., *The Rise and Fall of Liberal Government in Britain* (New Haven, CY: Yale University Press, 1983).

Peyrefitte, A., *The Collision of Two Civilisations: The British Expedition to China in 1792–4* (London: Harvill, 1993).

Philips, C. H., *The East India Company, 1784–1834* (Manchester: Manchester University Press, 1961).

Pratt, L., 'Family Misfortunes? The Posthumous Editing of Robert Southey', in L. Pratt (ed.), *Robert Southey and the Contexts of English Romanticism* (Aldershot: Ashgate, 2006), pp. 219–38.

Ragaz, S., 'Maturin, Archibald Constable, and the Publication of *Melmoth the Wanderer*', *Review of English Studies*, 57 (2006), pp. 359–73.

Ragaz, S., J. Belanger and P. Garside, 'Walter Scott, *Tales of My Landlord*: A Publishing Record', *Cardiff Corvey: Reading the Romantic Text*, <www.cf.ac.uk/encap/corvey/articles/database/landlord.html>.

Raimond, J., *Robert Southey. L'homme et son temps, L'oeuvre, Le rôle* (Paris: Didier, 1968).

Robbins, H., *Our First Ambassador to China. An Account of George, Earl of Macartney* (London: John Murray, 1908).

Sack, J. J., 'The Memory of Burke and the Memory of Pitt: English Conservatism Confronts its Past, 1806–29', *Historical Journal*, 30 (1987), pp. 623–40.

—, 'The *Quarterly Review* and the Baptism of the "Conservative Party" – A Conundrum Resolved', *Victorian Periodicals Review*, 24 (1991), pp. 170–2.

—, *From Jacobite to Conservative: Reaction and Orthodoxy in Britain, c. 1760–1832* (Cambridge: Cambridge University Press, 1993).

Saglia, D., *Poetic Castles in Spain: British Romanticism and Figurations of Iberia* (Amsterdam: Rodopi, 2000).

Savours, A., *The Search for the North West Passage* (New York: St Martin's Press, 1999).

Shattock, J., *Politics and Reviewers: The Edinburgh and the Quarterly in the Early Victorian Age* (Leicester: Leicester University Press, 1989).

Shine, H., and H. Chadwick Shine, *The Quarterly Review under Gifford: Identification of Contributors 1809–24* (Chapel Hill, NC: University of North Carolina Press, 1949).

Shunhong, Z., 'British Views on China during the Time of the Embassies of Lord Macartney and Lord Amherst (1790–1820)' (PhD dissertation, Birkbeck College, London, 1990).

S[mith], A. J., 'South African Water-Colours by Lady Barrow', *Africana Notes and News*, 11:9 (1955), pp. 331–7.

Sorenson, J., *The Grammar of Empire* (Cambridge: Cambridge University Press, 2000).

St Clair, W., *Lord Elgin and the Marbles* (Oxford: Oxford University Press, 1998).

—, *The Reading Nation in the Romantic Period* (Cambridge: Cambridge University Press, 2004).

Stamp, T., and C. Stamp, *William Scoresby, Arctic Scientist* (Whitby: Caedmon, 1975).

Stoddart, J., 'Cultures of Print: Mass Markets and Theories of the Liberal Public Sphere', in E. J. Clery, C. Franklin and P. Garside (eds.), *Authorship, Commerce and the Public: Scenes of Writing, 1750–1850* (Basingstoke: Palgrave Macmillan, 2002), pp. 171–85.

Stray, C. A., 'Curriculum and Style in the Collegiate University: Classics in Nineteenth-Century Oxbridge', *History of Universities*, 16 (2001), pp. 183–218.

—, *Classics Transformed: Schools, Universities, and Society in England 1830–1960* (Oxford: Clarendon Press, 1998).

—, 'From one Museum to another: The *Museum Criticum* (1813–26) and the *Philological Museum* (1831–3)', *Victorian Periodicals Review*, 37 (2004), pp. 289–314.

—, 'Scholars, Gentlemen and Schoolboys: The Authority of Latin in Nineteenth and Twentieth-Century England', in C. Burnett and N. Mann (eds), *Britannia Latina: Latin in the Culture of Great Britain from the Middle Ages to the Twentieth Century* (London: Warburg Institute, 2005), pp. 194–208.

—, 'Non-Identical Twins: Classics in Nineteenth-Century Oxford and Cambridge', in C. A. Stray (ed.), *Oxford Classics: Teaching and Learning 1800–2000* (London: Duckworth Publishers, 2007), pp. 1–13.

—, 'The Rise and Fall of Porsoniasm', *Cambridge Classical Journal*, 53 (2007), pp. 40–71.

Streak, M., *The Afrikaner as Viewed by the English* (Cape Town: C. Struik, 1974).

Sutherland, J., *The Life of Walter Scott: A Critical Biography* (Oxford: Blackwell, 1995).

Sweet, N., 'The *New Monthly Magazine* and the Liberalism of the 1820s', in K. Wheatley (ed.), *Romantic Periodicals and Print Culture* (London: Frank Cass, 2003), pp. 147–62.

Thomas, W., *The Quarrel of Macaulay and Croker: Politics and History in the Age of Reform* (Oxford: Oxford University Press, 2000).

Thorne, R. G., *History of Parliament: The Commons 1790–1820*, 5 vols (London: Secker and Warburg, 1986).

Thornton, M. J., *Napoleon after Waterloo. England and the St. Helena Decision* (Stanford, CA: Stanford University Press, 1968).

Todd, W. B., and A. Bowden, *Sir Walter Scott: A Bibliographical History 1796–1832* (New Castle, DE: Oak Knoll Press, 1998).

Varley, D. H., 'Sir John Barrow', in W. J. Kock and D. W. Kruger (eds), *Dictionary of South African Biography*, 5 vols (Cape Town: Tafelberg Publishers, 1968–87), vol. 2, pp. 34–6.

—, 'Mr Chronometer: Some Footnotes on Sir John Barrow', in J. G. Kesting, S. I. Malan, A. B. Smith and L. E. Taylor (eds), *Libraries and People* (Cape Town: C. Struik, 1970), pp. 141–9.

Varley, E. A., *The Last of the Prince Bishops: William Van Mildert and the High Church Movement in the Early Nineteenth Century* (Cambridge: Cambridge University Press, 2002).

Waquet, F., *Latin, or the Empire of a Sign* (London: Verson, 2001).

Ward, W. R., *Georgian Oxford: University Politics in the Eighteenth Century* (Oxford: Clarendon Press, 1965).

—, *Victorian Oxford* (London: Cass, 1965).

Warwick, A., *Masters of Theory: Cambridge and the Rise of Mathematical Physics* (Chicago, IL: University of Chicago Press, 2003).

Webb, T., 'Appropriating the Stones: The 'Elgin Marbles' and the English National Taste', in E. Barkan and R. Bush (eds), *Cleaning the Stones/Naming the Bones: Cultural Property and the Negotiation of National and Ethnic Identity* (Los Angeles, CA: Getty Research Institute, 2002), pp. 51–6.

*Wellesley Index to Victorian Periodicals 1824–1900, The*, vol. 1, ed. W. E. Houghton (Toronto: University of Toronto Press, 1966).

Wheatley, K., 'Paranoid Politics: The *Quarterly* and *Edinburgh* Reviews', *Prose Studies*, 15 (1992), pp. 319–43.

—, *Shelley and His Readers: Beyond Paranoid Politics* (Columbia, MO: University of Missouri Press, 1999).

— (ed.), *Romantic Periodicals and Print Culture* (London: Frank Cass, 2003).

Williams, O., *Lamb's Friend the Census-Taker: Life and Letters of John Rickman* (London: Constable, 1912).

Zeitlin, J., 'Southey's Contributions to *The Critical Review*', *Notes and Queries*, 136 (1918), pp. 35–6, 66–7, 94–7, 122–4.

# INDEX